THE SEXUAL DESIRE DISORDERS

Dysfunctional Regulation of Sexual Motivation

THE SEXUAL DESIRE DISORDERS

Dysfunctional Regulation of Sexual Motivation

HELEN SINGER KAPLAN, M.D., Ph.D.

Founder and Director
Human Sexuality Program
of the New York Hospital-Cornell Medical Center

Routledge
Taylor & Francis Group
NEW YORK AND LONDON

Published in 1995 by
Routledge
Taylor & Francis Group
711 Third Avenue,
New York, NY 10017

Published in Great Britain by
Routledge
Taylor & Francis Group
2 Park Square,
Milton Park, Abingdon,
Oxfordshire OX14 4RN

First issued in paperback 2015

Routledge is an imprint of the Taylor and Francis Group, an informa business

International Standard Book Number-13: 978-1-138-86940-0 (pbk)
International Standard Book Number-13: 978-0-87630-784-7 (Hardcover)
Library of Congress Card Number 95-15019

Library of Congress Cataloging-in-Publication Data

Kaplan, Helen Singer
The sexual desire disorders : dysfunctional regulation of sexual motivation / by Helen Singer Kaplan.
p. cm.
Includes bibliographical references and index
ISBN 0-87630-784-5
1. Sexual desire disorders. 2. Sexual desire disorders—Case studies. I. Title.
TV560.S46K37 1995
616.85'83—dc20 95-15019

informa
Taylor & Francis Group
is the Academic Division of Informa plc.

Visit the Taylor & Francis Web site at http://www.taylorandfrancis.com

and the Routledge Web site at http://www.routledge-ny.com

This book is dedicated to:

Phillip Agrippa, MSW, Miriam Baker, Ph.D., Barbara Bartlett, M.D., Cathy Beaton, MSW, Willa Bernhardt, Ph.D., Charlene Bird, Ph.D., Ellen Hollander, M.D., Peter Kaplan, M.D., Elaine Kleinbart, MSW, Richard Kogan, M.D., Ellen Lear, MSW, Lynn Merklinger, RN, Arlene Novick, MSW, Trudy Owett, MSW, Michael Perlman, Ph.D., Kenneth Rosenbaum, M.D., Sharner Striar, Ph.D., Carol Spero, MSW, Grace Sullivan, RN, MRN, MPH, Silvia Vitale, Ph.D., and Mildred Whitkin, Ph.D., who are currently participants in the Wednesday conference of the Human Sexuality Program of the New York Hospital–Cornell Medical Center in Manhattan, and also to the talented graduates and former members of the staff who have made many valuable contributions, but are too numerous to list here.

Contents

Tables and Figures

Case Studies

Page	#	Code Name	Case Description
59	4.1	"Juan Romeo"	Hyperactive Sexual Desire in a Well-Functioning Heterosexual Male in a Good Sexual Relationship
60	4.2	"Jossel Fromm"	Hyperactive Sexual Desire in a Heterosexual Male with a Concomitant Obsessive-Compulsive Personality Disorder, in a Poor Sexual Relationship
61	4.3	"Tyler Hummingbird"	Hyperactive Sexual Desire in a Married Bisexual Male
62	4.4	"Tina Jefferson"	Hypersexual Desire in a Depressed Heterosexual Female in a Good Sexual Relationship
68	4.5	"Paul Actor"	Mild, Partner-Specific HSD
70	4.6	"Frieda and Fred Aspen"	Lifelong, Severe, Global HSD in a Well-Functioning, Happily Married Woman
71	4.7	"Jack and Jill Priest"	Severe, Acquired, Partner-Specific HSD in a Married Man
77	4.8	"Regina and Roy Kaiser"	Sexual Aversion and Avoidance in a Married Woman with a Concomitant Personality Disorder
82	5.1	"May and Mark September"	Imbalance in the Sexual Appetites of Two Normal but Differently Sexed Individuals

Foreword

The creation of the sex therapies during the past quarter century was a major advance in the treatment of a group of disorders that handicap large numbers of people. Sex therapy took on even more importance and new dimensions in the era of AIDS. The brief period of sexual freedom that followed the discovery of the pill came to a grinding halt with the emergence of AIDS, and the need for safe sex now took priority over demands for sexual freedom; finding sexual satisfaction in mutual monogamy is now a matter of survival rather than moral or esthetic preference. The original work of Masters and Johnson represented an imaginative application of behavioral and learning theory to an area of psychopathology that had previously been regarded as entirely psychodynamic in origin. Their work paralleled tendencies throughout psychiatry to explore theories of etiology and treatment methods other than those psychoanalytically derived. Contemporary sex therapy began as one part of the movement away from the psychodynamic hegemony over psychiatry that existed in the United States after World War II. However, that necessary turn towards the proper introduction of newer pharmacologic, behavioral, and cognitive components into the psychiatric therapies threatened for a time to bury the vast and useful accumulated knowledge of psychodynamics. Fortunately, Dr. Helen Kaplan, one of the first to recognize the great value of these newer treatment modalities for the sexual disorders was a psychoanalyst, and she quickly became a leading practitioner and investigator of Masters and Johnson techniques. With her superb skills as a teacher, researcher, and administrator, she embarked on a major research and training program, using as her base the Outpatient Department of the Payne Whitney Clinic of the New York Hospital. She quickly became a legend as a teacher of unparalleled skills. Using videotape—then a new technology—and her extraordinary capacity for clear, jargon-free exposition of even the most complex issues, she educated several generations of medical students, psychiatric residents, nurses, and social workers in these newer techniques. Her seminars served her as a laboratory for the exchange of experiences and ideas and the pooling of case material.

Based on her systematic recording of the treatment experience and outcome of over 6,000 patients, and by recognizing and studying treatment failures as well as successes, she was able to discover the sexual desire disorders and devise therapeutic methods that have taken sex therapy far beyond the innovations of Masters and Johnson. Drawing on her psychoanalytic background, she continued to be interested in the personalities and the conflictual issues of patients with sexual difficulties, and when she found a group of patients who were unresponsive to the usual behavioral techniques, hers was the prepared mind that could conceptualize and explore the new categories of hypoactive sexual desire disorders that are the major topic of this very important monograph. Dr. Kaplan, in her pioneering work, has integrated the best of all sources of our knowledge of normal and pathological behavior and skillfully combined them to produce a range of sex therapies, aiming at an individualized treatment attuned to the specific diagnosis and individual circumstances of each patient. The case reports that are generously provided throughout the text are beautifully illustrative of the issues she presents. It is typical of Dr. Kaplan that she tells us not only of her successes, but also of those cases that achieved less than optimal results.

Dr. Kaplan is at the forefront of psychiatric therapy and research in adopting a genuinely integrated biopsychosocial approach—giving full weight to the neuro-physiological underpinnings of sexual behaviors, to the psychodynamic factors—past and present—that are influencing and shaping that behavior, and to the environmental determinants that are part of the immediate response. Kaplan's multiple-layer model of the sexual disorders allows the therapist to understand the presenting complaints and symptoms in terms of a series of influences, from 'superficial' and immediate to 'deep' and remote, with interventions ranging from simple to complex. Her attention to diagnosis is exemplary and the separation of the sexual desire disorders from the genital dysfunctions is a major achievement. The desire disorders are more subtle in presentation than are the genital disorders, and their treatment requires a far greater degree of sophistication and mastery, involving multiple areas of knowledge and skill. As this book makes clear, help is now available for large numbers of patients for whom we could previously offer very little.

Dr. Kaplan uses her psychoanalytic knowledge and clinical experience as a guide to more efficient use of behavioral and cognitive techniques, wisely seeing no conflict among the different viewpoints. Each addresses a different layer of feeling and behavior. Kaplan emphasizes the importance of providing the patient with comfort and support, including the use of anti-anxiety medication when approaching anxiety-provoking topics. Kaplan is a master at recognizing and using her knowledge of transference and resistance in the service of accomplishing her goals. She is also quite prepared to engage in insight-oriented uncovering therapy when that is indicated, making clear that there is little value to insight for its own sake, but it can be a necessary and highly effective tool when other techniques fail. Kaplan is a bold experimenter in her use of fantasy. A wise clinician, as interested in love as in sex, not diminishing the value of one or the other, Kaplan has a sophisticated therapeutic view of the role of fantasy in sexuality and the so-called perversions. In her view there is no such thing as a "sick" fantasy; all fantasies are attempts to attain pleasure or security and helpfully reveal aspects of the patient's relevant history.

It is fair to say that Dr. Helen Kaplan has created the exciting and effective field of integrated sex therapy. Her model of the sexual disorders is comprehensive, and the sections of the book on psychiatric and medical conditions and the effects of aging cover every conceivable source of sexual dysfunction. This book is a superb guide both for the therapist and the patient.

Arnold M. Cooper, M.D.
Professor Emeritus in Consultation—Liaison Psychiatry
Cornell University Medical College

Training and Supervising Analyst
Columbia University Psychoanalytic Center for Training and Research

Editor for North America
International Journal of Psychoanalysis

Deputy Editor
American Journal of Psychiatry

Thanks

I cannot adequately express my gratitude to my long-term friend, muse, and literary mentor, Bernard Mazel, my publisher, for his extraordinary efforts in facilitating the publishing of this book.

I would also like to thank Jennifer Moore and Gai Wright for their substantial parts in the production of this volume, and Sharna Striar for organizing the data and statistics.

My final thanks go to my husband Charles Lazarus, without whose support this book could not have been written.

Helen S. Kaplan

CHAPTER 1

Historical Perspectives and Current Status

HISTORICAL PERSPECTIVES

Almost two decades have passed since I first described the syndrome of *hypoactive sexual desire* and suggested that disorders of sexual desire constitute distinct clinical entities that are different from, and on a par with, erectile and orgasm phase dysfunctions (Kaplan, 1977).

Prior to that time, the motivational aspects of sex and sexual desire disorders had not been considered. Masters and Johnson, the originators of sex therapy, did not include sexual desire or desire disorders in their initial studies of human sexuality. The early work of those two great pioneers focused exclusively on the functions and dysfunctions of the genitalia (Masters & Johnson, 1964, 1970). And in this, the Masters and Johnson sex therapy method was so successful that it gained acceptance rapidly and by the seventies, large numbers of men afflicted with erectile and ejaculatory disorders, as well as women with anorgasmia and vaginismus, were being cured with the new intensive, two-week programs of sex therapy at facilities that were springing up everywhere. In the old days of lengthy and ineffective treatments, most of these men and women would have been doomed to lives of sexual inadequacy.

The new sex therapy approach radically changed the treatment of male and female genital dysfunctions and improved the outlook for these patients immensely. But the oversight of sexual desire disorders created problems in that this left large numbers of patients and couples whose complaints center around *inadequate sexual motivation* out in the cold. For effective as the new treatments were for the genital dysfunctions, patients with sexual desire disorders did not respond particularly well to the sex therapy of the era, and in some cases, actually reacted adversely.

Lessons From Treatment Failures

I first became aware of the existence of disorders of sexual desire in the early seventies as a consequence of analyzing our treatment failures. As I reviewed the charts, it became clear that we had failed to recognize a considerable subgroup of patients who had little or no desire for sex or for sex with their partners. These patients had developed impotence or orgasmic disorders mainly because they had tried to make love without feeling lust or desire, and we had been trying to treat these secondary genital dysfunctions without being aware of the underlying desire disorders. This meant that some of our so-called "resistant" patients were not resistant to sex therapy at all. We had simply been treating them for the wrong thing!

I also began to understand why patients with deficient sexual desire were often refractory to sensate focus-centered sex therapy. Masters and Johnson's treatment approach was based on the assumption that performance anxiety is the principal cause of all forms of sexual inadequacy. On that theory, they emphasized the sensate focus (SF) exercises, which are excellent for reducing performance pressures, in their treatment of evey kind of psychosexual disorder (Masters & Johnson, 1970).

However, by the seventies we had already learned that SF is effective primarily for psychogenic impotence, and only of limited benefit for other sexual dysfunctions. We also knew that this was so because other types of psychosexual syndromes are each associated with different and specific immediate causes (Kaplan, 1974, 1979).

In other words, the extensive clinical experience that had accumulated in the first decade of sex therapy confirmed that performance anxiety is indeed the primary cause of psychogenic erectile dysfunction and that SF-oriented treatment programs are highly effective for this syndrome. But, this was clearly not the case for other psychosexual disorders. For, although performance anxiety often plays an ancillary role in the pathogenesis of premature ejaculation (PE), retarded ejaculation (RE), anorgasmia, and vaginismus, these syndromes are each produced by the impairment of the sexual response cycle at different points, and via different pathogenic mechanisms. Thus, each requires a different and unique therapeutic approach (Kaplan, 1974, 1975, 1979).

For example, the immediate cause of vaginismus is not the patient's anxiety about her sexual performance, but an involuntary, reflex spasm of the muscles that guard the vaginal introitus. Consequently, the indicated treatment for this dysfunction is a behavioral program that centers around the gradual, progressive stretching and dilatation of the circumvaginal muscles, while the reduction of sexual anxiety is not curative per se.

Similarly, on the theory that in most cases the immediate cause of PE is the man's failure to register his erotic genital sensations, the behavioral exercises that are used to treat PE center around interrupted penile stimulation. This forces the patient to pay close attention to the rising erotic sensations in his genetalia as he nears orgasm (Kaplan, 1974, 1975, 1979, 1995).*

In addition to taking their sexual histories, this process entailed questioning literally thousands of patients and their partners closely and at length about the intimate details of their current sexual experiences. The inquiry went beyond a simple behavioral analysis and included questions about their thought processes before, during, and after lovemaking, their sexual behaviors and fantasies, their interactions and communications with their partners, and also assessments of their genital functioning.

Hypoactive Sexual Desire (HSD)

By thus examining the current sexual experiences of 2,109 patients and couples with chief complaints of deficient sexual desire.** I came to the conclusion that *the pathological decrease of these patients' libido is essentially an expression of the normal regulation of sexual motivation*

---

*I have hypothesized that patients with PE do not learn voluntary control of their ejaculatory reflex because they fail to register the erotic sensations that are premonitory to orgasm. The resulting sensory deficit interferes with the sensory feedback loop that is necessary for learning voluntary control over the ejaculatory reflex (Kaplan, 1974, 1975, 1989).

**The subjects were seen between 1972 and 1992, and represent the combined populations of patients with sexual complaints that were seen at the Payne Whitney Human Sexuality Clinic of the New York Hospital-Cornell Medical Center and in our private practice group.

gone awry. More specifically, sexual motivation or desire, just like other needs or motives, such as hunger or thirst, is regulated by a CNS control mechanism. Malfunctions of the system that normally adjusts and modulates the human sex drive result in disorders of sexual desire.

Further, my observations of patients with "sexual anorexia" or HSD indicate that the psychogenic form of this syndrome is caused by their active, albeit unconscious selectively negative cognitive and perceptual processes by means of which they literally "turn themselves off." In other words, while normal persons "accentuate the positives, and decentuate the negatives," (to borrow Johnny Mercer's famous lyrics), in order to maximize their sexual arousal and pleasure, patients with HSD inappropriately suppress their sexual feelings by dwelling on their partners' negative qualities, while they "decentuate the positives," that is, blind themselves to their attractive features.

Although I was perhaps the first to apply this paradigm to sexual desire disorders, the concept of dysregulation of motivational control mechanisms resulting in psychopathology is not my invention. This is the essence of Dr. Donald Klein's elegant hypothesis that panic disorder is the product of malfunctions of the "suffocation alarm response," a normal control mechanism which regulates breathing to insure adequate oxygenation (Klein, 1993). The same concept, namely psychopathology due to dysregulation, is also inherent in Dr. Judith Rappaport's fascinating hypothesis that OCD may represent a genetically mediated deregulation of the ancient grooming response (Rappaport, Ryland, & Kriete, 1992).

Sexual Aversion Disorders

The same minutely detailed clinical studies of 414 patients with *sexual aversion disorders* made it clear that the immediate cause of this syndrome is entirely different from that of "quiet" HSD. More specifically, the critical pathogenic element of sexual anxiety and aversive states is a tenacious and malignant link between fear and sexual contact with the partner.

Moreover, we found that the sexual aversions and fears of sexaphobics are often aggravated by underlying anxiety disorders. These conditions are more prevalent in sexaphobic patients than in patients with other psychosexual dysfunctions, and may constitute a predisposing factor (Kaplan, Fyer, & Novick, 1982; Kaplan, 1987).

The clinical implications of these differences in the immediate antecedents of the two sexual desire disorder syndromes, in terms of treatment strategies, will be detailed in Chapter 7.

Deeper Causes

Our observations confirmed the findings of others, that patients with sexual desire disorders tend to have more serious underlying emotional and marital problems.

Although there were many exceptions, as a group our patients and couples with desire problems were clearly afflicted with more severe intrapsychic sexual conflicts and difficulties in their relationships than those who were anorgasmic, vaginismic, premature, or impotent, and patients with sexual desire disorders also had a higher incidence of concomitant personality disorders.

These observations suggest that patients with relatively mild sexual anxieties who are in sound relationships and who, apart from their sexual dysfunction, enjoy good mental health, tend to develop impairments that affect the later phases of the sexual response cycle, the arousal and orgasm phases, while those with more intense and serious sexual fears, concomitant psychopathology, and marital problems are more likely to develop inhibitions earlier on, in the desire phase. This results in the abortion of the sexual experience from the onset.

The higher prevalence of significant concomitant psychopathology and the more serious marital problems that are more common in patients and couples with desire disorders, versus the better mental health of genitally dysfunctional patients, probably accounts, at least in part, for the fact that the prognosis for HSD is in general less favorable than that for the other psychosexual disorders (Kaplan, 1977, 1979).

Even when the outcome is ultimately favorable, in these complex cases resistances tend to be more tenacious and more difficult to resolve, and treatment tends to be lengthier. That is because with these more troubled patients and couples it takes more time and a greater therapeutic effort to establish that moment of harmony between the partners that is necessary for conducting meaningful sexual therapy.

A number of clinicians who have worked with HSD patients have reported similar findings (LoPiccolo, 1979, 1989; LoPiccolo & Friedman, 1988; Lazarus, 1988; Scharff, 1988; Leiblum & Rosen, 1988) which suggest that these observations are not unique to our population or to our treatment methods.

THE PSYCHODYNAMICALLY ORIENTED SEX THERAPY APPROACH TO DESIRE DISORDERS

Once again, by the 1970's, sex therapists had become very good at helping individuals with normal libidos who were attracted to their partners, but who had difficulty maintaining their erections, relaxing their vaginas, or achieving orgasm. But there was clearly a need for new and more effective treatments for patients with primary sexual desire disorders, who were not responding nearly as well. Therefore, we began to develop a treatment approach specifically for patients with disorders of sexual desire.

This method, which is still in the process of evolving, is based on the brief, integrated psychodynamically oriented sex therapy model that had been so successful for the genital phase dysfunctions, and uses the same basic treatment format (Kaplan, 1974, 1975, 1979, 1980, 1981, 1984, 1995).

The hallmark and the unique feature of the "new sex therapy" model is the integrated combination of behavioral/cognitive interventions, in the form of therapeutic sexual exercises that are used specifically to modify the immediate causes of the patient's sexual symptom, along with brief, active, psychodynamically informed psychotherapeutic management of the patient's resistances to treatment and exploration of his or her deeper problems.

This basic behavioral/psychodynamic format had to be modified in several ways to fit the special therapeutic requirements of patients with sexual desire disorders.

For one, as has already been mentioned, the conjoint and psychodynamic aspects of therapy tend to become attenuated and more complex with these more resistant patients. However, the most significant changes that had to be made were in the behavioral/cognitive aspects of treatment.

The primary objective of the sexual "homework assignments" for patients with HSD is to teach them how to maneuver their sexual desire in an upward direction. Thus, greater emphasis had to be placed on raising the patient's awareness of his or her tendency to engage in negative, countersexual mental processes during sexual encounters, and on cognitive restructuring to modify these processes. Meanwhile, less reliance is placed on the behavioral extinction of sexual anxiety, which is the major focus of the behavioral aspects of treatment for other psychosexual dysfunctions.

Libido-Enhancing Sexual Homework Assignments: Fantasy and Friction

A unique feature that has been incorporated into the psychodynamically oriented sex therapy approach to HSD, which distinguishes this method from long-term therapeutic modalities and also from standard sex therapy protocols for genital phase dysfunctions, is that in tandem with psychotherapy, explicit erotic materials, sexual fantasy, masturbation, and enhanced methods of genital stimulation are incorporated into the treatment format. By contrast, other approaches rely solely on *indirect* means of raising the patient's libido. Those therapies place their faith in fostering insight into the patient's unconscious sexual conflicts, improving the couple's communications, and/or reducing his/her sexual anxieties, on the theory that the patient's desire will automatically increase when the sexual performance anxieties, the emotional blocks, and the interpersonal difficulties that were getting in the way are resolved.

But in our experience, only a small proportion of low-desire patients and couples experience a significant increase in desire for their partners in response to standard individual and marital therapies. Most patients with low sexual desire need specific strategic interventions to modify their countersexual behaviors instead of or in addition to these more traditional treatments. I surmised this from the numerous patients we have seen who had gained insight into the deeper causes of their sexual difficulties, and whose individual or couple's therapies were successful in other respects, but whose desire did not improve until direct libido-enhancing strategies and interventions were added to their regimens.

In-vivo Desensitization

The therapeutic exercises for sexaphobic and aversive patients are quite different from those used for HSD, and center around individualized, systematic *in-vivo desensitization.* In other words, in order to extinguish sexaphobic patients' malignant sexual anxieties, they are physically exposed gradually and slowly to that aspect of sexual contact with the partner that is frightening or repellant to him or her. We have also found that sexually aversive patients with concomitant anxiety disorder generally do better when sex therapy is combined with antianxiety drugs. These and other treatment issues will be detailed and illustrated with case material in later chapters of this book.

CURRENT STATUS

Desire Disorders Rapidly Gain Acceptance by Sex Therapists

Quite independently, and at about the same time that my description of HSD was published (Kaplan, 1977), Harold Lief also concluded that desire disorders exist, and that these are as important as the genital phase dysfunctions (Lief, 1977). Further, he accurately predicted that once clinicians were alerted to the existence of these syndromes, disorders of sexual desire would turn out to be highly prevalent among patients with sexual complaints.

In 1978, I joined Lief in proposing the new diagnostic category of desire disorders to the APA's task force for sexual disorders for DSM-III, of which we were both members.

It was gratifying to observe that as soon as these articles on desire disorders appeared in the literature there was an immediate acceptance of and explosion of interest in these syndromes. Very soon, thousands of patients and couples with low sexual frequency and deficient sexual desire were being studied, evaluated, and treated in sexual problem clinics all over the country.

Masters and Johnson, themselves, lost no time in adding *inhibited sexual desire* (ISD)* and *sexual aversion disorders* to their list of human sexual inadequacies (Masters, Kolodny, & Johnson, 1979), and "without much ado" problems of deficient sexual desire disorders became a legitimate province of sex therapy (Leiblum & Rosen, 1988, p. 2).

Influences and Origins

I consider all my work an extension of William Masters' and Virginia Johnson's pioneering studies of the human sexual response and of their great invention, sex therapy. If I have gone somewhat beyond their original conceptions by including disorders of sexual desire, that is merely because one can sometimes see a little further when sitting "on the shoulders of giants."

But I owe my greatest debt, by far, to the remarkable group of dedicated and talented sex therapists who regularly participate in the postgraduate sex therapy seminars of the Human Sexuality Program of the New York Hospital-Cornell Medical Center. These seminars have been conducted weekly for the past 20 years at the Payne Whitney Clinic. Most of our meetings center around unedited videotaped sessions of my current treatment cases. Over the years, these have included patients and couples who represented the great diversity of ethnic groups and the wide spectrum of socioeconomic backgrounds that typify the populations served by the New York Hospital. Moreover, an extraordinary diversity of cases have been presented at

*The old term ISD (inhibited sexual desire) has now been replaced by the more accurate HSD (hypoactive sexual desire).

the seminars over the years; these have included every sexual dysfunction listed in DSM-IV, and then some.

The primary purpose of the videotapes is as a teaching tool to demonstrate our method of evaluating and treating common sexual disorders to the trainees and residents. But the videotapes also serve as catalysts for generating discussions that lead to new visions and insights about sexual disorders and their treatments. Possibly, this is their greatest value.

Each Wednesday, the staff of the Human Sexuality program and the graduates, trainees, and residents engage in intense, spirited interchanges on wide-ranging theoretical, research, clinical, and philosophical issues related to sex and sexual disorders. These symposia are often much more interesting, exciting, informative, and productive than the videotaped material itself, and I believe that it is mainly because of these rich and stimulating collegial interchanges that the Wednesday seminars have become, for many of us, the high point of our professional week.

It is my habit to bounce my new ideas, findings, insights, and hypotheses off the group every Wednesday, and I am always richly rewarded by the feedback. These seminars are the crucible from which many of the technical modifications and new insights have emanated, and it should be noted that a number of the ideas about desire disorders that are contained in this book were refined, revised, extended, or grew out of, and should be credited to, the contributions made by my colleagues in the course of these meetings.*

The Incidence of Sexual Desire Disorders Is Increasing

A number of scientific studies have been conducted by others since the first articles on *Disorders of Sexual Desire* were published in 1977, and those have left no doubt that sexual desire disorders are real clinical phenomena and that these syndromes constitute genuine pathological entities (Lief, 1985; LoPiccolo, 1979, 1989; Lobitz & LoPiccolo, 1980; Leiblum & Rosen, 1988; Crenshaw, 1985; Schreiner-Engel & Schiavi, 1986). As a matter of fact, just as Harold Lief had prophesied, sexual desire disorders are highly prevalent and patients with deficient libidos

*In addition to the current regularly attending members of the Wednesday conferences to whom this book is dedicated, over 150 residents and postgraduate professionals from the U.S. and abroad have undergone the human sexuality training program since 1972, and it is not possible to list all of these nor the former faculty members some of whom have made significant contributions.

and low sexual frequency constitute a significant proportion of the sexually dysfunctional population.

According to Leiblum and Rosen's recent survey (1988) of the current desire disorder prevalence literature, the incidence of sexual desire disorders ranged from a low of 1% in Germany (where they have only recently become aware of motivation dysfunctions) to a high of 55% in LoPiccolo's program in Texas. On average, approximately one-third of the patients who sought help at American and European sex therapy clinics in the eighties had complaints that centered around problems of sexual desire.

The findings of Leiblum and Rosen's survey are consistent with our own experience. More precisely, 38% of the 5,580 patients with diagnosed sexual disorders whom we saw between 1972 and 1992 met the criteria for sexual desire disorders (see Figure 1). Moreover, our data

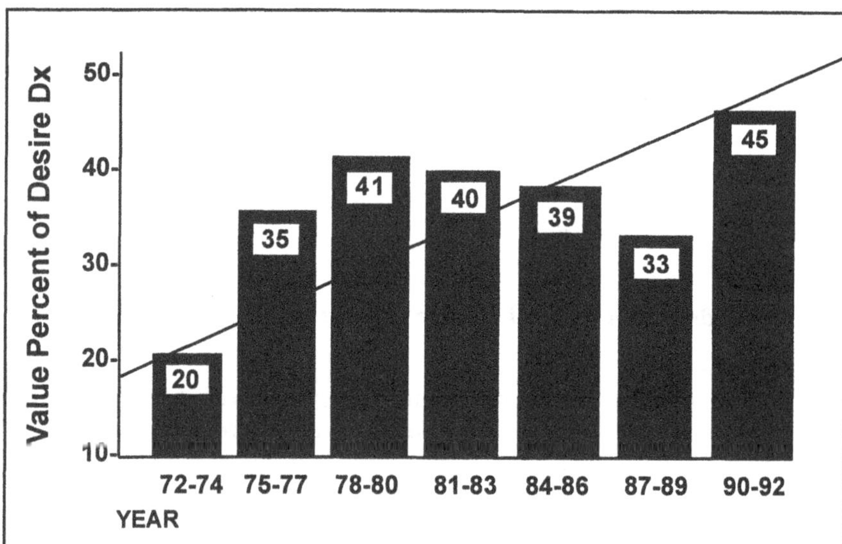

FIGURE 1. Percentage of patients with sexual desire disorders: 1972–1992.*

*These patients were seen at the Human Sexuality Program of the Payne Whitney Clinic of the New York Hospital-Cornell Medical Center, and in our own private practice group in Manhattan.

indicate that there has been a steady increase in the numbers of patients who are seeking help with desire problems in the past decade. The same phenomenon has been observed by others in the field.

There is good reason to believe that this upward trend is likely to continue. First is the steady increase in the number of elderly patients, a population that is particularly susceptible to desire disorders, who are seeking help for their sexual problems. Another factor contributing to the continuing growth of sexual desire disorders is the real and perceived danger posed by the sexual transmission of AIDS, for which there is as yet no end in sight.

ORGANIC SEXUAL DESIRE PROBLEMS IN OLDER PATIENTS

Sexual desire disorders due to medical conditions and drugs and to combined psychological/organic factors are on the rise. This increased prevalence is, at least in part, a consequence of significant improvements in American health care, which have increased the life expectancy of Americans by about 30% in the past two decades. Today, men and women are living healthier, longer, and better quality lives. Moreover, old age is being redefined in more positive terms (Friedan, 1993), with the result that more elderly people than ever before feel entitled to a good sex life and are looking for sexual health care.

Paradoxically, some of the very medications and treatments that are making all these good things possible also have serious sexual side effects, and this has contributed to the increase of sexual complaints in the elderly. For example, the drugs that are now being widely used to treat hypertension and coronary artery disease with great success are notorious for their adverse effects on libido and erections (see Chapter 10).

As another example, the new chemotherapeutic treatments for breast, prostate, and other cancers are increasing the disease-free and actual survival time of cancer patients. Unfortunately, these therapies frequently have devastating effects on male and female libido because cytotoxic agents impair the body's ability to produce sex hormones (Rose & Davis, 1980; Kaplan, 1992B; Kaplan & Owett, 1993).

Fortunately, these problems are being balanced out by recent advances in the medical treatment of the organic components of sexual disorders, together with improved psychosexual therapy approaches to deficient sexual desire that have made it possible to enhance and maintain the sexual desire and functioning of many elderly and handicapped patients. The treatment of elderly patients and couples can be most rewarding for therapists, and this topic is covered in Chapter 10.

THE NEW "HOT MONOGAMY"

In the past, older couples who have been together for many years and whose sexual interest in each other had diminished over time would assume relatively little risk by seeking new and more exciting sexual partners and novel sexual experiences. Hence there was a time in the 60's and 70's where there was a growing interest in such libido-enhancing activities as participating in orgies, joining sex clubs, or "swinging" with their neighbors' wives and husbands.

But today "the window of sexual opportunity" that was opened so briefly has been slammed shut by the fear of AIDS. The 25 short years of carefree sex that elapsed between the discovery of the "pill" in the 50's, which removed the threat of unwanted pregnancy, and the 80's, when the dangers of contracting HIV infections from sex with strangers surfaced, is over and sexual promiscuity has become more dangerous today than it has ever been in human history (Kaplan, 1993B).

But despite these real and perceived hazards, the "sexual revolution" has not been defeated by AIDS. The social forces that liberated people from the guilt and shame that had encumbered sexuality for the past 2,000 years, and which allowed them to feel freer sexually, have had profound effects that will not be eroded easily. In my opinion, once having experienced sexual freedom and tasted the joys of "hot" sex—sexual experiences enhanced by novelty, variety, erotica, fantasy, and variant sexual practices—people will never again content themselves with the lackluster, boring, passionless, mechanical sex that characterized so many marriages in the past.

I came to this conclusion in part because sex therapists are seeing increasing numbers of couples who are bored with their sex lives and no longer feel much desire for each other, but who are not willing to accept this passively.

More and more, these older couples are seeking professional help to enhance and revitalize their sexual relationship with their long-term partners when this has become boring and devoid of passion. Many modern senior citizens are no longer content to embrace celibacy, nor do they wish to risk their lives by engaging in the "Russian Roulette" that characterizes contemporary sexual promiscuity. These folk are looking for better sex, but only with their own husbands and wives, or with their exclusive lovers.

Sex therapists can often do quite a lot for couples who are engaged in this new quest for the "hot monogamy of the 90's." In other words, such couples may well reach their goals for better, more frequent, more passionate sex with their steady long-term partners through the use of therapeutic approaches that introduce novelty, fantasy, and flexibility into their sexual routines. These matters are discussed in Chapters 5 and 6 on treatment and also in the section on older patients in Chapter 10.

POPULATION

The great numbers of patients and couples we studied and treated made it possible to discern subtle clinical patterns and correlations, and my insights regarding the psychopathogenesis of sexual desire disorders grew out of these observations.

Between 1972 and 1992, I personally evaluated 7,663 patients with sexual complaints at the human sexuality clinic of the New York Hospital-Cornell Medical Center and/or at our private practice group in Manhattan. Of these, 5,580 were diagnosed with a sexual disorder, and the rest were asymptomatic partners. Of these, 3,552, or 64%, were males, and 2,028, or 37%, were female. The 5,580 sexually symptomatic patients included 2,122, or 37%, who met the criteria for sexual desire disorder. Out of these 1,695, or about 80%, were classified as HSD, 414, or 19%, had sexual aversion disorders and/or the phobic avoidance of sex, while 13 patients, or > 1%, were sexually hyperactive. Of the patients with sexual aversion disorders, 170, or 41%, were males and 244, or 59%, were females, while HSD was about evenly distributed between the genders.

A total of 787, or 14%, of the patients with sexual desire disorders were seen in consultation only. The remaining 1,335 patients received treatment at one of our facilities by myself and/or by members of the staff, who have all been trained in the brief integrated psychodynamically oriented sex-therapy method described in this volume.

Fourteen percent of the 1,003 patients with HSD who were treated and 35% of the 240 treated sexaphobics received psychoactive drugs in conjunction with psychosexual therapy. At this time, the proportion of patients with HSD who receive psychoactive drugs or hormones has risen to 25%.

Sixty percent of the sexually symptomatic patients were seen conjointly with their partners, and the remainder were seen by themselves, although most of these, about 75%, had partners who did not attend the sessions.

Our patient population was representative of the multiethnic community of New York City. Their places of birth encompassed every continent on the planet, and every major religious group and socioeconomic level was represented

Overall, 87% of our patients had sexual partners at the time they sought treatment, but the proportion of single persons who are seeking help for their sexual problems has been increasing in recent years and has now risen to over 20%.

The ages of our low desire patients ranged from 18 to 92 years. Of our patients diagnosed with HSD, 26% were 50 years or older. The men tended to be older than the women. More specifically, 31% of our male patients with low desire were over 50, while only 17% of the females were in this age group. Since 1992, which was the cut-off date for the study, the proportion of older patients has increased.

MODIFICATIONS AND NEW INSIGHTS

It makes me very happy to be able to report that the hypotheses and the preliminary ideas regarding the pathogenesis and the treatment of desire disorders, which had been based on our initial observations of only a limited number of patients and couples back in the 70's, have been confirmed and supported by this extensive clinical experience.

However, while I am pleased that my original ideas about desire disorders were basically on the right track, these early concepts were of necessity sketchy and incomplete. During the intervening years, I and my associates have had the opportunity to study and treat the large population of patients with desire problems, which was described above, and this experience has enabled us to refine, revise, and extend our hypotheses about the nature and origins of disorders of sexual desire. At the same time the new insights into the pathogenesis and the dynamics of these complex syndromes have fueled the continuous evolution and modification of our treatment methods, so that these have changed considerably from the initial format.

In short, we have learned a great deal about the causes and the treatment of sexual desire disorders in the past 16 years. It is definitely time for an update.

CHAPTER 2

Sexual Desire Disorders: The Dysfunctional Regulation of Sexual Motivation

On the level of subjective experience, sexual desire or lust is an urge that impels men and women to seek out, initiate, and/or respond to sexual stimulation. But sexual desire is not just a subjective sensation nor is this merely a mental event. Sexual desire is a motivational or drive state that is generated by specific neurophysiologic processes in the brain. In this respect, sex is exactly like the other drives or appetites that subserve individual and species survival.

In other words, subjective sensations of hunger, thirst, heat, cold and also sexual lust are generated by and are dependent on the activity of specially dedicated neural regulatory structures that lie deeply buried in the most ancient and primitive parts of the brain, the hypothalamus and the limbic system, a neural network that is also involved in the maintenance of homeostasis and emotional expression (Papez, 1937). Unless the structures that control sexual motivation, which are loosely referred to as the "sex-centers," are activated, it is impossible to experience sexual desire or to feel erotic pleasure.

THE SEX REGULATING STRUCTURES OF THE BRAIN

The sex regulating apparatus of the brain is in a certain sense still a "black box" (see Figure 2). By this, I mean that the precise neurobiological mechanisms that maintain physical homeostasis and regulate our drives remain to be elucidated. Thus, current concepts of drives and motives are based largely on inferences derived from observing the effects of incentive and suppressive stimuli, and also from the study of the behavioral deficits that follow certain experimental chemical manipulations and surgical ablations of different parts of the brain.

Such studies have made it clear that *bilateral clusters of hypothalamic nuclei* have important integrative and control functions over specific behaviors such as feeding, drinking, and reproduction. In other words if sensors in the neurones that make up the "thirst centers" pick up an impending state of dehydration from the blood that circulates through the brain, a subjective feeling of thirst is generated, and the creature will be seized by a compelling urge to drink water.

However, as Kupferman (1991) has pointed out "the idea of a specific drive regulatory center is an over simplification. In reality, the hypothalamic nuclei perform these control functions in concert with the limbic system and other neurocircuits that are distributed among several brain regions" (p. 755). The term "sex-center" is used here only as a kind of shorthand to avoid more cumbersome phrases.

The hypothalamic control nuclei are richly connected to other regions of the brain via the limbic lobe. If a set of these hypothalamic control nuclei or its connections are destroyed or physiologically inactivated, the motivation for the particular behavior which it regulates is impaired, and becomes over- or underactive.

The anatomy and physiology of hunger and sexual motivation are analogous in many respects and a comparison is instructive.

It has been well documented that the surgical extirpation of the *lateral hypothalamic nuclei*, or "appetite centers," and/or the inactivation of these structures by the local instillation of toxic drugs, causes an animal to stop eating and it will starve to death in the presence of an adequate food supply.

Conversely, the bilateral surgical ablation or chemical paralysis of the "satiety" centers, which are located close by in the *ventral medial nuclei of the hypothalamus*, produces voracious animals that eat incessantly and become grotesquely obese (Kupferman, 1991).

The effects of the destruction of the nearby hypothalamic "sex centers" are comparable. Thus, the bilateral ablation of the *anterior medial nuclei* of the hypothalamus effectively destroys an animal's sexual motivation and its ability to respond to sexual stimulation, while the removal of certain suppressor pathways in the hippocampus has the opposite effect and causes monkeys to become sexually hyperactive.*

*Monkeys with lesions in the hippocampal "sex-suppressor" areas exhibit the "Klüver-Bucy syndrome," which is characterized by a number of behavioral abnormalities, including a striking sexual dysinhibition.

Dual Control Elements are Involved in Sexual Motivation

According to Kupferman (1991), "all examples of physiological motivational control seem to involve dual effects—inhibitory and excitatory—which function together to adjust the system" (p. 751). Control of sexual motivation is no exception and also operates on such a "dual-steering" principle.

Once again, we can learn from the similarities between eating and sex.

More specifically, under normal circumstances, a state of starvation activates the ventromedial hypothalamic "appetite centers." This neurophysiologic activity produces a subjective feeling of *hunger* that compels us to hunt, gather, scavenge, or, depending on the social context, go to the icebox or to a restaurant to enjoy eating a good meal.

The appetite centers are normally "shut off" or become quiescent when certain sensors in the brain detect and signal that enough food has been ingested to maintain the body weight—in other words, that *homeostasis* has been achieved.

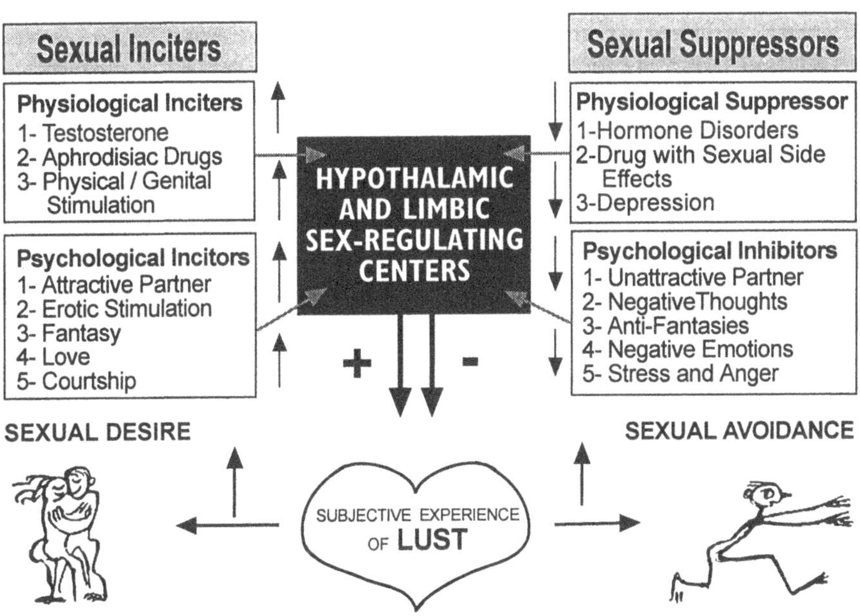

FIGURE 2. Dual control elements of human sexual motivation: A psychosomatic model

The same physiologic signal appears to galvanize the nearby "satiety centers" into action. On a subjective level, this shift in hypothalamic activity is perceived as a feeling of "fullness." In this sated state, the aroma and sounds of a sizzling sirloin steak, for which one "would have killed" half-an-hour ago when feeling starved, is now entirely unappealing.

However, satiety is only one of the signals that is capable of stopping hunger. The appetite centers and the urge to eat can also be overridden and inhibited by a number of external "suppressive stimuli," such as a disgusting smell or the perception of an imminent emergency. This is a built-in safety feature that is highly advantageous for the survival of the species.

Sexual motivation or desire is governed by a comparable "motor" and "brake" dual steering mechanism. When we have not had sex for a while and we come across an attractive sexual opportunity, such as an assignation with the one we love,* we are likely to feel intense lust or desire, presumably because our sex centers, which have been primed by the period of celibacy, are "turned on" by the sight, smell, and touch of an interesting and interested sexual partner.

But after the reproductive act is completed, most adult men feel "sated" and are refractory to further sexual stimulation.** The female satiation point is more variable, and while some women are satisfied after one orgasm, others want more, but eventually even the sexiest women become sated.

In addition to *satiety*, and even more important from a clinical perspective, is the fact that the "fight or flight" emergency emotions and the autonomic discharge that these generate have priority over and can override the desire to copulate, so that stressful and dangerous situations generally cause people to lose their "sexual appetite."

The built-in priority of emergency over the appetites was and still is important for the survival of the species, for "he who runs away, lives to mate another day." Even today, sexual "suppressors" keep our sexual desires in balance with our needs to avoid personal risk and to maintain our relationships with others.

*Dr. Michael Liebowitz has postulated that certain chemical changes occur in the brains of people when they fall in love, which heighten sexual desire on a physiologic basis (Liebowitz, 1983).

**Some adolescent or very young men do not feel sated until they have come more than once.

SEXUAL DESIRE DISORDERS: THE SEXUAL MOTIVATION DYSFUNCTIONS

Normal sexual desire depends on a good balance between the "erotic motor," which incites our desire to copulate, and the "sexual brakes," which keep our libidinous urges in check so that we do not crash headlong into disaster.

However, if the normal control mechanism that adjusts and modulates our sexual motivation goes awry, the person will experience an abnormal or dysfunctional increase or decrease of sexual desire.

In other words, I am suggesting that hyperactive and hypoactive sexual desire disorders are the result of malfunctions or dysfunctions of the sex-regulating mechanism that ordinarily modulates our sexual desires and adjusts these to the opportunities and hazards of the environment.

Once again, according to this paradigm, sexual desire disorders and eating disorders are analogous, in that both can be conceptualized as the resultants of important regulatory systems gone awry.

More specifically, both *hyperactive sexual desire* and *obesity/bulimia* represent a pathological or dysfunctional *lack of control* over the respective function, whereas *hypoactive sexual desire* and *anorexia nervosa* are analogous in that both conditions represent a loss of an appetite as a result of pathologically excessive overcontrol.*

What Causes the Sex-Regulating System To Go Awry?

According to a psychosomatic view of sexual desire, the sex-regulating apparatus of the brain represents the "final common pathway"** via which various biological and psychosocial factors influence the modulation and adjustment of human sexual desire (see Figure 2).

For example, a deficiency of bioavailable circulating testosterone or a shift in the balance of neurotransmitters from dopaminergic to serotonergic consistently results in a subjective decrease in sexual interest. However, subjectively and clinically, identical libido-decreasing effects are produced by psychological suppressive stimuli such as the perception of the partner as repulsive, by an imminent exter-

---

*It is interesting to note that the prevalences of the abnormal *over-* and *under-control* of eating and sex are reversed. Thus the lack of normal control over food intake, or *obesity,* is by far more common than *anorexia,* or the abnormal *over-control* of food intake. On the other hand, *hypersexuality* is a relatively uncommon condition, while the abnormal suppression of sexual desire, or HSD, is highly prevalent.

**The phrase "final common pathway" was originally used by the great neurologist Sherrington to explain the functions of lower motor neurones.

nal danger, or by anxiety and anger-provoking thoughts. Presumably, all these various classes of stimuli exert similar suppressor influences on the central sex-regulatory system.

Conversely, the urge to copulate is increased by physiologic factors such as the replacement of deficient testosterone, certain "aphrodisiac" drugs (see Chapters 7 and 10), and also by such environmental incentive input as the perception, seductive behavior, or the fantasy of a partner who personifies our sexual fantasies.

This psychosomatic view accounts for the fact that the regulatory mechanism that adjusts human sexual desire is subject to impairment by both physical and psychological stressors. This has important clinical implications.

More specifically, this model offers an explanation for the loss of sexual appetite that is experienced by patients who have certain kinds of sex-hormone abnormalities or who are taking drugs that chemically paralyze the sex centers of the brain. Such hormone-related or drug induced low-libido states constitute the *organic sexual desire disorders.*

But in humans (as opposed to other mammals that are hormone-driven), sex hormones and other physiologic factors are clinically important only if these are abnormal while the majority of low libido states are the result of psychological conflicts, difficulties in the relationship, stress, and depression.

The Psychogenic Dysregulation of Sexual Desire

The pathogenesis of psychogenic hyposexual desire disorders will not become fully understood until there is more complete information about the underlying neurophysiology of the regulation of the human sex drive.

However, despite the incomplete state of knowledge in this area, we have begun to learn something about what makes the sex-regulatory system go awry in persons who are by all appearances physiologically normal. The new insights have grown out of our extensive, detailed analyses of the sexual behaviors, thoughts, fantasies, perceptions, functioning and feelings, as well as the psychosexual histories of over 2,000 patients with HSD, before, during, and after they make love.

These observations have led to the conclusion, that patients with HSD unwittingly "turn themselves off" by manipulating the mental and psychological incentive and suppressive stimuli that ordinarily modulate human sexual desire in a negative direction. This results in the inappropriate and dysfunctional down-regulation of sexual motivation which typifies this syndrome.

How Do Patients with (Psychogenic) HSD "Turn Themselves Off"?

As was discussed in the preceding section, human sexual motivation is governed by a dual steering system by which lust can be increased or decreased, respectively, by the balance of certain so-called *sexual incenters* and *sexual supressors.*

As will be detailed in the following chapter on the evolution of human sexual desire, sexual incenters can be understood within an evolutionary context, according to which we have been genetically programmed to lust after and to copulate with fertile sexual partners who have "good genes" and will bring forth healthy children. Everything that facilitates this reproductive imperative is experienced as sexually arousing. Thus, sexual "turn ons" for women include the attentions of a "well hung," strong, attractive, successful, male, while men are stimulated by the flirtatious behavior of "well stacked," estrogen-primed, sexy young females, and both genders can also be aroused by the fantasies or mental images of the above. Another powerful erotic stimulant is physical stimulation, which both increases sexual arousal and prepares the quiescent genitalia for their reproductive functions.

But again, we have also been equipped with a "brake" mechanism to hold our sexual desires in check so that we do not imperil our physical safety, nor our place within our social group, by the rampant expression of our sexual urges.

The Normal Control of Sexual Motivation

Normal men and women who are free of sexual conflict instinctively manipulate the psychosexual stimuli that incite their sexual desires so as to maximize their erotic feelings and reproductive success when they are with the right partner in the right situation, and they call upon "suppressive" stimuli to down-regulate or decrease their sexual motivation only when sex would be disadvantageous.

A normal person who is in love "accentuates the positives" and *idealizes* his/her love object by selectively focusing on his/her good points thereby suppressing competing negative stimuli. At the same time, happy lovers "decentuate the negatives" and tune out any unattractive features that would interfere with the buildup of their passion.

Eager lovers "prime the pump" of their lust by anticipating their encounters with their beloved with pleasure, and by fantasizing about the erotic joys to come.

Unconflicted lovers make an effort to create quiet, private, beautiful, romantic environments that are conducive to seduction and to romance.

When they are courting a lover, normal people instinctively adjust their behaviors so as to entice the object of their desire, and to induce a positive, erotic state of mind in him or her.

Men and women bent on romance are careful about their appearance and hygiene, and they "put their best foot forward" to be appealing, for the opposites—rudeness, insensitivity, dirtiness, and sloppiness—pose the risk of "turning off" their partners.

Moreover, functional people who are eager to make love are careful not to sabotage the experience. They avoid overindulging in alcohol, drugs, or food, they make sure they are rested and in good shape when they meet their beloved, and they try to "tune out" their work-a-day worries. For getting "zonked," stuffed, loaded, obsessive, fatigued and stressed out are apt to put their "sex centers" out of commission.

In addition, unconflicted lovers skillfully exploit the erotic potential of physical stimulation, in the form of sensuous caresses and kisses, to inflame their partners and to become aroused themselves, and they know how to use the aphrodisiac powers of fantasy to enhance their sexuality.

Moreover, it has been demonstrated, by measuring cerebral blood flow, that attention to and the expectation of stimulation of one part of the body *physically* decreases the perception of competing areas (Dreverts 1995). In terms of sex, normal men and women focus on their genitalia and expect that their lover will stimulate them there and pleasure other erotogenic zones as well. This literally decreases extraneous and unpleasant sensory input so that an uncomfortable position or noises made by the children go unnoticed and do not compete with the buildup of erotic feelings.

The Dysfunctional Control of Sexual Motivation

Patients with hypoactive sexual desire disorders reverse this process. Hyposexual individuals misuse the normal suppressor mechanisms in the service of their neurotic fears of and conflicts about love, intimacy and sex. Thus they unconsciously down-regulate their sexual desires by selectively focusing on their partners' negative qualities or on other unpleasant issues, while they blind themselves to their lover's attractive features. In this manner their sex centers are "deceived" into "turning off" as though the sexual opportunity were hazardous or disadvantageous.

Further, they fail to exploit the natural sexual inciters by avoiding erotogenic physical stimulation of their bodies and genitalia and they suppress sexual fantasies or erotic imagery that might arouse them. In contrast to normal lovers, dysfunctional individuals focus on and expect unpleasant sensory input, which effectively decreases the experience of pleasurable, erotic sensations. In short, these patients engage in innumerable ploys and maneuvers to down-regulate their desire for sex, including such tactics as "turning off" their sexual partners by putting their "worst foot forward" and by creating sloppy, harried, disgusting environments that are not conducive to romance. According to this paradigm, such antisexual behaviors constitute the "immediate causes" or antecedents of HSD, as will be discussed in greater detail in later chapters.

Why Do Patients with HSD Turn Themselves Off?

The observations regarding the mechanisms and the behavioral/cognitive details of the immediate causes of HSD only concern the matter of *how* patients down-regulate their sex drives. However, this does not address the more complex question of *why* these individuals feel compelled to engage in these self-destructive, countersexual behaviors that rob them of sexual pleasure and spoil their relationships with their partners. This important issue is the topic of later sections of the book dealing with the deeper causes of disorders of sexual desire.

Implications for Treatment

The first step in the psychodynamically oriented sex therapy approach to hypoactive sexual desire disorders is to help patients recognize the self-induced elements in their dysfunctional lack of sexual desire, and to understand the means they use to down-regulate and suppress their lust when they are with their partners. This is a necessary preliminary to implementing the major treatment strategy of this approach, *which is to help the patient or the couple modify, reverse or eliminate their countersexual behaviors.*

This theme will be developed in subsequent chapters of the book devoted to the treatment of sexual desire disorders.

CHAPTER 3

The Evolution of Sexual Desire and Fantasy

Anatomic structures are seldom completely discarded as creatures evolve into more advanced life forms. For it is inherent in the process of evolution that outdated organs are "recycled" and adapted for the new purposes and needs of the emerging species. Thus, gills became ears and lungs, and fins turned into limbs as creatures climbed out of the ocean onto the land, and forelimbs evolved into wings for flight when creatures took to the sky. However, beneath the feathers, the wings of birds still retain the same set of bones that evolved into paws in terrestrial animals, and eventually into our very own hands and fingers.

The same conservationist principle has also governed the evolution of reproductive behavior, which has been similarly "recycled" and adapted to human needs. Thus, traces of primitive mating patterns are clearly visible in the palimpsest of human sexuality.

Although homo sapiens have evolved beyond estrus, which dominates the reproductive behaviors of other mammals, remnants of *the estrus cycle* are still discernible in human beings. Moreover, despite the fact that human sexuality has been virtually divorced from reproduction, the imprimatur of the biological imperative to *reproduce and to multiply* still gives shape to our sexual desires.

Further, some of the behavioral and hormonal elements of the ancient *maternal–infant bond*, which evolved to ensure the survival of helpless avian and mammalian newborns, appear to have been incorporated into human romantic love relationships.

Therefore, because we are so deeply rooted in our phylogeny, a brief look at the reproductive history of our species may extend our insight into our human sexual heritage.

ESTRUS

The reproductive behaviors of almost all infra-human mammals is organized around the female estrus cycle. With the exceptions of primates, female mammals are sexually quiescent, nonresponsive, and also of absolutely no interest to males when they are not ovulating. But as soon as they go into "heat," they become irresistibly attractive to males of their species and also highly responsive to sexual stimulation. Thus, the emergence of the estrus mating pattern resulted in limiting the sexual activity of females, (and therefore of males) to these brief time periods when the probability for conception is high.

This ancient energy-efficient reproductive dance is orchestrated by the interplay by the male and female sex hormones, *estrogen* (E) and *testosterone* (T).

Estrogen: The Hormone that Makes Females Attractive to Males

Estrus is produced in female mammals by surges of estrogen, which are seasonal in some species and induced by males in others. Estrogens are steroids that are synthesized and secreted by the ovaries. The flood of ovarian E results in the release of one or more eggs (ova) from the ovarian store, in a process that is called *ovulation*. Females are fertile and can be inseminated only during the few days that elapse between the release of the egg and its demise. At any other time, sexual intercourse is wasted from the viewpoint of reproduction.

In most mammalian species, the surge of estrogen that is secreted at ovulation also causes the odor, color, and shape of the female genitalia to change in ways that make the animal irresistible to males. For example, the female chimp's genitalia swell and turn purple during estrus, and this seems to drive male chimpanzees wild.

Human females do not go into heat when they ovulate, and there are no physical changes to indicate that we are fertile or receptive to sexual stimulation. We rely on more subtle, behavioral signals of body language, eye contact, etc. that let men know when we feel like having sex.

Another of estrogen's important functions in reproduction is the development and maintenance of more permanent female secondary sexual characteristics that are attractive to males but do not fluctuate with estrus. For example, estrogen is responsible for the development of the female genitalia and for female secondary sexual characteristics such as smaller size, female vocal quality, finer skin, and hair texture, etc. that distinguish males from females in sexually dimorphic species like ours.

In addition, the effects of estrogen on the brain are thought to be vital for predisposing the development of female behavior patterns. These entail the less aggressive, less territorial, and more nurturing, "maternal" behaviors that are characteristic of female mammals towards their young.

Although, humans have evolved beyond estrus, estrogen remains responsible for many of the physical features and emotional characteristics that attract human males to human females*.

Testosterone: The Masculinizing Hormone of Males and the Libido Hormone of Both Genders

Testosterone has the other lead in the pas de deux of the estrus cycle and reproduction, and its role is complementary to that of estrogen. This hormone masculinizes males physically, and T is also the "libido hormone" for both genders.

Testosterone and Masculinization

In males testosterone and other androgens are synthesized and secreted largely by the testes, and smaller amounts are contributed by the adrenal glands.

T plays a protean role in male sexuality that begins before birth, with the secretion of fetal T by the testes of XY embryos. This is critical for male development, for in the absence of fetal T, all mammalian fetuses develop into females, physically as well as behaviorally (McEwen, 1979, 1984).

In adult mammalian males, androgens are responsible for the development and maturation of the male genitalia and for maintaining these in a functional state, capable of erection and ejaculation, and this hor-

*The role of E in males is not well understood. However, it is known that E is needed for normal male as well as female skeletal development, and in addition both E and T are believed to play key roles in the normal embryological development of the male fetus.

mone also promotes the growth and maintenance of the male secondary sexual characteristics.

In sexually dimorphic species, like ours, T-mediated male secondary characteristics generally involve bigger size, greater strength, more massive muscular development, coarser fur, a deeper voice, and more aggressive, competitive, and territorial behavior tendencies, which are useful qualities for survival in natural settings.

In addition, T is responsible for purely decorative masculine features such as bright plumage, a gorgeous tail, symmetrical wing feathers, beautiful mating songs, impressive antlers, regal manes, etc., which serve primarily to attract the female of their species.

Androgens and Male Sexual Motivation

T is also vital and responsible for sexual motivation in all male mammals, including man. Presumably, this effect is produced by the direct action of this hormone on the T receptors of the neurones that make up the sex-regulating centers of the brain.

Androgen-driven male reproductive behavior has evolved into two distinct patterns: a seasonal and a permanent one.

Males of some species, like deer, elk, and moose, that live in temperate and arctic climates maintain a low level of circulating T during the winter months, when these animals have little interest in sex or in the company of females. But in the spring, during the mating season, their testicles swell and release a great tide of T, which presumably activates the subcortical sex centers. Then, the behavior of males changes dramatically, so that the active pursuit of females, who are now becoming fertile and going into heat, becomes their first priority, to the extent that some male animals, such as sea lions, do not bother to eat during the mating season, and a certain small Australian rodent copulates furiously until he dies of exhaustion.

On the other hand, the levels of circulating T in males of certain tropical and domestic species such as lions, dogs, cats, and homo sapiens as well remain constant and at a level that is sufficiently high so that they remain perpetually on the prowl and responsive to females in heat.

Testosterone Is the Libido Hormone of Human Males and Females

In humans, T retains its roles as the physical masculinizer of men, and as the "libido hormone" of both genders.

Testosterone and Male Libido in Humans

Adequate levels of bioavailable T are vital for the maintenance of human male libido. If this hormone is deficient, men become *hypogonadal*, and in that state they rapidly lose their sex drive, and, eventually, their ejaculatory and erectile functions as well (Segraves, 1988A; Schiavi, 1990; Davidson & Rosen, 1992). The signs and symptoms of hypogonadism are readily reversed by the administration of replacement T, as will be discussed in Chapter 10 on the Organic Sexual Desire Disorders.

The influence of T on human male sexual behavior begins at the sixth week of gestation, when the testes of human XY fetuses start to secrete fetal T. This hormone masculinizes the developing brain so that its behavior will become appropriate to the male gender (McEwen, 1984).

Circulating T remains relatively low in boys until there is a surge at puberty. This is associated with a sharp increase in sexual interest in adolescent males, along with the maturation of the male genitalia and the species specific secondary male sexual characteristics. In humans these include facial and pubic hair. Thereafter, the human testicles continue to produce sufficient levels of this hormone to maintain libido virtually to the end of the man's life.

Testosterone and Human Female Libido

The variegated influence of sex hormones on women has been well summarized in Money's dictum that E *makes females attractive to males while T makes them responsive to males.*(Money, 1961).

The importance of the androgenic hormones for *male* libido and sexual functioning has been known since the turn of the century. But, although Waxenberg and his colleagues clearly demonstrated in the early 50's that women who are deprived of endogenous androgens lose their desire for sex (Waxenberg, Drellick, & Sutherland, 1959; Waxenberg, Finkbiener, Drellick, & Sutherland, 1960), the fact that androgens are essential for normal human female sexual motivation has been accepted only recently, and only with some reluctance, by the medical establishment. However, while there can be no doubt that androgens are essential for maintaining a normal female sex drive, it is also true that women require much lower levels of circulating T than men, possibly because females have a greater neuronal sensitivity to this hormone (Sherwin, 1988).

All female mammals produce androgens. In human females, 50% of endogenous testosterone is produced by the ovaries and 50% by the adrenal glands.

The circulating levels of T rise in girls at puberty, thereafter remaining constant except for some slight fluctuations during the menstrual cycle. Thus, as has been emphasized in the previous section, since female libido is governed by androgens, women are unique among vertebrates in remaining amenable to sexual stimulation when they are not fertile and ovulating. In any season and throughout the menstrual cycle and even after menopause women secrete androgens and are sexually receptive, for the old association between heightened sexual motivation and fertility no longer exists in humans.

A number of circumstances can be associated with the development of clinically significant T deficiencies in women. These include advanced old age, hysterectomy with bilateral salpingo-oophorectomy, and chemotherapy for cancer with cytotoxic agents, which can all have deleterious effects on women's ability to synthesize and secrete androgens. Under these circumstances, women may develop what I have termed the *Female Androgen-Deficiency Syndrome* (FADS). This condition resembles male hypogonadism in that women also experience a complete loss or a marked decrease of libido, which can readily be reversed with T replacement (Kaplan, 1992B; Kaplan & Owett, 1993). See Chapter 10.

Pheromones.

The high surge of sex hormones that are synthesized and secreted during estrus causes the cells of the female genitalia to produce *pheromones*. Pheromones are aromatic chemicals that incite male sexual desire. These chemical aphrodisiacs are tremendously potent, as anyone who has witnessed a pack of male dogs pursuing a bitch in heat will attest to. Indeed, the power of pheromones as sexual incitor stimuli is such that a single drop of female mosquito pheromone suffices to lure male mosquitoes to their deaths in traps from miles around.

These sexual inciters are highly specific to their species so that animal pheromones have no demonstrable stimulating effects on the sexual desires of human beings.

Pheromones and Human Sexual Desire

Until very recently, it was believed that pheromones no longer play a role in human sexuality. But new evidence has been accumulated suggesting that humans may have retained some remnants of the capacity to respond to these ancient aromatic aphrodisiacs. Berliner (1993) and his group have found clusters of small receptors in human noses that respond actively to a wide variety of odorless chemicals that are produced by the human skin. Moreover, women and men respond to different chemicals. Berliner reported that when these so called pheromones are inhaled, they have a subtle tranquilizing and euphoric effect on the person's mood, and he has suggested that this might play a role in human bonding.

The significance of these tantalizing findings in terms of human sexual desire remains to be elucidated. However, while a whiff of their lover's genital aroma does not turn men into sex maniacs, as this does to rutting elephants or tomcats, the odor released by the lover can be arousing and exceedingly pleasurable for both men and women. In fact, many of our patients report that their partner's aroma is an attractant while the odor of others is strongly repellant. In other words, it would not be surprising if it eventually turned out that smell is a far more important element in human sexual desire and object choice, as well as in disorders of sexual desire, than current wisdom allows.

Oxytocin and Vasopressin: The "Love and Monogamy Hormones"?

Oxytocin and vasopressin are small peptide molecules secreted by the pituitary gland and also by certain neurons in the brains of vertebrates. Vasopressin and oxytocin and/or their biochemical precursors are ancient substances that have been with us throughout millions of years of evolution (Pedersen et al., 1992). The functions of these peptides in certain physiologic processes such as milk ejection (oxytocin) and water regulation (vasopressin) are well known, but their behavioral effects have been somewhat of a mystery until quite recently, when it was found that oxytocin and vasopressin play major roles in enhancing reproductive behaviors, and in facilitating pair-bonding and parental behaviors in vertebrates from toads to humans (Moore, 1992; Insel & Shapiro, 1992; Insel, 1992; Fakelman, 1993).

Oxytocin

Oxytocin is released simultaneously by the brains of mothers and their infants during suckling. It has been known for some time that this substance is necessary for the ejection of milk. But now it appears that oxytocin is also essential for the onset of normal maternal behavior, as well as for the formation of the mother/infant bond, in all mammalian species studied thus far (Pedersen et al., 1992; Insel & Shapiro, 1992; Insel, Carter, & Shapiro, 1993).

Oxytocin is also secreted simultaneously, and can be measured in the bloodstreams of both sexual partners during sexual stimulation. This parallel outpouring of oxytocin enhances the sexual functioning of both male and female mammals (Arletti, Benelli & Bertolini, 1992; Caldwell, 1992). and it has been postulated that oxytocin plays a role in human erection and desire as well (Davidson & Rosen, 1992).

In addition, it has been found that the simultaneous release of oxytocin by the sexual partners is associated with affiliative, non-aggressive behavior in both, and this, in turn, favors the formation of pair-bonding between monogamous sexual pairs (Arletti et al., 1992; Insel & Shapiro, 1992; Insel, Carter, & Shapiro, 1993; Fakelman, 1993).

It does not take a great leap of imagination to speculate that since the maternal-infant bond and mutual sexual stimulation are both associated with the simultaneous release of oxytocin, and both activities are characterized by a close, affectionate connection, the same basic hormonal-behavioral mechanism that produces maternal/infant bonding is also involved in the pair-bonding of sexual partners.

The notion that oxytocin is the "glue" that attaches babies and mothers as well as lovers to each other has recently been given support by the work of Insel and his colleagues who have demonstrated in a fascinating series of experiments that *partner selection* is enhanced by the release of oxytocin in *monogamous* mammals such as voles (Insel, 1992; Fakelman, 1993; Insel, Carter, & Shapiro, 1993). More specifically the investigators found that females are more likely to choose and attach themselves to a male who is secreting oxytocin than to one whose oxytocin release has been chemically blocked.

Vasopressin

This is another ancient peptide molecule that seems to have an active role in reproductive behavior. Recent evidence suggests that vasopressin may promote monogamous and paternal behavior in certain monogamous species. In addition to producing monogamous pair bonding and fierce "mate guarding" behavior in male prairie voles, vasopressin seems to inhibit male aggression towards their newborns, while enhancing affiliative "paternal" behaviors such as cuddling and grooming (Insel, Carter, & Shapiro, 1993). In short, vasopressin seems to make males better, less aggressive, and more nurturing fathers.

Oxytocin and vasopressin have been dubbed the "love and monogamy" hormones in the popular literature, but the signficance of these peptides in human sexuality, love relationships and parental behavior remains to be scientifically established. It is certainly possible that these fascinating peptides will be found to play a role in promoting monogamous love.

It may be speculated further that the simultaneous release of oxytocin by human sexual partners after sexual stimulation and orgasm is responsible, at least in part, for the peaceful, sensuous, affectionate "after-glow" that is so delightful after especially passionate and intimate sexual encounters. The happily sated lovers' blissful expression and body language, which reflect this sweet, floating, relaxed postcoital state, are strikingly reminiscent of the blissful, dreamy look that infants have after nursing, and which is mirrored in the tranquil feeling of their mothers. This parallel is suggestive of a common biological element in maternal and romantic love. If these speculations turn out to have any substance, oxytocin may yet prove to be the "resolution phase," or "afterglow," hormone, as well as the substrate of human mother–infant love.

THE PRIMACY OF PSYCHOLOGICAL INFLUENCES ON HUMAN SEXUAL DESIRE

In sum, in contrast to our animal cousins, sex in humans is no longer inextricably intertwined with reproduction, and our love lives are no longer dominated by the seasonal fluctuations of our sex hormones nor by the genital secretions of our partners.

Further, as we were freed from the constraints of hormones, pheromones, and the mating seasons, our reproductive behaviors became increasingly subject to experiential and psychological influences, to the point where the sexual desires of modern homo sapiens are shaped predominantly by learning, childhood experiences, and the social context in which we mate.

Human sexual tastes, though born of the basic phylogenetic reproductive imperative, are to a large extent acquired. This is very different from the instinctual sexual responses that lower animals have on a purely reflex basis to any and all fertile members of the opposite gender. Thus, compared to the bitch in heat who welcomes the attention of all the dogs in the neighborhood or the tomcat who pursues with equal vigor every cat that smells like she is ovulating, human beings are much more selective and finicky in their sexual desires and preferences.

In fact, human lusts and passions are distinguished by their remarkable diversity, malleability, and plasticity. Men and women are stimulated and aroused by a wide array of partners, erotic scenarios, sex symbols, and fantasies. Moreover, our interest in sex is greatly influenced by our emotional states and by the quality of our relationship with our partners, so that the slightest sign of rejection from a lover can completely "turn off" or override a sensitive person's sexual desire, even if the partner happens to be extremely attractive.

In one sense, this sensitivity places us above animals whose ardors are not diminished by the objections of their sexual partners or by ethical considerations. However, the inherent susceptibility of human sexual desire to negative psychological influences also has a downside in that this is the key factor in the malfunctioning of the sex-regulatory mechanism, that is to say, in the pathogenesis of disorders of sexual desire.

The Clinical Significance of Sex Hormones for Humans

Notwithstanding the unquestionable importance of experiential and emotional determinants of the human sexual experience, it would be a serious error to assume that we have entirely overcome our gonads. It should not be forgotten that adequate levels of the reproductive hormones, as well as a functional nervous system and a correct balance of neurotransmitters, remain absolute prerequisites for normal human sexual functioning and desire; conversely, severe sexual difficulties result from certain endocrine abnormalities that are clinically on a par with psychogenic sexual dysfunctions.

From the perspective of the clinician, however, *sex hormones are important only in their absence.* Given a normal reproductive hormone environment and the absence of diseases and drugs that interfere with the functioning of the CNS sex-regulatory structures, the ebb and flow of our patients' sexual desires are determined solely by their emotional states and by certain psychological variables such as the partner's physical beauty, love, and sexual fantasies, on the one hand, and the countersexual effects of disgust and anger or anxiety on the other.

The implication of this psychological dominance from a practical standpoint is that once drug-induced and endocrine-related organic factors have been ruled out, psychological interventions become the primary focus of treatment.

THE EVOLUTION OF HUMAN SEXUAL DESIRE AND FANTASY

I agree with John Money (1986) and others who feel that phylogenetic as well as ontogenetic influences determine and give shape to the sexual desires and fantasies of human males and females. More specifically, I believe that the *phylogeny* of our species provides the basic erotic theme, which is based on reproduction, while the individual's personal psychosexual development, or *ontogeny,* superimposes individual and idiosyncratic variations.

Phylogenetic Influences on Sexual Preferences

The point was made in the previous section that, although sex has become dissociated from reproduction to a large extent, human sexuality continues to be anchored in the logic of the reproductive imperative from whence it evolved.

Simply put, we have been selected as a species and are genetically programmed to desire, feel attracted by, and respond to members of the opposite gender* who have the physical and behavioral characteristics that indicate a high probability that the individual has "good genes" and will produce numerous healthy offspring, and also has the potential for becoming a protective, nurturing parent throughout the prolonged dependent period of human childhood.

Just as we have evolved to crave high-energy sugars and fats, presumably because food was scarce in our ancestral environment, human *males* are genetically predisposed to respond sexually to young, healthy, regularly cycling human females whose physical and emotional characteristics give evidence of their physical well-being, their fertility, and their fitness for motherhood. More specifically, human males lust after young women who posses such features as freely lubricating, sweet smelling genitalia, well-developed breasts and nipples, a feminine body shape that includes ample hips, and slim limbs, soft skin and hair, a clear complexion, and a relative absence of facial and body hair. These are all "turn ons" for men, as are feminine, seductive behaviors, graceful body movements, higher, softer voices, and warm, empathic, nurturing personalities.

It is no accident that these same physical and behavioral features are all dependent on high levels of estrogens, and that the physical attributes listed above all signify that the woman is in good health, fertile, and a sexually gratifying partner, while her nurturing "female" behavioral tendencies foretell that she is emotionally equipped to become a good wife and mother.

Women, on the other hand, have evolved to be drawn to strong, well muscled, and "well hung" men, with nice beards and deep, sexy voices, and to prefer those who are also intelligent, resourceful, energetic, active, and successful. However, while women tend to prefer "alpha males," they also favor men who have the capacity to form intimate, long-term, affectionate relationships, qualities that promise to make them faithful spouses and good parents.

Again, it is by no means serendipitous that most of these same phys-

*I am referring herein only to heterosexual normalcy. In many successful species there are nonbreeding members who undoubtedly have alternative genetically determined sexual scripts that are equally "normal" for these individuals.

ical characteristics are also indicative of high male T levels, which in turn are a prognostic sign of potency, virility, and fertility, as well as of the ability to be a competent provider and protector of the family.

Facial and corporal symmetry are not markers for sex hormones. However, symmetrical features happen to be a sign of normal early fetal development and, therefore, an indicator of a high probability that the individual will have normal, healthy offspring. Again, it is consistent with an evolutionary view of sexual desire that symmetry is a consistent factor in female as well as male partner preference, which cuts across many species and societies.

Although there are considerable cultural differences in what is considered attractive, these tend to be stylistic rather than substantive, and mostly involve such features as the length of hair, body weight, or mode of dress. But the biologically determined characteristics that were mentioned above have a more universal, crosscultural appeal, as is evidenced by the international popularity of certain movie stars. For example, Tom Cruise and Arnold Schwarzenegger, on the one hand, and Whitney Houston and Marilyn Monroe, on the other, are all amply endowed with the hormone-determined characteristics that we have been programmed to desire.

Gender Differences in the Magnitude of Sexual Desire

It is widely believed that males are genetically programmed to act the sexual pursuers. They are, therefore, equipped with a higher and more compelling sex drive that predisposes them to compete for and to copulate with as many fertile females as possible (Symons, 1979). On the whole, men have been cast in *proactive* and women in *reactive* sexual roles (Leiblum, 1988).

Recent, more female-oriented studies and theories give greater weight to active female mate selection and competition for "alpha males." Further, females of many species, including homo sapiens, have been found to be less exclusive sexually than had been thought in the past (Elia, 1986; Batten, 1992).

In my experience, there are definite male and female sexual styles, albeit there is considerable overlap. I have no doubt that the sex drive of human males is generally more compelling and less easily suppressed than that of human females, and that men are more interested in sexual variety and novelty. These gender differences are most pronounced in adolescents and young adults. As we mature, our gender differences diminish. Older men tend to experience a lessening of their sexual urgency, while women tend to become more assertive sexually and more adventurous.

The Evolution of Courtship Behavior

In addition to the urge to copulate, sexual behavior in males of many species includes *courtship behaviors*, the sole function of which is to lure and seduce females—and all male courtship behaviors are dependent on the presence of high levels of T for their expression. Courtship behavior patterns have evolved into species-specific rituals that vary in complexity from simple posturing to elaborate courtship dances, and from the mere display of sexual organs to the building of elaborate ornamental bowers, which male Bower birds construct on their territory for the sole purpose of being selected by females.

Courtship is a nonphysical, behavioral form of foreplay, which arouses a sexually receptive attitude in the love object. This is an extremely important element of the desire phase of the sexual response cycle, to the extent that in certain species, like voles and rabbits, female ovulation is actually triggered by the presence and courtship behavior of the male.

From an evolutionary perspective, courtship serves in the competition among males to select and be selected by fertile females and to insure the continuity of their genes. Courtship behavior and sexual selection essentially involve the male displaying his superior genetic qualities to the female, in the form of the size of his genitalia, his strength, and his ability to dance, sing, defeat rivals, or build bowers.

Human males also engage in courtship, territorial, and display behaviors, although these have become so subtle and symbolic that people are seldom fully aware of this.

The masculine physical and behavioral characteristics that remain attractive to modern women once indicated that the man was fertile and that he had what it took to be a superior survivor and a protective husband and father under conditions that prevailed long ago, when humans first emerged on the planet. And there is little doubt that human females still respond to the display of male virility and power.

For modern women, this is symbolized by a "hot car," or, better yet, a chauffeured limousine, a gold Rolex, a gorgeous "pad." Being dined and wined at expensive restaurants is also enticing, and it helps if the maître d' bows and scrapes a bit to attest to the gentleman's high status.

Such open displays of wealth and power may offend some finer sensibilities, but these are all signs of adequacy, intelligence, resourcefulness, and success in our culture. Together with physical "masculine" attributes—for example, strength and athletic prowess—these are very effective in luring human females.

Females of many species, including human females also have an armamentarium of seductive behaviors to entice and to compete for desirable males. Essentially, these involve the display of features that promise fertility and sexual fulfillment to the male and also signal her fitness for being a good wife and mother.

These include the seductive hip-swinging walk, perfume, shiny hair, a warm seductive voice, and sensuous clothes that reveal the shape of the breasts and the legs, as well as flirtatious, teasing, and submissive "stroking" and "grooming" behaviors, and it does not hurt if the lady provides a sumptuous home cooked dinner.

Courtship remains an important factor in human sexuality, and inadequate courtship behavior can play a definite role in the pathogenesis of HSD and low sexual frequency, as will be illustrated by two case studies in later chapters.

Monogamy vs. Polygamy: Is It Normal for Men and Women To Lose Sexual Desire in a Long-Term Relationship?

There has been much debate but little hard data on a question, which has considerable relevance for the treatment of couples with low sexual desire—whether humans have evolved a monogamous or a polygamous pattern of sexual desire. In other words, are we genetically programmed to feel lust only with new partners and to become sexually sated in long-term relationships? Or do we bond for life?

Some social scientists have proposed that, like chimpanzees, men, but not necessarily women, are basically polygamous creatures, with an inherent desire for new sexual partners, but forced into an unnatural state of monogamy by church, economics, and female politics.

Money has suggested that humans are serially monogamous, that desire remains high for three or four years and then fades unless the couple have a new baby, which will rekindle their passion for another four mating seasons (Money, 1986). To support their position, the "polygamy" group cites the decrease in sexual desire that occurs in many long-term relationships, the undeniable universal erotic appeal of sexual novelty, and also the high prevalence of extramarital affairs in most societies. This line of reasoning, which leads to pessimism regarding the treatment of low desire in long-term relationships, has been endorsed by the German sex-therapist Gunther Schmidt.*

But, say those who believe that monogamy is the "natural state," there are many successful animal species, like Hamadrias baboons and

*Unpublished presentation by Dr. Schmidt, as reported by Dr. Sharna Striar (Copenhagen, June, 1984).

prairie voles, who have evolved a monogamous pair-bonding pattern. Moreover, long-term monogamous relationships dominate the mating patterns of every human society, past and present. Further, the "monogamy" advocates point out, men who are divorced or widowed are often depressed and are more likely to develop medical illnesses, while those who are married and/or living with someone are on the whole happier, healthier, and longer-lived.

Actually, no conclusions regarding human mating patterns can be deduced from animal studies, because in nature both reproductive strategies—monogamy and polygamy—are successful in terms of survival.

We may never be certain about this question from a scientific perspective. There is evidence to support both positions, but I am inclined to think that monogamy is the winner, for clinical observations make it clear that humans of both genders have strong impulses to seek steady partners and form exclusive, long-term relationships. Moreover, remaining single is not good for human health and happiness, as is evidenced by the statistics that show that persons without partners are more likely to abuse drugs, develop fatal illnesses, and commit suicide. Further, the loss of a lover—by death or by rejection—is one of the most devastatingly painful of all human experiences. In short, most people are simply much better off emotionally and physically when they are involved in a happy, compatible, exclusive, long-term relationship than when they are alone.

However, the powerful aphrodisiac appeal of new sexual partners, as well as the decline in sexual frequency and passion that most couples experience after they have been together for a long time, have been well documented and are undoubtedly real phenomena. Yet this does not constitute evidence that we are by nature polygamists or polyandrists. For, in good relationships, desire and sexual frequency do not disappear altogether. Under normal circumstances, after five to 10 years a couple's lust and sexual frequency are likely to drop from daily to perhaps twice a week, and maybe to once a week 20 years after that, but this level of sex normally endures in healthy couples over time until advanced old age (see the section on aging in Chapter 10).

Rather than assuming that a couple's lust for each other normally disappears after a while, one can make a case that the erotic bond may simply lie dormant. The persistance of long-term sexual attractions can be surmised from the fact that passion is often rekindled when exclusive possession of the mate is threatened by a competitor.

Thus, while some decrease of passion is normal, I regard a marked or complete loss of sexual desire in a long-term relationship as pathological. Such declines are often due to the corrosive effect of marital hostility and disillusionment, and *not* to familiarity. If both patners of a long-married couple find the loss of their sexual desire distressing, I consider this a valid reason for treatment. Moreover, I see it as my task as a therapist to assist those of my patients who wish to achieve the goals of improved sexual relationships with their long-term partners.

In our experience, couples who have been together for many years and who have become asexual are often quite amenable to therapy, especially if this includes the introduction of novelty, variety, flexibility, and fantasy to loosen up their ossified sexual repertoires. (See Chapter 10.)

ONTOGENY OF SEXUAL DESIRE: CHILDHOOD ORIGINS.

Superimposed on the dominant genetic theme, to lust for partners with characteristics that favor species survival, we acquire our idiosyncratic sexual desires, preferences, and fantasies as a consequence of our individual histories, learning, and experience.

The specific content of people's sexual fantasies and desires is undoubtedly the product of complex interactions of multiple, epigenetic determinants. These historic cause-and-effect patterns lie hidden within the huge mass of data that is accumulated in the course of studying the past and current sex lives of a great number of sexually dysfunctional patients and their partners. And the "wheat" that is the kernels of genuine information is difficult to tease out and to separate from the great tangle of "chaff," or "noise."

Nevertheless, two major correlations that bear on the question of the early origins of sexual desire and fantasy have emerged clearly from our observations. The first, which is in concert with the predictions of psychodynamic schools of child development, is that *sexual fantasies and desires often, if not always, begin very early in life.* The other finding supports certain existing theories that hold that perverse or paraphilic sexual desires, fantasies and practices originate in childhood pain.

The Earliest (or Very Early) Erotic Experiences Are Highly Influential in Shaping Adult Sexual Destiny

Many of our patients have reported that they first began to experience their particular sexual desires or fantasies when they were very young, sometimes at the ages of three or four, and that these early fantasies persisted essentially unchanged into adult life. Further, people whose fantasies are "normal," that is, concern genital contact with a person of the opposite gender, usually don't remember any specific incidents that triggered their fantasies, whereas those with paraphilic or unusual fantasies often remember the originally arousing incidents that started their sexual fantasies. These observations *would suggest that an individual's first or very early sexually arousing experiences may become permanently imprinted on and give shape to his or her lifetime erotic "program," or "love-map."**

This observation is consistent with the implication that is inherent in Freudian theories of psychosexual development, that there is a critical period in early human psychosexual development, during which the individual's sexual desires are formed (Freud, (1919, 1964). Since Freud's original thoughts on this matter, numerous highly complex and elaborate theoretical formulations regarding the psychic processes by which the infant's early experiences with signficant figures become translated into subsequent sexual desire have been proposed. (Klein, 1975; Kernberg, 1974, 1977, Cooper, 1991; Roiphe & Galenson, 1981.)

In terms of learning theory, which occupies a different level of abstraction and neither supports nor contradicts the more elaborate psychoanalytic formulations of early psychosexual development, it may be speculated that any and all experiences that are *sexually arousing to the child and occur during a critical period of development* (possibly between the time the child is old enough to understand mentally what is happening to him or her, but before his/her sexual desires and fantasies have formed, that is, while these are still in an amorphous or malleable state) may become *permanently and indelibly programmed into his or her "erotic software."* More specifically, *I am proposing that the simultaneous experience of sexual pleasure and the mental perception of the arousing stimulus form an association via the principle of "sensory-sensory" integration* (Birch & Bitterman, 1949).**

Moreover, I believe that under certain circumstances these early fantasies may come to occupy the person's entire "love-map" or "sexual program," to the exclusion of any other subsequent input or deletion, so that this becomes and remains the person's exclusive sexual desire.

While most of our patients remembered that their erotic fantasies started at an early age and remained essentially unchanged into adulthood, some initially reported that their fantasies had changed over time. However, in all cases, closer scrutiny revealed that it was only the *embellishments* that were altered, while the *basic elements* of the person's fantasy or desire remained fixed. According to this notion, a man whose major sexual desire and/or fantasy since adolescence has been to have oral sex with a beautiful, long haired woman may substitute different

*Dr. John Money coined the term *love-map* to describe "the mental template of every individual's sexuoerotic fantasies and erotic practice." (Money, 1986, jacket cover).

**The theory of "sensory-sensory integration" holds that two simultaneously occurring perceived events become functionally and neurophysiologically associated or learned.

partners in his imagination or in his bed over time, but he is unlikely to shift to a shoe fetish or to a pedophilic fantasy.

The emergence into consciousness of latent sexual fantasies at a later point in life, regardless of whether the person discovers these by accident or through the process of therapy, may also seem like an apparent contradiction of the notion that fantasies originate early on and don't change much over time.

For example, one of my patients, an exhibitionist, had not realized until he was in his thirties, that exposing his penis to women would arouse him. Up to that time, he had never experienced exhibitionistic impulses or fantasies. At the age of 34, he felt an unexpected jolt of lust when a woman at a resort where he was staying accidentally walked into his room while he was undressed. From then on, exposing his penis or fantasizing that he was exposing himself to a woman became his favorite sexual activity.

But this patient's exhibitionism did not begin with the incident at the resort. The origins of his fantasy were later traced to pleasurable, exciting experiences that occurred when he was three to five years old. He remembered that he had enjoyed becoming aroused on many occasions when his nurse would stand him on a chair and undress and dress him, while his older sisters watched with interest. The patient had "forgotten" all about this until the memory was uncovered in therapy.

Some Speculations Regarding Normal Mother/Child Eroticism in Early Life and the Acquisition of Normal Sexual Fantasies and Desires

On the theory that the earliest experiences of arousal are among the primary influences that normally shape human sexual desire, it may be further speculated that the continuous and repeated mutually pleasurable intimate physical and emotional contact that small children normally enjoy with their mothers, fathers, and other family members—which include sleeping together, carrying, holding, cuddling, stroking, suckling, feeding, sniffing, licking, kissing, rocking, looking at, caressing, touching, holding, soothing, patting, joking, giggling, teasing, tickling, belly kissing, blowing, bathing, drying, dressing, grooming, playing with, rubbing, cooing, talking to, singing to, etc., etc., activities which all normal parents, including myself, remember regularly enjoying with their babies—are *inadvertently mildly erotically arousing to infants and young children, and sensously pleasurable for their parents, most especially their mothers, and that these experiences form the psychologic origins of normal sexual fantasies and desires.*

I do not mean to imply that such mutually pleasurable erotic experiences harm the child, as abusive and incestuous experiences certainly do. To the contrary, I am proposing the notion that these physical mother/infant (or parent/infant) love experiences may be *necessary* for healthy, normal psychosexual development, and that without such mutually pleasurable, familiar erotic contacts, children may never develop normal sexual feelings or desires within loving relationships.

Such hypothetical *normal*, as opposed to incestuous or *abusive*, familiar erotic stimulation probably occurs at a low level of intensity, like a low voltage electric current that does not shock, but only tickles, pleasantly and provides just enough stimulation to become conditioned and reinforced.

This scenario of parent and child experiencing simultaneous, pleasurable sensuous sensations is normally repeated continuously throughout the child's early years, and it may be speculated, that these ongoing, normal, nonabusive, physical, mutually mildly erotic, and pleasurable experiences of childhood are normally assimilated in a manner that predisposes youngsters to imprint erotically on love objects who are reminiscent of members of their families or clans, and on aims and activities that mimic this early, intimate, sensuous, mother–child love play.

These early memories and desires may not be remembered per se, but they are not "erased." They exert an influence that is generally outside of the person's conscious awareness. If all goes well when these children mature, they will desire, fantasize about, and eventually marry "a girl (guy) just like the girl (guy) who married dear old Dad (Mom)."

Negative Early Sexual Programming

When accidental or malicious exposures to painful, violent, negative, or inappropriate situations constitute the child's first significant sexual experiences, this hypothetical normal sexual "imprinting" process can go awry and result in linking sex with fear and/or in the acquisition of and fixation on atypical and possibly disadvantageous sexual fantasies and desires.

For example, one of my female patients had a sexual fantasy of watching a man masturbate. The origin of this fantasy became clear when she remembered that when she was a little girl she became highly aroused for the first time in her memory by seeing a man playing with his penis while sitting on a bench in the park. Thereafter, she would look for exhibitionists in the park, and follow them around to get a closer look, always while experiencing great pleasure and excitement.

As a further example, another of my patients was fixated on voyeuristic fantasies and desires. These were clearly connected to his early experiences when as a youngster, he used to become highly aroused night after night and masturbate while he watched his older sister undress through the semitransparent glass door which separated their rooms.

The sexual fantasies and desires of "Bill Kangaroo" (Case 8.2) whose case history and treatment will be described in a subsequent chapter provide another illustration of the powerful and pathogenic influence of early inappropriate sexual arousal. The patient was a 41-year-old man, a virgin with severe generalized HSD and sexual avoidance, who had a lifelong sexual fantasy and intense desire for stroking a woman's nude legs and thighs. This was a direct replay of the first experiences that had aroused him. From the age of five when his father died to age 14 when she remarried, Bill's mother would regularly ask him to "massage" her legs and thighs while she reclined on a couch, dressed in only a loose robe, with no underwear. These experiences were extremely arousing for the boy, and when he was 12 years old he surreptitiously began to rub against the couch and to ejaculate during these sessions.

The Erotization of Childhood Trauma

A number of authors have contended that painful and traumatic experiences in childhood are a source of atypical or pathological adult sexual desires and/or fantasies. My observations of patients with paraphilias and sexual obsessions strongly support this notion, which I have termed, "the erotization of childhood trauma."

More specifically, children sometimes eroticize painful and negative experiences, and transmute these into sexual longings. In other words, youngsters who are beaten tend to develop erotic desires, fantasies, and practices that involve receiving beatings from their sexual partners or they may become aroused by the idea or by the act of administering physical punishment to their lovers. The link between such "perverse" or atypical sexual fantasies, desires, and/or practices and childhood trauma is evident from the aberrant "love maps" of patients who were abused and traumatized as children. In fact, I can state unequivocally that in more than 7,000 sexual examinations I have conducted over the past 20 years, I have not found a single person with sadistic or masochistic sexual fantasies, desires, and/or practices who had not been subjected to significant cruelty as a child. As I reviewed and analyzed the family and psychosexual histories of patients with aberrant sexual fantasies, and sexual obsessions, it became crystal clear that events and persons who elicit fear, anger, and/or disgust in the youngster may eventually become sought-after objects of desire.

Although perverted fantasies and practices are much more common among men, the following example of this dynamic was a Jewish European woman who had been incarcerated as a child in a Nazi death camp where her entire family perished. To her utter bafflement and self-loathing, this woman could become sexually aroused only by fantasizing that she was making love to an SS guard.

Another clear example of the "erotization of childhood pain" is provided by the case of "Jack Priest" (Case 4.7), which will be described in a following chapter. This man was unable to feel the slightest desire for his beautiful wife, whom he loved dearly. However, he would become very aroused when he acted out his favorite sexual fantasy of having a prostitute spank his bare bottom with a wooden paddle, while crooning loving endearments to him. I was not surprised to learn that, as a youngster, this patient had suffered greatly at the hands of his disturbed sadistic mother, who, among other forms of emotional torture, would often pull down the boy's pants and, while paddling his naked behind with a hairbrush, coat hanger, or other hard object, she would softly tell him that she was doing this only because she loved him.

It goes without saying that the connection between childhood trauma and a specific erotic desire or fantasy is not always as direct or concrete as in these examples, which were selected specially to make the point. More often than not, the erotization of trauma or the erotization of the aggressor is expressed in more symbolic terms. Thus, a boy with a cruel, intrusive mother who emotionally beat him to the ground may grow up with the desire to be physically beaten to the ground or to do this to his partners.

The link between childhood pain and paraphilic adult sexual fantasy has been noted by several authors, each of whom interpreted the phenomenon in the language of his own theoretical persuasion. Robert Stoller (1975, 1991), a psychoanalyst whose major interest was sexual perversions, felt that sexual fantasy always represents the unconscious *revenge against the hated parents*, while Arnold Cooper (1991), feels that separation from the mother is the key trauma that shapes perverted sexual fantasy. Kernberg, also a psychoanalyst, attributes this puzzling phenomenon that he dubs "the recruitment of love in the service of aggression," to the consequences of early abusive object relationships. (Kernberg, 1974; 1977B)

Money (1986, 1988), who also observed the phenomenon of eroticization of childhood trauma although he did not use this term, coined the colorful and descriptive phrase, "vandalized love-maps" to identify the process by which paraphilic desires are acquired during childhood. Money, who is not a psychoanalyst, attributes this to "opponent-process conditioning," an arcane concept derived from learning theory, while Stoller, Kernberg, and Cooper employ complex psychoanalytic models of psychosexual development to explain how children come to lust after that which hurts them.

I cannot agree with Stoller that the primary dynamic purpose of paraphilic sexual fantasy is to express the patient's unconscious feelings of revenge against his parents (Stoller, 1975). For, while one can discern much vengeful material in sexual fantasy, to my mind this is not the only nor the primary aim.

My view is more similar to that of Money, who believes that "the shared principle of all paraphilic love-maps (fantasy) is to turn childhood tragedy into (sexual) triumph" (Money, 1986, p. 36). In other words, the process of eroticizing painful childhood events and relationships is seen as basically an adaptive mechanism that represents the child's attempt to cope with and survive the vicissitudes of his painful childhood. In a strikingly similar construction, Stoller, apparently contradicting his own earlier view, later expressed a similar belief that "erotic fantasy turns childhood trauma into triumph" (Stoller, 1975, p. 30).

I believe that insofar that this protects the youngster's budding sexuality and preserves it from oblivion, the erotization of childhood trauma is a defense that may be likened to a scar that forms a protective layer over a wound while it is healing, or to a callus that surrounds a fractured bone to stabilize it until it mends. By analogy, on a psychological level the erotization of trauma and pain, which is especially devastating to a child when this occurs at the hands of parents, makes this psychic wound less overwhelming and easier to bear, and helps the child to maintain its tenuous psychological integrity. In other words, by putting an erotic spin around the psychic wound, the youngster enables himself to continue to function and to maintain his critical but painful object relationships while trapped within his dysfunctional or malignant, family, until he matures and grows strong enough to separate himself from them.

As is true of all mechanisms of defense, the process of eroticizing the aggressor can backfire; when this happens, the person may have to pay a heavy price. This darker side of sexual fantasy will be discussed in Chapter 6 on the use of sexual fantasy in sex therapy.

SEXUAL FANTASY AS VIRTUAL EROTIC REALITY

Throughout this discussion, I have used the terms "sexual desire" and "sexual fantasy" interchangeably. This was by design and not by accident. What I meant to convey by this was that *sexual fantasies are, in fact, mental representations of a person's most ardent sexual wishes and desires.* As such, fantasies and desire are identical in content, differing only in that fantasy remains in the realm of virtual reality or mental simulation, while desire is fantasy that may actually be put into practice.

An immensely important evolutionary development of our brains is the ability to simulate reality and to solve problems in virtual reality without the costly and hazardous process of trial and error. As a fortuitous byproduct, this has endowed human sexuality with a unique new dimension, sexual fantasy. For the first time in biological history, *mental representations* of attractive *sexual incenters*, that is to say erotic fantasies, emerged as important determinants of human sexual desire.

The ability to create virtual reality in our minds is really a stunning evolutionary step. For *in all other animals*, sexual motivation is incited solely by the perception of an *actual sexual partner.* Thus one sniff of the genital odor of a cat in heat drives the Toms in the neighborhood wild, but a *picture* of a pretty pussy does nothing for the feline male.

Of course, humans have retained the ability to become aroused by the actual sight, touch, sound, and smell of an attractive partner. But in addition, the human brain has evolved to the point where we are now able to create *simulated sexual partners and scenarios* in our minds, and these *virtual sexual images* are powerful nonchemical aphrodisiacs that can be as arousing as the real thing, and in some cases even more so.

In terms of the "dual controls" model of the regulation of sexual motivation that was described in the previous chapter, the *virtual sexual reality of our fantasies* has the same power to incite human sexual desire as the *actual perception of a real sexual opportunity* has, presumably by activating the sex-regulating apparatus of the brain in a similar manner.

For example, the aforementioned patient, "Jack Priest" (Case 4.7) became extremely aroused when he was "lovingly" spanked by a pro, and he often (secretly) gratified this desire in actuality. However, mental images of receiving a spanking were also very arousing to Jack, and these served as his masturbatory fantasies.

The Priority of Self-Preservation: Anti-fantasies

On the downside, the ability of the human brain to create and respond to virtual realities can also make for difficulties, because simulation also works in a countersexual direction. In other words, negative, repulsive, aversive, and frightening mental images, as well as simulated disadvantages and dangers that evoke emergency emotional states, function as powerful "anti-fantasies" or suppressors of sexual desire. Thus, imagined or virtual "saber-toothed tigers" (see the following section) in the bedroom can inhibit the human sex drive with the force of a real predator.

Adaptive Sexual "Turnoffs"

The primary directive that is built into our genes is, above all, to survive. Thus, we have been engineered so that behaviors motivated by the avoidance of pain and injury have priority over everything else, including pleasure and reproduction.

To make this more graphic, picture a couple about to make love on the grass. Both are feeling very passionate, when they hear a saber-toothed tiger approaching. Chances are that they will instantly lose their desire for sex, (presumably because the "sex centers" have been shut down during this emergency), while their attention and energies shift toward coping with the tiger by running away or chasing it off.

As was discussed in the previous chapter, from the viewpoint of evolution, the primacy of survival over reproduction is highly adaptive. In fact, this basic motivational hierarchy that gives self-protection priority over all else has been so successful that this program has been selected and remains wired into our brains, essentially unchanged since before the stone ages. And even in modern "civilized" life, the built-in priority of our emergency-driven behavior over our sexual urges retains adaptive value as this frees up our energies to cope with emergencies. Warnings, in the form of mental images and memories of dangerous, unpleasant situations provide a check on our sexual urges in situations where the expression of such would be dangerous or disadvantageous. Thus, modern humans are saved from disgracing themselves by making love in public places by conjuring up frightening representations, such as mental images of a police officer, or of a punk-filled jail cell. Similarly, the virtual image of a sexual harassment suit has had salutory inhibiting effects on many a man's urges to seduce his patients or "come on" to his employees.

Maladaptive Sexual "Turnoffs"

However, the fact that physical and emotional pain, as well as negative mental images that evoke emergency emotions, can override and down-regulate sexual motivation and can also be a very large disadvantage. As was discussed in Chapter 2, the same control mechanisms that are normally there as a "brake" on our sexual urges, to keep us from self destructing, can malfunction or be misused to suppress sexual desire in the wrong situation, when lust should be given a free rein.

Chapter 5 lists some of the common psychological suppressor stimuli that patients with HSD unwittingly employ as "anti-fantasies" to "fool" the sex-regulating system into turning off by making it seem as though there were something wrong with the partner or some danger were inherent in the situation. These dangers are not real, and mostly represent symbolic hazards and imagined apprehensions about sex, love, and intimacy that grow out of the person's neurotic distortions. Yet these are as potent in destroying a person's sexual appetite in imagination as they are in actual reality.

Benign and Malignant Sexual Fantasies and/or Desires

The impact that a person's atypical, perverse, or paraphilic sexual fantasies can have on his/her life varies from playful, benign, and trivial, to malignant, invasive, and extremely destructive.*

In some persons, the atypical sexual fantasies that are the residues of the erotization of the abuses suffered when the patient was a child are confined to the bedroom. When limited to the sexual experience, the human ability to fantasize about sex or to create virtual sexual realities and to simulate arousing sexual scenarios is a definite plus, irrespective of content or origins. I consider sexual fantasy a "gift from the gods," merely a pleasant by-product of our "state of art brains," which can enrich and add new dimensions to the human sexual experience.

However, problems arise when paraphilic or atypical sexual desires are not confined to the sex act. For in some cases, the person's perverse fantasies take a malignant course and become invasive, and "metastasize" to destroy his or her ability to beget normal romantic relationships.

Thus, it is not uncommon for persons, who were emotionally damaged by their sadistic, disturbed, manipulative, rejecting, withholding,

*I am indebted to Dr. Ethel Person for pointing out the destructive potential of perverse sexual fantasies.

overly demanding, cruel, abusive, neglecting, narcissistic parents when they were children, to eroticize these very same miserable qualities that once hurt them so. When they grow up, these people fantasize about and are attracted to and become obsessed with partners who injure them in similar ways; even worse, they feel compelled to avoid decent, loving partners.

Later in the book, two case histories, one of a male patient with HSD ("Doc Scotch," Case 8.8), one of a woman who phobically avoided appropriate partners ("Lucinda Skier," Case 6.2), will be described, illustrating the potentially far-reaching destructive effects that childhood trauma and perverse sexual desire can have on the person's love life. The benign and therapeutic potential of sexual fantasy that is the residue of childhood pain will be illustrated by the case of a man ("Joe Senator," Case 8.7) who learned to use his sadistic fantasy to make love to his gentle and loving partner.

CHAPTER 4

Diagnostic Criteria and Clinical Features

PROBLEMS OF DEFINITION: WHAT IS NORMAL AND ABNORMAL SEXUAL DESIRE?

Current definitions of normal and abnormal sexual desire do not yet rest on scientific terra firma. But this does not trouble me greatly, nor does this detract from my work with patients, for precise diagnostic criteria are of greater importance to statisticians than to clinicians, whose primary focus is on treating patients who are in distress, regardless of diagnostic labels.

Unlike the erectile disorders, which can now be assessed with scientific precision thanks to such modern diagnostic procedures as Rigiscan NPT monitoring and doppler ultrasound penile blood flow studies, there are as yet no comparable laboratory tests nor imaging techniques that permit us to examine the anatomy or the functioning of the sex-regulating structures of the brain directly, nor are there any practical methods by which pathological manifestations of human sexual desire can be measured with scientific objectivity.* Therefore, statisticians

*One early method that was developed to quantify the strengths of various drives was to separate an animal from the object of its desire (food, water, a new mother's unweaned pups, or a female of his species in heat) by an electric grill that carried a specified charge. The magnitude of the rat's or cat's drives was measured by how often it would cross the grid and tolerate the electric shock in order to get to its food, water, babies, or sexual partners.

(Continued on the following page.)

and researchers have of necessity looked to behavioral and subjective parameters in their attempts to establish human sexual norms, despite the obvious limitations of this approach.

Sexual Frequency

Since *sexual frequency* is one obvious manifestation of human sexual desire, a number of attempts have been made to arrive at a definition of HSD based on a low rate of sexual activity. One of the most widely accepted is that of Schiavi and his research group, whose criteria for abnormally low sexual frequency is "sexual activity occurring less than once every two weeks, for persons 55 years or younger" (Schiavi, 1992).

For statistical and research purposes, this is reasonable enough. However frequency alone cannot be taken as the "gold standard" of sexual normalcy, nor as the sole indicator of sexual pathology.

Frequency and Desire Are Not Synonymous

A number of other biosocial variables, apart from sexual desire, determine the frequency of a couple's sexual relations. For example, many women who are in relationships they value will continue to engage in sexual intercourse for the sake of their partners, even when they do not experience desire or sexual pleasure. An example of the limitations of frequency alone as the criterion for sexual desire disorders will be provided by the case of "Mrs. Aspen" (Case 4.6), which is described later in this chapter. This patient was a married woman with severe, lifelong, global HSD, who had intercourse with her husband once every week for 31 years, despite her total lack of desire for sex and without ever deriving the slightest pleasure from the act.

Normal Fluctuations of Sexual Desire

Another limitation of using the frequency of sexual activity as the sole measure of sexual normalcy and abnormality is the natural ebb and flood of sexual interest. Some level of sexual motivation is present in men and women throughout life; however, this is by no means static, but tends to vary periodically.

The magnitude of human libido changes throughout the life cycle in a gender-specific pattern. More specifically, a high sex drive, which is

---

No comparable methods are available that could be used with humans. However, recent advances in non-invasive imaging cerebral functioning such as PET, functional NMRs, and optical scanning of cerebral blood flow, may in the future allow us to measure the activity of the sex-regulating areas of the brain directly.

characterized by a high frequency of sexual outlet, spontaneous sexual urges, and *proactive* sexual behavior, is more common in young men, particularly during adolescence, than it is for women and for men over 50. The libido of women of all ages and that of older men is more likely to be less urgent, and is typically associated with a lower frequency of sexual activity and a more *reactive* pattern of sexual behavior. In the absence of illness, however, the sex drive should remain sufficiently intense to enable men and women to respond to sexual stimulation until advanced old age (Kaplan, 1990A; Schiavi, 1990A,B; Schiavi et al., 1994; Bachman et al., 1985; Segraves & Segraves, 1992; Sherwin, 1992).

Libido also tends to change from an intense, high frequency, proactive level when a couple first fall in love to a lower but still pleasurable level as the relationship matures.

Nevertheless, human sexuality is highly variable and there are numerous exceptions to these general trends. There are, for example, some perfectly normal young men who have never experienced urgent, spontaneous, sexual desire or fantasy, and I have interviewed a number of women who appeared to have nothing wrong with them, who reported regularly experiencing spontaneous surges of sexual desire and fantasy, and at times, a compelling urge to have sex.

Similarly, while it is true that the intense passion that characterizes the early phases of romantic relationships often declines from a high to a lower level over time, even in good relationships, a few fortunate couples remain each other's sexual fantasies and continue to feel a rush of passion for each other, even though they have been lovers for decades.*

Psychopathology Is Not Strongly Correlated with Sexual Desire

It is interesting to note that our findings do not support the widely held belief that there is a strong link between psychopathology and sexual adequacy, although, of course, severely disturbed psychiatric patients are seldom very active sexually. We have observed all the gradations of sexual desire that are described below, from extreme hypersexuality to complete sexual anorexia, in males and in females, in the mature and in the young, in heterosexuals, bisexuals, and homosexuals, within happy and problematic relationships, in otherwise well-functioning individuals as well as in patients with significant concomitant psychopathology, and in persons of diverse socioeconomic and cultural backgrounds. These observations would suggest that the human sex drive is fairly independent of such psychosocial parameters.

---

*From an unpublished study of enduring romantic relationships.

DEFINITIONS, DIAGNOSTIC CRITERIA, AND CLINICAL FEATURES

Happily, the authors of DSM-IV chose to retain the two critical elements of DSM-III and III-R, which gave this system of classification a tremendous advantage over the old nosologies.

The most important of these features by far was the separation of disorders of sexual desire from the genital dysfunctions (DSM-111-R, 1986, p. 93). The second improvement that has been fortunately preserved in DSM-IV is the distinction that is drawn between *HSD*, or the "quiet" lack of desire of sex, and *sexual aversion disorder*, which is characterized by an active, phobic avoidance of sexual contact with the partner.

The Advantage of Separating the Sexual Motivation Disorder from the Genital Dysfunctions.

Since the 1980 edition of its Diagnostic Manual (DSM-III, 1980), the APA's classification of sexual disorders has been based on the physiologically oriented, triphasic model of human sexuality, which divides the psychosexual syndromes into impairments of desire, excitement, and orgasm* (Kaplan, 1977, 1979). This represented a significant conceptual advance over the old nosologic systems, which had not taken the underlying physiology of the human sexual response into consideration and therefore lumped all the sexual disorders of males and females—impotence, anorgasmia, premature and retarded ejaculation, and vaginismus, together with libido deficiencies, under the overinclusive "wastebasket" labels of "impotence" and "frigidity," which only served to confuse.

This faulty and obfuscating diagnostic system, which reflected the ignorance of the era with regard to sex and sexual disorders, was responsible, at least in part, for the poor treatment results that had been par for the course for all psychosexual disorders in the "old" days, before the advent of modern sex therapy.

DSM-IV not only retained the physiologically based model that conferred such a conceptual advantage on the DSM-III nosologies, but extended this further by describing and specifying the physiologic parameters of the four phases of the sexual response cycle that are

*There are actually *four* physiologically discrete phases of the sexual response cycle: desire, arousal (excitement), orgasm, and resolution. Since disturbances of the resolution phase are exceedingly rare, compared to dysfunctions of the other three phases, resolution phase disorders are seldom mentioned in the literature. Thus the phase-related classification system is usually referred to as the "triphasic" concept of sexual disorders, which is also easier to pronounce than "quadriphasic," which is technically more correct.

impaired in the orgasm, arousal, and sexual desire disorders (DSM-IV, pp. 493–494).

Hypoactive Sexual Desire vs. Sexual Aversion Disorders

The subdivision of the disorders of sexual desire into two separate syndromes was a real improvement that makes a great deal of sense from a clinical perspective. For the "quiet" loss of sexual desire, or HSD, and the "active" phobic avoidance of and/or aversion to sex differ in prevalence, gender distribution, and etiology. Finally, and most important, the two disorders respond to different treatment strategies (see Chapter 7).

Hypoactive Sexual Desire. (See Table 1.) In consideration of the tricky nosologic issues that were described in the previous section, the task force on DSM-IV, the American Psychiatric Association's (1994) current diagnostic manual, decided to stay with the convention that was started in DSM-III. They have based the diagnosis of hypoactive sexual desire

TABLE 1
Diagnostic Criteria for Hypoactive Sexual Desire Disorder (302.71) (DSM-IV)

A. Persistently or recurrently deficient (or absent) sexual fantasies and desire for sexual activity. The judgment of deficiency or absence is made by the clinician, taking into account factors that affect sexual functioning such as age and the context of the person's life.

B. The disturbance causes marked distress or interpersonal difficulty.

C. The sexual dysfunction is not better accounted for by another Axis I disorder (except another Sexual Dysfunction) and is not due exclusively to the direct physiological effects of a substance (e.g., a drug of abuse or a medication) or a general medical condition.

Specify type:
Lifelong Type
Acquired Type

Specify type:
Generalized Type
Situational Type

Specify:
Due to Psychological Factors
Due to Combined Factors

American Psychiatric Association: *Diagnostic and Statistical Manual of Mental Disorders, Fourth Edition.* Washington, DC. American Psychiatric Association, 1994. Reprinted with permission.

disorders on clinicians' interpretation of the meaning of the patient's complaints that their sexual frequency is disturbingly low.

More specifically, according to the current Diagnostic and Statistical Manual of the APA (*DSM-IV)*, the chief clinical features of hypoactive sexual desire (HSD) (302.71) are "persistently or recurrently deficient (or absent) sexual fantasies or desire for sexual activity. The judgment of the deficiency or absence is made by the clinician, taking into account factors that affect sexual functioning, such as age, and the context of the person's life" (p. 498).

Sexual Aversion. (See Table 2.) The diagnostic criteria for *sexual aversion disorder* (302.79), the second clinical subtype of disorders of the sexual desire phase, is made on the basis of the patient's "complaints (persistent or recurrent) of extreme aversion to, and avoidance of, all (or almost all) genital sexual contact with a sexual partner" (DSM-IV, 1994, p. 500).

Global vs Situational Desire Disorders

Sexual desire disorders continue to be divided into *generalized* and *situational* types in DSM-IV. Patients with generalized or *global* HSD experience a total "sexual anorexia" in that they lose interest in any

TABLE 2
Diagnostic Criteria for Sexual Aversion Disorder (302.79) (DSM-IV)

A. Persistent or recurrent extreme aversion to, and avoidance of, all (or almost all) genital sexual contact with a sexual partner.

B. The disturbance causes marked distress or interpersonal difficulty.

C. The sexual dysfunction is not better accounted for by another Axis I disorder (except another Sexual Dysfunction).

Specify type:
Lifelong Type
Acquired Type

Specify type:
Generalized Type
Situational Type

Specify:
Due to Psychological Factors
Due to Combined Factors

American Psychiatric Association: *Diagnostic and Statistical Manual of Mental Disorders, Fourth Edition.* Washington, DC. American Psychiatric Association, 1994. Reprinted with permission.

and all sexual activities, and are devoid of sexual fantasies. Similarly, patients with global sexual aversions are afraid of or repelled by any sort of sexual contact with all partners.

In the more common situational clinical form of HSD, the patient's desire is inhibited or he/she is repelled only by one or a certain class of partners, but retains interest in masturbating, fantasy, and/or other partners. Patients with situational sexual aversions panic only when they try to engage in a specific sort of sexual activity, or to have sex with their steady spouses, but they are comfortable with other activities or with other partners.

A total of 72% of our low desire patients had partner-specific complaints, while the sexual symptom was global in the remaining 28%.

In our patient population, partner-specific HSD was more common in males, while the global form was more prevalent in females.

Lifelong and Acquired Desire Disorders

DSM-IV continues the excellent practice that began with DSM-III, of subdividing the psychosexual dysfunctions into lifelong or primary, and acquired or secondary types. The majority of our patients with sexual desire disorders reported that their problem was *acquired*, that is, that they lost their sexual desire after some period of normal functioning. A smaller proportion of patients, 21%, had *never* experienced a normal desire for sex or had *always* been phobic of genital contact. In these patients the sexual symptom usually becomes manifest at adolescence, and is described as *primary* or *lifelong*.

In our population the incidence of primary sexual desire disorders was more common in women than in male patients.

The Destructive Impact of Sexual Desire Disorders

The committee for sexual disorders for DSM-IV has proposed the following addendum to the diagnostic criteria for desire disorders. "The disturbance causes marked distress and/or interpersonal difficulty" (DSM-IV, 1994, pp. 484, 490).

From the viewpoint of the clinician, this is an excellent addition. As health professionals, we have no business imposing our own or our society's moral values and standards of sexual behavior on our patients under the guise of scientific knowledge. As far as I am concerned, if a person and his or her partner are content to have sex once a month or just once a year, or if both enjoy having sex twice a day, it would be inappropriate to label this behavior as a disorder or to intervene therapeutically. As long as the patient's atypical sexual behavior does not create problems for either partner, the diagnosis of sexual desire disorder is not warranted.

Another improvement of DSM-IV over the older manuals is that the important problem of *desire discrepancies* between the partners is accounted for: "The clinician may need to assess both partners when discrepancies in sexual desire prompt the call for professional attention." In other words, a "complaint of *low desire* may actually represent the excessive need for sexual expression in the other partner. Or, both partners may have levels of desire in the normal range, but at different ends of the continuum" (DSM-IV, 1994 p. 496). The subject of desire discrepancies will be discussed further later in this chapter.

Another excellent feature of DSM-IV is the inclusion of three new diagnostic subcategories in recognition of the fact that sexual motivation dysfunctions are frequently of organic or mixed etiology: *Hypoactive Sexual Desire due to General Medical Conditions, Drug Induced Hyposexual Desire and Sexual Desire Disorders due to Mixed Factors* (DSM-IV, 1994 pp. 515–522). These organic and mixed desire disorders are discussed in Chapter 10.

A CONTINUUM OF HUMAN SEXUAL DESIRE

For the purposes of evaluating patients and formulating treatment strategies, we have found it useful to describe the manifestations of normal and abnormal sexual desire in greater detail, and to grade and categorize these more precisely.

More specifically, several of the most telling subjective and behavioral indices of sexual desire, such as frequency of sexual outlet and response to abstinence, have been placed on a hypothetical continuum. This is divided into six categories, with *hyperactive sexual desire* occupying the high and *sexual aversion* the low end of the curve.*

The six points on the scale are: 1. *Hyperactive Sexual Desire*; 2. *High-Normal Sexual Desire*; 3. *Low-Normal Sexual Desire*; 4. *Mild Hypoactive Sexual Desire*; 5. *Severe Hypoactive Sexual Desire*; and 6. *Sexual Aversion or The Phobic Avoidance of Sex*. (See Table 3.)

*I thank Dr. Ellen Hollander who made the suggestion, which I adopted, to add the sixth category of hypersexual desire.

Hyperactive Sexual Desire (Sexual Addiction, Compulsive Sexuality)*

The chief clinical feature of this condition is the dysregulation or lack of control over sexual motivation. Sexually hyperactive individuals have sex frequently, often having several orgasms each day.** They are typically preoccupied with sexual feelings and/or thoughts to the extent that this interferes with their functioning at work, and/or creates problems in their relationships. They usually respond to a wide variety of erotic stimuli and partners. Their sexual urges arise spontaneously, and they feel "horny" even in the absence of external sexual incitors. Persons

TABLE 3
Continuum of Sexual Desire

1. *Hyperactive Sexual Desire* (Sexual Addiction; Nymphomania; Don Juanism)	Intense, spontaneous sexual desire and fantasy; compulsive sexual behavior; high frequency; inadequate control of sexual impulses, distress.
2. *High-Normal Sexual Desire**	Spontaneous sexual desire and fantasy; proactive sexual behavior; normal sexual functioning; high frequency.
3. *Low-Normal Sexual Desire**	No spontaneous sexual desire or fantasy; reactive sexual behavior; normal sexual functioning; average or low frequency.
4. *Mild Hypoactive* Sexual Desire	No spontaneous sexual desire or fantasy; sexual avoidance; poor sexual functioning; low frequency, distress.
5. *Severe Hypoactive Sexual Desire*	No spontaneous sexual desire or fantasy; poor sexual functioning; sexual avoidance; very low-frequency or celibacy, distress.
6. *Sexual Aversion Disorder* (Sexual Phobia)	Active aversion to and/or phobic avoidance of sex; very low frequency or celibacy, distress.

*Normal levels of sexual desire

*The committees for psychosexual dysfunction for DSM-III, DSM-III-R and DSM-IV decided that the inclusion of hypersexuality was not warranted by the available evidence, and at this time hyperactive sexual desire is not officially a sexual disorder. This condition may, however, be diagnosed under "sexual disorder not otherwise specified"(302.70).

**Some normal homosexual individuals have reported that they have up to 10 orgasms per day, and that they have had sex with as many as 1,000 different partners a year (Bell & Weinberg, 1978, p. 85). This level of frequency is not considered a disorder unless the individual complains of distress.

with hyperactive sexual desire disorders typically find sex extremely pleasurable and sexual activity is associated with an elevation of their mood. Unless they have orgasms to excess, these individuals usually function well.

There is a driven quality to the hypersexual's need for sex, and the sex drive is so compelling in this condition and the controls are so inadequate that he will engage in sex even when he is aware that he is risking losing his job, his wife, or his life through AIDS. When they try to abstain, hypersexual individuals are likely to become tense, anxious, and dysphoric; in most cases, they soon resume their compulsive sexual activity. Hypersexual individuals often pressure their partners for more frequent sex, which may have a negative impact on the relationship.

A striking clinical feature of sexual hyperactivity, which underscores the failure of the normal regulatory mechanism, is that these individuals are *insatiable.* In other words, orgasm does not materially decrease their craving for further sexual stimulation, or does so only for a very brief period of time.

By contrast, men with high but normal sex-drives, are generally satisfied with one or possibly two orgasms on a single occasion. There is an exception. When otherwise normal individuals first fall in love, they may go through a phase where they, too, are insatiable and "can't get enough" of their lover.

It may be speculated that the initial phase of sexual bonding could normally be associated in both genders with biochemical changes that favor the intensification of the sex drive. Possibly, this involves the release of endogenous "aphrodisiacs" or simply making extra dopamine and/or endorphins available to the neurones of the sex centers in the hypothalamus.

Still, the sexual frenzy that typifies falling in love is different from the hyperactive individual's abstract craving for sex, for the latter is perpetual and may not be related to affection for a particular person. In fact, "sexual addicts" may have excellent sexual relationships with their partners, but this does not appease their voracious sexual appetites.

The following four vignettes, taken from our files, illustrate some of the typical clinical presentation of *hyperactive sexual desire.*

1a. Male Hypersexuality

CASE 4.1—"Juan Romeo": Hyperactive Sexual Desire in a Well-Functioning Heterosexual Male in a Good Sexual Relationship

The patient, Juan, a 26-year-old married man of Puerto Rican extraction, consulted me because his 23-year-old wife, Maria, had announced her intention to move out of the couple's apartment with their one-year-old baby because of her husband's promiscuous sexual behavior. Juan was devastated and desperate for treatment to reduce his unquenchable sex drive and keep his family together.

Juan drove a delivery truck while Maria worked the night shift as a P.N. in a hospital in their community. A strikingly handsome young man, Juan was preoccupied with sex. While he was making his deliveries, he habitually picked up girls and would invite them to join him in his vehicle where he would fondle them. He was often able to persuade them to have oral sex or intercourse with him in his truck. A phone call from one of these young women, who had become obsessed with Juan, had precipitated the current marital crisis.

When Juan could find no girls, he sat in his truck and masturbated to orgasm, sometimes four to five times a day. He also masturbated while looking at erotic magazines when his wife was at work and while he was home minding the baby. He reported that whenever he tried to desist he became restless and depressed and would quickly begin his sexual activity again.

In addition to all of Juan's sexual activity, the couple had sex about three times a week, which both described as satisfactory. Nevertheless, he often pressured Maria for more frequent sex.

The patient's psychiatric history was unremarkable, except for his hypersexual behavior.

CASE 4.2—"Jossel Fromm": Hyperactive Sexual Desire in a Heterosexual Male with a Concomitant Obsessive-Compulsive Personality Disorder, in a Poor Sexual Relationship

Jossel was a 31-year-old Orthodox-Jewish jeweler who had been married for six years and was the father of four children. The couple were accompanied to my office by his father, father-in-law, mother, mother-in-law, and several other family members. The family were determined to save this couple's marriage. They were also hoping to preserve their standing in the community which was being threatened by Jossel's irrepressible habit of masturbating, quite obviously through the pockets of his pants for hours every day without exposing his penis, while standing on a busy sidewalk in his neighborhood and staring at women passing by. He also did the same thing during his lunch break, on the corner of a street near the jewelry district where he worked.

Jossel admitted that he regularly masturbated to orgasm about four to five times a day, and that he almost never stopped rubbing his penis. He knew that according to his religion he was committing a sin, and he was quite aware that his family was acutely embarrassed. However, he claimed that he could not stop, and that his urge was especially compelling during the two weeks of the month when he was forbidden to have relations with his wife. He told me that his wife did not like sex, and that they had intercourse infrequently, even when this was permitted.*

The psychiatric examination revealed that the patient had been anxious and obsessive since childhood, and that he met the criteria for obsessive-compulsive personality disorder.

CASE 4.3—"Tyler Hummingbird": Hyperactive Sexual Desire in a Married Bisexual Male

"Tyler Hummingbird," a bisexual married man aged 34, consulted me because he was deeply troubled by his compulsive homosexual behavior, which he could not control despite the fact that he knew that this posed a serious threat to his career, marriage, and health.

He was especially concerned about not infecting his wife, who knew nothing about his compulsive homoerotic behavior.

This man, who was attractive, well-educated, and successful in his work as a broker with a conservative Wall Street firm, was continuously preoccupied with thoughts of touching and fellating young men. When commuting to work in the morning, Tyler habitually sought out (unprotected) oral sex in the men's rooms of the train station. This would satisfy him for several hours, but as lunch approached, he would again experience an irresistible urge to have oral sex with a man and he frequented erotic bookstores during his lunch hour to satisfy this craving. Hummingbird usually had sex again by rubbing the penises of young strangers, on the crowded train on his way home to the suburbs where he lived with his wife and daughter. Sometimes, he would get up at three in the morning, leave the marital bed, and go to all-night gay bars for more sex, and then proceed to his office.

This man reported that he had sex with his wife about once a week. Tyler expressed deep love for his wife, said that he found her "very attractive," and claimed that he had no problem functioning with her.

However, the patient did admit that he was always vaguely anxious and apprehensive about having sex with his wife, and he told me that she often complained about his "clumsy and adolescent" approach to lovemaking.

*According to Orthodox Jewish law, a husband and wife are not allowed to have sexual relations or touch each other while she is menstruating and for a week afterwards, and until she has undergone a rabbinically supervised ritual cleansing bath.

Hummingbird reported that he had had approximately 500 different sexual partners during the past two years, the great majority of whom he did not know.

On numerous occasions, this man had tried to stop his ego-dystonic, compulsive sexual behavior. But each time he did, he became dysphoric, depressed, and restless, and quickly resumed. In great despair, he told me, "Doctor I need help, I feel completely out of control."

1b. Female Hypersexuality

Ubiquitous legends about insatiable succubi notwithstanding, nymphomania is mostly a male fantasy. In actual fact, female hyperactive sexual desire disorders are extremely rare; certainly, they are far less prevalent than the male counterpart.

Out of over five thousand patients with sexual disorders (3,552 males and 2,336 females) whom I evaluated between 1972 and 1992, only 18 were clearly distressed by their excessive sexual needs, and only two of these were women. The following is a brief description of one of those two cases.

CASE 4.4—"Tina Jefferson": Hypersexual Desire in a Depressed Heterosexual Female in a Good Sexual Relationship

Tina Jefferson was a black, 42-year-old postal worker, married to Frank, a trucker aged 45. The couple, who had been married for 16 years and had two children, described their marriage as harmonious.

The Jeffersons had come to New York to consult me because Tina was becoming increasingly depressed and agitated as she could find no relief from her constant, intrusive, sexual urges. For the last 10 years, this woman regularly wanted to have intercourse and orgasms about three times a day. Mr. J., who loved sex and who had a high-normal sex drive, had no complaints about his wife's unusually high erotic interest, and he did his best to comply. But when he happened to be unavailable or too exhausted to make love, Tina would feel mounting and distressing pelvic discomfort, which was not relieved until she had intercourse.

Mrs. Jefferson's craving for sex was intrusive and interfered with her functioning at her office job. She often could not bear to sit at her desk more than two hours at a time before she would feel a compelling urge to have intercourse. She would gradually become too uncomfortable and "frustrated" to be able to continue her work.

The significant findings on Mrs. Jefferson's history were a chaotic early family life. This woman's childhood had been a nightmare on account of her father's alcoholism, chronic unemployment, and periodic violence. This was made worse by her mother's withdrawal and inadequate, passive response. The patient reported that she had experienced recurrent mild depressions since adolescence.

Normal High Sex Drive or Pathological Sexual Addiction?

Hypersexuality has been variously conceptualized as a form of compulsive behavior that represents the individual's attempts to ameliorate symptoms of depression and anxiety, as an impulse control disorder, as a dysinhibition, and as an addictive state (Assalin & Ravart, 1993).

The addiction notion has been widely publicized and its offspring, the "Sexaholics Anonymous" movement, has gained a considerable following.

The addiction model derives from some similarities between chemical addiction and hyperactive sexual behavior. More specifically, the irresistible craving for sex and the insatiability that characterize hypersexual individuals, as well as the intense pleasure and the mood elevation that is produced by a "sexual fix," clearly resemble the "highs" seen with dependence on certain addicting substances, while the mounting discomfort and the dysphoria that is experienced with sexual abstinence mirror the "lows" and withdrawal.

On the other hand, anyone who has worked with these patients must be impressed with the compulsive quality of their sexual behavior. In support of the obsessive-compulsive view, there have been some reports about the efficacy of SRRIs, medications that are often effective for OCD, for this condition.

However, without taking exception to the addiction or compulsion paradigms, I find it useful to think of hypersexual behavior in terms of a dysregulation of sexual motivation, which results in unbridled sexual expression.

I believe that multiple organic and psychological factors, some as yet not identified, can precipitate such a regulatory malfunction. The cause in any particular case will determine the thrust of treatment, although this is still largely empirical.

"Juan Romeo" was seen in consultation only, and I have no follow up information. "Jossel Fromm" and "Tina Jefferson" were treated pharmacologically. Jossel had a fairly good response to Prozac, combined with psychotherapy with an Orthodox Jewish counselor from his congregation.

Mrs. Jefferson, who lived in a rural community without good mental health facilities, experienced only partial relief with tricyclic antidepressant medication.

"Tyler Hummingbird" was determined to gain insight into and gain control over his sexual impulses, and he made a considerable commitment to treatment. He embarked on a program of psychoanalysis with an analyst specializing in his condition, in conjunction with a course of psychosexual therapy for himself and his wife. Eventually, the outcome was excellent.

For the clinician, the most important issue in these cases is to distinguish persons whose excessive sexual desire is disabling, distressful, and/or destructive to their relationships from individuals who are merely blessed with a strong, healthy sex drive. There is the danger, in uncritically labeling every person with an unusually high level of sexual activity as a "sexual addict," of regressing to the old negative, moralistic judgmental designation of all unconventional sexual behavior as "sick." There is also the risk of creating a population of normal, highly sexed individuals who accept the opprobrium of, and seek treatment for, their "sexual addictions."

Once again, as long as an atypically high level of sexual activity is not perceived as detrimental by the person or by the partner, and as long as this causes no harm to anyone, there is no scientific justification for categorizing a person's sexual behavior as pathological. Lest we forget, it was only a few decades ago that masturbation was dubbed pathological and that this "disorder" was "treated" by physicians and educators by the tying of children's hands, physical punishments, intimidation, and worse.

The following two points on the continuum of sexual desire describe gradations of sexual behavior that falls within the *normal range.* In other words the sex-regulating system of persons who exhibit these sexual behavior patterns appears to be functioning normally.

2. High-Normal Sexual Desire

Normal persons with high sex drives personify a *proactive* as opposed to the reactive pattern of sexual behavior, that characterizes persons whose libidos fall into the lower-normal range.

This category describes individuals who are similar to those with pathological hyperactive sexual desire in that their sex drives are also strong. These individuals, more often men than women, are also aroused by a wide spectrum of sexual scenarios and partners, and they, too, periodically experience spontaneous, fluctuating surges of sexual desire. In these highly sexed individuals, the urge to have sex is also internally generated and may occur in the absence of any external erotic stimulation. The sex drive of persons in the "high-normal" category is intense enough to compel the individual to actively seek out sexual partners and to initiate sexual activity.

These normal, highly sexed individuals also resemble the pathologically hypersexual patients described in the foregoing sections in their ability to function well and to enjoy sex, and also in their mounting frustration if they do not find a sexual outlet.

However, although the sex drive of these normal persons is intense, this is not destructive nor inappropriate. For, unlike the hypersexual, these normal people are able to control their sexual urges when they would be inappropriate or disadvantageous. But perhaps the most important differences between normally and abnormally sexy persons is that neither they nor their partners are distressed by their intense sexuality, and this tends to enhance rather than impair their lives and their romantic relationships.

3. Low-Normal Sexual Desire

The sex-regulating functions of individuals whose libido falls into the low-normal range are perfectly adequate, but their "sexual thermostat" is set at a relatively low level. These men and women do not experience spontaneous surges of sexual desire, and they are much less likely to actively seek out sexual opportunities or to initiate sexual activity. Moreover, "low-normals" do not suffer from the intense frustration that plagues persons with higher sex drives when they are abstinent.

However, although the range of stimuli that will arouse these individuals tend to be more narrow, they, unlike patients with pathologically inhibited desire, have an entirely normal response to sexual opportunities and to sexual stimulation. They do not lose their interest in nor do they avoid sexually appropriate and attractive partners.

Thus, individuals with normal, albeit low, sex drives typically have sexual relations on a regular but less frequent basis, enjoy sex, have normal feelings of arousal, have no problems with erections or vaginal lubrication, and are capable of having pleasurable orgasms. Moreover, persons with a low but normal interest in sex can be attracted to and enjoy good relationships with their lovers, whose approaches they welcome, just as long as these are not more than they can handle. Once again, these individuals do not find sex emotionally painful, and neither do their partners.

A 69-year-old patient, who had never masturbated and whose only sexual partner was and always had been his wife, described his experience of the passage from a high *proactive* to a lower *reactive* sexual status like this: "I used to get upset and cranky if I didn't have sex at least every two or three days. I would get this painful sensation in my groin. It was so bad that I was afraid to plan business trips that kept me away from my wife for more than a day.

"Now I can go away for a week, and I never even think about sex, and it doesn't bother me. That is, until I get home and Hilda gives me a kiss and starts to touch me. Then I get horny again right away."

A low sex drive can become a problem even when this is within normal limits if the partner's libido is substantially higher. When there is a significant discrepancy in a couple's sexual needs and interests, one of the partners is apt to feel under constant pressure to have sex, while the other feels perpetually rejected.

The difficulties that can arise from imbalances in a couple's level of sexual desire are further discussed in Chapter 5, where this issue is illustrated by the case vignette of "May and Mark September" (Case 5.1). Briefly, September's level of sexual activity was perfectly normal for a man in his 60's. However, his new, youthful wife was upset and felt rejected because in the past she had been accustomed to making love much more frequently with her younger lovers.

The normal age-related decline of the male libido from high-normal to low-normal can also create difficulties if the aging couple are not prepared for this. The increasingly common problem of sexual desire disorders in the elderly will be discussed in Chapter 10.

The next two categories on the desire continuum represent the pathological overcontrol or suppression of sexual desire. As such, these patterns of sexual behavior have crossed the boundary between normalcy and pathology, and fall into the category of psychiatric disorders.

4. Mild Hypoactive Sexual Desire

This category desire represents a mild to moderate level of overcontrol of sexual desire. The libido of patients with the milder forms of HSD is muted. These individuals do not experience spontaneous fluctuations of their sexual urges, least of all towards their partners, and they have little desire to engage in sexual fantasies or to masturbate. Moreover, the range of erotic activities and the kinds of partners that can arouse them tend to be quite narrow and specific. In contrast to men and women whose libido falls within the low-normal range and whose genital responses to sexual stimulation are entirely normal, these hypoactive individuals do *not* respond adequately to erotic stimulation with appropriate, attractive partners.

Patients with mildly impaired sexual desire find it difficult to become aroused, especially during sexual interactions with their significant or exclusive partners. Ordinary courtship behavior and physical stimulation fail to incite their desires sufficiently. Moreover, it may take very lengthy and intense physical stimulation, such as with an electric vibrator pressed tight against the clitoris or intense oral stimulation for half an hour or more, together with steady erotic fantasy or absorption in erotica, for the man or the women with a low-desire profile to be able to function and come to orgasm. Even then, the experience of erotic pleasure is likely to be fleeting. As a rule, the partners do not find sex gratifying under such unspontaneous conditions.

Patients with the global form of HSD may be described as *sexually anorexic* because they have simply lost their appetite for sex under any circumstances; in the language of the "dysfunctional control" model, their sexual motivation is down-regulated across the board. These men and women do not engage in sexual fantasy and, unless their partners push them, they can go without sex for months and even years without feeling frustrated.

Although desire disorders do not affect the excitement or orgasm phases of the sexual response cycle directly, if these low-desire individuals attempt to engage in sex despite their lack of appetite just to accommodate their partners, they may have trouble lubricating or maintaining their erections and/or coming to orgasm. When they do manage to function, the experience lacks pleasure and is typically described as mechanical, or as only " a release."

More often, the decrease in the patient's level of sexual desire is specific and selective. Typically, these individuals become severely blocked with regard to the act of sexual intercourse, as opposed to manual or oral sex, and the loss of desire is typically most severe for the marital or long-term partner. However, patients with situational HSD retain their capacity for normal lust, arousal and responsiveness to other partners, masturbation, erotic fantasy, or paraphiliac practices.

Paradoxically, even when sexual experience does turn out to be pleasurable, these patients are likely to be just as reluctant to have sex the next time they are approached by their partner. Both spouses may be puzzled as to why the sexually symptomatic partner's avoidance is impervious to positive sexual experiences. "I just can't understand it, Dr. Kaplan—My orgasm felt really good. Why wouldn't I want to do it again? It would make her so happy," is a common refrain in these cases.

The following case illustrates the down-regulation of sexual desire that occurred in this patient only with exclusive, committed partners. But the "brakes were off" when the symbolic meaning of the relationship with the sexual partner changed. This case also provides a good example of the relationship between the "deeper" and the more "superficial" or immediate causes of hypoactive sexual desire disorders.

CASE 4.5—"Paul Actor": Mild, Partner-Specific HSD

Paul Actor, a handsome, divorced, acclaimed author, aged 54, was highly ambivalent about and sexually "turned-off" by Evelyn, an attractive, voluptuous, divorced woman of 47 who was actively pursuing him. The couple made love infrequently. Evelyn tried to initiate sex quite often, but Actor usually avoided her approaches, claiming that "the chemistry" just wasn't right, and that Evelyn was simply not his "type."

On the rare times that this couple did have sex, intercourse was seldom Actor's preference. Their sexual encounters typically consisted of Evelyn's providing Actor with oral or lubricant-assisted manual stimulation of his penis, while the couple sat on a couch watching his favorite erotic fantasy on the videotapes she would rent for the occasion. He was turned on by the scenario of an older woman seducing an attractive young boy. Although under these circumstances Actor was able to become sufficiently aroused to have good erections and to climax, his desire was low and his orgasms were not pleasurable. Actor told me that he found it much easier to masturbate to his fantasy when he was alone, although even then his ejaculations were anesthetic (Kaplan, 1991).

This woman was determined to seduce Actor into a committed relationship and she spared no effort on that behalf. She once managed to persuade him to join her for a vacation at a beautiful house on a Greek island, which had been provided gratis by one of her friends. The ambiance was perfect: a moonlit night with celestial music playing over the speakers as Actor and Evelyn playfully swam together nude in the velvet waters of the shimmering pool.

Actor reported that he felt "nothing" and he went to bed in a separate room without making love to Evelyn, which hurt her very much. But he was amazed to observe that he had developed a strong erection that persisted for a long time. "Doctor," he asked me, "is it possible for my body to be aroused without my mind knowing it?"

Actor had put it very well. Patients with HSD behave as though they are "disconnected" from their genitalia. Or, to put it more precisely, in psychogenic hyposexual desire disorders, there is a dissociation between the motivational and the genital aspects of sex.

On the initial evaluation, it is often quite difficult or impossible to differentiate patients who are not attracted to their partners for realistic reasons, from those who are inhibited by emotional conflict. Final judgment on this matter must often be deferred until later, when the underlying pathogenesis of the patient's sexual problem and/or of the couple's dynamics have become clearer.

In this case, I could not reach certainty regarding this differential during my initial contacts with the patient. I was simply unable to decide whether he was repelled by some of Evelyn's truly undesirable qualities, such as her tedious tendency to talk too much when she became anxious or her dark, unspectacular Mediterranean looks (he preferred slender, spectacular Nordic blondes), or her age, 47, (which precluded Actor's starting the new family he yearned for), or whether his sexual disinterest possibly represented a neurotic inhibition.

However, subsequent events made it crystal clear that Actor's lack of desire for Evelyn was a product of *inhibition* and not an *absence* of attraction based on reality.

At Evelyn's urging, Actor agreed to try sex therapy. However, he was too ambivalent to continue, and I saw the couple together only a few times. Actor soon stopped coming to the sessions and Evelyn entered into individual therapy with me. It was thus that I learned that when this woman was finally able to give up her painful, obsessive pursuit of the unavailable Actor and married someone else, he suddenly became sexually obsessed with her. In fact after she had remarried, Actor actually managed to persuade Evelyn to carry on an extramarital affair with him!

Although this man had been turned off by the single Evelyn, he was extremely hot for the married Evelyn, and he even regained some of his ejaculatory sensations when they made love.

I received the final evidence that Actor's initial lack of desire for Evelyn had had a neurotic basis when he consulted me some years later. Actor, now 62, was having similar sexual difficulties with his new wife.

Actor had been quite smitten with the strikingly glamorous, 32-year-old Eva. He had felt very passionate about her prior to their wedding, while she was still married to her former husband. Soon after her divorce, however, on their honeymoon, he again felt completely "turned off."

This man's sexual desire was suppressed when he was in a close, committed, monogamous relationship with an available woman, while a "triangle" scenario with other men's wives served as a powerful erotic inciter stimulus. Clearly, this was a pattern of behavior that had little to do with the characteristics of his partner.

Actor's desire for Evelyn increased sharply when the unconscious meaning of their relationship changed. After she married a "father figure" and thus, became the symbolic "mother," he was able to play out his erotic fantasy of the little boy who sneaks into his mother's bed and makes love to her while father is away. This same fantasy also aroused his desire for Eva while she was still married to her wealthy first husband.

As is typical of patients with psychogenic HSD, Actor was entirely unaware of the deeper meaning of his sexual symptoms. He firmly believed that he had been drawn only to Eva's real blond Nordic beauty and youth. He had no idea that after Eva's divorce became final and they became man and wife, she lost her appeal because she was no longer part of an "oedipal triangle."

5. Severe Hypoactive Sexual Desire

In the most severe forms of HSD, it is impossible for the person to become sexually aroused even with the most intense physical and/or psychic stimulation. In the global form of this syndrome, the person develops a severe and total "sexual anorexia." To put it another way, the sex regulatory centers have shut down completely and nothing can stimulate them into action. These individuals do not enjoy love-making under any circumstance, nor with any partner, and no sort of stimulation will arouse them. They tend to avoid sex and with some exceptions, they are either totally celibate or they engage in sex very infrequently.

Typically, these patients experience no sexual frustration even after prolonged periods of abstinence. Their sexual experience, when they have one, is described as mechanical and devoid of pleasure, although nongenital contact with the partner may remain neutral or tolerable.

Sexually anorexic patients are perfectly comfortable with their lack of sexuality and claim that they do not miss sex. In clinical practice we see men and women with severe hyposexual desire states only when their lack of interest in sex has resulted in marital problems, or if their asexuality has interfered with their ability to form romantic relationships to the point where their loneliness and sense of isolation drives them to seek help.

CASE 4.6—"Frieda and Fred Aspen": Lifelong, Severe, Global HSD in a Well-Functioning, Happily Married Woman

This case shows that HSD, even when this is severe, is not always associated with low sexual frequency. The patient was a cheerful, 54-year-old, happily married woman with three grown children. She had never experienced any sexual desire nor had she ever had an orgasm. Except for her absent libido, Mrs. Aspen functioned perfectly well and led a full and satisfying suburban married life.

Frieda accepted her lack of sexual desire and pleasure with equanimity and did not see this as a problem. She had agreed to a consultation with me only to satisfy her long-frustrated husband.

For the past 31 years, ever since their honeymoon, which had been her first sexual experience, Frieda had permitted her husband to make love to her once a week, and no more, and always without feeling the slightest desire or pleasure. She remained entirely passive and removed during the act, occupying herself mentally with planning menus or making shopping lists. She steadfastly resisted her husband's tireless attempts to have sex more frequently and with more variety, although she admitted that he was a considerate, gentle lover.

Fred had remained very attracted to his wife, but he found her lack of responsiveness extremely frustrating. He told me that over the years he had tried "everything" to arouse Frieda—attempting to stimulate her breasts and genitalia (which she did not permit), bringing home erotic books (to which she strongly objected), trying to take her dancing (she refused to dance), planning romantic vacations and dinners, and giving her expensive presents—all to no avail. A course of marital therapy also proved ineffective, as she had no complaints about her husband or their marriage.

Frieda had never had any desire for sex with her husband, nor for sex with any other man or woman. She had never had the slightest interest in masturbating or in fantasy. Not surprisingly, she had absolutely no interest in entering sex therapy.

This case vignette demonstrates that it is possible for some women with HSD to fulfill the function of being sexual partners, even when they feel no desire and are basically passive. But men find it more difficult to attain and maintain erections without feeling desire; therefore, males with HSD have a greater tendency to avoid sex. This can be painful for the partner and often leads to the rupture of valued relationships. Some of the problems that can be created by HSD and sexual avoidance in married men are illustrated by the following case vignettes.

CASE 4.7—"Jack and Jill Priest": Severe, Acquired, Partner-Specific HSD in a Married Man

The patient, "Jack Priest," was a handsome, successful, 48-year-old business executive with an Irish Catholic background. He had been married for five years (his second marriage) to Jill, a stunning, sexy woman, aged 32, who had been a professional model. The couple had a small daughter whom they both adored. Apart from their sexual problems, their relationship was loving and harmonious.

The Priests had consulted me because Jack had not approached his wife sexually for the past three years, since the baby's birth. Whenever Jill attempted to initiate sex, Jack invariably refused, and, since he "didn't want to start what he couldn't finish," he also avoided all non-sexual physical contact with her, and she was feeling hurt and frustrated.

The couple had been married after a brief, "whirlwind" courtship. Initially, Jack had been very attracted to Jill, but soon after the wedding Jack began to lose his sexual desire for his exceptionally attractive wife, and he found it increasingly difficult to function with her. The frequency of the couple's lovemaking had declined precipitously after their honeymoon, and had ceased entirely after Casey's birth. Jill was devastated by the rejection, but she had stopped trying to initiate sex with her husband since it was clear that her requests for sex, as well as her complaints and tears, got her nowhere.

Jack expressed his own distress at his lack of desire for his wife as follows: "She's a wonderful, beautiful woman, it is not her fault, she's an excellent partner and would do anything to please me, but I just feel like a brother to her. I'm very guilty about this, I know I'm ruining her life and jeopardizing my marriage, but I just can't help it."

The Priests' lovemaking during the brief "good" period of their relationship had been entirely conventional, consisting of perfunctory foreplay, followed by "man on top" intercourse.

It was a deep secret that Priest regularly visited a dominatrix who dressed up like a nurse for him and spanked him "lovingly." As he lay across her lap, she would hit his bare bottom with a wooden paddle and croon "Jackie, I love you, I'm only doing this for your own good."

This scenario, which he felt he could never reveal to his "classy" wife because "it is vulgar and sick," played out his erotic fantasy and incited intense desire. Under these circumstances, his lust and functioning were excellent.

6. Sexual Aversion

Sexual aversion and/or the phobic avoidance of sex is the most severe form of sexual desire disorder. In these *sexual anxiety states*, sexual contact with the partner is associated with a feeling of imminent peril, and the accompanying emergency emotions override all sexual feelings.

Patients with the "quiet" forms of hypoactive desire, which were described above, simply have no appetite for sex, but they are not repelled by physical contact with the partner. By contrast, patients with sexual aversion disorders are intensely frightened of, or actively repelled by, and phobically avoid sexual activity.

The following description of this syndrome is taken in part from a chapter in *Sexual Aversion, Sexual Phobias, and Panic Disorder* (HSK, 1987, pp. 12–16).

Clinical Presentation

An element of phobic avoidance plays a role in and complicates all psychosexual dysfunctions, but this is the essential feature of true sexual phobias. For example, a premature ejaculator may appear to avoid sexual opportunities, but though he may overreact, his performance fears have a basis in reality. When their sexual symptoms improve in treatment, dysfunctional patients with secondary sexual avoidance rapidly begin to develop a sense of sexual confidence and soon begin to look forward to sex. On the other hand, the phobic avoidance of patients with sexual panic disorders is not related to performance fears or to a real sexual disability.

Total and Partial Sexual Phobias

Some patients are totally phobic of sex and experience panics or revulsion in response to any and all erotic sensations, feelings, thoughts, images, and opportunities. Even subtle sexual references or situations, such as pictures or films with erotic nuances, might disturb severely sexaphobic individuals. Thus, Mrs. Kaiser, who will be described later in this chapter, could not tolerate the sight of an explicitly sexual illustration from one of my textbooks that hangs on the wall of my office, and she always made sure to sit with her back to the drawing.

In other cases, the patient's phobic response is limited to, or most intense towards, a specific aspect of sex.

The following are the 13 most common specific sexual phobias we have observed in our patients:

1. Touching or caressing body (especially breasts, nipples, and thighs)
2. The sight of genitalia (own or partner's)
3. Touching the partner's genitalia

4. Kissing (mouth, breasts, genitalia)
5. Vaginal penetration (women: being penetrated with any object or with the penis only; men: penetrating)
6. Sexual secretions and odors (semen, vaginal secretions)
7. Sexual arousal (own or partner's)
8. Orgasm (fear of loss of control)
9. Oral sex (receiving or providing oral stimulation of the partner's genitalia)
10. Sexual failure (performance panic, more common in males)
11. Pregnancy (becoming or causing)
12. Contracting a sexually transmitted disease (AIDS, herpes, etc.)
13. Nudity (own and/or partner's)

Patients with such circumscribed sexual fears or aversions may actually enjoy other aspects of sex and function normally as long as they can manage to avoid their particular phobia. As a common example, women with specific penetration phobias tend to panic only when intercourse is attempted, but they are often able to enjoy foreplay and climax with clitoral stimulation. Providing that they are certain that this will not lead to vaginal penetration, they may fully enjoy all other sexual activities and are often sensitive and responsive lovers.

Thus, not uncommonly, patients with isolated penetration phobias have enjoyed kissing, caressing, genital stimulation and orgasm in their premarital sexual experiences, before they attempted coitus, and their phobic avoidance of intercourse may surface for the first time, often to their own amazement, during the honeymoon.

The Intensity of the Phobic Response

Patients with sexual phobias and aversion disorders will avoid sex as far as this is possible, but sometimes they get "trapped" into having sex by a partner's pressure, by the fear of losing a lover, or by a feeling of obligation to comply because of their love for the partner. Once they find themselves in sexual situations, there is considerable diversity in the intensity of the fear or aversion that sexaphobics experience.

Patients with mild phobias and aversions are able to calm themselves and, once they push themselves past the barrier of their anticipatory anxiety and avoidance, are even able to enjoy sex, sometimes to the point of orgasm. Once again, it is a paradox that such positive experiences do nothing to diminish the sexual phobic avoidance and these patients are often puzzled by their continuing and compelling urge to avoid sex despite the enjoyment and gratification they experience once they allow themselves to get involved.

Those with more severe phobic responses become so anxious that they cannot function nor feel erotic sensations. However, if they make the effort to do so, such individuals can often make themselves fairly comfortable by detaching themselves or by averting their attention from the erotic aspects of the experience. Some, while feeling little pleasure themselves, can go so far as to focus on and enjoy the intimate, physical contact with their partners, and are gratified by the fact that they have power to give pleasure to their lovers. Others feel used and angry because they continue to experience nothing, while their partners are having a good time.

Still other patients become so panicked and uncomfortable, and experience such intensely aversive feelings during the sexual act, that they cannot detach themselves. They merely endure the experience as best they can, comforting themselves with the thought that it can't last indefinitely and that no real harm will come to them. One patient told me it was very much like being in the dentist's chair, knowing that if she could just hold on it would be over soon.

Patients with severe sexual anxieties, especially those with concomitant anxiety disorders, may experience true anxiety or panic attacks, complete with the physical symptoms of autonomic discharge, if they cannot avoid a sexual situation. Feelings of terror, tremulousness, impending doom, palpitations, difficulty in breathing, faintness, feelings of depersonalization, amnesia, and actual loss of consciousness have been reported. All feel an urgent wish to escape. Some sexaphobics weep uncontrollably during or after sex, and one of my patients has vomited several times after she has had sex.

Patients with severe sexual aversions experience intense disgust and revulsion towards their partners. Many of these patients cannot tolerate the slightest physical contact with the partner, even in nonerotic contexts.

Some sexaphobic patients report that they feel intense postcoital psychic pain: "I feel as though I had been violated, raped," after a sexual experience. These "afterpains" can last from a few hours to several days.

Anticipatory Anxiety and Avoidance Patterns

Dr. Donald Klein has pointed out the important distinction between the phobic reaction itself, and anticipatory anxiety (Klein, 1980). All phobic patients, those who have underlying phobic anxiety syndromes as well as those with simple phobias, be these sexual phobias or other types of phobias, characteristically develop anticipatory anxiety and learn to avoid their phobic object. Thus, just as patients with claustrophobia will go to great lengths to avoid closed places, sexaphobic individuals make every attempt to avoid sex whenever possible. As with other kinds of phobias, these avoidance patterns are a major obstacle to the treatment of sexual phobias.

Sexaphobic patients typically become very anxious and try to escape situations where it will be difficult for them to avoid sex. Their anxious apprehension interferes with the pleasurable anticipation and the build-up of desire that people normally experience before a date or party, or a romantic evening at home, and they can think only of escape.

Sometimes sexual anticipatory anxiety takes on the dimensions of an obsession, and the individual's preoccupation with his or her sexual anxiety may interfere with work or social life.

In describing her experience, which is quite typical, a married woman with panic disorder and a phobic avoidance of sex told me:

> When we haven't had sex for a week or so, I start getting anxious and worried because I know he will want to soon. Coming home from work on the bus, I start to obsess: What if he wants sex tonight? God, he will really get mad if I refuse again. I'll try to distract him. Maybe I should invite the Smiths for supper. He'll get all involved with them and it will get too late for sex. I know, I'll get him a steak and make his favorite dessert, that will make him feel I care.
>
> By the time I get home I'm a wreck. Sometimes I take a drink, sometimes I binge eat and get myself sick. Sometimes, when sex is inevitable, I knock myself out with pot, then it's a little easier. I feel like a very selfish person. He is really very good to me. He's only asking for what he's entitled to.

Patients with sexual phobias and aversions who are in relationships develop ingenious and varied *avoidance strategies*. Often, these individuals are reluctant to refuse to have sex in a straightforward manner, and they try to conceal their avoidance by making themselves unavailable physically and emotionally for sex and intimacy.

They often *hide out in the office.*

When they are home, they remove themselves with *compulsive tasks*, lengthy *telephone calls*, or obsessive *watching of television*, which is possibly the most widely used vehicle for sexual avoidance in our modern society.

Many *use their children*, leaving the bedroom door open at all times "in case the kids need us."

Household pets can provide still another excuse for avoiding sex. For example, the girlfriend of one of my patients, a retarded ejaculator who was rapidly getting better, sabotaged their relationship by insisting that her two huge Dalmatian coach hounds sleep in their bed every night.

In the service of avoiding sex, sexaphobics may arrange a frantic round of *social and family activities* that never allows the couple to be alone together.

Some have learned to turn off their partners by *making themselves unattractive.* At home they wear curlers, face cream, and old bathrobes, smoke *smelly cigars*, or make a habit of not shaving, showering or brushing their teeth, unless they are going out.

Still others cloud their consciousness with *alcohol* or other substances when sex is in the air.

Patients may develop *somatic symptoms* and actually become ill to help them escape the dreaded sexual ordeal. The famous quote, "Not tonight dear, I have a headache," is no joke in these marriages.

Problems of the Married Sexaphobic

The following case study illustrates some of the difficulties typically experienced by married, sexaphobic or sexually aversive individuals, who must balance their repugnance of sex with their fears of destroying their relationships and/or losing their partners.

CASE 4.8—"Regina and Roy Kaiser": Sexual Aversion and Avoidance in a Married Woman with a Concomitant Personality Disorder

Regina Kaiser was a 54-year-old married woman with a severe aversion to having sex with her attractive, intelligent, successful, albeit somewhat controlling and compulsive, husband.

This was the patient whose aversion to all things sexual was so severe that she could not bear to look at an erotic illustration that hangs on the wall of my office.

This patient's anticipatory anxiety was overwhelming to the point that she could feel at peace only when her husband was safely out of town on one of his frequent business trips. A day or two before his anticipated return, her feelings of apprehension and panic would rise again, because she knew he would expect to have sex.

As is typical of married patients with sexual aversions, Regina devised a number of rather ingenious avoidance maneuvers. She trained her cat to sleep on the couple's bed, to which her husband strenuously objected. (When he more or less got used to the animal, she bought a second one.) When Roy was home on weekends, she kept herself compulsively occupied and emotionally removed. She engaged in lengthy telephone conversations, scheduled work sessions at her foundry (she was a gifted sculptor who created large metal pieces). She also spent much of her time attending church (she had become a devout born/again Christian, which drove her liberal, intellectual, secular-minded husband crazy). Regina, like many persons who fear intimacy with their partners, avoided going to bed when her husband did, making sure to busy herself until the late hours of the night, so that the couple had not gone to sleep while both were awake for the last 10 years.

As an additional avoidance tactic, this exquisitely coiffed, bejeweled woman who wore elegant Chanel suits, bathed very rarely, perhaps once a month, dousing herself with perfumes and deodorants so that she would be socially acceptable. However her aroma was not very appealing in bed.

Regina described her sexual encounters with her understandably frustrated husband, which occurred about once every two weeks, and only when she had exhausted all avenues of escape, as "tortuous and traumatic," although these were "mercifully" (her word) brief on account of his PE. "I feel like I am being lowered into a snake pit, as though I were being violated by a reptile."

The patient had a repetitive nightmare that symbolized her fear of and aversion to sex. She dreamt that she was being suspended over a chair, helpless, her legs apart, while lobsters were snapping their claws angrily at her exposed genitalia.

The Single Sexaphobic

Sexaphobic patients who are not married or in relationships develop comparable tactics to avoid potential sexual partners; these strategies often shape and distort their lives. Some become members of devout religious sects, such as Orthodox Judaism or Jehovah's Witness. This permits them to refuse to engage in sex on religious or moral grounds, and confine their friendships to people with similar values who will respect their wish to remain virgins prior to marriage. Others avoid dating altogether and behave in ways that discourage romantic advances. Sometimes, this entails relating as sisters or brothers or "pals" to members of the opposite sex. Some sexually avoidant individuals make a habit of becoming obsessed with totally unavailable individuals, others sabotage their sexual attractiveness by acting, dressing, and conducting themselves in a sexually unappealing manner, while still others throw themselves compulsively into their work or avocations to the exclusion of socializing.

The most extreme and tragic sequel of the phobic avoidance of sex is seen in individuals whose sexual problems engulf their entire existences to the extent that they remain virgins, single, and starved for affection in a world where everyone else seems paired.

Chapter 8 contains descriptions of the successful treatments of "Greta Biedemeyer," (Case 8.1), a 39-year-old, single, sexaphobic woman who had never had a date with a man, and of "Bill Kangaroo," (Case 8.2), a 41-year-old male virgin with HSD and sexual avoidance. These cases illustrate the potentially malignant sequelae of the avoidance of sex, in terms of the quality of life.

CHAPTER 5

Evaluation I: Patients with Desire Disorders— Establishing the Diagnosis

DOES THE PATIENT HAVE A GENUINE SEXUAL DESIRE DISORDER?

When evaluating a person who complains about a lack of libido, the first issue that must be cleared up in the examiner's mind is whether or not the patient is actually afflicted with a real or genuine sexual desire disorder, that is, if the diagnosis of HSD or sexual aversion is warranted.

The apparent straightforward question of whether the patient's sex drive is normal or abnormal is not as simplistic as it seems, because every man and woman who lacks sexual interest in the partner does not have a sexual desire disorder.

The diagnosis of sexual desire disorder is obvious when the sexual symptoms are severe. Almost all of the case histories cited in this book describe such patients. For example, this includes "Bill Kangaroo" (Case 8.2, the teacher who was still a virgin at age 41); "Greta Biedemeyer" (Case 8.1, the 39-year-old, sexaphobic woman who was sexually molested as a child); "Mrs. Traveler" (Case 8.6, a woman who developed a sexual aversion towards her husband after she learned that he had had an extramarital affair and had exposed her to gonorrhea); and "Paul Actor" (Case 4.5, the man who could feel sexual passion only for married women, but was totally blocked in monogamous relationships).

These case studies were selected for didactic purposes to illustrate the clinical features of sexual desire disorders. However, in clinical practice one sees many borderline cases where the diagnostic picture is not as clear cut, and it is often difficult, especially during the initial evaluation, to determine whether the patient who complains that his/her libido is deficient actually *has* a genuine desire disorder.

Discrepancies in the Partners' Sex Drives

In many cases where the couple come in complaining about one partner's deficient desire, it turns out that the other's needs are, in fact, excessive. Alternatively, both partners' sex drives may be within normal limits but at opposite ends of the range, and the couple's distress is due to a discrepancy in their sexual needs.

A significant difference in the partners' desire for sex is a fairly common cause of sexual and marital difficulties (Zilbergeld & Ellison, 1980; Lazarus, 1988), and the consequent stress on the relationship may be sufficiently severe to require therapeutic help regardless of whether or not either partner meets the criteria for a sexual desire disorder.

In a typical scenario, the partner with the more urgent sexual desire feels perpetually rejected and accuses the other of having a sexual disorder, while the one who wants sex less frequently feels incessantly pressured and guilty.

However, I have recently seen a number of couples where the accusation of sexual abnormality was reversed, in that it was *not* the low-desire partner who was accused of being "sick." Rather, a normally sexed man with a high level of desire had been labeled a "sexual addict" by his wife and sometimes by his counselor.

There are, of course, genuine cases of hyperactive sexual desire, as was illustrated by the four case vignettes of hypersexual patients described in Chapter 4. However, not uncommonly, the real issue behind such complaints is the discomfort experienced by the lower-desire partner because the spouse's high-normal sexual appetite exceeded his/her own.

I am not troubled when the dynamics of an imbalance in a couple's sexual needs does not become clear on the first interview. As a matter of fact, I generally take this opportunity to use my uncertainty to create a small therapeutic crisis. I often say to the rejected, frustrated, high-desire individual, who has dragged his/her reluctant spouse into my office and who is complaining bitterly about the other's "frigidity" or lack of libido: "I can see how hurt and rejected you must feel. But it is not clear to me as yet whether your wife's lack of interest in making love to you is abnormally low or whether your expectations are unrealistically high, or whether it might be a combination of both."

The disclosure of my bafflement can serve to engage the couple and to start them on the process of reevaluating their entrenched, locked-in, countersexual positions.

In the following case, the partners got into trouble because of a discrepancy in their sex drives, although neither had a true desire disorder.

CASE 5.1—"May and Mark September": Imbalance in the Sexual Appetites of Two Normal but Differently Sexed Individuals

May, a 29-year-old woman who had recently married 62-year-old Mark September, consulted me because her husband would make love to her "only once" during their sexual encounters. She complained that she expected him to have intercourse at least twice when they made love, as she had been accustomed to with her former, much younger partners. She also wanted him to make love to her every day. Extremely frustrated, May could not understand why this man, who was loving and generous in every other way, was "withholding sex" from her.

The sexual status examination revealed that the couple made love about three times a week, that Mark was an attentive lover, and that both enjoyed their sexual encounters.

But May wanted more. "Dr.," she said to me, "My second orgasm is really much better than the first. After I have the first one, I'm all wet and aroused and I enjoy it so much more. You understand, don't you? My husband has a real problem with this. It probably was his mother's fault. Do you think you can help him?"

But the examination of this couple's sexual status clearly indicated that the husband did not have a desire disorder, nor was he "withholding" sex. His libido was normal for a man in his sixties, and although he found his wife extremely attractive, he simply could not exceed the biological limitations imposed by his age. Hence, any attempts on my part to enhance this man's libido would have been inappropriate and doomed to failure.

However, the wife's level of sexual desire was also entirely normal. May was blessed with a strong libido. She was one of those fortunate women who experienced spontaneous surges of desire and multiple orgasms, and she simply loved sex. In short, May's sex drive was in the high-normal range. Moreover, she did not feel sated after a single orgasm. But she certainly could not be described as pathologically hypersexual.

May's problem was really not so much that she felt sexually frustrated. She was hurt and angry because she mistakenly took her husband's lower sex drive as a sign that he was rejecting her and withholding his love.

This couple was a victim of a biological discrepancy in the magnitude of their libidos. In the language of the six-point continuum of sexual desire, it was simply a matter of a "High-Normal-2" married to a "Low-Normal-3" (see page 58).

The aim of therapy in such cases is to help the couple arrive at mutual accommodations and compromises. This can be quite successful in terms of improved marital satisfaction, providing both partners are well motivated and the couples can be persuaded to approach the imbalance in their sexual needs constructively, with loving understanding, and without taking this as a personal rejection.

The Septembers were crazy about each other and both were eager to make their relationship work. Under these circumstances, it was not too difficult to get May to understand the realities of the male aging process, and for Mark to accept the idea that he did not have to match each of his wife's orgasms with one of his own. By the end of therapy, May was able to adjust to having sex less frequently in exchange for a better quality of sex and greater intimacy and emotional security with her husband.

Nonpathological Lack of Sexual Attraction: Sexual Incompatibility

The term *sexual discrepancy* denotes a difference in the magnitude of the partners' sex drives, *while sexual incompatibility* refers to a lack of attraction between the partners, which is a more serious problem.

There is a myth in our culture that men who are sexually sound are supposed to feel the urge to copulate with any and all available partners, unless these are grossly inappropriate.

But sometimes a lack of sexual interest in the partner represents a normal response. After all, we are not designed to respond indiscriminately to any fertile member of the opposite gender, as do insects and dogs. For humans, sexual attraction and partner preference are far more subtle and complex. A feeling of attraction depends on the right look, the right odor, the right touch, the right voice, the right personality, the right behavior, and, above all, on the right fantasy.

Some people are not attracted to each other for good reasons, and it makes no sense to attempt to "treat" an individual with a normal, nonpathological low-desire state for a psychiatric disorder.

Sometimes, the lack of attraction or desire is due to obvious sexual deterrents, such as extreme ugliness, severe deformities, serious age discrepancies, crippling physical disabilities, mental retardation, and poor hygiene. Grossly bizarre or unattractive behaviors, as occur in certain psychiatric disorders, are also sexual "turn offs" for most normal persons. Further, there may be clear and specific sexual incompatibilities between two people—for example, between an exclusive homosexual and a member of the opposite gender who simply does not arouse him or her.*

Similarly it is not surprising if a man whose sexual fantasy and ideal is a slim, buxom, youthful partner has little sexual interest in his matronly, Rubensesque wife who might appeal to a man with different sexual appetites, nor if the woman who is "turned on" by articulate, intellectual men is sexually unresponsive to her crude, muscle-builder, jock date (who might be another's dream).

Problems Arising Out of Sexual Incompatibility

A lack of sexual desire for the spouse or an outright sexual aversion can create serious family and marital problems that require therapeutic intervention, whether or not this is actually pathological.

I have frequently seen such situations in couples who marry for reasons that do not include sexual attraction, as in some arranged marriages (which are still common among East Indians, Arabic Muslims, and Orthodox Jews, among others), and also in marriages that are contracted primarily for economic or social gain.

The following five cases all involved marriages that were arranged by the couples' families. All the brides and grooms were virtual strangers when the wedding ceremony took place, and all were in trouble because one of the partners was sexually aversive to the arranged-for spouse. However, each case differed with respect to the underlying dynamics, and each required different, individualized, therapeutic interventions.

---

*Alfred Kinsey devised a six point scale of sexual orientation wherein "sixes" are exclusively and "fives" predominantly homosexual. These individuals have no or virtually no desire for sex with the opposite gender, while "zeroes" and "ones" are exclusively or predominantly heterosexuals, that is uninterested or aversive to sex with partners of their own gender. "Twos," "Threes" and "Fours" are *bisexuals* who have the capacity, in varying degrees, for hetero- as well as homo-erotic desire and arousal (Kinsey et al., 1948).

CASE 5.2—"Dr. Zubin Raj": Arranged Marriage I—Partner-Specific Lack of Sexual Desire and Aversion in the Husband

"Dr. Raj" was a handsome, tall, 32-year-old physician from Bombay who had been working in the U.S. for some five years. He was seeking help because he and his wife, Indria, had not been able to consummate their marriage. Dr. Raj was accompanied to my office by his father-in-law, who had made the long trip from India to New York because he wanted to consult with me in person to see if I could "cure" his son-in-law's "sexual disorder" and thereby save the marriage

The young couple's betrothal had been arranged by their families in India. They had been married for one year, during which time Dr. Raj's many attempts to have intercourse with his wife had failed.

In the beginning, he simply could not become aroused sufficiently to maintain his erection, although he admitted that she was a most cooperative partner. Lately, he had developed an active aversion to his wife and for the past three months had avoided all physical contact with her.

Both families were in an uproar about the young couple's failure to consummate their marriage. The crisis was escalating because the Raj family was now claiming that the problem was entirely Indria's fault and that she was an "unfit wife" for their son. Thus, there was more at stake here than the matter of resolving the couple's sexual problem. The outcome could have a serious impact on the young woman's entire future, for if she were to be labeled "unfit" for marriage, she would be, in her father's words, "worse off than a homeless person."

Dr. Raj did not agree with his family's assessment. He was exceedingly ashamed and guilty about his inability to make love to his wife. He felt she was blameless and regarded the sexual problem as entirely his fault.

The initial session with the family was followed by separate interviews with the husband and the wife.

Indria was a petite, intense, dark-skinned, not unattractive young woman, who was dressed in a beautiful, traditional Indian sari. Her command of English was very good, although she spoke with a heavy accent.

Indria was anxious during the interview. She had a slight facial tic, and her speech was rapid and pressured. As she leaned forward, a stream of invectives against her husband poured out of her mouth. However she insisted that she could, and wanted to, learn to love him if he would "only behave like a proper man." She was understandably hurt and bitter because she had done her best to be a good wife, cooking delicious Indian food for him and diligently trying to practice the various erotic techniques that had been suggested by her mother, aunts, and cousins. She felt increasingly hurt, angry, and helpless because the more she approached her husband sexually, the more he seemed to avoid her. She felt humiliated by the problems she was causing for her family, and worried about her own future.

The trouble which Dr. Raj revealed to me in private was that he was deeply in love with another woman, a beautiful, tall, blonde, athletic, American physician. It was a well guarded secret that they had been having a passionate affair for two years, that Dr. Raj was very aroused by this woman, and that he functioned perfectly well with her. He had terminated their relationship only because he knew his family would not accept an American wife. But this blond American woman doctor was his sexual fantasy and ideal, and he still longed for and fantasized about this lover.

By contrast, he had never liked his wife's petite, dark, physical type. Moreover, he felt they had little in common, since this traditional Asian woman knew nothing about Western medicine and science, which was his whole life.

Although Dr. Raj was quite American in speech and dress, he was also deeply imbued with his culture's traditions. A responsible young man, he felt honor bound to try to make the marriage work, and he told me that he was prepared to make every effort to overcome his aversion to his wife. However, on a deeper level of consciousness, he was rebelling by not consummating a marriage he did not want. The doctor didn't know it, but he was acting out his desire to remain faithful to the woman he loved.

The dynamics of the following case, also a desire problem in an arranged marriage, are entirely different. In this instance it was the wife who had a sexual aversion to her husband. Moreover, the woman had a primary, global sexual desire disorder that probably would have surfaced with any partner.

CASE 5.3—"Esther and Shlomo Solomon": Arranged Marriage II—Sexual Aversion with Concomitant Panic Disorder in the Wife

The Solomons were Orthodox Jews of a Hasidic Sect. The husband, Shlomo, a gifted 19-year-old Talmudic scholar and the eldest son of a distinguished rabbi, and his 18-year-old wife, Esther, had been married for three months. As in the previous case, this young couple's marriage had been arranged. Worried family members, the groom's father and the bride's aunt, eager to preserve the young couple's faltering marriage, accompanied Esther to every session, often bringing other relatives along.

Both families, Esther's and Shlomo's, were extremely upset because the young woman was refusing to have sex with or even to stay in the same room with her husband.

As was the custom in the Hasidic community, the marriage had been arranged between the two families. Esther had met her husband-to-be briefly before the marriage contract was signed; at the time, she had felt no objections to the betrothal. On the wedding night, when she found herself alone with Shlomo for the first time, she remembered becoming extremely anxious. After they had intercourse, she found herself weeping uncontrollably. Esther assured me that intercourse had not been painful and that her husband had not been brutal or inconsiderate in his lovemaking. She confessed that she had been puzzled at the depth of her despair.

Since that time, she had developed increasing feelings of loathing and aversion to her husband, to the point that she could not tolerate being in the same house with him. She even found the sight of Shlomo on the street extremely difficult to bear.

To test the intensity of the patient's aversion, I asked Esther to look at her husband from a safe distance and to tell me how this made her feel. I tried to keep the distress this assignment might cause at a minimum by suggesting that she glance at him from the safety of the women's balcony, which was upstairs and screened from the men, while he was at prayer in the men's section on the ground floor of the synagogue. But the mere sight of Shlomo precipitated a severe panic attack and Esther had to be taken from the synagogue.

After this incident, Shlomo's family sent him to Israel to study, in order to avoid a public scandal, and also to give Esther time for treatment.

I asked the young woman to bring her husband's picture to the next session. The snapshot depicted a tall, thin, fine-looking young man with a full dark beard, dressed in typical Hasidic garb. I said, "He looks kind of handsome to me. What is it that you don't like about Shlomo?" With that, Esther jumped up, spit on the picture, and tore it into little bits which she threw on the floor. Then she proceeded to stomp on the pieces.

This patient had a concurrent panic disorder with agoraphobic features. Her mother, with whom she had been very close, had died when the child was eight. Since that time, Esther had experienced panic attacks. She had apparently developed a school phobia and dropped out of school at the age of 12. Although she worked part-time in a relative's store near her house, she phobically avoided traveling outside of her neighborhood.

Esther reported that when she was about 11 years old she had once been molested sexually by a dark-haired, bearded man who physically resembled her husband. He was a relative of a friend she was visiting. The man had pushed the terrified little girl against the wall and rubbed his genitalia against her. She had a clear memory of feeling exceedingly frightened and repelled.

Although on a manifest level the sexual symptoms of the aversive spouses in the last two case vignettes were not materially different, there was little similarity in the dynamics of these two problematic arranged marriages.

Dr. Raj's lack of interest in his wife was not pathological, nor was this amenable to treatment. He was simply in love with another woman who was much closer to his sexual ideal and a much more compatible partner.

Dr. Raj deeply appreciated our understanding and support of his wish to be with the woman he loved. His sessions gave him the strength to stand up to his family.

Happily, we were also able to help him work out the annulment of his marriage in a way that protected his young wife's future.*

In contrast, Esther's sexual aversion to her husband was clearly pathological. If she were to have a future in a community that accepted nothing less than marriage and motherhood for their women, she would have to undergo treatment to overcome her aversion to sex. On that basis, the young woman agreed to enter individual therapy. However, she was adamant that she could not possibly tolerate her husband and she threatened suicide if she were not released from her marriage vows. Finally, despite their deep reluctance, the families had to acquiesce.

---

*My associate, Dr. Richard Kogan, who treated Dr. Raj after I completed the evaluation, and I gave Indria a letter to take back to India, stating that we had examined her and found her to be a fully fit wife. Some two years after we saw the Raj's, I received from Bombay a beautifully printed announcement of Indria's impending wedding. This was accompanied by a graceful letter from Indria's father in which he admitted that at the time he had found my advice, "not to worry about saving the marriage, but to worry about saving my daughter *from* the marriage," very difficult to accept. But he finally did, and the marriage was eventually dissolved. The father thanked me for rescuing his daughter from "an irretrievably devastating marriage." He went on to express his joy at Indria's happiness with her new husband to-be, the well educated son of a high-ranking Indian family, of an "appropriate age" (32) who was deeply in love with his daughter, and who "is the gentle, caring kind."

The following case vignette of a couple from a different culture is similar.

CASE 5.4—"Ali and Shanda Al Husa": Arranged Marriage III—OCD in the Husband; Sexual Aversion in the Wife

A family of Jordanian Muslims recently consulted me because their brother's new 18-year-old wife was refusing to have sex with him. Shanda was a strikingly beautiful young woman who had come to America from Jordan for her wedding. The two families, old friends, had arranged the marriage between Shanda, the daughter of the clan who remained in Jordan, and Ali, the youngest son of the Arab family who had emigrated to the United States and had built up a lucrative business here.

The couple had seen each other only briefly once before the wedding. That was nine years ago in Jordan, when Shanda was 9, and Ali was 21.

Ali, a dark handsome man of 30, was delighted with his gorgeous bride, but Shanda did not like him and would not let him touch her. The hidden problem was that Ali, unbeknownst to his wife and her family, had a severe obsessive-compulsive disorder for which he was receiving treatment. Shanda was totally mystified and repelled by her husband's strange behavior. She actively resisted his attempts to consummate the marriage, keeping her legs clamped together and twisting away from him whenever he attempted intercourse. Ali was unable to force the situation, despite his older brother's threats to "beat him up" if he did not "perform."

The family's pressure on this young couple escalated when Shanda's father flew to New York from Amman to tell his daughter that "this marriage is your destiny" and to urge her to accept Ali as her husband.

I do not mean to imply that arranged marriages are necessarily associated with desire problems. To the contrary, healthy young men and women, especially if they are from similar cultural backgrounds, are more likely than not to feel attracted to one another even though they are strangers. Such couples share common cultural values and enjoy the full approval and support of their families, which are very positive elements in new marriages. Thus, Ali's older brother's marriage had also been arranged and both spouses were very happy. It is my impression that the majority of these prearranged nuptials turn out well, with many of these couples enjoying excellent sexual relationships.

A case in point is the couple described in the following case vignette, who loved each other deeply, even though their marriage had been arranged. This case also demonstrates that the fact that a marriage was arranged may be immaterial in the dynamics of a couple's sexual problems.

CASE 5.5—"Ida and Ira Diamond": Arranged Marriage IV—Sexual Aversion to Intercourse in a Woman with a Concomitant Panic Disorder

Ida, age 20, and Ira, age 24, were extremely upset because they had not been able to consummate their marriage, which had taken place one year prior to the consultation. The reason for this difficulty was Irma's sexual phobia and vaginismus, which made their attempts to have sex an ordeal.

This couple, like the previous one, were Orthodox Jews and their marriage had been arranged. But these two young people were absolutely crazy about each other. In fact, Ira felt so protective towards Ida that he was almost ready to commit the sin of foregoing having children. He told me that he would rather give up sex and face God's anger than see his beloved wife go through such terrible pain and distress every month. Ida was exasperated with her uncontrollable panic attacks and the vaginismus she experienced every time her husband approached her, and she was completely beside herself because of her inability to make love to him.

"I want to be a normal woman, Dr. Kaplan," She pleaded with me, "I love him, I want his children."

Ida's sexual symptom was probably to some extent the consequence of the emotional damage she had sustained during her painful childhood, which had been rendered even more toxic by her underlying panic disorder.

Ida had been born to a Jewish mother and an Italian father. After the father abandoned the mother and child when Ida was three, the grandparents, Orthodox Jews who had been distraught over their daughter's marriage to a Catholic, determined to make good what in their eyes was a terrible sin. They had the child spirited away from their daughter and brought secretly to an Orthodox community located in a different state. There, Ida was raised by an exceedingly devout, strict, elderly, childless couple, who provided the child with an ultra-Orthodox Jewish upbringing, but not with very much warmth.

Ida had dreaded her impending marriage, anticipating an unappealing choice by her foster parents. She was pleasantly surprised when she instantly felt attracted to her handsome husband-to-be and he also fell "head over heels" in love with her at first sight.

Ida was bitterly disappointed when she found herself unable to have intercourse. However, this young woman adored her husband and she was highly motivated to solve the problem. On his part, the husband was a most cooperative and loving partner. Thanks to this fortuitous combination, this case was brought to a successful conclusion in 14 sessions.*

A COMPREHENSIVE DIAGNOSTIC PROCEDURE

Every patient or couple who has been seen in our program since 1972 has undergone a standard comprehensive diagnostic procedure that was especially designed to evaluate patients with sexual complaints. This is comprised of a structured interview, which is supplemented when the loss of libido is not clearly psychogenic by a physical examination of the patient's genitalia, and laboratory tests of circulating sex and gonadotrophic hormones. Further, when this is indicated, the patient is referred for additional specialized medical diagnostic procedures (Kaplan, 1983, 1984).

We have found this diagnostic instrument extremely useful in that it enables the examiner to obtain all the information that is needed to differentiate between organic and psychogenic desire disorders, to select appropriate candidates for sex therapy, and to formulate the initial stages of treatment, rapidly and reliably.

How Much Time Should Be Devoted to the Evaluation?

Some therapists maintain that each partner of every couple with a sexual disorder should be examined separately in addition to a conjoint diagnostic session, with every interview lasting about 40–45 minutes (Masters & Johnson, 1970; Tiefer & Melman, 1983, 1989; Tiefer, 1992). But I believe that three full sessions are not always necessary for a competent sexual assessment, nor is this justified economically. I prefer a more flexible approach wherein the couple or the patient is seen only as much and as often as is necessary to fulfill the objectives of the evaluation, and no more.

I would estimate that in about 60% of our cases the entire evaluation was completed in a single 40 minute session with the couple, or with the

*After I conducted the initial evaluation, this couple was treated by Cathy Beaton, MSW, of our group.

symptomatic patient alone. A second session was necessary in about 20% of our cases, and this was mainly to discuss the results of laboratory tests and/or to make provisions for adjuvant medical treatments such as hormone replacement for patients with endocrine deficiencies or intra cavernosal injection (ICI) treatments for men with erectile difficulties. In the remaining 20% of our patients, it was necessary to see the couple three or four times to complete the evaluation because they had problems that were especially complex, or one or both partners had a "secret" (an affair, an abortion, homosexuality, etc.) that necessitated solo sessions.

The Information

The following information encompasses all that the clinician needs to know to establish the diagnosis of sexual desire disorder and to commence treatment. This data can be broken down into eight sets of questions:

1. Does the patient have a genuine desire disorder? What kind? (HSD? Sexual Aversion?)
2. Is the desire problem lifelong or acquired?
3. How severe is the patient's desire disorder?
4. Is the patient experiencing distress because of his/her desire disorder? Is this damaging the relationship with the partner?
5. Is the disorder of sexual desire primary or secondary to another pathological condition? (Psychiatric? Medical?)
6. What is the cause? (Organic? Psychogenic? Mixed?)
7. If the problem is psychogenic, what are: (A) the immediate causes of the patient's loss of desire or aversion? (B) the deeper causes?
8. Is the lack of desire or aversion generalized or specific to the partner? (What, if any, are the contributions of the relationship? Does the patient have a pattern of losing his/her desire with familiar partners?)

THE STRUCTURED DIAGNOSTIC INTERVIEW

The structured diagnostic interview was expressly designed to elicit the eight points of information listed above. It has been divided into eight portions, which are pursued consecutively:

1. The *chief complaint* (CC) and the *history of the chief complaint* (Hx of the CC); 2. *The Sexual Status Examination*; 3. *The Sexual History*; 4. *The Family History*; 5. *The Medical and Drug Histories*; 6. *The Psychi-*

atric Histories; 7. *The History of the Patient's Current and Past Relationships*; and 8. *Review and Recommendations*.

The information that is needed to answer the first question posed on the preceding page and to establish the diagnosis of sexual desire disorder is discovered from the first two portions of the diagnostic interview: the *CC and Hx and of the CC* and the *Sexual Status* examination. These same parts also supply the answers to questions 2, 3, and 4, (See page 92) namely, how severe and distressing the loss of desire is for the symptomatic patient and/or the partner, whether the patient's low libido is lifelong or was acquired after some period of normal functioning, if the patient's lack of sexual interest or revulsion is specific to the partner or across the board, and also if the patient's current sexual symptom represents a pattern of pathological behavior that would surface with any partner, or whether this particular relationship is sexatoxic.

The Chief Complaint and the History of the Chief Complaint

First, the patient and/or the couple are asked to describe their sexual problem as they see it and the history of its onset in detail. From this, we learn how severe the patient's sexual difficulty is, whether his/her lack of desire or sexual fears are lifelong or acquired, and in the latter case what the circumstances of the onset of the sexual symptom were. This information establishes the diagnosis of sexual desire disorder, and can also provide important clues as to the causes or precipitating factors of the patient's sexual symptom.

For example, a 32-year-old married man complained anxiously that he had lost all desire for sex, and that this was ruining his marriage.

In answer to my query about the onset of his problem, he said that he first noticed that he was no longer approaching his wife for sex about 2½ years prior to the consultation. He did not remember experiencing any particular stress at the time. He also told me that he had never had this problem before.

Closer questioning revealed that the onset of the decrease of this patient's sexual desire could be pinpointed to the time he learned that his wife as pregnant. Both had wanted a child and were very happy, but he temporarily became overwhelmed with the responsibility and the permanence of his situation. In this crisis-laden environment, he experienced a few episodes of erectile failure, related to performance anxiety, and thereafter he lost his desire for sex.

After the nature of the patient's *chief complaint* has been elucidated and when it has become clear when and under what circumstances the patient's libido decreased or vanished (and/or he/she became repelled by sex), the examiner proceeds to a detailed examination of the patient's current sexual status.

The Sexual Status Examination

The sexual status examination is the most important part of the diagnostic interview. A powerful diagnostic and research instrument, a well conducted sexual status examination is also a virtual treasure trove of information, providing the examiner with insight into exactly what the patient does to down-regulate his/her sexual desire.

As the picture of the couple's current sexual experience unfolds during the sexual status examination, I begin to envision strategies to modify their malignant antisexual behaviors and interactions. Each new bit of information about the manner in which the couple make love and what goes on in the patient's head organizes and focuses the direction of the remaining portions of the interview.

The sexual status examination is a unique feature of the diagnostic interview and invaluable for assessing patients with sexual complaints. Its purpose is somewhat similar to the physical examination that provides the internist with a comprehensive mental picture of the current status of the patient's vital organs, in that this detailed, problem-focused inquiry provides the examiner with a comparably comprehensive and detailed mental picture of the vital aspects of the patient's and/or couple's current sexual experience. This includes his/her genital functioning, sexual behaviors, mental processes, perceptions, emotional state, and the interaction between the partners.

This information is the basis for judging whether or not the patient's libido is, in fact, deficient, and if a diagnosis of sexual desire disorder is warranted. In addition, in the hands of a skilled and experienced sex therapist, the sexual status examination goes a long way towards illuminating the nature of the immediate causes of the patient's inadequate sex drive or of the specifics of his/her phobic avoidance of sex. In other words, this part of the examination yields a clear image of the patient's anti-fantasies and his/her unwitting countersexual behaviors. The inquiry also clarifies precisely what repels or scares him or her about sex, and how the partner fits into the picture. This information is, of course, essential for developing the behavioral and cognitive treatment strategies that will be used to modify the patient's countersexual behaviors, as will be described in subsequent sections.

I usually devote the first portion of the initial interview, right after I have clarified the nature and the onset of the patient's deficient libido or sexual aversion, to assessing his/her/their current sex life in great detail. I do not move away from the sexual status part of the inquiry until my mental image of their current sexual experience has become crystal clear and I have learned exactly how the patient manages to down-regulate his/her sexual desire, or, in the case of patients with sexual aversions, just what frightens or repels them about sexual contact with their partner, even if I have to defer their sexual and family histories to future sessions.

I generally begin the sexual status examination by ascertaining the *frequency* of the patient's sexual outlet and how this has changed, if it has, over time. As the picture begins to unfold, I zero in on the desire phase.

I first ask some open-ended questions: "When was the last time you made love? Was that typical of your recent sexual experiences?"

If the answer is yes, I ask them to describe this to me in detail: "I'd like a clear picture, a 'mental videotape,' of your last sexual encounter."

Few patients spontaneously provide the necessary details in response to such general questions. Most have to be gently but firmly prodded with further and more specific queries in hazy areas until my mental picture is crystal clear.

"Where did you make love? In the kitchen? In the bedroom? Is that usually where you have sex? What time of day was it? Was it light or dark? Were you undressed? What were you wearing? Who started this time? Last time? How do you let each other know that you are interested in having sex?"

When evaluating patients with sexual desire disorders, it is also important, apart from their responsiveness to the partner and to sexual stimulation, to establish whether they have noticed any changes in the spontaneous fluctuations of their libido and if they can tie this to any particular events.

What Turns the Patient "On" and "Off"?

It is critical when evaluating patients with hypoactive sexual desire disorders for treatment to ascertain what they find arousing, i.e., what their fantasies and desires are, and also what they find unattractive, what "turns them off," and how this relates to the current situation. More specifically, the examiner especially needs to understand patients' erotic reactions to their partners, and whether the partner is perceived as attractive, neutral, or unattractive, for this is often the critical issue in these cases.

It is also essential to obtain a mental image of what is in the patient's mind, what he/she thinks about and feels, and how he/she behaves prior to and during the process of making love, and afterwards also. It is especially important to gain a clear sense of how the partners interact with each other, whether they facilitate each other's functioning, or whether the partner's sexual behavior is a "turn off" for the patient that will have to be modified in treatment.

If these issues are not clarified by the patient's verbal "videotape" of his current sexual experience, specific questions may be needed to fill in the blanks.

Perhaps a clinical "mini vignette," a fragment of a recent sexual status examination, will make this clearer.

A couple who had been married for four years were referred by the husband's psychopharmacologist (who had been treating him with Nardil and supportive therapy for depression) for the evaluation of his very low interest in sex, which was placing a strain on the couple's otherwise excellent marriage.

The frequency of the couple's sexual relations had diminished from two to three times a week at the beginning of their marriage to about once every two months. But, because they knew they had the appointment with me coming up, they managed to have sex twice during the past week.

I asked them for a mental "videotape" of these recent encounters and supplemented this with a few direct questions.

"How did you feel when you touched your wife's body?"

The husband, an extremely intelligent and articulate man, answered, "About 5% anxiety, 20% revulsion, and the rest was arousal." He told me he found his wife attractive (she was), but that some "parts of her" were displeasing to him. "What parts?" I asked. "She is too skinny, and her breasts are too small"—but, he replied to my question, he loved "other parts" of her, for example, "Her bottom is excellent."

As he was making love to his wife, this man's mind switched from her "exciting bottom" to her small breasts. When I asked him if large breasts were his sexual fantasy, he told me that in the past he had never found large breasts arousing, but that he had recently begun to fantasize about women with large breasts because, "I think I am using this as a negative about Ellie."

In other words, my gentle but unrelenting probing of the details of this couple's sexual experience had uncovered the immediate cause of this man's sexual "turn off," namely that he switches the focus of his attention from an erotic positive, his wife's "excellent bottom," to obsessing about her "small breasts," which he had managed to make into a negative.

It appeared that this man had been unconsciously down-regulating his sex drive and had overridden his desire for sex with his wife by immersing himself in anxious and aversive feelings. However, he demonstrated his sexual potential when he was motivated by the upcoming sex therapy appointment, as he managed to "tune out" the "5% anxiety and 20% revulsion" and focus on the "75% erotic positives" of the experience.

In order to elicit such critical details, the examiner may have to ask very personal questions about the most intimate details of the couple's sexual experience:

"Do you find your partner attractive? Very? Do you like the way he/she looks, moves, touches you, sounds, smells, feels? Is she/he your sexual type or fantasy? Do you think you are his/hers? Is there anything particularly unattractive about him/her? Does this intrude on your lovemaking? When you make love, is he/she clean? How is his/her/your genital hygiene? Does he/she/you take showers prior to going to bed? Shave? How is his/her genital odor? Breath? Does he/she smoke? Do you?

How do you respond when he/she touches, kisses, caresses your breasts, nipples, clitoris, genitalia? Is he/she a good lover? Why not? Is he/she a good kisser?

"Is he/she relaxed about sex? Up-tight? Do you think he/she is attracted to you?

"Is he/she nice to you? How is he/she not nice? How does she respond if you come too fast? Lose your erection? Does she carry on? Does she blame you? Is she considerate, supportive, sensitive?

"How does he react if you don't have an orgasm on intercourse? Do you ever get the feeling he gets tired stimulating you?"

Some persons are turned on when the partner is seductive to them, while others feel pressured by this and need to be the one who initiates. Therefore, it is important to find out how the couple initiate sex, how they signal each other, and what their courtship behaviors are like.

"Who usually starts? How? How do you know he/she wants sex? How do you let him/her know you are in the mood?

"What are you usually feeling when you initiate sex? What do you do when you are 'horny'? How do you communicate about sex to each other? Do you know his/her special likes? dislikes? Do you know each other's sexual fantasies? Do you want to tell each other how?

"Do you often have sex out of a sense of obligation? How do you usually react when your partner approaches you? Happy? Excited? Apprehensive? Worried about disappointing your partner? Do you anticipate frustration? Disappointment? How do you feel as you approach him/her?"

Absorption in the Sexual Experience

Patients with sexual desire disorders are often unable to "let go," that is, to abandon themselves to the sexual experience. The examiner should always try to get a feel regarding the patient's level of *absorption* in the erotic sensations and in the erotic experience.*

"How absorbed do you become when you have sex? Do you lose awareness of street noises? Of your body? Of how you look? Does a 'tape' play in your head that distracts you?"

Is the Symptom Global or Situational?

The detailed examination of the patient's current sexual experience also reveals whether the problem is *global* or *situational.*

This is not always obvious. For example, a handsome, trim, 62-year-old, thrice-married man was referred by his internist for evaluation of the loss of his libido after endocrine testing had revealed a normal profile of sex hormones.

The patient was despondent and thought he had gone into a permanent sexual decline. "Sex has always been very important to me doctor. I'm really going to miss this part of my life," he told me sadly.

In answer to my questions, he told me that 10 years ago he was having sex three to four times a week, five years ago the frequency had declined to two to three times weekly, and for the past year the couple had had sex only once every two or three weeks. This description of the gradual progression of his symptom suggested that the patient was not imagining things. The sexual decline that was troubling him seemed to be a real phenomenon.

He also felt fewer and less intense surges of spontaneous sexual desire. However, the patient admitted that he still reacted erotically to pretty, scantily dressed girls at his beach club. He also told me that with an old love, a woman he still saw occasionally, he had felt intensely passionate at their last encounter several months ago.

This was the clue that the decline in this man's libido was essentially situational and most severe with his wife, whom he loved dearly.

Further questioning cleared up the mystery. The wife had lost her libido when she became seriously depressed about a year ago. Prior to this, the couple had had a good sex life. She was now feeling better, but her libido had not returned and she had lost her ability to have orgasms.

*We thank Dr. Ellen Hollander for calling the important issue of absorption in the sexual experience to our attention (Wednesday conference).

Possibly, the latter was due to the high doses of Prozac she was still taking. In addition, she was subject to painful bouts of cystitis that were related to intercourse. Despite all her problems, this woman never refused to have sex with her husband. But when he went to make love to her, the following thoughts were on his mind:

1. She would not enjoy sex.
2. She would not have an orgasm.
3. She was doing him a favor.
4. He better hurry up so she would not get cystitis!

After I "played" this back to him, the patient recognized that this negative symphony was the perfect recipe for dampening anyone's sexual desire. He felt encouraged that the loss of his desire for his wife had a rational explanation and was not a sign of an irreversible, age-related loss of sexuality.

Sexual Fantasy

Sexual fantasy is one of the most important areas of inquiry in the evaluation of patients with sexual desire disorders.

More specifically, the examiner will want to know whether the patient has erotic fantasies and/or is aroused by erotica, and what the content of the fantasies are. Are these typical? Perverse? Atypical?

Next, one needs to know how the patient and the partner feel about the fantasies. Is the patient guilty? At ease? Have the partners shared their fantasies? How does the partner feel about the symptomatic person's fantasies? Is he/she accepting? Does he/she feel they are "wrong?" "sick?" Does she or he take this as a personal rejection? Is she or he angry about the partner's fantasies?

What role do the patient's sexual fantasies play in his/her sex life? How dependent is the patient on these fantasies? Does he/she use the fantasies or erotica when masturbating? While making love with the spouse? With other partners? Do the couple act out their fantasies with one another? Why not?

In other words, it is most important to establish whether patients use their fantasies to enhance their sex life, or if they suppress these out of guilt or shame. This is a critical point of information, since guilt and shame about sexual fantasies, as well as the suppression of fantasies, are common immediate causes of psychogenic HSD.

If the patient's sexual fantasies and desires are atypical or paraphilic, e.g., sado/masochistic or fetishistic, the examiner should keep in mind that at some point it will have to be determined whether these are confined to the bedroom or if they also affect his/her object choices adversely. The clinical implications of this issue are discussed further near the end of the chapter.

The Sexual Fit

If the patient's loss of desire is specifically for the partner, it is essential to determine if the partner is *congruent* or *at variance with* the patient's erotic desires and fantasies, for this can certainly matter. Is the partner the low-desire patient's sexual fantasy? The kind of lover he/she has always wished for? Or does he or she yearn for a taller/shorter, thinner/fatter, lighter/darker, younger, smarter, richer, more elegant, more beautiful lover?

The "fit" between the symptomatic patient's sexual preferences, practices, and desires and those of the partner is an important determinant of the quality of a couple's relationship, and explicit questions may be required to shed light on this rather subtle matter.

Each partner is asked how he/she feels about the other's erotic preferences and fantasies in order to ascertain how compatible these are. How do you feel about oral sex? Giving? Receiving? How do you think your partner feels? How do you feel about taking his penis in your mouth? Swallowing his semen? How do you feel about going down on her? How about anal sex? Sexual games? Dressing up? Porno? Talking during sex? Do you find "talking dirty" exciting? Does talking during sex distract you? How do you feel about leaving the lights on or off? Do you like to be in control? Do you like your partner to be the one in charge?

There are, of course, no problems when one person likes to lead and the other loves to follow, or if both are "morning" or "evening" people. But we often see couples whose fit in the area of sex is poor—both want to dominate or both want to be dominated, or both become aroused only if they remain passive or both vie for the active role. And there are also couples where one functions best in the morning, while the other "must" make love at night to feel aroused, where one likes it hot and the other likes it cool, where one needs intimacy while intimacy during sex turns the other one off. Then there are couples where one likes it fast while the other must have slow foreplay. Such erotic and stylistic differences are frequently misinterpreted as power and control struggles. This is often so. But it may also be that the partners' sexual fantasies and desires are incongruent, and each is merely trying to create the conditions that he/she finds necessary to become aroused.

Masturbation

Many patients experience normal desire when they masturbate alone with their fantasies, but not when they are with their partners. Much can be learned about what down-regulates the patient's sexual desire by comparing the patient's mental processes during sexual encounters with the partner with those during masturbatory experiences. Often one finds that the patient is relaxed and absorbed in fantasy when he/she masturbates, but with the partner becomes anxious and distracted. Such information, together with the patient's response to other lovers, establishes whether the loss of sexual desire is global or if it is specific to the partner.

Contraception

The sexual status exam is not complete unless the examiner understands what, if any, contraception the couple use and how this affects their sexual experience.

As an example of the potential clinical importance of this material, many men, especially those over 50, experience difficulty maintaining their erections when they attempt to use a condom. "Condom impotence" is a common phenomenon that has not been widely publicized, and women often misinterpret their lover's refusal to use condoms as a sign of hostility or a lack of caring, when in reality the man is simply afraid that he will lose his erection. Such misunderstandings can lead to friction between the partners.

Further, some women act out their ambivalence about having sex with their partners, by constantly complaining about the difficulties of using a diaphragm, or by making a habit of inserting it during sex so that this interrupts the flow of lovemaking.

Genital Functioning

The primary aim of the diagnostic interview of patients with desire problems is to clarify the behavioral and emotional antecedents of the patient's low sexual desire or fear/aversion to sex. Therefore, the focus of the sexual status examination is on the motivational aspects of sex, what the partners think, feel, and do, what attracts and repels them, their erotic fantasies, and how good their sexual fit between them is. However, since the functioning of the genitalia exerts considerable influence on sexual desire, in order to obtain a complete picture of the patient's sexual problem, it is also important to learn something about the orgasm, excitement and resolution phases of the sexual cycle as well.

Therefore, part of the sexual status examination of male patients with desire problems is devoted to detailed queries about their erections and ejaculations, including such matters as the state of their morning and nocturnal erections and their ejaculatory control on masturbation by manual and oral stimulation and during coitus (Kaplan, 1983).

Analogous inquiries are included in the evaluation of women with sexual desire disorders. Female patients are asked to describe their vaginal lubrication and the need for lubricants, and they are asked about pain or discomfort on intercourse. If the woman admits to genital pain or discomfort, a physical examination of the genitalia is always indicated in order to determine the specific source and cause of the pain.

The female orgasm is assessed in similar detail. Our women patients are asked about the manner in which they climax: "Clitoral stimulation? Vaginal penetration? Both?" They are also asked whether they use vibrators and what positions they prefer, whether they receive long enough and sufficiently effective foreplay to become aroused, and whether they are distracted by their concern that their partner feels that the task of stimulating them is tedious.

If this line of inquiry indicates that the patient has a primary genital dysfunction, the focus of the sexual status examination shifts to illuminating the immediate causes of the particularly syndrome in question, for that must be treated first.

Within this context, although dysfunctions of the *resolution phase* are rare and seldom involved in the pathogenesis of sexual desire disorders, an inquiry into the nature of the couple's postcoital experience can reveal problematic discrepancies in the partners' capacity, need for, and tolerance of intimacy. If I suspect this may be the case, I might ask, "What happens after you climax? Do you feel like falling asleep? Energized? Do you like to cuddle? Do you (or your partner) get up and take a shower?"

Problem- and Treatment-Focused Inquiry

The above are representative samples of the questions that are asked in the course of examining patients' and couples' current sexual status. In actual practice, one would not, could not, and should not ask all these of any one patient. On the other hand, different questions not mentioned herein might well be included in other cases.

The questions are asked so as to obtain a clear picture of the patient's level of sexual desire in order to establish the diagnosis of sexual desire disorder. This portion of the diagnostic interview also provides a picture of his/her affect, thoughts, behavior, and interactions with the partner. The purpose of the latter line of inquiry is to determine what factors in the patient's current sex life are responsible for dampening his/her sexual desire, so that these can be modified in treatment. This cannot be accomplished by a pre-set list of questions, nor formatted as a standard sexual-functioning questionnaire.

Once the examination of the couple's current sexual status has established that the patient has a genuine sexual desire disorder and the parameters of the sexual symptom have been delineated, the examiner proceeds with the medical, drug, psychiatric, and historic portions of the diagnostic interview, to determine the etiology.

In contrast to the sexual status exam, which is always pursued slowly, carefully, and in detail, as was described above, the remaining parts of the diagnostic interview are in the form of brief screens or surveys only, and are pursued just long enough to rule out any significant pathological issues that might be material. During the initial session, the examiner delves into these portions of the diagnostic interview in depth only if there are definite positive findings that may be relevant for making decisions regarding disposition and treatment.

IS THE LOSS OF SEXUAL DESIRE PRIMARY OR SECONDARY TO ANOTHER PATHOLOGICAL CONDITION?

Once it has been established by means of the chief complaint and the sexual status exam portion of the diagnostic interview that the patient's sexual desire is truly abnormally low, the next question, which is of utmost importance for the appropriate management of patients with hypoactive sexual desire disorders, is whether the symptom is primary or secondary to another pathological condition.

Urologic and Gynecologic disease states that result in dyspareunia, as well as fatigue, stress, and chronic anxiety, can result in a secondary loss of sexual desire and/or sexual avoidance in patients who have normal hormone profiles, who are not taking drugs with sexual side effects, who are devoid of intrinsic sexual conflicts and whose relationships are basically sound.

All such underlying conditions must be detected during the evaluation because the appropriate course of action in such cases is to see to it that the underlying problem is treated first, before the patient is considered for psychosexual therapy.

Some of the information that is pertinent to answering the question of whether the patient's loss of desire is primary or secondary has already been elicited on the sexual status examination. For example, the analysis of the couple's current sexual experience will reveal if intercourse is painful, or if the patient is usually exhausted when he/she tries to make love. Further data on these points is elicited by the physical examination of the patient's genitalia and by the psychiatric portion of the diagnostic interview.

Is the Loss of Sexual Desire and Sexual Aversion Due to Painful Intercourse? The Physical Examination of the Genitalia

Masters and Johnson conducted physical examinations on all their subjects, while some sex therapists never include genital exams in their workups. I do not deem it necessary to examine the genitalia of all sexually dysfunctional patients. However, I regard it as crucial to examine every patient and partner who admits to physical discomfort on intercourse.

It goes without saying that the repeated association of sex and pain can lead to a loss of sexual interest and/or the development of a phobic avoidance of sex. If the sexual status examination suggests that dyspareunia may be a causal factor in a patient's desire problem, it is essential that the *exact location and the cause of the pain be identified by physical examination of the genitalia.*

Painful conditions of the genitalia are often missed on routine gynecologic exams because the lesions are not always obvious. Moreover, patients frequently don't tell their doctors that sexual intercourse hurts, so that the gynecologist or urologist may not know what to look for. For these reasons, I prefer to conduct the examinations of the genitalia myself, although this can, of course, be done by medical colleagues who are knowledgeable about and interested in sexual disorders.

When I examine a female patient, I always ask her to identify the painful area by touching it with her finger or by showing this to me in a mirror, and I try to reproduce the pain during the examination of the patient's genitalia, by touch, or by stretching the vagina as would occur during coitus. This method makes it possible to detect subtle sore spots on the vaginal mucosa, small tender nodules in the submucosal tissues, connective tissue shrinkage not apparent when the vagina is collapsed, and tiny scars and painful vaginal muscle spasms. All of these, as well as other conditions, can cause female dyspareunia.

It is equally important to examine male patients who complain about pain on sex, even after they have been cleared by their urologists for conditions that may make sex painful. These include subtle painful areas in the scrotum, hypersensitive areas on the skin of the penis, sensitive plaques, and small tender areas along the urethra, which are best found by stretching the penis.

Since it is not feasible to examine patients with erections, I will, when this is important for diagnostic purposes, as for example in Peyronie's disease, ask him to bring in a polaroid picture of his erect penis.

If the physical problems are found, a treatment plan should be formulated in consultation with a sexually sensitive gynecologic or urologic specialist. Naturally, all sex therapy assignments that entail physical stimulation of the genitalia or intercourse must be deferred until sex no longer hurts (See Table 9 in Chapter 10).

The Psychiatric Screen: Is the Loss of Desire Secondary to a Psychiatric Condition?

The psychiatric portion of thc interview is devoted to detecting underlying and concomitant psychiatric disorders so as to determine if the loss of desire is symptomatic of another psychiatric condition, such as depression. The psychiatric examination also serves the important function of screening out patients, as well as their partners, who have emotional problems that put them at risk of reacting adversely to sex therapy.

For the purpose of evaluating patients with sexual desire disorders for possible treatment, the psychiatric history needs to be pursued in detail only if there are positive findings. To orient me as to the direction and extent of the psychiatric examinations that will be necesary in a particular case, I ask both partners to fill out a brief questionnaire before they are interviewed. This is to ascertain whether either partner has had or is currently having psychiatric problems or undergoing treatment and, if so, to establish the nature of the psychiatric diagnosis and of the treatment modality.

With patients who behave normally in the office, who have no histories of prior psychiatric difficulties or treatments, the psychiatric portion of the interview is extremely brief. However, if the questionnaire or the patient indicates that either partner may be afflicted with a psychiatric disorder, or if I sense this because they relate to me and/or to each other in an aberrant manner, or if either partner's demeanor, affect, speech, or orientation raises doubt about his/her psychiatric status, the evaluation shifts into a lengthier, more thorough psychiatric examination.

The patient's psychiatric history is pursued in sufficient detail and depth to make the examiner feel comfortable that the patient's and/or the partner's psychiatric status will not pose a problem in case the couple are accepted for the treatment of their sexual complaint. Until this is accomplished, the remainder of the interview is deferred.

Emotionally Fragile Patients

Apart from detecting patients with psychiatric disorders who should be treated for these prior to considering sex therapy, another purpose of this portion of the diagnostic interview is to screen out emotionally fragile individuals for whom the process of sex therapy might prove psychologically hazardous.

The brief, active, and frankly erotic process of sex therapy can be quite taxing, much more so than slower forms of psychological treatments. For one, the therapeutic sexual homework assignments can be highly emotional experiences that expose patients to erotic and intimate situations they have previously avoided because these were too threatening. Moreover, the therapy sessions in the doctor's office can also be traumatic. The interpretations that are made during this active, dynamic, interactive process can at times be relentlessly confrontational. Further, in the course of the therapy sessions, both partners may unceremoniously be stripped of their customary psychological defenses. For these reasons, this procedure can make fragile patients, as well as fragile partners, feel exceedingly vulnerable.

Although sex therapy is not absolutely contraindicated for emotionally fragile and highly rejection-sensitive patients, in order to do no harm to such individuals, one should identify them so that they can be treated more carefully and at a much slower pace. With these precautions, emotionally vulnerable individuals can often derive considerable benefit from sex therapy. But if they react adversely after a few careful trial sessions, the therapist should be prepared to steer them towards longer-term therapies.

Depression

It is particularly important before one initiates sex therapy with patients who complain about a decrease of their sexual interest to rule out underlying depression. The loss of libido is one of the cardinal signs of this highly prevalent psychiatric disorder, and this may occur even in individuals who are only mildly or subclinically depressed.

If the patient's loss of libido is due to an underlying depression, it is inappropriate to treat him or her for a desire disorder. Depressed patients should first be treated for their depressive symptoms with the indicated psychological therapies and antidepressant medications (American Psychiatric Association, 1993). In many cases, the patient's libido will return to normal spontaneously, soon after the depression has lifted. Patients in whom the symptoms of low libido persist after their mood has improved should be reevaluated for sex therapy about three weeks after their antidepressant medication has been discontinued. This delay is recommended because the sexual side effects that many of the antidepressant drugs have should have worn off by then.

Anxiety Disorders

A significant proportion of patients with sexual aversion disorders and sexual phobias are afflicted with concurrent panic disorders. The susceptibility to anxiety and panic that characterizes individuals with these conditions predisposes them to develop fears and phobias in many situations, including sex. Not surprisingly, multiple phobias, including the phobic anxiety of heights, enclosed places, open spaces, public speaking, flying, and socializing, are frequently found in patients who also have sexual phobias (Kaplan, 1987).

It is important to detect patients with underlying panic disorders and other anxiety disorders during the evaluation, because in some cases medication should be prescribed to facilitate their treatment (see Chapter 7).

Alcoholism and Substance Abuse

The loss of sexual desire is very common among alcoholics and substance abusers. Therefore, we routinely screen out patients or couples who are currently abusing alcohol or other substances. In addition to the fact that these drugs decrease sexual desire on a physical basis, I consider such individuals to be unsuitable candidates for sex therapy because they are presently too self-destructive to benefit from this treatment. In our program, substance abusers and alcoholics are referred for treatment of their addictions and may be reevaluated for the treatment of their sexual problems after a period of recovery.

Personality Disorders

The psychiatric screening part of the diagnostic interview is geared to identify low-desire patients with concomitant personality disorders. Although sex therapy is not necessarily contraindicated for patients with personality disorders, concomitant Axis II diagnoses of obsessive/

compulsive, narcissistic, or borderline personality disorders in the low-desire patient and/or in the partner indicate that the prognosis is poor, that the patient is apt to be resistant to sex therapy, and that treatment is likely to be complex and difficult.

Stress

A common underlying cause of low sexual frequency in contemporary society is prolonged unrelieved stress and fatigue. Sex therapists are frequently called upon to help couples whose low sex frequency is due to their self-imposed, compulsive, overloaded, stressful lifestyles.

The human animal is not designed to reproduce under dangerous, stressful, energy-depleting conditions, and a serious loss of libido is often associated with such modern-day personal disasters as unemployment, bankruptcy, malpractice suits, etc., and sexual anorexia is almost endemic during difficult divorce proceedings.

I recently saw a patient who had experienced a dramatic loss of libido directly after he learned that he was the subject of a highly threatening sexual harassment suit. This man, a member of a minority, was a conscientious, high-ranking executive with a long and impeccable record in a large public company. He told me that the accusation that had been made against him was politically motivated and entirely without substance, but he felt helpless about being able to prove his innocence. When a group of his fellow executives marched in and summarily ordered him to vacate his office, he felt totally "castrated." After that incident, he had been unable to feel the slightest sexual interest or desire. The loss of this patient's libido persisted throughout the many stressful, litigation-filled months that it took to clear his name.

This patient needed strategic support and reassurance, rather than sex therapy.

In cases where overwhelming, inescapable, and chronic stress appears to be material in a person's decreased sexual desire, his or her total life-situation must be assessed carefully with the aim of deciding if the timing for sex therapy is appropriate. Often in such situations, the person first needs time and/or help to resolve the stressful situation. A high level of ongoing stress is not conducive to successful sex therapy, even as soldiers fighting in the heat of battle would not be given sexual homework assignments until the war was over. In many cases, the person's libido returns to normal spontaneously after the crisis has been resolved.

Stressful Lifestyles

Apart from unavoidable, catastrophic stresses, like death and taxes, we often hear complaints of low sexual frequency from a couple, only to learn that the husband is an associate in a law firm, trying to make partner, working a 60-hour week in addition to many weekends, while the wife regularly gets up at 6:00 A.M. in her struggle to care for several small children, manage a large, complex household, and try to organize an active social life.

There is simply no way a person's sex life can be expected to survive unscathed under such stressful conditions. This issue is further discussed and illustrated with case studies in Chapter 8.

Is the Patient's Low Sexual Desire Due to Primary Genital Phase Dysfunctions and/or Performance Anxiety?

During the sexual status part of the diagnostic interview, it was determined whether either partner had any difficulties with orgasm/ ejaculation and/or erection/lubrication (see page 85). The main purpose of this inquiry was to try to figure out which came first—whether the low libido is due to a genital dysfunction or whether the patient's sexual responses are sluggish because he/she was trying to make love without interest.

The three phases of the human sexual response cycle—desire, arousal, and orgasm—are controlled by separate nerves, modulated by different neurotransmitters, and involved with different parts of the genital anatomy. This physiologic arrangement makes it possible for orgasm, arousal (erection/lubrication), and sexual desire to be impaired separately, without affecting the other phases (Kaplan, 1977, 1979). See Tables 4 and 5.

In other words, the "separate wiring" arrangement of the three phases explains why many patients with erectile disorder are able to feel normal sexual desire and ejaculate normally although their penis may remain flaccid. Further, this accounts for the numerous women who cannot achieve orgasms with their partners, but who nevertheless still feel intense desire, lubricate normally, and feel satisfied after sexual contact. And it explains why a high proportion of men with ejaculatory disorders have excellent erections and high sex drives. This neurophysiologic discreteness of the three phases also accounts for the fact that patients with HSD are often able to have erections, lubricate, and reach orgasm.

However, the three phases of the sexual response cycle are also intimately related and interconnected so that they normally function in harmony. Thus, desire, excitement, and orgasm overlap in time and, under normal circumstances, blend into a single, pleasurable, harmonious, subjective experience.

From a clinical perspective, what is most important about the dynamic relationship between sexual desire and genital functioning is that the genital phases of the sexual response cycle and sexual motivation also appear to *exert considerable reciprocal psychophysiologic effects upon each other.* More specifically, functional "feedback loops" exist between erotic desire and the genitalia that produce positive or negative sensory input that increases or decreases the magnitude of the response of the other phases.

Thus, a high level of sexual desire or lust *facilitates and maximizes the erection-lubrication and orgasm-ejaculation responses and sensations, while lowering the threshold for the genital reflexes.* In other words, it takes less time and less stimulation to achieve an orgasm or an erection when a person is feeling "hot," or passionate, than when he is in an asexual state. Conversely, the perception of a firm erection or the sensory awareness of a copious lubrication-swelling response acts as an incenter stimulus to increase sexual desire to further heights.

The reciprocal feedback loop also acts in a *negative manner,* and this is of considerable clinical importance. For example, when a person's desire for sex is low, the thresholds for orgasm and for erection are raised, so that it becomes very difficult and a lot of work to maintain an erection or achieve an orgasm. Furthermore, although men are capable of achieving erections and ejaculating even in the absence of lust or passion, genital functioning becomes a pleasureless, sterile, mechanical experience at best, and repeated episodes of mechanical, joyless sex are likely to lead to eventual chronic erectile failure.

Similarly, women who try to accommodate their partners, even though they themselves are not interested, may experience vaginal dryness, discomfort, and difficulty in reaching a climax because the orgasm threshold is raised when desire is low. If this becomes habitual, a negative cycle is created and these women may eventually lose their interest in sex and avoid it altogether.

The feedback loop also works in the other direction from the genitalia to the sexual motivation control apparatus, so that poor genital functioning often results in a circular, secondary loss of sexual desire. Patients who cannot control their ejaculations or maintain their erections often develop a sense of sexual inadequacy and on that account lose their desire for sex. Presumably, men who have ejaculatory or erectile difficulties tend to avoid sex in order to protect themselves from the

TABLE 4
The Four Phases of the Human Sexual Response Cycle

<table>
<tr><th></th><th colspan="2">Physiology</th></tr>
<tr><th></th><th>Male</th><th>Female</th></tr>
<tr><td>DESIRE</td><td colspan="2">Activation of the sex-regulatory centers in the hypothalamus and limbic system is associated with the subjective urge to copulate and to engage in sexual fantasy. Testosterone is needed for normal libido in both genders; Males require 10 times the levels that females do.</td></tr>
<tr><td></td><td colspan="2">Vasocongestion of genitalia prepares these for their reproductive functions.</td></tr>
<tr><td>AROUSAL
(Excitement)</td><td>Dilation of penile arteries increases inflow; relaxation of mouth cavernosal muscles impedes outflow, results in Penile Erection</td><td>Diffuse vasocongestion results in Vaginal Lubrication/Swelling</td></tr>
<tr><td></td><td colspan="2">Reflex, Pleasurable, Clonic, Spasms of Genital Muscles</td></tr>
<tr><td>ORGASM</td><td>1. Emission-contraction of smooth muscles of internal male reproduction organs gathers bolus of ejaculate in posterior urethra

2. 0.8 per second contractions of the bulbo-cavernosii and ischio-cavernosii muscles propel ejaculate out of external urethral meatus.</td><td>1. No emission.*

2. 0.8 per second contractions of the circum vaginal bulbo-cavernosii and ischio-cavernosii muscles.</td></tr>
<tr><td>RESOLUTION</td><td colspan="2">Return of genitalia to quiescent stage; sated feeling (may be associated with the simultaneous release of oxytocin by both sexual partners).</td></tr>
</table>

*It has been claimed that there are a few women who express fluid from residual prostatic tissue (The Grafenberg, or "G" spot, during orgasm.) This phenomenon has been termed "female ejaculation.

humiliation of sexual failure and from the anticipated rejection by their partners. But these men ordinarily have no insight into the defensive nature of their sexual withdrawal. They are aware only that they are no longer interested in making love.

When the decrease in the patient's desire is fueled by erectile or orgasm disorders, or if this is due to sexual performance anxiety, these symptoms, not low desire, should be treated first.

TABLE 5
The Sexual Disorders

Phase	*Male*	*Female*
DESIRE	1. *Hypoactive Sexual Desire (HSD) (302.71)*: The absence or marked decrease in the urge to copulate or engage in sexual fantasy. 2. *Sexual Aversion Disorder (302.72) (Sexual Phobia)* The fear, repulsion, and/or phobic avoidance of sexual contact with the partner, or a specific aspect of sexual contact	
AROUSAL (Excitement)	*Erectile Disorder Impotence* (302.72): The inability to attain or maintain an erection until the completion of the sex act; a decrease in erectile firmness.	*Female Arousal Disorder:* (302.72): The inability to attain or maintain adequate vaginal lubrication/swelling until the completion of the sex act.
ORGASM	1. *Premature Ejaculation* (302.75): The lack of adequate control over the ejaculation reflex; the tendency to ejaculate with minimum stimulation 2. *Male Orgasm Disorder* (Retarded Ejaculation) (302.74): The delay or absence of ejaculation after adequate stimulation	*Female Orgasm Disorder:* (302.73): The delay or absence of orgasm after adequate stimulation (the inability to climax on vaginal penetration in a woman who can have orgasms with a partner on clitoral stimulation is not considered a disorder)
RESOLUTION	Rare; pain or discomfort after ejaculation due to residual vasocongestion	Rare; pain or discomfort after intercourse due to residual pelvic congestion
Sexual Disorders Associated With Genital Muscle Dysfunction Plus Sexual Pain Disorders	1. *Post Ejaculatory Pain Syndrome*: male genital muscles spasms 2. *Male Dyspareunia* (302.76): Other types of psychogenic sexual pain disorders	1. *Vaginismus* (302.51): Reflex involuntary spasms of the muscles of the vaginal introitus 2. *Female Dyspareunia* (302.76): Other types of psychogenic sexual pain disorders

The patient's sexual interest is apt to return when his functioning improves, without additional treatment. The positive effects on libido that can sometimes be provided by the restoration of potency are best exemplified by the rapid return of sexual desire, sometimes to very high levels, which is often seen after a patient's erectile capacity has been restored with intracavernosal injection treatments (ICI). A case that illustrates this sequence of events is presented in Chapter 8.

A similarly negative effect is produced on female sexual desire by a chronic lack of lubrication or anorgasmia.

CHAPTER 6

Evaluation II: Determining the Etiology

After it has been determined that the patient's desire is, in fact, abnormally low and that this is not due to an underlying psychiatric condition or to painful intercourse, the next question that must be addressed concerns *etiology.*

Is the cause of the patient's desire problem psychogenic? Organic? Or is it due to combined factors? And if the etiology is psychological, what are the A, immediate and B, deeper causes?

Since organic and psychogenic desire disorders are often indistinguishable on the basis of the clinical presentation alone, physical causes must be ruled out in all patients unless the sexual symptom is clearly situational. The evaluation of organic and mixed desire disorders will be described in Chapter 10, while this chapter is devoted solely to the psychosexual evaluation of patients with psychogenic desire disorders.

THE "MULTIPLE-LAYER" MODEL OF PSYCHOPATHOGENESIS

According to the "multiple-layer" model, sexual symptoms are not the product of a single psychopathologic agent, but result from the interplay between multiple determinants that are conceptualized as operating on "deeper" and on more "superficial" psychic levels (Kaplan, 1979, 1987, 1995).

This paradigm has proven enormously useful for organizing the evaluation and treatment of psychosexual disorders.

More specifically, the *superficial or immediate causes* refer to the patient's currently operating sexual anxieties, negative thoughts, and malignant interactions with the partner, which interfere with or block the development of sexual desire in the "here and now." The therapeutic behavioral homework assignments are expressly designed to eliminate or modify these.

On the other hand, the patient's *intrapsychic sexual conflicts and neurotic interactions with the partner,* which presumably have their origins in childhood difficulties, are regarded as the *deeper causes* of psychogenic desire disorders. These same underlying conflicts operate outside of conscious awareness to maintain the patient's sexual symptom and mobilize resistances to treatment. Again, one of the major objectives of the psychodynamically informed aspects of psychosexual therapy is to help patients gain insight into these deeper, unconscious sexual fears and conflicts and into the meaning of the resistances to treatment which these spawn.

ASSESSING THE IMMEDIATE CAUSES OF SEXUAL DESIRE DISORDERS

In Chapter 2, sexual desire disorders were cast as manifestations of the normal controls of sexual motivation gone awry. More specifically, it was proposed that the immediate cause of psychogenic hypoactive sexual desire disorder is the patient's unwitting, self-destructive misuse and dysfunctional down-regulation of the control mechanisms that normally modulate and adjust the human sex drive.

One of the most important functions of the assessment procedure is to spot these immediate causes and to outline them precisely, so that these countersexual behaviors can be modified in therapy.

The immediate causes of HSD are detected by examining the current sexual experience of the couple in detail, as was described in the previous chapter in the section on the sexual status examination.

Since it helps if the examiner knows what to look for, the more common of the numerous countersexual behaviors that we have observed in our patients with HSD are contained in the following discussion. (See Figure 3.)

All of these are variations on the major HSD theme, namely the *selective focus on the negative aspects of the partner, with simultaneous denial of positive qualities.*

To put it more graphically, when they are with the right person in the

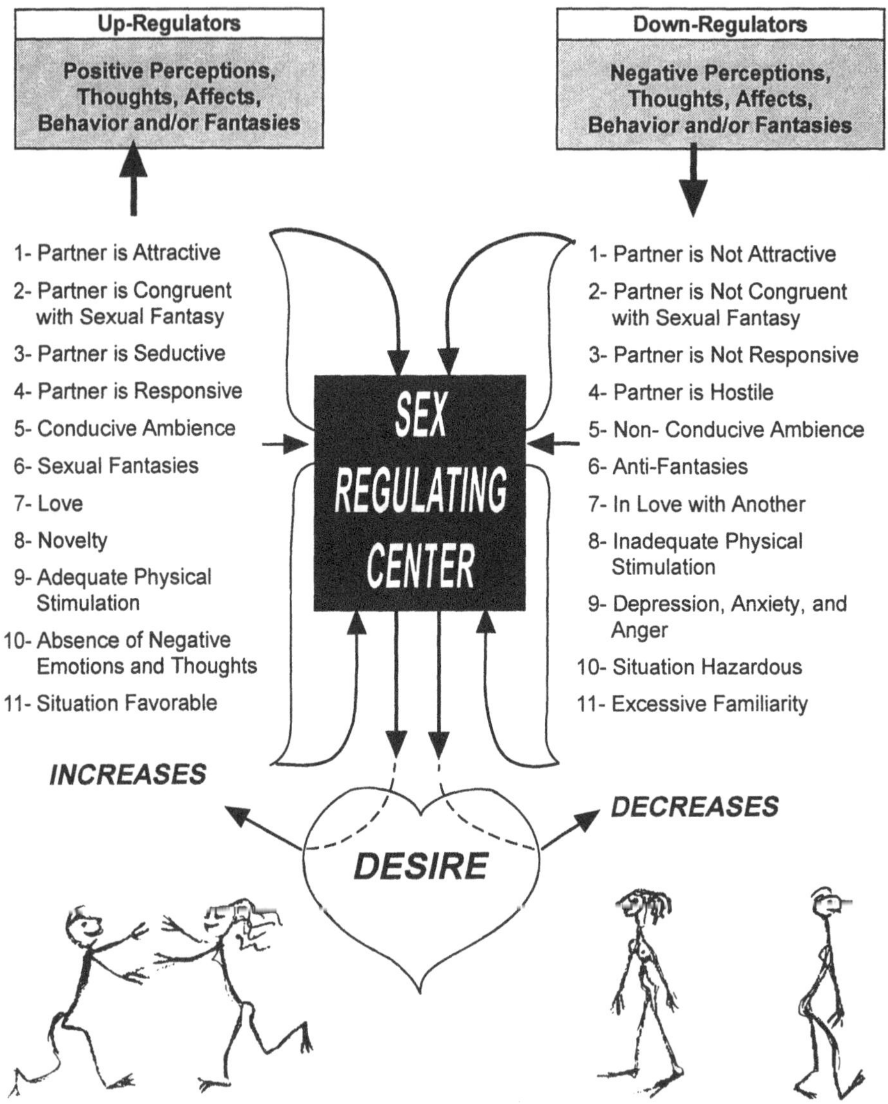

FIGURE 3. Psychological incenters and suppressors of human sexual desire.

right place, instead of getting into gear and stepping on the gas, patients with HSD keep their foot on the brake or shift into reverse, so that they never get anywhere, sexually speaking.

It should be noted once again that patients with sexual motivation dysfunctions typically have *no insight* into the self-induced elements in their lack of sexual interest in the partners; they tend to blame this on "poor chemistry."

Selective Focus on Negatives

Some of the cases that have been cited previously, as well as others that will be described later, illustrate the critical role that *selectively negative cognitive and perceptual processes* play in the pathogenesis of HSD.

The case of "Paul Actor" (Case 4.5) is especially interesting because of the spontaneous shift from countersexual to prosexual behaviors that took place when the deeper meaning of his relationship with his partner changed. "Paul Actor" had no sexual interest in his girlfriend when she was single, but he felt great passion for her as soon as she married another man.

A critical immediate cause of Actor's lack of desire for Evelyn when she was available was his self-induced, exaggerated, and selective focus on her negative qualities, such as her age and her unprepossessing appearance. This focus on the negatives was buttressed by his perceptual defenses against registering her positive features, for example, her voluptuousness, intelligence, and deep love for him.

When Evelyn was single and pursuing him, Actor would fill his mind with critical thoughts: "She's too aggressive, she talks too much, her breasts are too large, she is not good looking enough." Moreover, he would indulge in negative anticipations prior to their dates: "We're not going to have a good time at the party, the place will be filled with her dull academic friends (Evelyn was a history professor), she will embarrass me with an open display of affection." Or, if they were going to a play she selected, "it would be no good, a waste of time, they would get home too late," etc., etc.

After Evelyn married someone else, a man who happened to be a powerful "father figure" so that on a symbolic level she now fulfilled Actor's "triangle" fantasies, his thought processes suddenly shifted to a prosexual mode. More specifically, his perceptual defenses against his partner's positive and erotic qualities melted away, and he now called Evelyn "my queen of fantasy" and eagerly looked forward to their clandestine meetings. He no longer seemed to notice that "she talked too much," or that she was "too old" (she was 47). Instead, he admired her keen intelligence and began to see her as the sexy, voluptuous woman she was. Once (after she was married), when she was reluctant to remove her robe because on a previous occasion (before she remarried) Actor had been cruelly critical of her body, he exclaimed with genuine bafflement, "Why cover it up? You have the most beautiful breasts!"

Simultaneously, all his negative perceptions regarding Evelyn were blocked, and he became obsessed with her.

Sexual Defenses Are Evoked at the Beginning of the Sexual Response Cycle

Also typical of the pathogenesis of HSD was the fact that *Actor's defenses became operative early on in the sexual response* cycle before the sexual encounter actually took place. By contrast, the sexual anxieties of patients with erectile or orgasm dysfunctions come into play later, when they are already engaged in making love and are aroused or ready to climax. Such later occurring sexual anxiety interferes only with the excitement or orgasm reflexes, but does not decrease the individual's desire.

The negative feelings of desire disorder patients typically surface *before* they enter the bedroom, thereby destroying any possibility of a normal build-up of their sexual desires.

Once again, patients use various permutations and combinations of all the different immediate causes that were listed in Figure 3 to down-regulate their sexual desires in the service of their pathological needs.

Avoidance of Erotic Stimulation

For example, in addition to his countersexual behavior, Actor also *avoided physical stimulation* when he was in his negative mode, but eagerly pursued this after Evelyn was married.

A shift in Actor's sexual stance, this time in the reverse direction, from prosexual to countersexual, reoccurred some years later with another woman, Eva, his new wife. Prior to their marriage, Actor had been smitten with Eva. He could see only his young wife's beauty, while blinding himself to her faults. At that time, he enjoyed kissing and touching her, and the couple would sleep intertwined all night long. However, after they married and had a baby, this all changed. Once more, Actor began to focus on negatives, although the content was different. This time these involved Eva's "narcissism" and her "neglecting" him. He also became annoyed because she was not his "intellectual equal."

By the time the couple consulted me, he could not bear to touch her and slept rigidly on his side of the bed each night.

The powerful erotogenic effects of physical stimulation of erotic areas of the body and of the genitalia, that is, kissing and foreplay, are normally exploited to increase sexual arousal. But as in Actor's case, patients with HSD tend to keep away from erotic physical stimulation to avoid becoming aroused.

In the first phase of their relationship, Actor avoided the single Evelyn's kisses, would pull away when she tried to hold his hand, and would never sleep in the same bed with her. With the married Evelyn, however, he happily shared intimate caresses and kisses all evening long and was hurt when she couldn't stay over night and sleep in the same bed with him.

"Mrs. Frieda Aspen" (Case 4.6) exemplifies how effectively patients with HSD can down-regulate their sexual feelings simply by *avoiding erotic stimulation.*

Although Frieda had allowed Fred to have intercourse with her once a week for 31 years, she had never touched or looked at his genitals or, for that matter, at her own (for example, she never used tampons). She did not allow Fred to touch or kiss her breasts or nipples or her clitoris, and she always slept in a long nightgown. In addition, she avoided looking at any erotic pictures or reading books with sexual content, nor did she permit any "off color" jokes or sexual banter in her house. In short, this woman managed to avoid anything that might have aroused her sexual desire, all throughout her life.

Suppression of Sexual Fantasy

The suppression of sexual fantasies when with the partner is another immediate mechanism that some patients with psychogenic, situational HSD use to down-regulate their sexual desires when they are with their partner. Some individuals cannot function without evoking their special erotic images to incite their sexual desire. Such fantasy-dependent individuals usually use their virtual images freely when they masturbate. But when they are with their partners, they may suppress or withhold these, especially if the content is paraphilic or if this involves a different partner.

Patients offer various rationalizations for not making use of their sexual fantasies while making love to their partner—it is "disloyal," "not fair," "not nice," "sick," "I want real intimacy," etc. However, the withholding of erotica and fantasy, as well as the consequent inability to become aroused and to function with the partner, is often symptomatic of deeper underlying conflicts about sex and intimacy. A case that hinged on freeing up a patient's fantasy will be described later (Case 8.7).

Tapping into the Incest Taboo

"Highjacking" the antisexual effects of the universal, latent "incest taboo" is another subtle but highly effective method of deactivating the sex centers. The incest taboo, that learned program of sexual inhibition that once helped us negotiate the steamy, turbulent waters of our early psychosexual development within our erotically charged families, lies dormant in adults. But this is not erased and can be reactivated by one's relating to potential sexual partners as though they were sisters, daughters, brothers, or pals.

The use of the "incest taboo mechanism" to control inappropriate sexual desire is not pathological per se. In fact this is a socially useful device that helps keep sexuality under control in situations like the workplace, which often takes on the trappings of a family. This taboo-related desexualization mechanism, like the other normal suppressor mechanisms, becomes a problem only if this is used to serve dysfunctional, self-destructive purposes.

"Greta Biedemeyer." (Case 8.1), the 39-year-old woman with the severe aversion to sex who has been mentioned previously, was a prime example of the defensive use of the "incest taboo." Among the multitude of defenses against sex that this patient developed, her habit of relating to every man she met like a "pal" or a "sister" was one of the most effective. As a backup, this woman also perfected the art of "*sexual invisibility.*" Not only did she cloak all her attractive features by wearing unbecoming clothes and hairstyles, she also let herself become seriously obese. This patient's "ugly sister act" was so "successful" that she ended up without any social life at all.

Another patient who became an expert at relating to attractive potential partners as though they were "sisters" and "pals" was Bill Kangaroo, the 41-year-old teacher with severe, life-long HSD, who had been seduced by his mother. (See Case 8.2.) His asexual way of relating reduced Bill's sexual anxiety, but also effectively kept him from having romantic relationships.

Unattractive Behavior

Counter-courtship maneuvers, or unpleasant behaviors that spoil the partner's appetite for sex, are among the most common and effective defenses against sexual desire and good sex.

Except for individuals who have genuine masochistic or sadistic desires, and actually become aroused when they are hurt or humiliated by their partners or when they inflict misery, negative interactions with a partner are incompatible with passion and desire.

When one observes couples who have fine marriages and good sex lives, the one thing they have in common is that the partners are instinctively sensitive and considerate towards one another. He pulls out her chair, she brings a sweater for him; he cuts out an article that might interest her, she spends hours tracking down his favorite coffee.

Yet, there are a number of case studies in this book in which the opposite takes place, and a partner's insensitivity, hostility, obsessiveness, obnoxiousness, withholding, tantrums, betrayal, or provocations caused the other to lose sexual interest. Such negative behaviors create a downward spiral of mutual and reciprocal angers, along with hostile environments that are incompatible with lovemaking.

It is astonishing how many of our patients have not grasped the simple fact that lovers should be good to each other, and that they should as a matter of course treat each other with consideration. They seem to believe that their mate should be pleased to go to bed with them even though they sit around the house in their dirty underwear, don't brush their teeth, and display rude, critical, or selfish behavior. But that belief is totally unrealistic, and even animals know enough to control their aggressive behavior and put their best foot, tail, or song forward when they have the urge to mate.

As an example of such a failure to understand the basic affiliative nature of human love relationships, in a recent consultation a 62-year-old woman told me that she and her husband had never had good sex in the 40 years of their marriage, and for the past two years they had had no sexual contact at all. With tears in her eyes she told me that she did not want to die without having felt "like a real woman."

I was touched and eager to help.

The 65-year-old husband listened quietly to his wife's lamentations and then described what turned out to be the immediate cause of the low sexual frequency in this marriage. He explained that he was turned off by his wife's constant criticisms and verbal abuse. She interrupted him to let me know that her husband was completely unreasonable in that he kept insisting that he could not get into a romantic mood and make love to her unless she were "nice to him *the whole day.*" The wife considered this much too much of a demand. "Dr. Kaplan," she intoned, "why can't he make love to me if just I'm nice to him at dinner? Isn't that enough? Why should I have to kiss his ass the whole day?"

When I pointed out that people who are not "nice" to each other can't expect to have a good sex life, and suggested that if she really wanted to experience better sex with her husband before her life was over she might have to start by being less critical and demeaning to him, she was astounded and offended. She explained to me that she couldn't possibly be expected to be nice to him on a consistent basis because she had had a difficult childhood.

ASSESSING THE IMMEDIATE CAUSES OF SEXUAL AVERSION DISORDERS

The immediate cause of sexual aversions and sexual panic states is an irrational feeling of terror and/or revulsion of sexual contact with the partner. However, unlike patients with HSD, sexaphobic patients do not unconsciously down-regulate their sexual motivational states with negative input. While these patients avoid sex out of fear, they do not necessarily lack sexual desire. As was pointed out in Chapter 4, some patients are repelled or frightened by and avoid any and all sexual contact with any partner, while patients with *partial phobias and aversions* are repelled only by their spouses or by *specific* aspects of sex, such as kissing, touching of the breasts, or vaginal penetration.

It is an important mission of the *sexual status examination*, to identify and delineate the parameters of the patient's sexaphobic responses precisely so that appropriate and specific in-vivo desensitization programs to modify these can be instituted.

ASSESSING THE DEEPER CAUSES OF PSYCHOGENIC DESIRE DISORDERS

The deeper causes of sexual desire disorders are explored by a review of the patient's sexual and family histories.

When the sexual status exam is complete and I have a good fix on the immediate causes of the patient's decreased desire, and/or on the exact parameters of his/her aversion to sex, I turn to the *sexual and family histories* to begin to look for deeper causes.

Problem-Focused Sexual History: Was the Patient's Psychosexual History Normal or Abnormal?

Patients with disorders of sexual desire have the same types of underlying intrapsychic conflicts, marital problems and guilt about sexual pleasure as are found in patients with orgasm and arousal phase difficulties. It is only the nature of the immediate causes that is unique and distinguishes the different psychosexual syndromes from one another.

Similarly, although the immediate causes of HSD and those of sexual panic states are distinctively different, no comparable differences can be discerned with regard to the deeper intrapsychic psychopathology or in the relationship difficulties of patients with those two syndromes.

Further, the deeper psychological causes of the sexual disorders vary widely both in nature and severity. Patients with psychosexual disorders, regardless of specific type, have sexual histories that may be perfectly normal or else involve dysfunctional family backgrounds, sexual trauma, and antisexual conditioning. Thus, I first want to know if the patient's psychosexual development was, in broad terms, normal or abnormal. To get a sense of this, I ask a few brief questions about such sexual developmental landmarks as masturbation and the first sexual experience and I also ask whether the patient remembers any incest or abuse. I also attempt to get an idea of the patient's adult sexual experience—sexual frequency, functional adequacy, sexual orientation, number of partners, marriages, divorces, pregnancies, abortions, etc.

Many patients with sexual desire disorders have unremarkable sexual histories, and this is a good prognostic sign. In such cases, I quickly move on to the *family history portion* of the interview and I fill in the details of the patient's sexual history later on, as therapy proceeds.

However, if the patient's answers are indicative of abnormalities in his/her psychosexual development, the sexual history is explored in greater depth.

Masturbation History

An abnormal masturbation history can yield valuable clues about early disturbances in the patient's sexual development.

Most boys in our society begin masturbating around puberty, stimulating their penis manually while imagining erotic scenes or looking at erotic pictures in magazines. A suspicion of possible difficulties is raised if the boy did not masturbate at all* or avoided touching his genitalia, bringing himself to orgasm in atypical ways, such as rubbing himself against the bed, putting his penis between his thighs, rocking back and forth, or stimulating his penis through his underwear.

Since only about 40% of girls report masturbating, the absence of self-stimulation is less significant in female sexual histories.

*About 98% of U.S. males report having masturbated at some time in their lives. But this does not include Orthodox Jews and devout Roman Catholics. These religions strongly prohibit self-stimulation and the absence of Onanism is not indicative of abnormal sexual development in persons who belong to these subcultures.

First Sexual Experience

A sexual landmark that I try to touch on in the first interview is a brief description of the *patient's first sexual experience.* Often, there is little of importance to be learned from this inquiry, but once in a while one discovers the beginning of a long-term destructive sexual pattern.

For example, "Regina Kaiser's" (Case 4.8) sexual aversion to her husband began on their honeymoon, which was the occasion of their first attempt at intercourse.

Roy had gone to considerable efforts to make the beginning of their lives together special, and he had rented for their exclusive use a magnificent, fully staffed villa in the Caribbean. Regina was moved by his thoughtfulness. But, unfortunately, it was hot and there was no air conditioning, so Roy simply stripped and presented himself stark naked with the beginnings of an erection, to his bride, who gasped in dismay. It may be speculated that this woman's negative reaction, which set the unfortunate tone of this couple's subsequent sexual relationship from that day on, occurred because Roy's exposed, erect penis recalled a traumatic incident that occurred when she was a little girl (see below).

Sexual Trauma and Abuse in Childhood

All patients are asked whether they recall having been sexually abused, subjected to incest, or traumatized. If the answer is affirmative, I ask the patient to tell me about the incident(s) in exact detail. The key to the pathogenesis of these patients' sexual symptoms, as well as the success of treatment, often depends on the therapist's understanding of the particulars of the traumatic experience(s).

In several of the case studies that are cited in this book, it was possible to trace the patient's current sexual symptoms to the specific events of the abusive episode(s).

For example, "Greta Biedemeyer's" (Case 8.1) sexual symptoms were a direct reflection of the manner in which she had been molested as a child.

Between the ages of eight and 12, this patient had repeatedly been forced to endure the "disgusting" kisses of her middle-aged malodorous neighbor. The man would grab the child and hold her fast. He would then kiss her and keep his mouth on hers, while he forced her to stimulate his penis; he did not let the little girl go until he had ejaculated. These experiences forged a link between kissing and Greta's feelings of revulsion; this link was the core of her phobic avoidance of sex. These details were very useful in the planning of this patient's treatment, which involved "bypassing" her kissing aversion, as will be described in Chapter 8.

"Regina Kaiser's" (Case 4.8) sexual aversion could be traced to a single violent incident that occurred when she was five years old. The reader is reminded that this woman was so sexaphobic that she could not bear to look at an erotic illustration that hangs on the wall of my office, slept with two cats in the marital bed, and seldom bathed, all in the service of avoiding sex with her husband.

Regina revealed that she had been molested by the director of a summer camp at the age of five. This had been a most unpleasant and traumatic experience. To this day, she had a clear and still painful memory of the man forcing her to go behind some bushes with him, where he exposed his erect penis, stuck this in her face, grabbed her hair, and made her kneel down in front of him and fellate him.

Prior to this incident, the child's sexual development had been uneventful, and she had exhibited a normal healthy curiosity about sex and about male genitalia. She recalled that prior to this traumatic event, when she was about four years old, she had once watched with some amusement her father's penis bobbing in the bath water of the tub and she remembers being told to leave the room when she asked if she could touch it. At about the same time, she also recalls questioning her governess, with a similar sense of amused curiosity, about an exhibitionist in the park and having the embarrassed woman whisk her away.

But after the incident with the camp director, her benign attitude towards penises changed and she became extremely phobic of erect phalluses. The patient remembered clearly at age seven screaming hysterically when she saw a man exhibit his erect penis on a bus, and she had a similar negative reaction when she saw her husband's penis on their honeymoon.

The destructive effects of sexual child abuse are not limited to females. We have a considerable number of cases in our files of adult male patients who were badly traumatized by early homosexual abuse by older boys, teachers, priests, and camp counselors. When they grew up, men who had been abused by homosexual pedophiliacs developed a variety of severe and disabling sexual, as well as post-traumatic, emotional symptoms.

Adult Sexual Trauma

Sexual trauma in adult life may also affect sexual desire adversely. The undigested memories of sexual trauma suffered by adult women often persist and become a source of resistance to treatment.

I have seen a number of patients whose loss of sexual desire or phobic avoidance of sex was precipitated by rape, and by unusually painful deliveries (particularly when these were assisted by pitocin, and without epidural blockage). The loss of sexual desire is also very common in couples who have been traumatized by lengthy and invasive treatments for infertility.

Sexual Desire Disorders and Treatments for Infertility

Infertility and its treatments are frequently sexually traumatic for both spouses. The past decade has witnessed a revolution in reproductive technology which has enabled many formerly childless couples to become parents to healthy babies. Unfortunately, modern methods of assisted reproduction can also be intrusive, expensive, invasive, emotionally taxing, and so stressful that few couples, even those with iron-clad egos and marriages made in heaven fail to succumb to these repeated, traumatic assaults on their reproductive organs, their self-esteem, their privacy, their pocketbooks, and their sex lives. In fact it has been reported that the majority of men and women who undergo treatments for infertility eventually develop sexual and emotional problems (Stotland, 1990).

Infertility problems and treatments revolve around the fact that human females are fertile for only three to four days of the month after ovulation, usually about two weeks after the end of the menstrual period. Sperm must be introduced to the egg during this brief period to achieve fertilization.

Therefore, the management of infertility usually begins with compulsory, regimented, daily intercourse during the few days of each month when there is a viable ovum in the woman's reproductive tract.

If this does not work, the next step is usually artificial insemination with the husband's sperm, which the doctor inserts into the woman's vagina or cervix on the fertile days.

This is followed by a progressively more technically complex, painful, expensive, and invasive sequence of diagnostic and treatment procedures. These include various monitoring methods, for example sophisticated hormone tests and imaging techniques, microsurgical procedures by which occluded fallopian tubes and surgically severed spermatic ducts can be reopened, and advanced hormone manipulations that result in increased egg and sperm production. Finally, a growing number of increasingly sophisticated *in-vitro methods of fertilization* have been developed that involve the surgical removal of ova from the woman's reproductive tract, mixing this with the husband's sperm outside the body, and later reimplanting the embryo into the mother. These include GIFT and ZIFT, egg drilling and zona drilling, various types of surrogate techniques by which one woman can bear the fertile ovum of another. Further, advanced methods of sperm, ovum, and embryo preservation and freezing, which can postpone conception are available.

Lamont and Anderson (1993) have pointed out that the wife and the husband experience different kinds of stresses at each step in assisted reproduction: admission of the problem, investigation, treatment, failure to conceive and the exploration of alternatives.

In general the investigation of the problem and the early phase of treatment, with its rigorous performance demands, tend to be more difficult for men, while the technically advanced, later procedures are often more difficult for women, who are more likely to be subjected to daily blood tests and injections, whose bodies have to yield more frequently to repetitive and painful invasive surgical procedures on their reproductive organs, and who have to suffer the emotional destabilization which is the frequent side effect of fertility drugs.

The most common sexual problem for which couples undergoing infertility treatments are referred to us is the husband's inability to perform on the days that his wife is fertile. This can be devastating for him, as for the rejection-sensitive wife, who often takes this as a sign that her husband doesn't love her or that he is ambivalent about having a baby.

But those are only rarely the real reasons. The most common immediate causes of infertility-related male dysfunction are *performance pressure* and *the loss of sexual desire.*

As has been detailed in the previous chapter, one fairly common cause of the loss of sexual desire is a harried, pressured environment that is not conducive to romance. The obligatory, "love on demand" for reproductive purposes that creates a pressure-cooker atmosphere each month, when the woman ovulates surely qualifies for that designation.

To put it more graphically, when a husband tries to perform after his wife has informed him that her temperature is up, that she is ovulating, and that she needs to be "serviced" right now, and when he knows that she will be devastated if another cycle goes by without her becoming pregnant, he is not likely to feel very lustful.

Under these circumstances, sex becomes a duty, a performance coerced by the demands of reproduction and the act loses all semblance of spontaneity and romance. This is a perfect breeding ground for performance anxiety impotence, which further decreases the desire for sex. The damage that almost all couples sustain when they are undergoing lengthy treatments for infertility is escalated when this synchronizes with the patient's preexisting psychopathology and/or the couple's marital disharmony. The following case vignette is illustrative:

CASE 6.1—"Sam and Sandra DeBopp": The Loss of Sexual Desire Due to Infertility and Treatment for Infertility

The husband Sam was 50 years old, short, bald, smart, and a highly successful businessman. His second wife, Sandra, was a 41-year-old, tall, slender, beautiful, well educated but insecure, emotionally fragile and highly obsessive woman.

The couple had been married for four years. Their relationship had been stormy, especially so since Sam's children from his former marriage had come to live with the DeBopp's two years prior to the consultation. (His first wife had been confined to an alcoholic rehabilitation program and the patient happily agreed to assume custody of his son and daughter.)

Sandra found it increasingly difficult to be warm and even civil to her little stepchildren, since she was consumed with wanting children of her own.

Until her late thirties, she had been engrossed in her career as a buyer in an upscale department store and ambivalent about becoming a mother. Then suddenly, after her husband's daughter came to live with them, she became obsessed with having a baby. He reluctantly agreed, but Sandra did not become pregnant.

The couple were referred by their fertility specialist. After enduring the "reverse rhythm method"* for over a year, Sam had become impotent with his wife. Even worse, he had become so anxious about his sexual performance that he arranged to be away on business trips during his wife's last two periods.

Sandra became increasingly frantic as the months rolled by and she still did not become pregnant. Her obsessions had recently begun to center on Sam's erections; whenever Sam had a problem, she angrily accused him of rejecting her and unconsciously denying her a child.

This man had a history of having had transient episodes of premature ejaculation and erectile dysfunction with new partners. However, in the past these had always resolved spontaneously as soon as he became comfortable in the relationship.

*"Reverse Rhythm" is the term I use to describe the "sex-on-demand-when-the-wife-is-fertile" procedure, because this is the reverse of the "Rhythm" method of contraception, where the couple *abstain* from sex during the wife's fertile periods.

During the first two years of this couple's marriage, after his usual, brief, initial period of dysfunction, their sexual relationship had been quite passionate and satisfying for both. However, for the past year, a few cycles after they began to try to get pregnant, Sam developed the aforementioned desire and erectile problems, which had now become chronic.

Part of what Sandra said was true—Sam *was* somewhat ambivalent about having more children at his age. But his love for her was stronger than his reluctance, and having resolved his initial reservations, he was now perfectly willing to become a father again.

Sam's conflict about having another baby was not the critical cause of his impotence, nor did this issue need to be addressed in therapy at this time. The immediate cause of Sam's desire and potency problems was *partner pressure.* In her frantic desire to have a baby before it was too late, Sandra was sabotaging the effort by putting enormous performance pressure on this man, who was already prone to erectile problems related to performance anxiety.

Sandra never let Sam forget how important it was for her to get pregnant and how disgusted she was with his impotence. For example, once when Sam did manage to penetrate and ejaculate, she undermined him by accusing him of not putting his penis and his semen deeply enough into her vagina!

Sandra had no insight whatsoever into her contribution to Sam's lack of desire and his erection difficulties. She completely denied the role that her own unconscious conflicts about becoming a mother might be playing, and she blamed the problem entirely on Sam.

I tried to "bypass" Sam's anxiety by suggesting that he become absorbed in erotica and fantasy while making love to his wife. But this strategy was not effective in this case, as it was simply impossible for Sam to "tune out" the intrusive, pressured environment that was created by his agitated, anxious, and angry wife.

I felt for Sam in his desperate sense of pressure to perform and I was also sympathetic with Sandra's intense wish for a baby. Under these circumstances, I thought it best to try to detour around this couple's problem with a trial of "at home" artificial insemination.*

Since Sam had no problem masturbating, the couple were able to make good use of the device. Not surprisingly, however, Sandra com-

*Grace Sullivan, RN, MPH, a member of our group, has developed a simple, practical device which we give to couples, along with instructions for use at home. It serves to insert the husband's sperm into the wife's vagina when she is in her fertile period.

plained that if Sam "really, truly" wanted to have a baby with her, he wouldn't have to resort to this.

Sexual and emotional symptoms that result from sexual violence, including the attenuated violence of assisted reproduction, may be considered as *post-traumatic sexual stress syndromes*. Like other types of post-traumatic disorders, the symptoms tend to persist, sometimes for many years after the original trauma occurred, but they are often amenable to treatment.

Antisexual Messages

Next, I attempt to discover the nature of the messages about sex that the person received during his/her formative years.

If the patient was brought up in a home with permissive, liberal sexual values, and if sex was discussed openly with the parents during childhood, culturally induced guilt about sex is ruled out as a deeper cause and I proceed to the next area of inquiry.

On the other hand, if the patient tells me that he/she was brought up in a highly traditional home with antisexual values, or if the family belonged to one of the fundamentalist Judeo-Christian religious groups that consider any form of sexual expression that is not for procreation as sinful, shameful, and dangerous, and especially if that person attended parochial schools, where the families' antisexual messages are strongly reinforced, I look for evidence of residuals of *malignant, early antisexual programming,* which is another common, deeper cause of sexual desire disorders.

Family History: Was the Patient's Family of Origin Normal or Abnormal?

The family is the crucible out of which sexual pathology emerges, and the family history is arguably the most important source of information about the deeper psychic infrastructure of the patient's sexual desire disorder.

However, I do not try to take a complete family history as part of the initial evaluation. Even though I must have a complete grasp of the patient's current sexual status and the immediate causes of the sexual symptoms prior to commencing treatment, I do not require a comparably detailed understanding of the family history at that time.

During the first interview, I am interested just in getting a general sense of the early developmental origins of the patient's deeper conflicts and deficits, only the highlights. I fill in the details of the history and revise my initial hypotheses about the nature and severity of the underlying psychopathology gradually, as therapy unfolds and as resistances to the therapeutic homework assignments begin to emerge.

All I really need to know about the patient's family of origin to fulfill the objectives of the evaluation and to commence treatment is whether the patient's family was, in general terms, functional and if she/he was properly nurtured and cared for as a child, or if the youngster suffered abuse at the hands of a family that was chaotic and dysfunctional. I also want to know how the patient related to his mother and father. This basic information is the key to understanding what role if any, intrapsychic conflicts play in the patient's lack of sexual desire or in the design of his/her sexual terrors.

Sex is a natural function, and I believe that a child can be expected to develop a normal capacity to love, to desire appropriate partners, and to function well sexually providing she/he is reared in a relatively stable family, receives reasonable parenting and nurturing, has an essentially loving and constructive relationship with the parents, and is not taught to feel guilty about or afraid of sex during its formative years.

The importance of normal developmental conditions, and conversely, the damage to sexual development that can be caused by inadequate parenting and by abuse are so basic that these have been demonstrated in infra-human primates. In Harlow's experiments (Harlow, 1958; Harlow & Lanersberg, 1974; Harlow & Harlow, 1965), baby chimps were separated from their mothers at birth and placed in cages where they were fed and "raised" by "surrogate mothers." These were wire structures, roughly the size of an adult chimp, to which bottles of milk were attached. When these experimentally abused animals reached adulthood, they were frightened by potential sexual partners and completely unable to mate.

Comparable damage to human sexual development occurs when the home is chaotic; when a parent is alcoholic or disturbed; when the child is emotionally starved, or neglected, or physically or sexually abused; if the parents are hostile, competitive, or punitive towards the youngster; if they involve the child in their battles with each other or, worse, if they don't protect the child from sexual abuse or incest; if there are no gender-appropriate role models, and/or the child is brainwashed with antisexual propaganda. Under such conditions, the unfortunate little creature is likely to eroticize the tragic events of his/her childhood and to grow up with aberrant sexual desires and serious deficits in his or her ability to form romantic relationships.

I usually can get a sense of whether the patient's family provided a basically normal nurturing environment for the patient from a brief vignette of the family of origin: its composition, whether the parents cooperated in raising the child, how the family meals and holidays went, and if the parents' relationship was stable. If they divorced, I want to know how old the child was and how he/she fared. Also it is important to know if the family were emotionally uncommunicative or expressive.

The Parents

Although I may not get to this during the initial interview, at some time soon I like to know how the parents got along together, so I can gauge what kind of role model for romantic relationships my patient grew up with. Did the mother and father love each other? Were they empathic, sensitive, nice to one other? Did they fight? Were they cruel to each other? Were they faithful to each other? Which parent was dominant?

Information on the parents' relationship is useful for many reasons, including the fact that many people unconsciously *mirror or rebel against* the kind of relationship they observed between their parents when they were growing up.

I always try to get some sense of the kind of person the father and the mother are or were, and how they related to the patient. Often, I can get this information by asking the patient to tell me "in one sentence or less" how he/she got along with mother and with father, and what they were like.

This rapidly gives me a picture, to be revised later as more information unfolds, about the deeper causes and dynamics of the patient's sexual desire disorder.

Among the case histories in this book are some that illustrate the complex relationships that can exist between a patient's early, destructive relationships with his/her parents, and the genesis of the sexual desire disorder.

The case of Bill Kangaroo (Case 8.2) provides an excellent example of the malignant consequences of inappropriate seductiveness and incestuous behavior on the part of the *opposite gender parent.*

Bill's mother regularly invited the boy to touch her intimately. One could say that this young man won the Oedipal contest, but it was a Pyrrhic victory that fixated his sexuality pathologically on his mother to the extent that he was later paralyzed with appropriate partners.

Another patient, "Joe Senator" (Case 8.7), was in double jeopardy from the seductions of his mother and the intimidation his scary father seemed to relish subjecting him to.

Joe's father, a cold, distant, tyrannical man, an executive in a company making electronic weapons, regularly went out of his way to frighten and harass the boy. The father also set up an inappropriate sexual competition in that he bragged about his numerous sexual peccadillos. At the same time, he put Joe's mother, his wife, on an unrealistic "pedestal," admonishing his sons that nice women are fragile creatures who should be protected and that "fucking" was a hostile, dirty, demeaning act reserved for "cheap" women or sluts.

As if this were not sufficient to damage the boy's sexuality, Joe's "angelic" mother also played an active role in the genesis of his desire disorder in that she was inappropriately seductive to the boy.

As it happened, Joe *turned the trauma* caused by his mother's flaunting of forbidden sexual temptations under the shadow of his father's "castrating" (or at least frightening) shadow *into a triumph* by eroticizing the whole sick scenario. In other words, his "bad whore" fantasy preserved the boy's masculinity and protected his sexuality from irreparable damage. However, this cost him the ability to relate normally to women when he grew up.

Another patient who exemplified what could be described as an underlying Oedipal problem and who also eroticized and became fixated on the painful events of his childhood was "Paul Actor," the patient who was aroused only by married women (Case 4.5). This patient's erotic triangle scenario could be traced directly to the eroticization of this painful and traumatic relationship with his parents.

Actor's father was a domineering, narcissistic man, who regularly humiliated and teased the sensitive little boy, who grew to hate and fear him. Paul, an only child, was much closer to his mother, who unfortunately was a highly self-absorbed woman who exploited the child's need for maternal love. The mother was phobic of being alone, and when Paul's father went away on one of his frequent business trips, she would use little "Paulie" as her companion. At these times, she would spend much of her time with him and would often invite him to sleep in her bed.

When the elder Actor returned, she would immediately turn all her attention to her husband, while completely ignoring little Paul, who would be left out in the cold.

This painful scenario of alternating seductions and rejections was repeated again and again, and this left its mark on Actor's sexuality. His favorite masturbation fantasy was a revengeful one of a young boy making love to an older woman, while an older man watched. It does not take a great stretch of imagination to hypothesize that on a symbolic level Actor had reversed the painful rejections of his childhood to where the mother was making love to *him* instead of to the father, while the latter was relegated to watching.

Actor's triangle obsession was not confined to fantasy. In real life, Actor could become aroused only with a married woman, who symbolically became his mother. Each time he made love, he was unconsciously displacing the hated "father."

The Same-Gender Parent

It is well known that the parent of the opposite gender is in a position to exert malignant influences on his or her child's sexual destiny, as was illustrated in the cases cited above. Less attention has been paid to the potentially destructive impact of the other, isogender parent. However, I have come to believe that a good relationship with the same-sex parent confers considerable immunity against subsequent sexual psychopathology.

Boys who have encouraging fathers and girls whose mothers give them unqualified support for becoming attractive and sexually successful women have a headstart on their psychosexual development. These fortunate youngsters are likely to grow up free of the guilt and fear of hell fire and brimstone, and free of the dread of vengeance from sexual competitors that often makes sexual cripples out of the unfortunate offspring of competitive and unthinking same-gender parents.

In our patient population, the great majority of women with HSD and sexual aversion disorders had not received proper encouragement from their mothers, and they had for the most part been unable to form healthy female identifications. The mother–daughter relationships of our female patients were poor for a variety of reasons, including the mother's unavailability, cruelty, alcoholism, narcissism, or her own emotional problems.

There are a number of cases in this book in which a female patient's sexual inadequacy was clearly associated with her destructive relationship with her mother.

For example, Greta Biedemeyer's mother (Case 8.1) was depressed and agoraphobic, and she could not and did not give the child proper parenting. The relationship between that mother and daughter was so impoverished that the child could not bring herself to tell her mother about the sexual abuse she was enduring for all these years, and she suffered alone in silence.

To cite another example, "Esther," the phobic Orthodox Jewish woman who had a severe, intractable aversion to her husband, had lost her mother at the age of eight and was brought up haphazardly by a number of relatives who were overburdened by their own large families (Case 5.3).

Ida, another Orthodox Jewish woman, was too phobic to consummate her marriage (Case 5.5). This patient, too, had a history of poor maternal care. At the age of four, she had been spirited away from her mother by her fanatical grandmother and raised by elderly, cold, ultra-religious foster parents who seemed to have been more interested in religious ritual than in the child's emotional welfare.

Regina Kaiser (Case 4.8), the woman with the sexual aversion to her husband, had a mother who was described as narcissistic, extremely self-involved, and seemingly not bothered that one of her children, Regina, had to live with the fact that she openly preferred her more attractive older sister.

A comparable type of sexual and emotional protection is afforded boys who have relationships with fathers who are close, encouraging, and supportive, and who provide the youngster with a healthy male role-model. The father's influence is so important and so predictably effective that if the patient's family history reveals a warm, loving, constructive father-son relationship, I make the tentative assumption (to be modified later, if this is not confirmed) that the patient's desire problem is likely to be situational and that his prognosis is favorable.

On the other side of the coin, the key to much of male sexual pathology lies in *faulty father–son relationships*. A predominant feeling of fear or loathing towards the father or a sense of emotional distance and discomfort with him robs the boy of the opportunity to make a loving alliance with a constructive male and of forming a healthy masculine identification. As a result, when such boys grow up, they are subject to a great deal of sexual anxiety and symptomatology.

BENIGN AND MALIGNANT SEXUAL FANTASIES AND PARTNER CHOICES

In Chapter 3 sexual fantasies were defined as mental representatives of our sexual desires, which retain the erotic power of real incenters.

Further, I expressed the opinion that the impact of the fantasies that grow out of the child's early emotional pain, irrespective of their content, are often *benign* and do not interfere with the person's ability to love and to enjoy intimate love relationships. As a matter of fact, I regard such fantasies as harmless reminders of the past. These are encapsulated, non-malignant remnants of the eroticization of painful events that took place in the person's childhood, which have retained their erotic power and are there to be enjoyed.

Some authors disagree with this point of view, feeling that "perverse" or atypical fantasies are by nature always alienating and damaging to intimacy. Thus, Dr. Shandor Lorand, a psychoanalyst who has published extensively in the area of sexual perversion, expressed a pessimistic position regarding sexual fantasy, one that is shared by many, as follows: "the fetishist (person with paraphilic desires) cannot become completely involved in a heterosexual relationship" (Lorand & Schneer, 1976, p. 981).

Although there is no doubt that this is true in some cases, I have seen many persons whose traumatic childhood experiences have spawned atypical, perverse, or paraphilic fantasies who use these erotic images playfully and constructively in the service of enhancing their sexual feelings and functioning with loving, intimate partners. Thus, we have numbers of histories in our files of men who have sadomasochistic desires, as well as others who are aroused by different paraphilic desires such as cross-dressing, who contracted excellent marriages, had nice children, followed good careers, and enjoyed a fine quality of life. These men did not give up on either their variant desires nor their family life; they compromised by confining their enjoyment of their atypical desires to fantasy and play-acting with accepting partners.

Similarly, it is not unusual for a woman who is aroused by the fantasy of being mistreated and dominated, but prefers gentle, considerate partners in real life, to have her cake and eat it, by slipping into the virtual sexual reality of the fantasy that she is being tied up and violated, while she makes love to her decent husband.

Further, I believe that under certain circumstances the aphrodisiac power of fantasy can be exceedingly useful for some patients with HSD, and I do not hesitate to encourage patients who are unable to sustain sufficient feeling of desire for their partners to use their fantasies to "bridge over" their anxieties or their lack of attraction. This can help them function with their spouses and to enhance their marriages.

The case of "Joe Senator," which will be described in the next chapter, illustrates this point clearly (Case 8.7). This patient felt no desire for his beautiful fiancée, whom he loved deeply. Joe could function only with the aid of a sadistic, misogynistic sexual fantasy that consisted of thinking or saying, "You whore, you slut, you deserve a good fucking" to his sexual partner. But Joe, who was basically a very nice fellow, found these crude and hostile images unacceptable and incongruent with the loving, protective, and respectful feelings he had for his fiancée, and he could not get himself to fantasize when he was with her. As a result, he was unable to function. The successful treatment of this case centered around freeing the patient up to exploit the erotic potential of his sadistic fantasies in the service of improving his loving relationship.

Paraphilic Sexual Fantasy and Destructive Object Choice

Problems arise when the person's paraphilic sexual desires are not confined to the sex act, but take a malignant course. In some cases, the person's perverse desires "metastasize" from their original genital site in the bedroom, so to speak, and invade and destroy his or her ability to form healthy object relationships.

Thus, it is common for men who were hurt by rejecting, withholding, demanding, controlling, cruel, elusive, or sadistic mothers to eroticize the very same destructive qualities that caused them so much pain when they were children. When they grow up these men may feel attracted only to women who hurt them in similar ways, but they are unable to form attachments to decent women.

The case of "Doc Scotch" (Case 8.8) provides a good example of such an erotization of childhood trauma (See Chapter 3). This patient had no sexual interest in his kind, loving, generous girlfriend. Doc lusted obsessively only after sexy, disturbed, manipulative women whom he despised. This scenario was a direct replay of Doc's pathological relationship with his mother. Doc's mother was a nasty, disturbed, manipulative woman who had repeatedly and systematically rejected him. She placed him in a series of foster homes before he was one year old, and she kept switching him to a different family as soon as she saw the child had grown attached to his foster parents. When he was 12, she finally relented and allowed Doc to live with her, but she was critical, cruel, and abusive to him and after nine months, she had him committed to an institution for wayward boys.

When he grew up, this man was severely handicapped by the very defenses that had allowed him to survive emotionally, namely the eroticization of his mother's cruelty. Although he was starved for affection, Doc was completely unable to respond erotically to women who were decent and loving. It is of interest that the only time he could remember feeling a surge of attraction for his loving girlfriend, Marie, was when she uncharacteristically yelled at him for a trivial oversight!

The following case illustrates a young woman who had a similar history and developed similar symptoms.

CASE 6.2—"Lucinda Skier": Erotization of Childhood Sexual Trauma and the Phobic Avoidance of Good Sexual Relationships

"Lucinda Skier," age 32, was a highly successful attorney at a prestigious Wall Street firm. Tall, slim, attractive, and elegant, Lucinda was divorced and lived with her little daughter.

Lucinda had no problem attracting men. In fact, they were drawn to this beautiful "trophy" woman as though she were a magnet. Wherever she went—to the office, law court, her gym, ski trips, and the many social events she was always being invited to—the stunning Lucinda was invariably the object of male attention. This suited Lucinda, who loved sex, and she had had a number of affairs since her divorce two years ago.

But Lucinda never seemed to be able to make relationships work. This young woman was invariably interested in men who were physically attractive but, without exception, unavailable, elusive, withholding, and sometimes downright sadistic to her. Some of her lovers were married or deeply involved with other women; others had clear track records of avoiding long-term relationships.

At one time, she was obsessed with a psychopathic French ski instructor, who abandoned her alone in Paris after having asked her to make the transatlantic flight (at her own expense) to meet him there.

Moreover, Lucinda managed to bring out the worst and most sadistic qualities in men, so that even those who might have had the potential for becoming decent partners wound up treating her shabbily.

On the other hand, whenever a warm, decent, substantial man showed an interest in Lucinda, she became extremely anxious. If her anxious, panicky behavior did not turn the man off, Lucinda immediately shifted into the next line of defense. She would then become hypercritical of her hapless suitor and lose all interest. In other words, instead of feeling attracted to men who were kind, generous, and admiring, Lucinda was sexually and emotionally repelled.

Thus, a handsome, warm, wealthy, intelligent investment banker who pursued Lucinda ardently was "too short," while an athletic, successful, young entrepreneur who fell madly in love with her was "too inexperienced sexually."

Another of Lucinda's suitors, the handsome heir to a famous family fortune, arranged to meet her while she was in London on a business trip. Adam procured two tickets for a play Lucinda had wanted to see. He hired a limo stocked with iced champagne and brought her an orchid. After the play he took her to a delightful party at Buckingham Palace. When she returned from her trip, Lucinda announced that she was through with Adam because he was "simply too materialistic" for her (a curious objection from a woman whose own earnings were in the six figures and who adored luxuries). Lucinda promptly introduced Adam to one of her friends, to whom he is now happily married.

This patient's sad history is typical of persons who are destined to become enslaved by their erotic fantasy of yearning for love and approval from the very persons who had treated them cruelly when they were children. This young woman's father was a sadistic man and a drug addict who had openly rejected Lucinda, forbidding her to come to his apartment although he lived in the same neighborhood. Never much of a presence in the house, her father abandoned the family altogether when Lucinda was eight years old; he went to live openly with an 18-year-old model, to the patient's great embarrassment.

Since the father was chronically absent and Lucinda's mother was regularly incapacitated in an alcoholic stupor, the child was often left in the care of her older brother. The brother was a handsome, charming and popular boy who had problems of his own. He alternated between acting lovingly and protectively towards his little sister and rejecting her in an incredibly cruel manner, without any apparent provocation on Lucinda's part.

Yet, Lucinda never gave up trying to please her sadistic brother and her psychopathic father, seeking to win their affection even though both often left her in tears.

It is important to note that this patient, like many others with similar problems and similar histories, was entirely unaware of the self-induced elements of her aversion to appropriate partners, which was ruining her life. Moreover, she initially resisted my attempts to make her aware of the connection between the emotional damage she had sustained as a child at the hands of her parents and brother and her current difficulty with men.

Rejection Sensitivity

I always look for signs that a patient has a tendency to overact to rejection and criticism, for this can be a most important issue in the psychopathogenesis of sexual desire disorders.

The excessive sensitivity to rejection probably has a constitutional element that is often present from early childhood on and acts to amplify the malignant consequences of all the painful experiences of childhood. Moreover, excessive rejection sensitivity is frequently the critical underlying cause of a couple's marital problems or of a patient's lack of desire for the partner.*

Rejection-sensitive individuals are so vulnerable to rejection that they may be virtually disabled emotionally by the slights or put-downs directed toward them by their partners. These individuals often unconsciously protect themselves from the toxic and devastating effects that rejections by their lovers can have on them by avoiding intimacy, commitment, and monogamous attachments altogether. "Putting all their eggs in one basket," that is to say, for a man to allow himself to love a woman and also to feel sexually drawn to her, or for a woman to permit herself to lust after a man on whom she is dependent, may, on an unconscious level, represent an unacceptable emotional risk for extremely rejection-sensitive, vulnerable persons. Without being fully aware that this is motivated by their underlying fears of rejection, many of these people have learned to protect themselves by drawing away from their partners, emotionally and sexually, at the first hint of criticism or the slightest indication of less than absolute approval or acceptance.

The importance of detecting a history of rejection sensitivity during the evaluation, apart from clarifying the deeper causes of a couple's sexual desire disorder, is that the conduct of treatment will have to be especially adapted to the patient's ultra sensitivity to criticism. This can make the process of sex therapy a little difficult. This topic is discussed further in Chapter 9, which deals with the subject of psychopathology in the partner.

ASSESSMENT OF THE RELATIONSHIP

When psychoanalytically oriented therapists conceptualize and formulate the pathogenesis of sexual desire disorders, they focus primarily on the nature and the origins of their patients' intrapsychic sexual conflicts and on the deficits in their object relationships. Consequently, in their evaluation of patients with HSD, psychodynamically oriented clinicians tend to look for oedipal and pre-oedipal material (Kernberg, 1974A, 1974B; Scharff, 1982; Person, 1988).

On the other hand, systems-oriented therapists believing that the

*Excessive rejection sensitivity is similar in some respects to, and may be confused with, narcissistic personality disorder, but lacks the malignant dimension of that syndrome.

couple's pathological interpersonal interactions and their dysfunctional marital systems are the critical causes of sexual dysfunctions focus their inquiry on the dynamics and the structure of the couple's relationship and on the quality of their communications (Masters & Johnson, 1970; Masters et al., 1994; Verlust & Heyman, 1979; Lief, 1985).

I believe that sex therapists ought to remain eclectic on this issue, first because there is no inherent contradiction in these two approaches, and also because both have merit and are valid in different clinical situations.

Sometimes the symptomatic partner clearly has significant intrapsychic conflicts, which would surface in any relationship, about melding sexual passion with emotional closeness; in other instances, the sexual desire problem is obviously the product of the couple's specific pathological interactions. And in some cases the therapist must deal with a complex network of intrapsychic *and* interpersonal pathology.

The question of whether the patient's sexual desire disorder is due primarily to his or her intrinsic sexual conflicts, fears, or guilt, or to the couple's interpersonal problems is of more than theoretical interest, because this will, of course, determine the thrust of treatment.

If the low-desire patient has a pattern of repeatedly losing sexual interest in long-term relationships, or if the sexual aversion is clearly the product of early sexual abuse, the psychotherapeutic aspects of treatment will focus on bypassing or resolving the symptomatic patient's inner conflicts about sex, love, and intimacy, or on working through his/her memory of the sexual trauma.

On the other hand, if the deeper cause of the patient's sexual avoidance is the hostility that is poisoning his/her current relationship, it becomes the aim of the conjoint therapy sessions to work on the couple's malignant interpersonal interactions so as to defuse their anger, resolving their power struggles or improving their inadequate communications.

I usually leave the assessment of the relationship for the last part of the diagnostic interview.

By this time, I have a fairly good sense of their sexual interactions. Now I want to get a quick "snapshot" of the couple's life together, apart from their sexual functioning, and also a very brief history of their relationship.

The Current Relationship: Love and Anger

I usually begin this portion of the interview by asking a few open-ended questions about mundane and trivial aspects of the couple's life together. This can reveal a great deal about how they treat each other, how sensitive or insensitive they are to each other, if they love each other, and how solid their relationship is. A review of the details of their daily transactions may also begin to reveal what sorts of problems they have.

"How do you get along apart from sex? How much time do you usually spend together? How do you feel when you hear his key in the door? What does he/you do when he first comes home? What do you like to do together? Do you miss him/her when he/she is away? Do you like to tell him about your day? Listen to his/hers? Does anything particularly annoy you about him/her? What does he/she do that makes you mad? Do you fight about anything in particular? What?"

The answers, plus the partners' affect and body language, give me a good, quick sense of the status of the couple's relationship.

Anger

Anger at the partner is the most common and serious underlying cause of partner-specific loss of desire. The examiner should try to gauge the depth of the anger that the partners feel toward each other and to judge how serious their differences are. It is especially important to figure out what it would take to defuse the couple's quarrels. Buried anger is probably the most important deeper relationship cause of sexual desire disorders and, unless the anger between the partners can be resolved, at least to the point where they both want to improve their sexual relationship, sex therapy is likely to fail. I agree with Harold Lief's position (personal communication) that couples whose relationship is in serious trouble are poor candidates for sex therapy. These patients should be offered marital therapy and then reevaluated for the treatment of their sexual dysfunction after their relationship has improved to a point where helping them make love together starts to make sense.

The case of "Peter & Pearl Traveler" (Case 8.6), which will be described more fully in Chapter 8, illustrates how anger can destroy sexual desire and how the resolution of anger can pave the way for sexual recovery.

Pearl was a traditional woman who had suppressed a good deal of ambivalence towards her husband for many years. Her anger erupted out into the open when she learned that Peter had been unfaithful to her and had exposed her to a venereal disease. She subsequently developed a severe aversion to him.

Peace was restored in this marriage and sexual relations were resumed only after the couple renegotiated their marriage contract and changed their lifestyle so that this was more in concert with Pearl's needs.

However, the scars that deep anger leave cannot always be removed. The next case is one of a group of six I have seen wherein the anger of the injured parties was so deep that, even though they remained in the relationship, they never had sex with their partner again.

In this case, the husband redressed the grievances of his outraged spouse. Even though this succeeded in defusing her anger, his repentance and generous reparations had no impact on her sexual aversion, which was never resolved.

CASE 6.3—"Alex and Alexandra Hollywood": Sexual Aversion Due to Marital Anger

The patient, Alexandra, was a beautiful young model, age 28, who was married to Alex Hollywood, a dapper, 68-year-old, thrice married, extremely successful and wealthy real estate developer, who was known for his generosity to charitable organizations and liberal political causes.

Initially, Alexandra had been genuinely and deeply in love with her husband, and the couple had enjoyed a wonderful sexual relationship that was rich, playful, fantasy-spiced and mutually gratifying. However, the shrewd old man tricked his wife into signing a predatory pre-nuptial agreement, that would have left her penniless if the marriage were ever dissolved.

Initially naive, it did not take this bright young woman long to figure out that she had been duped. At first, she could not believe that "her wonderful, generous Alex," whom she had trusted completely, could have deliberately put her at such a disadvantage. At first she blamed the lawyers for having drawn up such an unconscionable contract, and she pleaded with her husband to modify this. He flatly refused and told her that their prenuptial agreement was not negotiable. This tough, old "wheeler and dealer" could not stop himself from treating his young wife like a business adversary, and the couple got into a bitter struggle.

When Alex stonewalled Alexandra, she was seized by a smoldering rage and lost all interest in having sex with him. Finally, feeling totally frustrated, she moved out of the house, proceeded to have an affair with a handsome and athletic young surgeon, and filed for divorce.

When he learned of Alexandra's new romance, Alex became completely obsessed and begged her to come back to him. He wept and pleaded and promised her millions of dollars if she would only forgive him.

Eventually, this couple remarried, this time without any prenuptial agreement and with a generous cash settlement for her up front, to boot.

But Alexandra could never regain the passion she had once felt for Alex before the struggle about money, and the deception surrounding it, poisoned their relationship. Even though on a conscious level Alexandra was no longer angry with her husband, her sexual aversion to him persisted. Moreover, she resisted all my attempts to resolve this in therapy.

Alexandra stayed with Alex until he died, several years later. However, she distanced herself from him emotionally, and occupied herself by starting her own business (with Alex's generous help). Although she was unfailingly attentive and kind to her husband, and very solicitous during his terminal illness, she never slept with him again.

The male libido is not immune to the corrosive effects of anger, as will be illustrated by the case of "Solomon Weiser" (Case 9.2). This man's frustration and rage at his difficult, provocative, obese, castrating, borderline wife was such that, even though he could have made love to her and on a conscious level thought he should, he could not get himself to boost his desire with fantasy in order to do so.

I do not mean to imply that these angry patients deliberately withhold sex in order to punish their partners. Some persons do this, of course, but willfully avoiding sex does not constitute a sexual desire disorder. In genuine HSD, the decrease in sexual interest is entirely beyond the person's voluntary control.

The History of the Couple's Relationship

The history of the couple's relationship is rarely explored in depth during the initial evaluation, except if this seems particularly germane. In those cases, the couple might be asked to talk about any crises they have weathered together, such as illness, bankruptcy, problems with children, etc., and to tell me how these were resolved and how this affected their relationship. Once again, particular attention is given to uncovering any smoldering resentments that might have been left over from the past and could still be impacting negatively on the sexual aspects of the marriage.

Love at First Sight

It is my custom to ask each couple how they met, and how they felt when they first saw each other. I ask this because the partners' first reactions to each other can sometimes provide clinically relevant information.

In a small unpublished study of long-enduring romantic relationships, I found to my surprise that both partners of every one of the 19 couples I had selected for the study, because they still felt intense sexual desire for each other after they had been together for 20 years or more, reported that they had literally fallen in love at first sight, or within the first few minutes of their meeting.

It was striking that these men and women, who came from a wide range of socioeconomic and ethnic groups, all told the same story, and in very similar words. In each case, both partners maintained that the first time that they looked at each other, they had felt an instantaneous, deep excitement and sexual attraction. They all claimed they "knew" that something "special" had happened when they first caught sight of each other. In addition to the sexual attraction, every person reported that he or she had also experienced a simultaneous welling of affection. Each described this as a feeling of closeness, familiarity, and tranquility. "I felt at home with him/her," or "I felt complete," or "I felt relief—like I had found what I was looking for" are typical expressions of this aspect of the experience. Each person reported that he or she "knew" absolutely and instantly that they would marry, and these pairs seldom if ever parted after their first meeting. These fortunate folks tend to treasure their relationships, and sparkle in animation when they talk about each other.

I have speculated that these men and women were describing the experience of bonding romantically with their partner, very rapidly. Further, I believe that such rapid, mutual bonding occurs only between two people who are each other's sexual fantasy. In contrast to most human pairs, these rapid, intense bonders seem to remain each other's sexual fantasy until death does them part.

I do not mean to imply that excellent marriages and relationships cannot develop between two people who did not fall in love at first sight, and who are not exactly each other's fantasy. There is no question that "slow starters" can have wonderful, rewarding, erotic relationships, and there are many excellent marriages between people who do not fit each other's sexual ideal precisely.

But as a diagnostic marker, a history of an instant mutual attraction may well denote that the two partners are destined to remain each other's sexual fantasy, and that the romantic bond between them is likely to endure.

Pathological Relationship Patterns: The Inability to Meld Erotic Passion and Emotional Closeness

There are people who seem to be "unlucky in love," whose romantic relationships never work out. These unfortunate individuals fall into two categories: Some always pick the wrong partners, and the others find nice partners, but always manage to destroy their relationships.

The last item of information that the examiner needs to determine is to this point. In other words, prior to commencing treatment, one should know whether the patient's lack of sexual interest in, or aversion to, the partner represents an intrinsic repetitive pathological pattern or is due to a specific fault in the current relationship.

The first of these pathological patterns, the *habitual attraction* to *inappropriate, unavailable, or destructive* partners, has already been discussed on page 137, and was illustrated by the case of Lucinda Skier (Case 6.2). The other malignant dynamic that is frequently seen in couples with sexual desire disorders is the *inability to sustain passionate feelings within a close committed relationship.*

The capacity to meld emotional closeness with sexual passion is a fundamental requisite of monogamous pair bonding. A person's inability to fuse these two major components of romantic love is a frequent and challenging issue in partner-specific HSD.

This pathological pattern can be readily detected by a history of a serial loss of sexual interest in long-term committed relationships.

Individuals with intimacy-passion splits are perfectly capable of *falling* in love, but they have trouble *staying* in love.

These men and women experience normal feelings of desire and passion in the early stages of a relationship. However, if the partner looks for more of a commitment or a greater degree of intimacy, at a certain point, a point that exceeds these individuals' psychic "safety zones," they shift into a critical, countersexual mode, and lose their erotic interest in the partner. Arlene Novick (personal communication, Wednesday conference) has characterized this pattern as an "addiction to the courtship phase," because such persons feel "high" when they are pursuing a new love, go into "withdrawal" when the courtship ends, and often develop the habit of frequently changing partners.

The family histories of patients with intimacy-passion splits often reveal one of two types of "deeper" causes: 1) the *reawakening of the incest taboo,* and 2) *painful early emotional attachments.*

Both issues have been discussed in earlier parts of the book. To recapitulate very briefly, the *incest taboo,* which results in an inhibition of sexual desire, can be reactivated in adults by situations reminiscent of the early family structure. This includes living in very close quarters, sharing the same facilities and the same space, and especially using the same bathroom as the partner. In several of our cases, a change in a couple's living arrangements, to more romantic and less incestuous, had a therapeutic effect on the couple's level of desire.

The inability to meld emotional closeness with sexual passion is hardly surprising in persons who sustained substantial emotional damage in early life. These individuals simply feel safer reserving their erotic feelings and desires for strangers who cannot get close enough to hurt them.

The tendency to split passion and intimacy has been called the "Madonna-whore" complex. This is a misnomer because, although this conflict is more often seen in males, some women are also afflicted by the inability to experience sexual passion within a long-term committed relationship.

TERMINATING THE DIAGNOSTIC INTERVIEW

The initial session marks the beginning of the therapeutic process. In addition to eliciting the massive amount of information that is required in order to understand the patient's or the couple's sexual problem and to advise them properly, an equally important objective of the first visit(s) is to *engage the patient and the partner in the treatment process, and to begin to form the crucial therapeutic alliance with them both.*

For the couple's comfort and for the sake of the future therapeutic relationship, it is wise to leave sufficient time at the end of the interview to sum up the examiner's impressions of their situation clearly and to make treatment recommendations. Time should also be reserved for addressing any questions and concerns that may have been raised by the interview.

The examiner should try to balance veracity with regard to the seriousness of the couple's sexual problem with emphasis on the positive aspects of their relationship, as this will set the tone for future sessions.

And, above all, one should try to leave with these strangers who, at your behest, have shared the intimate details of their sex lives with you and risked exposing their vulnerabilities, the impression that you understand and are empathetic with both partners' pain and frustration and that you will do your very best to help them.

CHAPTER 7

Treatment I: Patients with Desire Disorders—Theoretical Considerations

The psychodynamically oriented sex therapy approach to psychogenic disorders of sexual desire is a brief form of treatment that combines behavioral/cognitive concepts and techniques with psychodynamic interventions. More specifically, therapeutically structured sexual interactions in the form of behavioral "homework assignments" are used to modify the immediate cause(s) of the patient's deficient libido, and these are integrated with brief, active psychodynamically oriented explorations of the couple's deeper emotional problems and their resistances to treatment (Kaplan, 1974, 1979, 1987, 1995).

This same integrated therapy model has been widely used to treat the genital phase dysfunctions. However, the behavioral and cognitive therapeutic interventions that were developed to treat orgasm and erectile disorders are not very effective for HSD, and the therapeutic homework tasks assigned to these patients have evolved into very different forms. Further, as will be discussed below, completely different behavioral protocols are used for the two kinds of sexual desire disorders.

However, no special differences have ever been found in the character of the deeper causes. Therefore, since the same underlying problems must be dealt with, the psychodynamic aspects of therapy are essentially the same for all patients with psychosexual dysfunction. Once again, the only consistent difference that distinguishes this phase of the treatment of patients and couples with sexual desire disorders is that therapy tends to be lengthier than the 14 office sessions that are average for patients with psychogenic genital dysfunctions, since there is likely to be more resistance to treatment.

THE BEHAVIORAL/COGNITIVE ASPECTS OF TREATMENT

It is the express purpose and design of the behavioral/cognitive interventions to modify the patients' compulsive countersexual behaviors that constitute the immediate causes of HSD. *This is critical because, once again, it is a basic axiom of integrated sex therapy that a successful treatment outcome for patients with sexual desire disorders depends entirely on the elimination or modification of the immediate cause(s) of the sexual symptom.*

In other words, the patients' sex drive will increase only as long as the immediate, currently operating causes of their deficient desire can be permanently modified. However, if patients continue to engage in their habitual countersexual thought processes and behaviors, their sexual motivation will remain down-regulated and their sex life will not improve, regardless of whether or not they gain insight into their underlying conflicts and/or the couple have resolved the difficulties in their relationship (Kaplan, 1979, 1980a, 1980b, 1987, 1995).

Modifying the Immediate Causes of Hypoactive Sexual Desire: Some Common Therapeutic Sigs*

Different specific behavioral treatment protocols have been devised for each of the genital phase dysfunctions.** This kind of therapeutic specificity was feasible for erectile and orgasm dysfunctions simply because the immediate causes of these syndromes tend to be singular.

For example, the *immediate cause* of psychogenic erectile dysfunctions almost invariably involves sexual performance anxiety, and every treatment program that is used for this syndrome is built around a sequence of "non-demanding" sexual exercises, to reduce the impotent patient's performance fears (Masters & Johnson, 1970; Masters et al.,

**Sig* is from the Latin "sigma," a term which refers to the physician's directions regarding the manner in which the prescribed medication is to be taken, and is used here to denote the *behavioral prescriptions* which are given to patients in psychosexual therapy.

**The behavioral treatment of the psychosexual dysfunctions has been described by a number of authors including Masters & Johnson, 1974, 1994; Kaplan, 1974, 1975, 1979, 1980a; Leiblum & Rosen, 1988; Apfelbaum, 1988; Althof, 1988; Barbach, 1976; LoPiccolo & LoPiccolo, 1978; Araoz & Bleck, 1982.

1994; Kaplan, 1974, 1992a, 1993a, 1995; Zilbergeld, 1992; LoPiccolo, 1988, 1992; LoPiccolo & Lobitz, 1978; Althof, 1988).

In the same vein, the standard treatment for vaginismus, on a behavioral level, is the gradual, systematic dilatation and stretching of the patient's spastic vaginal muscles, since this is the sole *immediate* cause of that disorder (Kaplan, 1974, 1975, 1987; Leiblum et al., 1988).

In contrast, the negative behaviors and cognitive processes by which patients with HSD down-regulate their sexual desires are subject to countless individual variations. This complexity and diversity have made it necessary to develop multiple treatment strategies and tactics to counteract each of these. Therefore, it is impossible to provide a single, standard therapeutic formula for this syndrome that is comparable in terms of uniformity to protocols that have been devised for the other sexual dysfunctions.

In the following section, some of the behavioral assignments and cognitive maneuvers that are commonly used in the treatment of psychogenic HSD are described. The list of possible assignments is huge and this represents only a sample to give the reader a sense of what transpires in psychodynamically oriented sex therapy with these patients.

It goes without saying that these interventions must be shaped and tailored to suit each individual patient's and couple's special dynamic needs. In clinical practice, innumerable combinations and permutations of these therapeutic interventions have been used in the treatment of different HSD patients. In fact, although there were similarities, in all the cases I have treated over the past 20 years, I have never once repeated the identical homework assignment.

Raising the Patient's Consciousness

As was mentioned in the previous chapter, most patients are totally unaware that they are unwittingly "turning themselves off." They tend to attribute their lack of sexual desire for their partners to "poor chemistry," and many resist the idea that this could be their own doing.

The first step in therapy is to raise the patients' level of consciousness about their countersexual behaviors and the anti-fantasies by which they have been suppressing their desire for their partners automatically, without conscious awareness, and to help them realize that they could gain a greater degree of voluntary control over their sexual feelings.

This is an important phase of treatment, as no improvement can be expected unless the patient first owns up to his/her role in the origin and maintenance of his/her desire problems.

Towards this goal, we confront patients with evidence of the specific negative antisexual thoughts, emotions, and behaviors they are using to "trick" their sex centers into behaving as though the person were facing a real danger and shutting down.

More specifically, at the beginning of each therapy session, the couple's experience with their last assignment is reviewed in detail and depth. This analysis provides the therapist with the information needed to identify the specifics of the patient's antisexual behavior(s).

For example, one of our trainees (Sara Rosenthal, MSW) recently asked a young woman with partner-specific HSD to look at an erotic videotape with her boyfriend. During the following session, the patient reported that she had not become aroused. The therapist's astute interrogation regarding the details of the patient's experience elicited the following highly relevant facts:

1. The patient remembered thinking that the tape was "silly."
2. She was annoyed by the "phony" way the couple got "right into fucking."
3. She was worried that her boyfriend would be turned off (he was not).

The couple did not make love that evening, but the next day, when the young woman was alone, she recalled the videotape, became highly aroused, and masturbated to orgasm.

The exploration of this incident gave the therapist the opportunity to point out to the patient that she actively down-regulated and suppressed her sexual feelings when she was with her lover, and that she did this by dwelling on negative thoughts and avoiding registering the stimulating parts of the tape. By contrast, when she was alone, she did not engage in negative thinking and she allowed herself to become aroused.

It is important for the therapeutic alliance that the therapist point out the self-induced elements of the patient's lack of desire, carefully and in an empathic, nonjudgmental, and supportive manner that avoids creating the impression that the patient is being blamed for the sexual problem.

Once patients have recognized and accepted the fact and understand the means by which they turn themselves off, they are ready to proceed with the cognitive/behavioral exercises, which are designed to help them control and modify these compulsive negative behaviors.

Accentuating the Positives and Decentuating the Negatives

The major thrust of the cognitive interventions for patients with HSD is to reverse their habitual selective focus on negative perceptions, images, thoughts, and emotions, along with their concomitant avoidance of positive psychic and physical erotic input, and to get them to focus on the positive elements of the situation instead.

In other words, we attempt to get these patients to allow themselves to fantasize and to expose themselves to erotic physical stimulation. At the same time they should focus on the partner's attractive features and ignore the negatives as do normal people who wish to have a good time in bed with their lovers.

Assignments that help patients recognize and learn how to counteract their dysfunctional antisexual thoughts and negative emotional processes vary according to the particular circumstances and to the particular defenses against sexual arousal that each patient uses.

Patients who become or make themselves too tense to get absorbed in the sexual experience may be taught a variety of relaxation techniques that they can use to make them comfortable before they initiate sex. Towards this end, we may suggest that they take a warm shower or listen to music or to more formal relaxation tapes that can be prepared for individual patients. With others, we may suggest that they spend some time communicating their feelings, concerns, and vulnerabilities to their partners prior to physical lovemaking, and that they make close emotional contact, which can go a long way to relieve the tension. And in some cases, we prescribe short-acting, antianxiety substances.

"Priming the Pump"*

Many HSD patients interfere with the buildup of their sexual desire by commencing their countersexual obsessing prior to entering the bedroom. To counteract this defense against sexual desire, we give these patients the responsibility for putting themselves into an erotic state of mind *before* they attempt to initiate sex with their partners.

Patients with deficient desire for their partners are always admonished against attempting to have sexual intercourse if they are unable to manage to "prime their pump," or to turn on their "pilot light"** If

*The phrase, "priming the pump," was coined by William Masters (Schwartz & Masters, 1988).

**This expression should be credited to Arlene Novick (Wednesday Conference).

they are unable to put themselves into a receptive frame of mind, they are asked to postpone having sex until they succeed in putting themselves in the mood. This therapeutic intervention serves to interrupt the cycle of negative reinforcement and functional difficulties that may occur when a person tries to make love without feeling desire, and then finds difficulty in functioning.

In addition and at the same time, patients may be given mental and physical assignments that entail fantasy or erotica to heighten their arousal and to distract them from their sexual anxieties and their anti-fantasies.

Sexual Fantasy as a Therapeutic Tool

As has been discussed previously, erotic fantasy is a powerful inciter of sexual desire and an integral part of normal human sexuality. I believe that people who *think* that they don't have sexual fantasies are probably among those lucky individuals whose partner actually happens to *be* their sexual fantasy. In other words, when the lover approximates the person's sexual ideal or fantasy closely, virtual and actual erotic reality are so congruent that they appear to be identical.

Persons whose fantasies are not what they wish them to be—feminists who are aroused by rape fantasies; liberals who have sadistic erotic fantasies; macho men who are turned on by masochistic fantasies of being dominated by a woman, etc.—often ask therapists to help them change these.

But there is no such thing as a "sick" fantasy. Our sexual fantasies are the logical consequences of the developmental cause and effect processes discussed in Chapter 3. More specifically, it was postulated that the origins of paraphilic fantasies and desires involve the child's eroticization of painful early relationships and traumatic events, and that any youngster who is emotionally or sexually abused is likely to develop atypical sexual fantasies.

I am firmly convinced that usually, by the time a person reaches adulthood, his or her erotic fantasies are permanently "set" and impervious to outside influences. I further believe that it is useless and potentially harmful for professionals to attempt to tamper with their patients' erotic fantasies.

Rather, I feel it to be my task to help patients to take full advantage of the erotic potential of their sexual fantasies, be this for the purpose of improving their sexual relationships or simply to increase their own sexual pleasure when they masturbate.

Some persons habitually use erotica and fantasy to distance themselves from their partners, and this represents an undesirable defense against intimacy. But the *temporary* focus on fantasy and/or erotica to block out the patient's awareness of the partner can serve a major therapeutic function by "bypassing" sexual anxiety and allowing the patient to function. Fantasy training is especially useful with patients whose obsessive overconcern for pleasing their partners, performance anxieties, and/or fears of intimacy interfere with the buildup of their desire and functioning. Becoming absorbed in their fantasies may allow these persons to become sufficiently aroused to have successful sexual experiences with their partners. Further, the knowledge that they can rely on their fantasies to help them function can give these individuals the confidence they need to overcome their avoidance of sex.

With good responders to fantasy training, it is sometimes possible to shape the patient's erotic behavior gradually towards greater intimacy with the partner to a point where fantasy may no longer be a necessity. In other cases, however, the use of fantasy becomes a permanent part of that person's sexual behavior. Perhaps such an outcome is less than ideal, but the reliance on the use of and the sharing of sexual fantasy with the lover is certainly a better alternative than not having sex at all.

Arousal and Distraction

The capacity of fantasies to *arouse* and to *distract* can be exploited in sex therapy in various ways.

As has been mentioned above, patients can make good use of fantasy to "turn on their pilot light," that is, to put themselves in an erotic mood before they approach their partner. Also, the powerful aphrodisiac effects of sexual fantasy and erotica frequently provide a way to detour around the blocks erected by the patient's underlying sexual anxieties and fears of intimacy. This capability to"bypass" anxiety and ambivalence is perhaps fantasy's most valuable function in sex therapy.

Depending on the patient's particular needs, a variety of fantasy assignments may be given in the attempt to circumvent his/her sexual anxiety. Most commonly, patients whose desire for the partner is blocked are asked to immerse themselves in their favorite fantasy or in watching an erotic tape, and to "tune out" the partner, while making love.

If the situation warrants, we may suggest that the couple share their fantasies. Shared fantasy assignments may entail a couple taking turns providing physical genital stimulation to each other, while the receiver becomes absorbed in his/her sexual fantasies. However, any number of variations may be suggested. For example, the partner may be asked to verbalize the lower-desire person's fantasy out loud while making love. That is highly arousing to some normal people. However, before giving this assignment, one should be aware that other equally normal men and women are distracted and turned off by the partner's making sounds or talking during sex.

Or the assignment may entail that the couple stimulate each other while watching erotic videotapes together. In still another version, the lower-desire partner is asked to watch an erotic videotape that is known to arouse him or her or to look at erotic pictures or read arousing passages in a book as a "warm-up" prior to approaching the partner.

The aphrodisiac effects of fantasy and erotica can also be useful in facilitating sexual functioning *when the partner is not the person's sexual fantasy*, but the relationship is in other respects loving, compatible, and advantageous to both.

The aphrodisiac effects of shared fantasies are especially useful for enhancing the flagging sexual desires and improving the functioning of older couples who no longer turn each other on, as they did in the past, but who want to continue making love together.

Similarly, erotic fantasy can facilitate the continuance of sexual activity when one of the partners develops a physical problem that interferes with his/her own or the partner's sexual desire. For example, after undergoing a mastectomy, some women lose their desire to make love to their partner and/or are reluctant to risk making love to new sexual partners since some men are turned off by the missing breast. And yet, a loving, romantic, supportive relationship is an important element in the healing and well being of women with breast cancer (Spiegel et al., 1989; Kaplan, 1992b). Thus, the resumption of sexual activity is a worthwhile medical as well as psychological goal for such patients and couples, and the judicious and sensitive introduction of fantasy can form a "bridge" that facilitates their sexual recovery.

The use of fantasy to supplement the physical stimulation provided by the partner is often the only way to help maintain a sexual connection in couples who wish to stay together and have sex together, but where one of the partners is aroused by a noncongruent or variant fantasy, such as cross-dressing, bisexuality, group sex, pedophilia, S & M, etc., that does not interest the other. Nevertheless, the acceptance of the partner's incongruent fantasy can be a benefit to both. The incorporation of that particular fantasy into the couple's sexual behavior produces desire and arousal in the partner who could not function without this, and this very arousal and desire, irrespective of what the stimulus is, can become exciting to the other even if this fantasy did not originally arouse him/her. On that basis, therapy-assisted acceptance and use of fantasy has salvaged many otherwise positive relationships that would have foundered because the sexual fit between the partners was poor.

Erotica: Therapeutic and Diagnostic Functions

Erotica, like the fantasies it depicts, can also be used as a therapeutic tool to enhance sexual desire, bypass sexual anxiety, and distract patients from their antisexual thought processes. However some authors have objected to erotica because they believe that some types, such as sadomasochistic pornography and heterosexual x-rated material that depicts women in submissive roles, create violent and misogynistic sexual behaviors in consumers. But this is a myth. I am convinced by our clinical experience that *only that particular erotic material that taps into the person's preexisting sexual fantasy life*, which has been present since childhood, is consistently arousing. All other scenarios that are incongruent with the person's inner "love map" quickly become boring or may be perceived as negative.

The ability of erotica to target and illuminate latent erotic fantasies, which I consider akin to buried treasure, also makes this an ideal diagnostic instrument for detecting the hidden sexual fantasies of persons who have no conscious awareness of or access to these.

Some individuals with deficient sexual desire report that they have no sexual fantasies. In such cases, we make the assumption that these persons have blocked, repressed, or suppressed their sexual fantasies. With fantasy deficient low-desire patients, erotica can be employed in *a diagnostic capacity* as a probe to reveal potentially arousing hidden fantasies. More specifically, the patient is provided with the opportunity to react to a wide menu of erotic material, in the form of books, pictures, and videotapes. The patient's reactions to these are then analyzed during the therapy sessions. This process can lead to the discovery of unsuspected, latent, or previously suppressed sexual fantasies and desires, which then become accessible and useful in therapy.

The choice of material that we assign in the attempt to discover a patient's latent fantasies is dictated by the patient's cultural and educational background. We have suggested the works of Anais Nin, Nancy Friday, Henry Miller, D.H. Lawrence, and "Anonymous" Victorian paperbacks, as well as erotic letters and pictures in *Playboy* and *Hustler*.

Erotic and/or pornographic videos are especially effective in uncovering repressed fantasies, because people can get deeply absorbed in such visual material. Available films include some that were clearly produced for the purpose of sex education. These videotapes can be given to more traditional, inhibited patients, who might be offended by coarse or raunchy material. However, while such educationally oriented, "soft core"* videos are good for sex education and for desensitizing sexual anxiety, many persons don't find them very arousing.

Women patients who sometimes object to images of erect phalluses spurting semen may find romantic "soft-core" porn films, such as the "Emanuelle" series and *The Last Tango in Paris,* easier to tolerate as a first exposure to erotica. For similar reasons, the female-oriented, erotic videotapes produced by "Fem Productions" are acceptable to some women who are put off by male-oriented films. These products are especially useful for discovering latent female fantasies.

There are also vast numbers of excellent homoerotic porno films available that can be extremely arousing to homosexual and bisexual men and women, as well as to heterosexuals of both genders.

In our experience, for most low-desire patients, the XXX-rated, "hard core" videotapes, that depict explicit erotic scenes, sexual body parts, and a wide variety of "normal" as well as atypical, perverse, or paraphilic themes are potentially the most arousing and therefore the most useful for probing for latent erotic fantasies and also as adjuvants to therapy.

The recent advent of "*telephone-sex*," which enables men to dial a number and for a fee hear a female voice describing a variety of explicit erotic scenes on the phone, has added another erotic diagnostic tool and nonchemical aphrodisiac to the sex therapist's armamentarium.

The Therapeutic Uses of Masturbation

Masturbation, like sexual fantasy, is a normal, integral part of human sexual behavior.

Masturbation is the earliest form of human sexual expression. Most babies reach for their genitalia as soon as hand coordination permits; reinforced by the pleasurable sensations that this yields, the activity can soon become habitual. However, early masturbatory behavior can also become the occasion for the beginnings of sexual shame, guilt, fear, and conflict, when parents who are uncomfortable with their own sexuality, as well as those with moralistic, antisexual attitudes, greet their youngster's early masturbatory explorations with disapproval, embarrassment, rejection, and even harsh physical punishment.

Despite the subsequent guilt and shame about masturbation that is the frequent residue of such punitive attitudes towards youngsters' earliest sexual expressions, the majority of men and women in our society

---

*"Soft core," erotica, by definition, depict no erect or ejaculating peni.

have experienced their first orgasm through self-stimulation and, while masturbatory orgasms are seldom as exciting or as pleasurable as the ones that are shared with a lover, self-stimulation remains for most women and also for many men the easiest and most reliable way to achieve a climax.

Masturbation assignments are valuable therapeutic tools in sex therapy, where they are deployed to serve numerous purposes.

Masturbation sigs are often given to sexually blocked patients as a starting point from which their sexual ranges can later be expanded to encompass sexual partners. As will be described in Chapter 8, masturbating by herself while using fantasy was one of the early therapeutic homework assignments prescribed for Greta Biedemeyer" (Case 8.1), the severely sexaphobic and aversive patient who has been mentioned in previous chapters. Therapist-guided self-stimulation together with fantasy was also a critical intervention in the treatment of "Mrs. Traveler," the sexaphobic wife of the unfaithful husband (Case 8.6) and that of "Bill Kangaroo" (Case 8.2), the 41-year-old virgin who had been seduced by his mother.

Depending on the situation, masturbation sigs may be assigned for the patient to do alone, as mentioned above, or during or after sexual contact with the partner.

For patients who are blocked with their partners, but who have a normal response with self-stimulation, we may assign "parallel masturbation" sigs. In these exercises, the couple begin their lovemaking with foreplay and/or genital stimulation, or they may watch an erotic videotape together. At a certain point of arousal, both the low-desire and the high-desire partner "finish off" with self-induced orgasms.

In other situations, the low-desire partner may be asked to let the high-desire partner stimulate him or her, and to stop when his/her arousal plateaus. Next, the patient is asked to masturbate to orgasm in the partner's presence. When the patient's sexual inhibition is especially severe, we may "reduce" the assignment and ask him/her to masturbate alone in another room, after engaging in erotic foreplay with the partner.

The clinical application of this therapeutic masturbation sig will be illustrated in the treatment of "Joe Senator" (Case 8.7), the patient who would not allow himself to fantasize in the presence of his partner.

Many patients are initially ashamed of or embarrassed at self-stimulation assignments and resist them, especially if these entail masturbating in front of the partner. But if the partner is supportive or, as is frequently the case, actually *aroused* by watching the lover masturbate, this can be very salutary in beginning the process of moving the couple towards greater intimacy and shared eroticism.

The therapist's view of masturbation as a natural act, as well as his/her encouragement and "permission" for patients to enjoy self-stimulation, especially when this is supplemented by the partner's positive responses, can be a corrective emotional experience and very liberating for individuals whose negative view of onanism contributes to their inability to function with their partners.

Adverse Reactions

A word of caution is in order. Fantasy, the enjoyment of erotica and masturbation, or "spilling seed," are regarded as mortal sins by Orthodox Jews and devout Roman Catholics, and these exercises should *not* be assigned to patients belonging to these denominations except as a last resort. Even though they are powerful remedies, these interventions are not absolutely essential for curing patients with sexual desire disorders, and the creative therapist can usually find alternatives.

For example, when an Orthodox Jewish man told me he was not allowed to visualize women other than his wife in erotic poses, I asked him to put his wife into the "picture." Imagining *his wife's* genitalia and breasts was effective in arousing this young husband's desire, without his having to commit "adultery in his heart."

Sometimes a partner objects to the therapist's suggestion that the symptomatic patient fantasize or use pornography to boost his sex drive. This presents a therapeutic dilemma that must be handled with upmost sensitivity (see page 188).

Modifying Maladaptive Masturbatory Techniques

Most men masturbate by stimulating their penis manually, in a rhythmic back and forth motion, while the majority of women reach their climax through a rhythmic rotary motion of their index finger on the clitoris. These common masturbation techniques translate readily into partner-oriented foreplay and intercourse.

However, some patients are accustomed to masturbating in atypical ways that do *not* transfer easily to partner-related sex. In fact, atypical masturbatory techniques may actually get in the way of sexual intercourse and can play a role in inhibiting a person's sexual desire.

When the sexual status examination has revealed that the patient's masturbatory behavior follows an idiosyncratic pattern that appears to be a factor in his/her inability to feel normal arousal and desire with the partner, "masturbatory retraining sigs" may be assigned to the patient alone before involving the partner in treatment.

Male maladaptive masturbatory techniques commonly entail methods of stimulation that allow the man to avoid touching his penis with his hands. These include "humping" against the bed, or transmitting friction to the penis by placing the organ between the thighs and tightening the setorius and other thigh muscles rhythmically.

Women who use atypical or nonmanual methods of stimulating themselves may also need "masturbatory retraining" as an important step in their sexual rehabilitation. These include women who habitually come by exposing their clitoris to running water and those who have accustomed themselves to climaxing when lying on the stomach and rhythmically tightening their thigh muscles or moving their genitalia against a pillow.

Sigs that Enhance Physical Stimulation: Sexual Skills Training

Physical stimulation is a powerful inducer of sexual desire in the partner in many species. For example, a certain type of male mosquito stimulates his partner orally by vibrating his proboscis at extremely high frequencies against her genitalia to get her in the mood, while the male otter bites the female's nose, and it is said that giraffes inflame their mates by gently nuzzling their necks.

Physical stimulation is also a very big "turn on" for human males and females. More specifically, both men and women, but especially women, become aroused by the lover's gentle or teasing touch, caress, and kiss. The skin of the entire body surface is potentially erotically responsive to sensitive and gentle stimulation, and certain erogenous areas tend to be especially exciting. Erogenous zones are highly individual and may in different people involve the breasts, buttocks, nipples, neck, toes, ears, thighs, etc.

Steady rhythmic stroking or sucking of the penis or the clitoris with the hands, mouth, and body, and during coitus, is the ultimate sexual incentor of human sexual desire and this orchestrates the crescendo of erotic sensations that leads to the climax.

There are gender differences with respect to erotic responses to physical stimulation, and these can lead to sexual difficulties in couples who do not communicate well in the area of sexuality. As a rule, women require more of a "warm-up" period of "foreplay" in the form of gentle, slow, body and breast caressing and kissing and teasing before they are fully receptive to the steady, rhythmic stimulation of the genitalia that precedes orgasm. On the other hand, men tend to become aroused more rapidly and are said to be more responsive, as a group, to visual than to tactile stimulation. But as men age, they increasingly need physical stimulation of their genitalia in order to attain and maintain their erections.

Skillful and unconflicted lovers know how to exploit the erotic power of physical stimulation to enhance the excitement of lovemaking.

For sexually open people, both *giving* and *receiving* sexual stimulation are important elements of their sexual fantasy, and arousing the partner and being aroused by him or her are equally exciting.

However, this may not be the case for patients with HSD. Many of these patients have problems and blocks about the giving and/or receiving of pleasure. In such cases, the improvement of the couple's sexual skills and techniques becomes a major goal of treatment. A number of therapeutic homework assignments and strategies are available for this purpose.

A patient recently asked me, after I suggested that her husband, whose poor lovemaking skills she (legitimately) complained about, needed to learn how to become a better lover, "But isn't sex a natural act? Can lovemaking really be learned?"

The basics of copulatory behavior *are*, in fact, genetically "hardwired" into our brains. However, as is true of all complex human functions, learning and experience are very important ingredients in shaping the final product, and all sorts of things can interfere with this process. Thus there are a number of reasons why lovers fail to provide each other with adequate physical stimulation. These range from simple shyness, physical clumsiness, and lack of experience in perfectly healthy individuals to severe aversions and revulsions, and the phobic avoidance of the partner's body and genitalia, which may constitute expressions of profound emotional and sexual conflict.

Many low-desire patients, more often women than men, fail to become sufficiently aroused because their partners do not know how to kiss them or how to stimulate their genitalia effectively. Even worse, some women complain that they are turned off because their partners are clumsy, irritate them, or hurt them, and are tense, awkward, and annoying when attempting to stimulate their genitalia. A common complaint of women is that men reach for the clitoris before they have had sufficient time to become aroused.

Their partners' precipitous "grabbing" of their genitals is a major turn off for most women. Since most males can be instantly aroused by the manipulation of their penis, men often fail to realize that their lovers react differently.

Men have also been known to blame their partners' poor sexual skills for their own lack of interest. Common male complaints about their wives and lovers include excessive passivity in bed, lack of responsiveness, sexual awkwardness, poor kissing, and unwillingness to provide oral sex.

The low-desire partner's complaints about the other's poor sexual technique are often merely a rationalization that serves to cover up his/her own sexual inhibitions. But there are cases where these complaints are legitimate and where the partner truly needs to improve his or her sexual skills.

Improving the Couple's Communications

On the assumption that most persons want to become better lovers and would enjoy pleasuring their partners if they knew how, sexual skills training often begins in the therapist's office with working on the couple's communications about sex. The partners are encouraged to air their experiences, complaints, and wishes in this sensitive area during the office sessions, under the protection of the therapist's constructive presence.

The therapist has the dual tasks of facilitating the couple's communications and also of intervening actively to preventing destructive interchanges.

For example, Mrs. Hummingbird, the wife of the hyperactive, bisexual man described previously (Case 4.3), responded to my question, "Tell me what you don't like about your husband's lovemaking," with a tirade: "My husband is a total disaster in the bedroom—he is infantile about sex—he calls it 'doing the dirty deed'—can you imagine that? Besides that, he is clumsy, awkward, and tense when he touches me, and he slobbers all over me when he kisses. No one could get turned on with this klutz!"

As she went on, the husband's body language began to resemble that of a beaten dog, and I spent much of the rest of the session trying to help Mrs. H express herself in a less judgmental, less accusatory, and ultimately more effective and constructive manner.

Sometimes, the problem is the reverse in that the low-desire patient does not speak up sufficiently. Not uncommonly, people are too shy or guilty to express their sexual wishes. In other cases, the mates of silent partners are overly sensitive to criticism and have subtly intimidated their partners into keeping their complaints to themselves. These long-suffering individuals are reluctant to make any suggestions regarding sex because they have learned that there is simply no way they can do this without upsetting their partner. Sexually silent persons should be coaxed to communicate their sexual feelings and complaints to their spouses, who in turn must be helped not to take such expressions as personal attacks.

Foreplay and "Dry Touching"

A variety of therapeutic assignments are used in sex therapy to improve, when necessary, the quality, duration, and intensity of the erotic physical stimulation that serves as a prelude for sexual intercourse. The first of these were the famous *sensate focus* exercises (SF). These therapeutic exercises were invented by Masters and Johnson in the 60s and remain a cornerstone of the treatment of psychogenic erectile dysfunction to this day (Masters & Johnson, 1970; Masters et al., 1994).

The SF exercises can provide patients with the opportunity to learn to enjoy the pleasures of slow, gentle, nonpressured, intimate exchanges of physical caresses of the nongenital parts of the body, and to attend to these physical sensations free of the performance pressures that can be so destructive to sexual feelings.

As was mentioned in the introductory chapter, these exercises are excellent for the treatment of performance-anxiety related genital dysfunctions, but SF can backfire when assigned to patients with sexual desire disorders. That is not to say that the SF exercises should never be used for patients with HSD. The SF exercises can be useful for carefully selected patients with low-desire syndromes, but only in specific situations. For example, the SF experience can help women who have low desire because their partners hurry through the "preliminaries." In these cases, the SF exercises can be effective for teaching the couple the techniques and enjoyment of touching and foreplay, as well as for improving their sexual skills.

However, when they are prescribed routinely and indiscriminately, without insight into the deeper dynamics of the patient's sexual anxieties or the couple's destructive interactions, SF can be countertherapeutic in patients with sexual desire disorders. That is because these patients do not suffer as much from *sexual performance anxiety* as they do from *sexual intimacy anxiety.*

In other words, many patients with HSD and sexual aversions have serious intimacy conflicts and these individuals feel uncomfortable about touching and being touched by their partners even when this is not a prelude to intercourse. Thus, they tend to experience the SF exercises as an unpleasant *intimacy pressure.* A number of our patients have complained that the assignments actually aggravated their negative feelings about physical intimacy with their partners. Some of these individuals reported feeling "exposed" and "trapped" by the therapist's SF assignments and pressured by their partner's expectation that they should enjoy this.

Similar considerations apply to the "*intimate shower exercises.*" This modification of the Masters and Johnson SF technique, which was developed by Dr. Mildred Witkin (personal communications, Wednesday conference), can be an excellent intervention for enhancing the quality of pre-intercourse physical stimulation, but, like SF, only in selected clinical situations.

For this exercise, patients are instructed to take showers together and to wash each other's bodies playfully and erotically. After they finish, they are supposed to dry each other, gently and tenderly. Sometimes the partners also powder each other and caress each other's body with lotion.

While this can be a delightful and salutary experience for certain patients with good libidos who are inhibited or performance-driven, physical-intimacy exercises such as SF and "intimate showering" can be pure torment for sexaphobic individuals who are devoid of sexual lust. For these reasons, I consider these interventions contraindicated for patients with desire disorders who are conflicted, frightened, and turned off by intimacy with the partner. *Paradoxically, intimacy-phobic, low-desire patients do much better, and their desire is much more likely to increase, when they are given "permission" to avoid intimacy by "tuning out" their partners with erotica or fantasy. When these emotionally claustrophobic individuals are not pressured by their therapists or badgered by their partners to behave intimately to a point that exceeds their "comfort" zones, they are more likely to be able to immerse themselves in their erotic feelings.*

Enhancing Intimacy

That is not to say that intimacy conflicts should always be ignored and "bridged over" with fantasy. Sometimes sex with a non-intimate partner can be very beautiful, esthetically satisfying, and arousing. But intimacy adds a profoundly human quality to the sexual experience, while sex with an attractive passerby is more like "a recreational experience," like a wonderful dance between two strangers.

While intimacy cannot be forced on a person by the therapist, there are a number of strategies that we use with couples where the lack of intimacy is a problem. Primarily, these involve helping the patient gain insight into the deeper and unconscious causes of his/her fear of emotional closeness and to trace their childhood origins. But in this brief format, we also rely greatly on the transference to and identification with the "intimate" therapist to modify the patient's behavior towards greater intimacy with the partner. Transference is a powerful change agent and to encourage intimacy, I frequently "model" the open exchange of feelings and thoughts and use (carefully limited) self-disclosures of my evoked feelings and similar experiences with couples during the therapy sessions. I also encourage the couple to do the same with each other while I "eavesdrop" and comment on the interchanges, "rewarding" expressions of intimacy with my approval.

It should be noted in this context that while sexual fantasy can be used to avoid intimacy, it is not in itself anti-intimate. To the contrary, genuine intimacy is created when one partner can admit to the other that he/she is aroused by a certain atypical fantasy, and when the other lovingly accepts this as an integral aspect of the beloved person.

Kissing, "Wet" Genital Stimulation, and Coital Positions

Dry touching paves the way for the even more exciting wet touch and kiss. Guiding a couple towards improving their "wet sex" skills usually begins with frank, detailed, explicit discussions during the office sessions about kissing, about manual and oral methods of stimulation, and also about various coital positions and techniques when this is relevant to the couple's sexual problem. It goes without saying that meaningful instructions can only be given by therapists who are experts about sexual techniques, and this is an important issue in our training program.

The couple are then asked to experiment with specific sexual techniques at home, and the results of their sexual explorations are scheduled for discussion for the next therapy session.

"Show me/teach me/and I'll show you/ teach you" homework is often assigned to raise the level of "wet-sex" skills. During these assignments, the couple take turns kissing each other and stimulating each other's genitalia manually, sometimes with lubricants, sometimes orally, sometimes with a vibrator, and so forth. We usually suggest that the partners give each other feedback about what feels good, better, and best to them, and what does not. Sometimes they communicate by "showing" and sometimes by "telling."

Taking Turns

"Taking turns" assignments can be useful for patients who have trouble focusing on their own sensations because they are distracted by their compulsive need to "do for" their partners. Individuals who are too embarrassed to communicate their sexual wishes openly to their partners can also benefit from the separation of the giving and the receiving of pleasure.

There are many variations of this exercise. For example, the couple may be told that one week it is the low-desire partner's turn to *receive* stimulation, while the other takes the role of "*giver*." The "receiver" is asked to remain entirely passive and to concentrate only on becoming absorbed in the sensations he/she is receiving. The following week, the roles may be reversed and the higher-desire partner becomes the recipient. This maneuver provides the couple with the opportunity to fine-tune their sexual interactions, that is to learn to "hear" each other, and to develop sensitivity to each other's erotic sensations, likes, and dislikes in the privacy of their home, with the luxury of reporting back to their "personal sex trainer" for guidance.

"Staying with the Pleasure" Sigs

Some patients are not able to *accept* the skillful body and breast caressing, nor the perfectly adequate genital stimulation that their lovers are willing and eager to provide. As was mentioned in Chapter 6, these individuals, more often women than men, become anxious when they feel themselves becoming aroused and losing control. At a certain point of excitement, these patients abort the incoming stimulation by interrupting their partners and preventing them from continuing with their caresses or kisses, so that they never have the chance to become fully aroused or absorbed in their sexual feelings.

We attempt to counteract this cause of deficient desire by giving the patient "stay with the stimulation" or "stay with the pleasure" assignments, where we ask them to try to "endure" the arousing erotic stimulation for progressively longer periods of time. Depending on the situation, genital stimulation may be provided by the patient him or herself or by the lover.

Electric Vibrators

Electric massagers or vibrators are highly effective for stimulating the clitoris.* As a matter of fact, the intense stimulation provided by an electric vibrator can override the milder forms of inhibition and the defenses that some women with desire problems have erected against the inflow of erotic sensations, so that many women experience their first orgasm with vibrator-assisted stimulation. The use of a vibrator by

*Some electric massagers are shaped liked an erect phallus and designed to be inserted into the vagina. Such devices are not useful for helping women achieve orgasm. However, electric massagers that have vibrating heads are excellent for this purpose when they are held against the clitoris.

the patient herself and/or together with her partner can enhance female erotic feelings, which in turn can arouse the partner. These devices are often incorporated into the homework assigned to patients with HSD.

While not as useful for male sexual problems, electric vibrators do have a place in enhancing sexual feelings, erections and ejaculations in men with physiologically diminished penile sensations, which is a common consequence of diabetic peripheral neuropathy and also occurs in a number of other circumstances, including advancing age.

Courtship and Dating Sigs

Courtship behavior normally precedes and paves the way for sexual intercourse by inducing a state of heightened sexual desire in the partner and making him/her more responsive to sexual stimulation.

As was discussed more fully in the section on the evolution of sexual desire, courtship is an ancient and elemental aspect of reproductive behavior that can be observed throughout the phylogenetic scale (Mitchell, 1979). Thus, to co-opt Cole Porter's immortal lyrics to "Let's Fall in Love": "toads do it" (by clinging to the female for hours until she lays her eggs); "peacocks do it" (by displaying their gorgeous tail feathers); "bower birds do it" (by building splendidly decorated courtyards—and the bird with the biggest tail and the nicest yard gets the most sex).

Courtship behavior also plays an important role in human sexual desire or the lack of thereof. Some sexually conflicted persons engage in "anti-courtship" behaviors. Instead of displaying their best qualities and creating a lovely intimate ambiance to please the object of their desire, they sabotage their sex lives by putting themselves in the worst possible light. Their harried, stressful, lifestyles and the dirty, sloppy, unattractive environments they present to their partners are not conducive to passion and romance. When this sort of counterseductive behavior is material in a couple's low sexual frequency and decreased sexual desire, we attempt to break up the malignant pattern by getting the partners to behave in a more courtly, enticing, seductive, and sexually tempting manner towards each other.

Couples who have neglected the romantic parts of their lives are often given "dating" sigs in the attempt to resurrect their old romantic courtship behaviors.

Therapeutically structured "courtship" interactions were used successfully in the treatment of "Nick and Toni Black" (Case 8.4), which will be described in detail in the next chapter. Briefly, Toni, the wife of this hardworking pair, had completely lost the passion she had once felt for her husband in their early years together. The restoration of this couple's sex life was accomplished, at least in part, by getting them to replay the initial courtship phase of their relationship. Their "date" assignment served its purpose by showing Nick and Toni that they could recapture the passion of their early years by behaving in more erotic ways with one another. This experience also provided them with insight into how they had allowed their sexuality to get lost in the frenzy of their pressured, overactive life.

It should be noted here that "dating" sigs, like the other behavioral and cognitive tactics and maneuvers described in this section, are effective in permanently changing the countersexual behaviors of patients and couples who do not have severe underlying conflicts. For massively angry, ambivalent, or incompatible couples, it does *not* get "better in the Bahamas," that is it say, romantic vacations are not curative, although a miserable experience in a beautiful romantic spot may well convince a couple of the necessity to resolve the deeper problems that are at the heart of their sexual difficulties.

Courtesy Towards the Partner Sigs

In a related maneuver, "prescriptions" that involve "being nice to the partner outside the bedroom" are often helpful in resolving a couple's sexual avoidance and/or their defenses against sexual feelings.

These interventions are useful in cases where the patient undermines his own and his partner's sexuality by failing to behave in a sufficiently pleasing or courteous manner, or by being elusive, distant, or downright obnoxious to the partner, thereby creating an unpleasant, hostile, uncomfortable, anti-intimate, antisexual atmosphere.

Certain persons don't know how to behave in an appropriate affiliative, warm and courteous manner towards their spouses, or they actively avoid doing so. Some of these individuals may have seen their own parents behaving badly towards each other, and they may not have had a model of appropriate marital behavior to emulate. Others simply express their angers and frustrations by treating the partner badly. Whatever the underlying reasons, this sort of behavior must change before there can be any hope of improving a couple's sexual relationship.

When inappropriately hostile behavior or a clearly counterseductive manner plays a role in a couple's lack of passion and in their low sexual frequency, their homework assignments may entail the straightforward corrective strategy of being *nice to the lover outside the bedroom.*

The process of prescribing "Be Nice" assignments provides an opportunity for the therapist to model *generosity and sensitivity to the partner's needs.* This is an appropriate intervention for couples where a partner's insensitivity or self-involvement is at the root of their difficulty.

The therapist must intuit what would have special meaning for the low-desire partner. Since this is so different in every case, the suggestions given to couples are by their very nature highly individualized and varied. Thus, I have suggested cooking the husband a special dinner, taking the wife out dancing, listening sympathetically to the other's problems, cleaning up a messy bedroom, letting him have a TV set in the bedroom, taking showers and brushing teeth and shaving prior to going to bed, giving up cigars, giving up pets, giving up TV for the evening, wearing silk negligees, bringing flowers, buying a special present, arranging a birthday party. In one case, a successful assignment for a serious, scholarly young husband, who was turning off his young bride with his endless, obsessive, joyless Talmudic preoccupations, consisted of taking her to her favorite Kosher pizza parlor prior to going home and making love to her.

When they are deployed with an understanding of the couple's underlying dynamics, these simplistic sounding suggestions can have very powerful impacts. When a formerly inconsiderate or insensitive partner begins to behave more courteously, the other often responds in a positive manner, and this can begin an upward spiral of improvement in the couple's relationship.

This is what actually happened after the seemingly silly "Kosher Pizza Parlor" sig. The young bride began to see that she had not, as she was beginning to fear, entered into a joyless life of drudgery with a man who was oblivious to her feelings, and she melted towards her husband who, in turn, was very touched by this and made a greater effort to please her.

However, some patients simply cannot bring themselves to be loving and warm to their partners. They resist the "Be Nice" sigs, on account of their deeper angers and defenses, which then become grist for the therapy mill.

The Therapist's Professionalism and Comfort with Sex

The therapeutic sexual homework assignments that were described above are much more likely to be on the mark if these are shaped by the therapist's understanding of the deeper dynamic infrastructure of the patient's inability to give and/or to receive effective sexual stimulation, than if the exercises are dispensed in a mechanical, cookbook fashion. Further, patients are more likely to comply with the therapeutically structured sexual interactions that are given to them as "homework" for improving their sexual skills, and these are more likely to be effective if the therapist is knowledgeable about human sexuality and experienced in treating sexual disorders.

Above all, it is important for the therapist to be comfortable with his/her own sexuality, so as to be able to ask the highly explicit questions that are necessary to design these assignments properly and also to give the patients the detailed instructions about how they are supposed to look at, kiss, touch, caress, smell, lick, suck, and rhythmically manipulate the partner's body and sexual parts, in a professional manner, without embarrassment, seductiveness, or voyeuristic gratification.

MODIFYING THE IMMEDIATE CAUSES OF SEXUAL AVERSIONS AND SEXUAL PHOBIAS

It was previously pointed out that the immediate causes of sexual aversions and sexual phobias are distinctly different from those of "quiet" HSD. It follows, therefore, that the behavioral aspects of the treatment of these two syndromes are also significantly and distinctly different, and the libido-enhancing therapeutic strategies that were described in the foregoing sections are not appropriate for sexaphobic patients.

The *immediate cause of sexual anxiety and panic states is the malignant link between fear or aversion and sex.* This destructive association must be extinguished if the patient is going to improve. *Sex education* and *in-vivo exposures* to the feared sexual situation are the major behavioral/cognitive strategies for making this so.

Sex Education

Sexual fears sometimes arise, at least in part, from a patient's sexual inexperience and lack of knowledge. This is more often material in the sexual aversions and phobias of young couples from ultra religious and conservative backgrounds. Some of these individuals have had no sex education whatsoever, and they do not know what to do or what to expect on the honeymoon. However, sexual ignorance can also be a factor in the sexual aversions of older, sexually "uptight" individuals, who come from all segments of society, so the therapist can never assume that the patient in his or her consulting room is knowledgeable about human sexuality.

I keep life sized rubber models of the male and female genitalia in various states of excitement in my office. I use these models to illustrate the "facts of life" to inexperienced couples, and to teach these patients, some of whom have never seen the genitalia of the opposite sex (or even their own!), what to anticipate in the bedroom.

We also use the models to help couples communicate with each other so they can learn what hurts and where, and how and where it feels good to be touched. In addition, the replicas of the genitalia are sometimes useful for the first stages of desensitization of severely sexaphobic patients.

For the same purposes, I sometimes lend patients videotapes to view at home. The content of the tapes, as well as the couple's reaction to viewing them, is then discussed during subsequent sessions.

Excellent videotapes are available that depict a wide variety of sexual techniques in an educational, nonthreatening manner, ranging from holding hands, to caressing, to kissing, to oral sex, and to intercourse in a variety of positions. Some tapes even demonstrate the use of fantasy as part of normal sexual expression (see pages 156–157).

Extinguishing the Sexaphobic Response

The patient's phobic sexual anxiety and/or aversion to sex is eliminated or reduced by systematic and gradual exposure to the feared and avoided genital contact with the partner, or to that specific aspect of sex that triggers his or her panic or revulsion. This process, which is called *in-vivo desensitization* (Mowrer, 1974; Dollard & Miller, 1950), is the central strategy for helping patients with sexual anxiety states to overcome their avoidance of sex.

The therapeutic *in vivo* desensitization assignments are structured so that the patient is exposed to the feared or repellent sexual situation gradually and progressively under calm, "safe," and supportive conditions.*

More specifically, *the globally sexaphobic or aversive patient* is instructed to attempt to remain physically in the presence of a small, manageable piece of the feared and previously avoided sexual situation. This might involve, for example, the sexaphobic's looking and touching her own genitalia. Or, with very avoidant and frightened patients like "Bill Kangaroo" (Case 8.2), the first therapeutic homework assigned to him was merely to accustom him to undressing in the partner's presence.

Patients with *specific sexual fears and aversions* are exposed, under therapeutic control, to those aspects of sex that are frightening or repellant to them, which may entail, in different cases, kissing, touching the breasts, caressing the genitalia, etc. The exposures are repeated until

**In vivo desensitization* should be distinguished from *systematic desensitization*, a technique developed by Joseph Wolpe which uses imagery but no direct physical exposure to the phobic situation (Wolpe, 1958). In our experience, systematic desensitization is not effective for treating sexual disorders.

the patient's negative feelings have abated. He/she advances to the next step only after becoming entirely comfortable.

In a common example, women who are severely phobic of vaginal penetration are typically so frightened that they avoid even the sight of their own genitalia. As a first assignment, such a patient may be encouraged to simply look at her vulva in a mirror. Although patients are typically quite anxious when they are first asked to do this, most become accustomed to the view after a few repetitions. The next assignment might be to place the tip of her index finger at the introitus of her vagina, perhaps for two minutes a day. After the patient's anxiety has abated sufficiently so that she can do this easily, we might begin desensitizing her to her husband's genitalia according to the same principle, namely, slow, gradual, progressively increasing physical exposures.

According to learning theory, the repeated pairing of the previously feared and avoided sexual situation with the newly acquired state of inner tranquility progressively weakens the old, unwanted sex-fear or sex-aversion associations. Ultimately, in good responders, this opens up the possibility for the establishment of new and desirable connections between sexual contact with the partner and feelings of sexual pleasure.

Phase I: Overcoming the Avoidance of "Giving"

The treatment of sexual aversion disorders is often divided into two discrete phases. The aim of phase I is to help the patient overcome his/her avoidance of *giving* the partner sexual pleasure, or of providing the partner with sexual stimulation and gratification. During the first phase of treatment, no attempts are made to modify the patient's lack of desire and his/her avoidance of sexual stimulation by the partner. This is deferred until the second phase.

This division is useful for two reasons. First, except for individuals with very severe sexual panic states who find all sexual contact with their partners intolerable, it is far easier for most sexaphobic patients to overcome their avoidance of *giving* their partner pleasurable sexual stimulation than it is for them to allow themselves to be kissed and touched and to *respond* to the partner.

Responding erotically to the lover is the most threatening aspect of sex for most sexaphobic individuals. On the other hand, many sexaphobic and aversive patients, especially women, because they don't have to perform like men do, don't find it all that difficult to use their hands, mouth, and body to pleasure their partners and bring them to climax. This sort of "giving" sex can become quite comfortable, especially if the woman has learned to remain removed and in control of her feelings while she pleasures her partner. This allows her to avoid what for most of these patients is the most frightening part of sex, the part that makes them feel the most vulnerable, namely, to allow themselves to be "swept away" by their sexual feelings when they are with their partners.

Helping sexual avoidant patients to overcome their avoidance and aversion to giving satisfaction to their spouses to the point where they can do this comfortably, even if this is not exactly thrilling, can make life much easier for them. It is not surprising that the spouses of sexually avoidant individuals are frustrated and often make the phobic spouse the target of their rage. While receiving an orgasm from a dispassionate partner may not be satisfying in the long run, this usually suffices to defuse the frustrated spouse's anger for the time being.

Moreover, the therapist's beginning the therapeutic process by enabling the sexaphobic spouse to give pleasure to her partner, as a first step towards the couple's sexual improvement, sends a clear message to the sexually asymptomatic partner that his needs will not be neglected, that the therapist is sensitive to his feelings and is doing his/her best to see that he gets some relief. This strategy has the enormous benefit of enlisting the partner's unqualified cooperation in the difficult therapeutic process to come.

Phase II: Increasing Desire

The aim of the second phase of treatment is to increase the symptomatic partner's sexual desire and to help him/her to become absorbed in the sex act with the partner. Usually, this is the more difficult part of treatment. However, in some cases, the patient's libido rises to normal levels spontaneously, after his or her phobic avoidance of sex has been resolved. This was the experience of "Lucinda Skier" (Case 6.2), the beautiful, young, divorced woman who was described in Chapter 6. This woman habitually chose younger, less accomplished, nonthreatening men, "shmohawks" (her word), preferably ones who treated her badly. Meanwhile, she phobically avoided appropriate men. When, with my relentless confrontations and encouragements, Lucinda finally accepted a date with a smart, rich, and handsome man of an appropriate age, she experienced profound anticipatory anxiety, to the point where she asked for medication.*

Lucinda's anxiety persisted throughout the whole evening of her first date with Doug, and this was heightened when he showed a definite

*Dr. Richard Kogan, who saw this patient when I was away, prescribed 0.25mg of Xanax each night, and an additional 0.25mg in case she felt anxious during the day.

interest in her. On one level, she desperately wanted to escape, but this highly motivated patient was determined to overcome her avoidance of romantic attachments to appropriate men, so she gritted her teeth and agreed to go to bed with him. She reported that she had felt literally numb and anesthetized by anxiety as they first undressed, but when he kissed her she was suddenly "swept away" by intense erotic feelings. Thereafter, Lucinda, who had previously described Doug as "too homely" to go to dinner with, now saw him as "movie star handsome."

But more often patients show intense resistance to this second phase of treatment. Further, only about half of our sexually aversive patients were fully *cured.* The majority of the remaining patients became entirely comfortable when they engaged in sexual intercourse or when they stimulated their partners to orgasm, but they never went on to experiencing normal desire for or pleasure in sex with their partners.

Such was the outcome with "Regina Kaiser's" therapy (Case 4.8). By the end of treatment, she had become completely at ease about having intercourse with her husband and with stimulating him manually. She was "thrilled" that she could do this because it made her life much less stressful, and her former analyst considered this "a miracle." However, I was not happy with the outcome of this case, because Regina seldom felt much desire with Roy, and she continued to prefer to masturbate. After we terminated therapy, I suggested that she resume her long-term psychoanalytic treatment.

Optimal Level of Anxiety

The notion that the patient's anxiety should be modulated and adjusted so that this remains within a *therapeutic range* is seminal to the treatment of sexual panic states. This is necessary because the experience of a certain amount of anxiety is required for the success of the process of desensitization. If the behavioral assignment does not evoke any fear whatsoever, no extinction can possibly take place. However, excessively high anxiety levels are equally countertherapeutic, since the patient might have a panic attack while engaging in the therapeutic sexual exercises with the partner. In that event, the association between sex and fear is not extinguished. To the contrary, excessive anxiety can actually reinforce the phobic response, which may become more severe than ever.*

*The behavioral literature reports some success with the technique of "flooding" the patient with intense anxiety for the treatment of (nonsexual) phobias. However, in our experience, the exposure of the patient to the phobically avoided sexual situation while he or she is in a panic state is cruel and may aggravate these conditions.

In practical terms, this means that, for the purpose of extinguishing the sexaphobic response, the assignments must make the patient sufficiently anxious so that positive conditioning can occur, but this must not be so intense that the patient ends up becoming even more phobic and avoidant of sex.

In order to succeed in this critical task, the therapist must continually monitor his patient's responses to their therapeutic homework assignments closely. Such tight surveillance is an absolute necessity for providing the necessary feedback that is required to fine tune the pace and the intensity of the therapeutic exposures so as to maintain the patient's anxiety within a range that is optimal for the purpose of extinction.

SEXUAL ANXIETY DISORDERS

It is somewhat surprising to me that *every* patient with panic disorder does not develop a sexual phobia along with his or her other phobias and anxieties. After all, patients with low anxiety thresholds are susceptible to becoming anxious and phobic in response to any of the numerous situations they encounter, and that must surely include sex. In fact, we did find a significantly higher incidence of multiple phobias as well as concomitant anxiety disorders in our patients with sexual aversions and sexual phobias than in patients with other sexual dysfunctions.*

Very Gradual Exposure

The treatment of sexually aversive patients with concomitant anxiety disorders is complicated because in highly anxious individuals the association between fear and sex or aversion and sex is particularly intense, tenacious, and difficult to extinguish. Therefore, the therapeutic exposures for these patients must be adjusted to accommodate to their high anxiety levels.

More specifically, severely anxious sexaphobics often panic in response to the standard therapeutic SF exercises, and they require a much slower pace of desensitization. Therefore, with sexaphobics who have underlying anxiety disorders, we use very small increments of exposure. In some cases, it may be necessary to repeat each tiny step as many as 20 to 30 times before the patient's anxieties abate.

*Of the 5,580 patients with sexual disorders seen in our programs between 1972 and 1992, 414 met the diagnostic criteria for sexual aversion disorder. Of these, 35% had concomitant diagnoses of anxiety disorder. The incidence of anxiety disorders in the remaining patients who carried the diagnosis of HSD or one of the genital phase psychosexual dysfunctions was 10%. (unpublished study)

As an example, one of the most severely sexaphobic patients I have ever treated was so panicky that she could not tolerate the slightest physical contact with her loving (and incredibly patient) husband. I thought I had given a benign assignment when I suggested that the couple hold hands and exchange only one kiss. But I was wrong. The patient panicked when she tried to comply, and then wept bitterly in frustration about her "failure." But we did not give up. I reduced the next therapeutic exposure to a "homeopathic" dose, which consisted of having the couple lie on their large, king-sized bed, fully dressed, while they both simultaneously stroked their beloved dog. I felt amply rewarded for my patient persistence when, after two years of treatment, this couple succeeded in having normal intercourse.*

Anti-Anxiety Medication

It is often difficult and frequently impossible to control the fears of patients who have underlying anxiety disorders and to keep this within a therapeutic range with psychological tactics alone. Very anxious patients may not improve, because even the most painstaking, slow, well conceived, therapeutic exposure assignments may evoke intense, uncontrollable anticipatory anxiety and panic in these patients. Moreover, even if these anxious patients do not actually experience full blown panic attacks in response to their desensitization assignments, they still tend to *remain* in an intensely anxious state while they are being exposed to the feared sexual stimulus.

Under these circumstances, there is no opportunity for deconditioning to take place, since the extinction of the unwanted fear response can occur only if the patient's fear actually *diminishes* in the presence of the anxiety provoking situation. It is only if fear declines during the exposures that the new calm-sex association can become established. Unfortunately, these overanxious patients simply don't calm down sufficiently during their exposures to become reconditioned, no matter how "small" these are made.

The adjunctive use of anti-anxiety and/or panic blocking drugs has resolved this therapeutic dilemma in many cases by reducing the patients' anxiety down to manageable levels (see pages 193–196). This makes these medications invaluable for facilitating the therapeutic *in vivo* extinction of anxiety in patients who would otherwise be too anxious to cooperate with or to benefit from sex therapy.

By themselves, the drugs generally *do not* cure sexaphobic patients,

*This case has been described in a previous publication (Kaplan, 1987).

since their effects are transitory. This point will be illustrated by the treatment history of "Greta Biedemeyer." (Case 8.1), to be described in the following chapter. This patient's agoraphobia had been completely cured with a combination of cognitive therapy and Tofranil (imipramine). However, even though she no longer experienced panic attacks, there was no corresponding improvement in her phobic avoidance of sex.

Nevertheless, once again, in good responders like Greta, the panic-blocking medication can reduce anxiety sufficiently during the *in vivo* exposures to facilitate the permanent extinction of the sexaphobic response.

THE PSYCHODYNAMIC MANAGEMENT OF RESISTANCE

In virtually every case, patients and couples with sexual desire disorders resist the libido-enhancing interventions as well as the desensitization exposures of sex therapy. In this respect, disorders of sexual desire are like all the other psychosexual dysfunctions (Kaplan, 1974, 1979, 1980b, 1995).

The forms that resistances take to psychosexual therapy vary widely. Resistant patients miss their appointments, "misunderstand" the therapist's instructions, fail to comply with their assignments, start fights with their lovers, get "too busy," get pregnant, get ill, get into accidents, don't pay their bills, have affairs, attack the therapist, tell lies, hold back important information, fill the sessions with irrelevant material, etc., etc., etc.

Sometimes, resistances come from the low-desire patient only, whereas the partner is cooperative. In other cases, it is the partner without a desire problem whose anxiety is raised by the symptomatic patient's improvement, and who resists treatment on that account. In many cases, both partners take turns sabotaging treatment.

Resistance to the Process of Sex Therapy

Resistances may be mobilized by the *process* of sex therapy or by a favorable *outcome.*

Some patients become resistant primarily because the process of sex therapy involves assignments that are threatening or objectionable to them for reasons apart from sexual functioning. For example, very religious Christians and Jews may feel too guilty to comply with assignments that involve masturbation, erotica, and/or fantasy on moral grounds, while other patients are especially threatened by and resist procedures like SF that foster too much intimacy and openness with their partners.

Process resistances seldom pose insurmountable obstacles to treatment. As long as patients are conflict-free about improving their sexual functioning, if the therapist is flexible and uses a little imagination, it is usually possible to find alternatives to the particular intervention that is mobilizing the resistance. For example, some patients resist any and all assignments simply because they cannot tolerate feeling "controlled" by the therapist. Since this treatment is brief and time-limited, it is not appropriate to analyze or to try to resolve the patient's problem with control. In such cases, I might attempt to "detour" around this issue by joining the patient's resistance to taking directions. Often, the case will progress nicely if you let these patients create their own homework assignments with as little guidance from you as possible.

"You really know yourself better than anyone else ever could, so why don't you suggest this week's homework?" After the patient comes up with a task, one can gently tinker with it: "That's a great idea, but what do you think about waiting just a little longer before you and Harriette try to have intercourse?"

Resistance to the Outcome of Therapy

More commonly, the source of the low-desire patient's resistance is ambivalence, on an unconscious level, about a successful treatment result. In other words, the goal of treatment, that is, the attainment of increased sexual passion and closeness with the partner, poses a threat. Resistances that grow out of such inner conflicts are usually more difficult to resolve than those that involve the process of treatment.

The resolution of resistances to treatment is an exceedingly important aspect of the treatment of sexual desire disorders. The therapist's astuteness in analyzing the hidden sources of the couple's resistances and his/her technical skill in managing these effectively is the key to the successful outcome of the majority of cases and constitute the true art of psychosexual therapy.

"Bypassing" the Unconscious Sources of Resistances

According to the psychodynamic sex therapy model, if the patient and/or the partner resists, the assumption is made that these obstacles are manifestations of their deeper unconscious intrapsychic conflicts and/or ambivalence towards the partner, which gave rise to their sexual symptoms in the first place. However, although we proceed on this theory, we do *not* switch to insight-promoting therapeutic interventions as soon as the first resistances emerge.

Our first-line strategy for dealing with resistances to the libido-enhancing maneuvers and anxiety reducing *in-vivo* exposures is to attempt to "bypass" their presumed deeper sources with an orderly and systematic sequence of gradually intensifying behavioral and cognitive interventions that are aimed at progressively "deeper" psychic levels. These progress from simple *repetition of the assignment*, to *reduction of its intensity*, to the *cognitive reframing of the problem*, to *confrontation* (Kaplan, 1979, 1987, 1995), and finally to *insight into the patient's underlying conflicts*.

When resistances first begin to surface, our first move is to simply ask the patient to *repeat* the therapeutic homework assignment, several times if necessary. Repetitions, which are bolstered by the therapist's unfailing support, encouragement, and "permission" to enjoy sexual pleasure, often suffice to resolve the therapeutic impasse.

If encouragement and the repetition of the assignment do not diminish the patient's anxiety sufficiently to resolve his/her/their resistances, we then *reduce* the assignment so that this entails smaller and less threatening steps.

The rationale for maintaining a therapeutic level of anxiety and for conducting the therapeutic *in vivo* exposure programs in very small increments with anxious sexaphobics has been discussed in the foregoing section (pages 173–175). The same principle, namely, making sure that patients move into previously avoided territory, while at the same time preventing their becoming excessively anxious during the assignments, also governs the treatment of highly anxious and resistant patients with "quiet" HSD.

For example, in a recent case, a married woman with a generalized, severe lack of desire for sex found the assignment to watch an erotic tape with her husband too threatening, and she resisted, finding many excuses for not doing this. But when the homework task was reduced to watching a five-minute segment of the tape by herself, she was able to comply to this and then progress gradually from there.

But I want to reiterate that the patterns and sources of sexual anxiety are highly idiosyncratic and differ widely in this patient population. Further, the effectiveness and power of the therapeutic assignments depend to a large deree in the therapist's empathy and intuition. Therefore, it is impossible to recommend a single hierarchy of desensitizations that will suit every case, and there is simply no escaping the fact that the systematic desensitization programs have to be individually designed.

For example, another patient, also a woman with HSD, resisted for several weeks my suggestion that she look at some erotica by herself. I had assumed that, as with the patient in the last case, this would provoke less anxiety than watching with her sexual partner. It took me a while to realize that this woman's anxiety was raised to countertherapeutic levels when she was alone. As it turned out, this tapped into her old, unresolved guilt about masturbation. She experienced much less anxiety when she looked at erotica together with her husband.

If repeated and reduced assignments continue to mobilize resistance, we may *reframe* a particular point of resistance and reconceptualize this in terms that are less "toxic" emotionally.*

As a common example, resistances to the use of erotic fantasies can be expected if patients view these as signs of their depravity or evil nature. In such cases, it is often helpful to reconceptualize the meaning of erotic fantasy in terms that will provoke less guilt, as a natural phenomenon that is the logical result of a patient's particular childhood experience.

Similarly, I often attempt to neutralize the guilt which is so common in our culture and the resistances to the masturbation exercises by encouraging the patient to change his/her old perception of masturbation as a "dirty and impure" act, and to embrace the more rational notion that masturbation is a normal phenomenon and functions as a healthy rehearsal for eventual partner-related sex.

If patients continue to resist after repetition and reduction of the assignment, and if the therapist's reconceptualization of the anxiety provoking issue has failed to move treatment forward, we then *confront* the patient with his resistances in the attempt to make him aware of his sexual self-sabotage.

For example, I recently said to a patient who had repeatedly missed appointments and who "could not find the time" to do his assignments: "I know that one part of you wants very much to feel more sexual desire. You waited a long time to get these appointments, you always pay your fee, you go through an awful lot of trouble to get to the clinic. But it looks like another part of you, a part you don't seem to be aware of, is sabotaging this effort.** How else can you explain why you didn't do your 'home-

---

*I thank Dr. Peter Kaplan for introducing the concept of "toxic relationships" to the Wednesday seminars.

**Credit for the "Part of you wants to, but another part doesn't" formulation of resistance, which a number of us have adopted, should go to Arlene Novick (Wednesday conference).

work' for the last three weeks? Or why you didn't have the 'time' to look for erotic videotapes? Or why you yelled at your beautiful girlfriend and made her so mad she wouldn't make love to you? Do you really think it was only because she offered your dog some chocolate?"

Insight Into the Deeper Causes

Often, these brief therapeutic maneuvers, which can be characterized as "superficial" in that they do not deal directly with unconscious material, succeed in "bypassing" or "bridging over" the deeper sources of the patient's resistances. There are many cases in our files in which patients' sexual functioning and desire improved to normal levels, even though they had gained virtually no insight into the unconscious roots of their sexual symptoms, or their resistances to treatment. This is illustrated by the first three case histories that are described in the following chapter, which all had positive outcomes despite the fact that no insight-fostering, psychodynamic interpretations or clarifications were employed.

However, we have also seen many other cases where the patient and/or the couple were impervious to the libido-enhancing assignments, *in vivo* exposures, repetition, reduction, medication, restructuring, support, permission, and confrontations. When low-desire patients show no improvement in response to such behavioral and cognitive interventions, *in sharp contrast with therapists who don't believe in unconscious motivation nor in insight therapy* (Schwartz & Masters, 1988; Lazarus, 1988; LoPiccolo & Friedman, 1988), *we do not give up on the case. Rather, we shift into our second line, psychodynamic mode.*

Many patients who were initially unresponsive to behavioral and cognitive approaches have been rescued from becoming treatment failures by the addition to our treatment regimen of psychologically "invasive," insight-promoting, psychodynamically oriented interventions.

Chapter 8 contains a description of the treatment of "Joe Senator" (Case 8.7), which illustrates the method of salvaging resistant patients by shifting to psychodynamic, insight-fostering techniques.

As is typical of this approach, the psychodynamically oriented methods were deferred until it became quite clear that the patient was truly resistant to the cognitive/behavioral approaches.

One reason that psychodynamic methods are not introduced earlier is that these are not particularly effective in the initial stages of treatment, before resistances arise, when the thrust of treatment is to heighten the patient's awareness of the fact and the means of his/her sexual self-sabotage. Moreover, psychodynamic interventions are not always necessary for a successful outcome. While there is little doubt that the vicissitudes of early life play a significant role in shaping adult sexual destiny and psychopathology, it does not necessarily follow that each patient's childhood history needs to be explored extensively, nor that patients must always obtain insight into the deeper causes and the early origins of their sexual inhibitions and/or their resistances to treatment in order for their sexual desire and their functioning to improve.

THE PSYCHODYNAMIC ASPECTS OF SEX THERAPY

To describe the behavioral and cognitive strategies used in the integrated treatment of sexual desire disorders with clarity is a relatively straightforward task. However, it is nearly impossible to do justice to the complexities of the psychodynamic aspects of this method with equal lucidity, nor is it possible to put into words a valid description of the dynamic interplay that regularly takes place between the therapeutically structured sexual experiences and the active, relentless, psychodynamically informed interpretations and clarifications that characterize the process of brief psychosexual therapy. I think I can present this best by limiting this discussion to basic theoretical foundations and relying on the case studies presented in the following chapters to convey the essence of the method and to illustrate the didactic points.

Since the psychodynamic aspects of treatment of the sexual desire disorders are essentially identical to those of all the other psychosexual dysfunctions, this topic has also been considered in a number of my earlier publications on sex therapy, to which the reader is referred for further information (Kaplan, 1974, 1979, 1980a, 1980b, 1981, 1987, 1995; Kaplan & Moodie, 1984).

The Analysis of the Resistance

When patients remain resistant after a reasonable trial of the behavioral/cognitive maneuvers of sex therapy, the therapeutic objective shifts from *bypassing* the deeper causes and resistances to *insight and resolution.*

This phase of treatment requires an extensive and detailed analysis of the patient's deeper sexual conflicts. The general outline of the deeper psychic infrastructure of the patient's sexual symptoms that sufficed during the initial stages of treatment is not adequate for this purpose. At this point, the patient's psychosexual and family histories, as well as the history of the couple's relationship, which had only been sketched out in general outline during the evaluation, are now explored in greater detail and depth. This analysis is pursued until the significant pathogenic circumstances of the patient's early life emerge clearly, particularly with respect to a deeper understanding of his/her formative object relationships with the significant members of his family.

The therapeutic sexual exercises are *not* suspended during the psychodynamic phase of treatment. In fact, these assume additional importance because they *now became vehicles for analyzing the patient's resistances and for fostering insight.*

I believe that astutely devised assignments that are shaped by the therapist's understanding of the patient's and couple's inner dynamics can be very powerful transducers of insight and extremely effective triggers for significant memories. I have come to this conclusion on the basis of my own experience and also because a number of psychoanalysts, whose patients I was seeing for the treatment of their sexual symptoms while they were continuing their analytic work, have remarked about the great increase of significant dreams, associations, and memories that were precipitated by the patient's experiences in sex therapy.

Thus, after the shift to a psychodynamic mode, the therapeutic assignments are used in a dual manner, behavioral and psychodynamic. In other words, the exposures whose purpose it is to promote the extinction of sexual anxiety continue, but the patient's reactions, associations, and resistances to these structured therapeutic experiences are used to illuminate the patient's unconscious sexual conflicts, and this material is now interpreted on a deeper level, with the aim of fostering insight and resolution.

Dreams

Dreams, which the partners bring into therapy, are also now analyzed in great depth. In some cases the patient resists the therapist's attempts to interpret his dreams, but the case is nevertheless brought to a successful conclusion. This is what happened with the sexaphobic patient, "Greta Biedemeyer" (Case 8.1), who dismissed my suggestion that the umbrellas in one of her dreams might represent her defenses by characterizing my efforts as "reading tea leaves." But in other cases, the astute interpretation of a resistant patient's dream can illuminate and produce insight and resolution of resistances, rapidly and dramatically. The case of "Senator," the man who could function only with the aid of his "dirty whore" fantasies, but who could not use these with his fiancée (Case 8.7), will provide an example. This patient, who was in a resistant phase, had a dream about a bandit brandishing a gun. His associations led to his father and to the fear he had of the man, and this in turn clarified the deeper meaning of the patient's resistances. The process of working through the dream material enabled Senator to understand his sexual symptom and his resistance to treatment in the context of his early, painful history within his dysfunctional family. These insights were followed by a rapid improvement.

In brief psychodynamic sex therapy, dreams are frequently interpreted as "messages" from the patient's unconscious. Often, these messages represent warnings of impending psychic danger. For example, "Doc Scotch" (Case 8.8) brought in a dream in which he was in bed with a beautiful woman when two tigers jumped out of the wall and started to devour them. The tigers seemed to represent the patient's unconscious fears of women and of sex, but on a more immediate level the dream was also a warning about the danger posed by his unconscious, aggressive, self-destructive impulses. In other words, I believe the tigers represented Doc's own unconscious, murderous, self-destructive needs to "punish" himself for having sex with a symbolic "mother figure." Unfortunately, the patient acted these out before I could make any interpretation to this effect.

In the case of "Tim and Mary" (Case 7.1), which will be described shortly, the warning of danger in the patient's dream was so clear that this actually caused me to alter my therapeutic strategy.

Balancing Confrontation With Support

I like to think of confrontation and support as the two reins by which the therapeutic process is kept on track and moving forward.

More specifically, in the service of proceeding with therapy as rapidly as is possible without compromising a successful treatment outcome, I will "relentlessly" strip away the patient's defenses, rationalizations, and "cop outs" whenever and as soon as these get in the way of therapeutic progress and/or insight.

Such an extremely active, rapid, relentless style of confronting the couple with potentially threatening and previously repressed or avoided material typically causes both partners to feel exposed and highly vulnerable. This strenuous therapeutic process can be effective only if both partners are highly motivated and only if both have a strong therapeutic alliance with the therapist, which includes complete trust in him or her.

To make it possible for patients to tolerate the painful therapeutic interventions that are sometimes necessary to diffuse their defenses against good sex and to minimize the emergence of resistances, each confrontation should be carefully balanced by the therapist's equally active, vigorous, and unqualified emotional support of both partners, and also by the continuous affirmation of their relationship.

When a partner's resistance creates an obstacle to therapeutic progress, it may sometimes be wise to see the resistant partner alone for a few sessions, until he/she has gained some insight into his/her destructive behavior and stops sabotaging the low-desire partner's improvement. But most of the time there is an advantage to conducting the sessions conjointly.

Thus, even though I allow no therapeutic obstacle to go unnoticed and have been accused of going after resistances like a "bloodhound," I am also unfailingly congratulatory, and I do not hold back on expressing the genuine joy that I feel when a patient makes gains in his or her capacity to experience sexual pleasure. I have watched myself on the videotapes literally glow with pleasure when the couple I am working with manage to become more intimate and more sexual and succeed in making each other happy.

Equally important, at the same time that I am actively confronting and supporting the sexually symptomatic patient, I continually monitor the partner's reactions also, and I take every opportunity to support him or her with equal vigor. I make it a point to accentuate the partner's contribution to the symptomatic patient's improvements and to comment on the positives in the couple's relationship. However, I do not hesitate to confront and interpret destructive behaviors and sabotage on the partner's part.

Motivation

The importance of motivation cannot be overstated. As was indicated in the foregoing discussion, the process of sex therapy is often emotionally arduous for patients with sexual desire disorders, and this enterprise can succeed only if both partners are highly motivated. It is especially important that the individual with low desire genuinely *wants* to feel more lust in the relationship, out of motives of affection. However, the partner must also value the relationship sufficiently to be prepared to make the changes that might be required to make it so.

Patients who are angry at their partners, ambivalent about wishing to feel more passion for them, and not really serious about wanting to have sex more frequently are likely to fail or drop out of treatment. Therefore, I do not recommend commencing with sex therapy, and certainly not with assigning "sexual homework," until the therapist feels comfortable that the patient has resolved his/her conflicts on this score, genuinely *wishes* to feel more desire for the partner, and is not just "doing the right thing" and bowing to external pressures by entering sex therapy.

Transference in Sex Therapy

Once again, I am prone to confront resistances that get in the way of therapeutic progress and the patient's sexual improvement relentlessly, as soon as they appear; this includes *transference resistances.*

Although it is brief, the process of sex therapy lends itself to the formation of rapid and intense transferences towards the therapist by both partners. This may be attributed, at least in part, to the frank encouragement of erotic pleasure and the explicitly sexual nature of the material that is dealt with in this form of treatment.

When it seems that the therapeutic transference is being used in the service of blocking therapeutic progress, I handle this as I do any other form of resistance, namely, by direct confrontation and with explorations and interpretations of the deeper meaning of the patient's transference resistances. These usually involve his or her fears of and/or avoidance of sex and intimacy with the partner.

However, transference resistances are rather *uncommon* in this form of therapy. Much more frequently, patients and couples form strong positive transferences and make good projections onto the therapist, identifying with the therapist's constructive sexual attitudes. When this happens, I shamelessly exploit the transference to boost the therapeutic process.

Thus, I never interpret or clarify a patient's positive transference to me if treatment is going well. Rather, I use the exaggerated positive feelings and the couple's irrational wishes to please me, which are products of transferential states, to enhance their intrinsic motivation to overcome their antisexual behaviors and to feel more sexual desire for the partner.

As long as the couple's sexual functioning and their desire for each other genuinely and permanently improve, I don't care if they work hard at their therapy in order to make me happy.

THE COUPLES ASPECT OF THERAPY

Enlisting the Partner's Cooperation

I stand by my often repeated statement (Kaplan, 1974, 1980b, 1987, 1995) that enlisting the partner's unqualified cooperation is an absolute prerequisite for a successful outcome in the treatment of couples with sexual difficulties. Nowhere is this more true than with patients who are afflicted with sexual desire disorders.

The ebb and flow of a sensitive person's desire and passion can hang on the fine nuances of the partner's behavior and on the subtle flow of the couple's emotional connection. Thus, with just a slightly disapproving look, a bit of coldness in the voice, and an almost imperceptible emotional distancing, a partner can effectively sabotage treatment.

For these reasons the therapist's inability to engage the partner fully in the therapeutic process is a major cause of failure in the treatment of sexual desire disorders. Therefore, a great deal of the therapist's time and efforts are devoted to forming a strong alliance with the nonsymptomatic partner and to overcoming his/her resistance to the spouse's sexual growth.

Preventing Partner Resistance

A meaningful, comprehensive description of the couples aspects of therapy is beyond the scope of this chapter. The following are simply a few precautions I have found useful to minimize partner resistance.

When working within a couples context, the therapist must always remain aware of the impact that his/her confrontations with and interpretations to one partner are having on the other. In a sense, *the relationship is the patient,* rather than either partner, and while the therapist constantly turns towards one and then the other, like a slalom skier, he/she always swings back to the center line, the improvement of the couple's relationship.

When it is necessary to confront a patient sharply, one must be careful not to place him/her in a poor light vis-à-vis the wife or husband, as this risks undermining their relationship as well as the therapeutic effort. Therefore, all negative confrontations should be simultaneously balanced by positive remarks about the person or about the couple's relationship.

In addition, the therapist must be very sensitive to the vulnerabilities of the sexually asymptomatic partner, especially if he or she happens to be fragile emotionally. One must be very careful that the interpretations made to the sexually symptomatic partner do not raise the anxieties of the other one excessively. For example, I was trying to shore up a husband's self-esteem by telling him that his poor self-image had no basis in reality and that he was actually a handsome, brilliant, successful, and highly desirable man. This was all true, of course, but as I was praising the husband, I could sense that his wife was becoming uneasy. In trying to correct the husband's distorted self-image in the service of helping him become a better lover for his wife, I had inadvertently mobilized his wife's fears of rejection and abandonment, and her suspicions of me. I forestalled the potential damage to the therapeutic process by rapidly shifting my remarks to the wife and by being equally and realistically supportive and complimentary to her, especially highlighting the wonderful life she had made for her husband.

The same considerations, namely, simultaneous, unremitting sensitivity to both partners' needs and vulnerabilities, also apply to the *homework assignments*. It is the primary purpose of the therapeutic behavioral sigs, such as asking the patient to use fantasy or erotica or to try a vibrator, to heighten the symptomatic partner's deficient libido so that ultimately the couple will have a better sex life together. But little is gained, if the assignment to rent a porno tape is insensitive to the wife's insecurity and throws her into a rage.

CASE 7.1—"Tim and Mary Ruffino-Smith": PE in the Husband of an Emotionally Vulnerable Wife with HSD

This case vignette provides an example of systems-oriented behavioral interventions. A young couple, "Tim and Mary," had come to the clinic to seek help for the husband's PE.* However, it was soon apparent that this was of less significance in the couple's unhappiness than Mary's loss of desire and her avoidance of sex.

When I treat a patient with PE, I often get a good enough fix on the case to be able give the first therapeutic homework assignment at the end of the initial session, and I almost invariably do so when I see them for the second time. In this case, however, I was reluctant to start this couple with partner-provided, manual stop-start assignments** and I did not do so until the eighth session, when Mary despairingly complained that treatment was getting nowhere.

I held off because the dynamics of Mary's depression and her sexual avoidance were very complex, and I felt I should not ask her to do anything sexual with her husband until I fully understood the cause of her emotional pain and the reason she had lost her sexual desire.

I eventually learned that Mary felt betrayed by her husband for being insensitive to the pain that his rapid ejaculations had caused her. She could not forgive nor forget that Tim had waited two years before seeking help. Mary's sense of betrayal and her anger had been further inflamed because when they first married, Tim had sided with his

*After I had seen this couple for 14 sessions, treatment was continued by Dr. Ellen Hollander and her team.

**The "stop-start" exercises, or intermittent manual penile stimulation, through masturbation or by the partner, are usually the first behavioral interventions in the treatment of PE (Kaplan, 1974, 1975, 1989a).

mother against her instead of protecting her, on a number of issues where she had been innocent of wrongdoing. These incidents had tapped into the well of pain born of the emotional pain and neglect that Mary had suffered as a child.

It was not until after some highly confrontational sessions that Tim genuinely understood and acknowledged that he had, albeit unwittingly, hurt his wife badly. Tim was truly repentant. He also distanced himself from his difficult mother, and with that Mary began to feel better about their relationship. At that point, it seemed to make sense to begin the interactional homework assignments.

But this vulnerable woman was still not ready to give her unqualified cooperation to sex therapy, so I turned my attention mainly towards supporting and trying to "hear" her on a deeper level during the therapy sessions.

So as not to lose time while I was concentrating on Mary in the sessions, I gave Tim some solo "stop-start" and "slow-fast" sexual homework assignments (Kaplan, 1989a). However, because these assignments can have powerful emotional impacts on both partners, I did not give him these exercises until I had first satisfied myself that Tim's masturbating would not disturb Mary and until I had secured her agreement.

Tim did very well with the masturbation exercises, and feeling that I had exercised proper caution regarding Mary's vulnerabilities, I gave the couple their first interactional homework assignment, the "quiet vagina" exercise*

But things did not go well between the couple during the following week. They did not do the vaginal containment exercise and they had several quarrels. Mary brought in a frightening dream that helped me understand the hidden meaning of her resistance.

She dreamt that she was swimming in a pool. At the bottom she saw many dead bodies, and "poisonous wasps" were swimming all around her, trying to kill her. Mary barely escaped injury by swimming to the shallow end of the pool, where she felt safe. She woke up feeling very frightened.

I chose to regard this dream as a message from Mary's unconscious. I felt that she was trying to say that the "deep water," which I took to be a symbol for sexual intercourse, was still too dangerous for her, emotionally speaking, and that she needed the safety of "shallow water"

---

*This "quiet vagina" exercise entails the woman assuming the superior position, while the man keeps his erect penis in her vagina without thrusting, and tries to focus on his penile sensations. The purpose of this assignment is to accustom the man to vaginal intromission.

which was perhaps symbolic of a less threatening assignment, one that did not entail intercourse with her husband.

On the basis of this dream and the patient's associations, which lent support to the notion that intercourse was emotionally still traumatic for her, I deferred any further vaginal containment exercises until we had had a chance to work through her painful associations to intercourse. It turned out that Mary was still caught up in the memory of beginning to make love to her husband and then being repeatedly "stung," that is, hurt and "abandoned" or "killed" in an emotional sense, when Tim would ejaculate after two or three strokes and then withdraw into his own guilty misery.

Relationship Countertransference

The discussion of the preceding case during the Wednesday conferences evoked some intense countertransferential reactions towards Tim and Mary's *relationship.*

When we reviewed the videotapes of my sessions with this couple, some of the trainees and staff expressed strong objections to what they regarded as my unfair emphasis on the wife's needs over the husband's. These observations were correct. I actually *was* much more confrontational with Tim, and much more supportive of Mary. Moreover, I kept encouraging Tim to become more sensitive to Mary's feelings, but I hardly ever confronted Mary with her unkindness towards him.

The reason I did what I did was based on my feeling that this young man was crazy about his admittedly emotionally unstable, needy, difficult, and vulnerable wife.* Moreover, the constant support and solicitousness that she required of him and my admonishments to him to act in a super-solicitous manner were actually, on a deep level, very pleasing to Tim.

Mary had responded rapidly to my empathy, understanding, and especially sensitive and supportive behavior towards her during the conjoint sessions. This, as well as my "hearing" her and my unfailing acquiescence to her, was necessary both to engage her in treatment and also served as a model, showing Tim what it would take to live in peace and happiness with his wife, if that is what he wanted.

Fortunately, on an unconscious level, the fit between this couple was excellent, and they both found this arrangement extremely gratifying. Mary's thirst for affection was unquenchable. She had repetitive dreams

---

*Mary met the criteria for the narcissistic personality disorder.

of literally standing in water, feeling very thirsty, but she was never able to get a drink. In fact, through a process that has been termed *projective identification,* which is a frequent dynamic in the pathogenesis of sexual and marital problems, Tim went beyond a simple mother transference to his wife. He actually set her up to *behave* like his demanding mother. The patient was not aware of it, but I used this insight to improve the couple's fit.

Tim did not resist my suggestions to act the compliant "good boy." On the contrary, I suspect that he had always secretly yearned for this role, but he had been a little ashamed. Now he was relieved that an "authority figure" had given him "permission," and he complied wholeheartedly.

This young husband was the ever-eager supplier, and he was happiest when he succeeded in being "mother's best boy" and managed to make the woman in his life happy.

All of us have a notion of what a good relationship should include: mutual sensitivity, intimacy, love, trust, mutuality, an equal sharing of power, etc. In reality, however, there is no way of knowing if there is such a thing as an ideal human love relationship, and what this would be like.

On a strictly empirical level, I consider a relationship "good" if it makes both partners happy, and "bad" if this is destructive to one or both.

The arrangements that work for different couples are infinite in their variety and frequently quite unconventional. From the viewpoint of the clinician, social conventions and politics should be irrelevant as long the relationship, works for both partners.

Dr. Stella Chess, who studied the fit between parents and children, made an important point when she judged relationships good between two partners, "as long as the bumps on his head fit into the holes in hers" (personal communication). The same concept of "fit" is expressed in the European folk saying, "Every pot finds its cover."

One of the most important qualities of a good sex or marital therapist is the ability to visualize what it would take to make a couple's relationship work better for them.* The therapist's own prejudices and biases can get in the way of this by blinding him or her to potentially constructive but unconventional strategies and solutions. Therefore, lest their own prejudices interfere with their helping couples work out their own chosen styles of relating, it is essential that therapists become as keenly aware as possible of the countertransferential distortions that grow out of their needs and requirements for their own relationships.

---

*Elaine Kleinbart made this insightful observation during a Wednesday conference.

Once again, for the purpose of sex or marital therapy, neither the husband nor the wife is the patient. It is their *relationship* that is ailing and needs to be healed. If the therapist wishes a good outcome in this, he/she must put aside all personal bias, be this feminism or chauvinism, and focus exclusively on perfecting the harmony of the couple's interactions.

Some of the members of the Wednesday conference wanted me to help Tim become more assertive. They had not realized that this would have been a disaster for him, for her, and for their relationship. The last thing this man wanted and needed was to become more assertive with his wife, and that was surely the last thing she needed as well. What Tim wanted more than anything else, and what I gave him, was my "permission" for this couple to enjoy their complementary roles. I legitimized Mary's sense of entitlement to be continuously "fed" by Tim, and also his wish to please her in his own compliant, submissive manner, which felt familiar and comfortable to him.

This was what it took to make this relationship work and I helped the couple move towards that goal, even though this may not be politically correct and even though this is absolutely not what I myself have or want in my own marriage.

Improving the Fit Between the Partners

Sex therapy is a brief form of treatment with the limited and defined goal of improving the patient's or the couple's sexual functioning. This often entails helping the couple perfect their emotional and sexual fit. But one cannot hope to, nor should one attempt to, effect basic changes in a person's personality or in the fundamental architecture of a couple's relationship in the context of this brief goal-oriented kind of intervention. That is a job for lengthy, reconstructive psychoanalytic and long-term couples treatments.

Without judgments or prejudices of what relationships "ought" to be like, we should limit ourselves to trying to establish that moment of harmony between the partners that is a necessary condition for the conduct of sex therapy. As I see it, it is the therapist's job to try to resolve issues that get in the way of the couple's harmony, without fiddling with the fundamental structures of their relationship.

Common Sources of Anger in the Treatment of Low Desire

In that spirit and within these limitations, the sources of anger we commonly try to resolve within the context of brief psychosexual therapy include *power struggles*, which often center around money and children, *contractual disappointments* of various kinds, feelings of betrayal on account of one partner's extramarital affair(s), as well as *discrepancies* in the couple's sexual needs and wishes for attention, intimacy, and communication, mutual parental transferences, and neurotic projective identifications that get in the way of a happy married and sexual life.

The role of such interpersonal issues in the pathogenesis of sexual desire disorders will be illustrated in the following two chapters, which contain a number of case histories in which treatment is centered primarily on problems in the couple's marital system.

DRUGS IN TREATMENT OF SEXUAL DESIRE DISORDERS

Three types of medications are potentially useful adjuncts in the treatment of selected patients with psychogenic HSD and sexual aversions: 1. Anti-anxiety and panic-blocking medications; 2. Antidepressants; and 3. Non-steroidal Aphrodisiacs.

1. Anti-Anxiety and Panic-Blocking Drugs

Anxiety-Lowering Medication for Sexual Aversions and Sexual Phobias

Psychoactive medications, and most particularly tranquilizers, find their greatest usefulness in the treatment of patients with sexual aversions and sexual phobias who have concomitant panic and other anxiety disorders. The logic and effectiveness of combining behavioral and pharmacologic modalities for the treatment of phobic anxiety states such as agoraphobia, school and social phobias have been well documented (Klein, 1980, 1987, 1989; Klein & Rabkin, 1980; Klein, Gittelman-Klein, et al., 1980; Noyes et al., 1990).

We have been using a comparable combination of sex therapy and anti-anxiety drugs for sexual phobias and sexual anxiety states since the 70's (Kaplan, Fyer, & Novick, 1982; Klein, 1987). As was discussed in a previous section (pages 174–175), many patients with severe sexual anxiety states are too agitated to cooperate with or benefit from sex therapy without the adjunctive use of anxiety-lowering drugs.

Highly anxious patients who are undergoing sex therapy should receive anti-anxiety drugs in doses that are high enough to block their panic attacks without interfering with their sexual functioning. It is also desirable to avoid doses that are sufficient to put patients to sleep or to obtund their consciousness, as this can interfere with the learning process.

The medication should be administered daily in order to achieve a steady blood level, preferably in a single, night-time dose. However, if a patient experiences withdrawal sensations during the day with shorter acting drugs like alprezalam, he/she can be given the medication in divided doses, twice or three times a day.

There are several classes of effective anxiety-lowering medications currently available. These have different side-effect and toxicity profiles that can limit their usefulness for patients with sexual disorders.

Because new and improved psychoactive drugs are constantly coming on the market, the following suggestions about medications may be outdated before this book is in print.

At this writing, *our first line drug for patients with sexual panic states who are undergoing sex therapy is Xanax (alprezalam)* in low to moderate doses (0.25–1.5 mg/OD). I prefer this medication because of the excellent reduction of anxiety many patients experience at doses that are low enough to be only infrequently associated with unpleasant systemic and sexual side effects.

Other anti-anxiety agents, such as the diazepoxides, e.g., Valium and Atavan, may be substituted for patients who cannot tolerate Xanax. Of special interest is Buspar (buspirone), an anti-anxiety agent of the azaspirodecanedione type that are selective 5HT-1A receptor antagonists, has been reported to have low incidence of sedative effects and addictive reactions (Faludi, 1994; Buspar, 1994). There is reason to believe that Buspar will prove to be useful for unwelcome compulsive sexual states. However, it is too early to tell if the azaspirodecanes have significant advantages over agents currently used for the treatment of patients with sexual motivation dysfunctions.

Desyrel (trazodone), also in low to moderate amounts (50–100 mg) in a single nighttime dose, is my second choice drug for sexaphobic patients in sex therapy. Although in our experience this is generally not as effective as alprezalam in reducing sexual anxiety, the side-effect profile is excellent at low doses. Trazodone is a particularly interesting drug for this patient population because it tends to improve erections* (Segraves & Segraves, 1992; Lal, Rios, & Tharundayil, 1990).

Tricyclics (TCAs), chiefly Tofranil (imipramine), Norpramine (norimipramine), Elavil (amitryptaline), and Aventil (nortryptaline), are currently my third choice for treating sexual anxiety in combination

*The erection-enhancing effects of Trazodone can result in priapism, a rare but worrisome complication when this drug is used with male patients.

with sex therapy. Although these substances have long been known to be effective blockers of panic attacks (Klein, 1980, 1987; Klein & Rabkin, 1980; Noyes et al., 1990; Liebowitz, 1989), the high incidence of unpleasant systemic side effects makes them less than optimal for treating sexually dysfunctional patients. At low doses, these effects include sweating, constipation, and dry mouth with bad breath; at higher doses, there can be the additional problems of serious cardiac complications, as well as loss of libido and impotence in males. (See Chapter 10, Table 8.)

The older MAOIs (monoamine oxydase inhibitors), for example Nardil (phenelzine) and Marplan (isocarboxazide), with the exception of Eldepril (selegiline), are not my favorite adjunctive drugs for sexaphobic patients, although they are effective anti-panic agents. These MAOIs carry the risk of serious, albeit rare, life-threatening side effects. They also require dietary restrictions. Moreover, because the MAOIs are notorious for retarding ejaculation in males and delaying orgasm in women (Segraves, 1988b, 1992; Segraves & Golden, 1992; Segraves & Segraves, 1992), these drugs are unsuitable for treating sexual anxiety disorders except for carefully selected patients.

A new group of selective MAOIs, the so-called RIMAs (reversible inhibitors or monoamine oxydase), is currently being developed here and abroad. For example, the selective beta MAOI, Arorax (meclobinate) is said to be beneficial for patients with atypical depressions and those with excessive rejection sensitivity. (Angst et al., 1993). It has been speculated that the improved sexual side-effect profiles of these new agents will make them suitable for use with sexually dysfunctional patients, but this is yet to be proved.

Although the *SSRIs* (selective serotonin reuptake inhibitors) can be effective in lowering sexual anxiety, the same side effect, namely impairment of the male and the female orgasm reflexes, also limits the usefulness of such drugs as Prozac (fluoxitine), Zoloft (sertraline), and Paxil (paroxitine) for patients with sexual anxiety states (Liebowitz, 1989; Kline, 1989; Herman et al., 1990; Zajecka et al., 1991).

There is an interesting exception, however. The orgasm-delaying effects of some of the SSRIs can be beneficial for treating PE.* There-

*We and others have found that low doses of Prozac (5mg–20mg) as well as low doses of other SSRIs (Zoloft, Paxil) are effective adjuncts to the stop-start method of sex therapy for anxious patents with severe PE. Although it has recently been reported that long-term administration of the SSRI drugs and Anafranil (clomipramine) can have salutary effects on ejaculatory control by themselves (Assalin, 1988; Segraves & Golden, 1992; Segraves et al., 1993). We prefer the combined approach because of the additional benefits, in terms of enhanced sexual behavior, conferred by sex therapy (Kaplan, 1994).

fore, in cases where patients lose their desire for sex or become hesitant about initiating sexual relationships because they feel humiliated about their poor ejaculatory control, drugs with ejaculatory-delaying side effects, such as the SSRIs and also Anafranil (clomipramine), may be considered as part of the treatment plan.

Treating Sexaphobic Patients without Medication

For a variety of reasons, we have treated a number of sexaphobic patients who have concomitant anxiety disorders without medication. Most of those were seen before we were using anti-anxiety drugs for these conditions. In some cases, I was reluctant to prescribe medication for female patients who did not use birth control because of the possibility that they might become pregnant during the course of treatment.*

With persistence, a great deal of support, and very careful, slow, and gradual desensitization, it is possible to achieve successful outcomes with some sexaphobic patients with psychosexual therapy alone. However, without the aid of medication, this is far more difficult for the patient and for the partner, and also much harder on the doctor.**

Anti-Anxiety Drugs and HSD

Patients with HSD have a significantly lower incidence of concomitant anxiety disorders, and the benefits of anti-anxiety medication are not as striking for these patients. However, these drugs can be helpful for the occasional patient with HSD who is too anxious to abandon himself fully to the sexual experience.

2. Antidepressant Drugs

Drugs that have antidepressant effects, such as the SSRIs and the MAOIs, are on the whole more helpful for patients with HSD than benzodiazepines such as Valium or Xanax. With good responders, an

*I could find no data implicating anti-anxiety medication in human fetal damage, but I feel there are too many unknowns to be sanguine about prescribing psychotropic drugs to women in their first trimester.

**Of the 1003 patients with HSD who were treated in our program between 1972 and 1992, 138 or 14% received psychoactive medication. Of the 247 treated patients with sexual aversions/phobias, 85, or 35%, were medicated. This number has now increased to where about 75% of the sexaphobic patients who are currently in treatment in our programs are receiving anti-anxiety drugs.

SSRI like Prozac or an MOAI such as Nardil can on occasion facilitate the process of sex therapy in difficult, chronically depressed, angry, narcissistic, rejection-sensitive, or emotionally fragile, low-desire patients as well as in partners with those characteristics, by elevating their mood and stabilizing their emotions. These drugs certainly don't help every difficult patient with HSD who resists therapy, but the effect can be remarkable in some cases.

As an example of a good response, Mary, the difficult, demanding wife of Tim, whom I treated at the clinic (Case 7.1) became amazingly more cooperative and loving to her husband after I prescribed low doses of Prozac (20 mg OD). The change in Mary's behavior was so striking that one entire Wednesday conference was taken up by a spirited discussion about whether it was my intense support of Mary, the Prozac, or the combination that had resulted in the amazing change.

3. Non-Steroidal Aphrodisiacs

Chapter 10 contains a discussion of the powerful aphrodisiac effects of testosterone replacement for hypogonadic men and for women with female androgen-deficiency syndrome. More specifically, T replacement in low-desire patients with androgen deficiencies rapidly restores libido to entirely normal levels. However, the administration of sex hormones to persons who have no demonstrable T deficiencies is medically inappropriate and not effective.

More specifically, high, supraphysiologic doses of T do not raise the libidos of eugonadal men (Segraves, 1988a), unless their circulating androgens represent a drop from previously higher levels (See Chapter 10).

The picture is more complicated in women. The administration of exogenous T raises the libido of T-deficient women just as this does for T-deficient men (Kaplan, 1993; Davidson & Rosen, 1992; Schiavi & White, 1976; Sherwin, 1988). But androgens do not have this effect on physically normal women with HSD (Carney et al., 1978). However, supraphysiologic doses of androgens do seem to increase the female sex drive in some cases, but since this may have irreversible virilizing effects, T should never be used as a sexual stimulant for female patients who have no hormone deficits.

However, there are a few *non-steroidal drugs* that may have true aphrodisiac effects. These medications can be prescribed for men and women with low sexual desire states who have normal sex-hormone profiles and would therefore derive no benefit from testosterone. Non-steroidal drugs that raise libido may also be tried for patients who have

T deficiencies and would respond, but who cannot take androgens because they have medical conditions for which these hormones are contraindicated. The latter include patients with T-sensitive malignancies and congestive heart failure, among others.

The following are some of the non-hormonal medications that are currently used for their possible libido-raising effects.

1. *Bromocriptine.* This is an anti-prolactin drug that has no aphrodisiac effects per se. However, the administration of bromocriptine can indirectly raise the libido of patients with prolactin-secreting adenomas of the pituitary gland by suppressing the abnormal secretion of prolactin (Goodman & Gilman, 1993; Davidson & Rosen, 1992).

2. *Yokon* (yohimbine) is a drug that is said to act on the penis in a way that enhances erection. This substance, providing the patient is a good responder, is particularly useful in men whose impotence has contributed to their lack of desire. However, our experience with Yokon is not very impressive, as only a small number of patients seem to derive any notable benefits from this drug. There are recent reports that Yohimbine may be more effective when this is used in combination with Trental (pentoxifylline), a vasodilatory substance (Nessel, 1994; Korenman & Viosca, 1993).

3. *Dopaminergic Drugs.* Dr. Taylor Segraves, after reviewing the extensive literature on this subject, has concluded that substances that shift the balance of neurotransmitters in the brain towards serotonin tend to lower libido. The opposite effect, namely, an increase in libido, is produced by drugs that increase the brain's supply of dopamine (Segraves, 1988a,c). An example of the former is the serum serotonin release-inhibitor group of drugs (SSRIs), which increase serotonin and are well known to decrease the sex drive. The aphrodisiac effects of the following list of substances may possibly be attributed to their ability to make more dopamine available to the neurones of the sex-regulating structures of the brain.

Wellbutrin (bupropion) is an antidepressant drug that has demonstrable libido-enhancing effects in patients with low desire who are *not* depressed (Crenshaw, 1985). The aphrodisiac potential of Wellbutrin has been documented by well controlled clinical studies, and this drug is widely prescribed by medical sex therapists for low-desire states in male and female patients.

Further, Wellbutrin is the antidepressant of choice for depressed patients who complain of a loss of sexual desire due to other antidepressant agents, particularly the SSRIs, MAOIs, and TCAs. A number of studies have been published that are consistent with our own clinical experience (unpublished study) that such patients often report that their desire improved after they were switched to Wellbutrin (Segraves, 1992).

Our experience suggests that the effects of this drug are unpredictable. Some nondepressed patients with low libido states report that they experience a definite increase in their sexual feelings in response to bupropion, while others do not. No predictors of drug responsiveness have been identified as yet; this can be determined in any particular case only by a trial of medication.

Desyrel (trazadone) is an antidepressant drug that has the unique side effect of enhancing erections in some men, and this drug has been used to treat erectile disorders (Lal et al., 1990). Although not all patients react in this manner, erectile enhancement is occasionally so profound that patients must be cautioned about the risk of priapism. Men whose libido is depressed due to their erectile difficulties or to depression may do very well with this drug.

Eldepril (selegeline, deprenal). There are anecdotal reports, but no controlled studies, that *Eldepril*, a selective MAOI inhibitor that is used for depressed patients with Parkinson's disease, enhances libido. This effect is said to be especially likely to occur in older patients. We have noted this effect in a number of patients.*

L-dopa is a direct precursor of dopamine. This drug was one of the first to be used for Parkinson's disease. According to Segraves, the scientific evidence for L-dopa's libido-enhancing qualities is equivocal, but there have been a number of impressive and convincing case reports of Parkinson patients who claimed marked increases in their sex drive after they began taking L-dopa (Segraves, 1988a; Segraves & Segraves, 1992). These reports are promising, but the side effects are such that I know of no clinician who is currently using L-dopa for patients with low libido.

Recreational Dopaminergic Drugs. There is a considerable body of anecdotal evidence to the effect that acute doses of small amounts of *cocaine and amphetamines* stimulate libido and enhance sexual performance. However, it is generally conceded that *chronic usage and high doses* of these stimulants are associated with a definite, and sometimes long-lasting depression of sexual interest and responsivity.

Similarly, there is a wide belief that *marijuana (THC) and alcohol* are dysinhibiting and sexually stimulating. This observation is proba-

*As an example of the potential aphrodisiac effects of *Eldepril,* I saw a 81-year-old woman, who had been given this drug for Parkinson's disease, who complained of intense sexual feelings for an elderly gentleman and the urge to masturbate. This celibate, devout Roman Catholic woman was distressed by these unaccustomed feelings, which promptly abated when the medication was discontinued.

bly valid if these substances are taken in small amounts, on occasion. But once again, high doses and chronic use of alcohol and THC have the opposite effect. Alcoholics frequently lose their desire for sex and, for reasons that are not entirely clear, this may persist after years of sobriety.

It may be speculated that the libido-raising effects of these substances, which are all dopaminergic, are temporary because the long-term use of high doses of these substances can be expected to result in a down-regulation, or even a permanent "burnout," of the dopamine receptors in the pleasure and sex centers of the brain.

Current Status of Aphrodisiac Drugs

It is my impression that all the aphrodisiac drugs and substances listed above can, in fact, increase the libido of some men and women to some degree. However, these are, relatively speaking, not very potent agents, and the responses of most patients with HSD are disappointing. Even at best, the libido-enhancing medications and substances that are currently available are unreliable, and they cannot compare to the astounding efficacy of testosterone replacement in T-deficient men and women.

Despite many advances, the neurophysiology and pharmacology of the sex-regulating apparatus of the CNS are still largely unexplored. As more knowledge about the molecular biology of the anatomical structures, hormones, and neurotransmitters that drive these neural centers accumulates, we can expect the development of more powerful and less toxic aphrodisiacs. This would be of immense benefit to patients with low libido states, regardless of whether the deficit is psychogenic or the result of such physical assaults as cancer treatments, the deterioration of old age, or accidental injuries to the gonads.

However, I foresee an ethical dilemma that might impede the commercial development of new aphrodisiacs. Our society unhesitantly endorses the healing of the sick and doctors receive unqualified approval for restoring the deficient sex drives of patients with sexual desire disorders. Yet, I wonder how the establishment is going to respond if it should turn out that these same substances can also rev up the libido of normal men and women who might want to use these "smart drugs" just to have a good time.

CHAPTER 8

Treatment II: Case Studies

The following eight case studies were selected to illustrate the clinical and dynamic heterogeneity that characterizes patients and couples with sexual desire disorders, the flexibility with which the principles of psychosexual therapy can be employed to meet the needs of different patients, and also the diversity of the responses to treatment.

The first three patients presented in this chapter responded primarily to the libido-raising behavioral/cognitive exercises and *in-vivo* exposures described in the previous chapter. The rest required supplemental psychodynamic insight therapy to varying degrees.

In five of the cases, therapy was mainly directed towards resolving the low-desire partner's underlying intrapsychic conflicts and sexual anxieties, whereas the focus of the therapeutic effort in the remaining three cases was on ameliorating the couples' toxic interactions.

The cases also varied considerably in complexity. This is reflected by the wide differences in the duration of treatment, which ranged from a brief six sessions in one case to one couple whom I saw for more than five years.

The patients' psychosexual histories were also diverse. Two patients, a man and a woman, had been sexually abused when they were young. Two others had suffered severe emotional abuse and/or neglect as children, while the families of origin of three other low-desire patients were only mildly to moderately dysfunctional. In one case both partners come from functional, stable family environments.

The eight case histories provide samples of the entire spectrum of treatment outcomes, from the successful establishment of normal sexual desire and frequency in four cases to two that were outright treatment failures. The remaining two patients reported that their sexual desire had improved only partially.*

The first two cases involved single patients, five were treated as couples, and one patient preferred to be seen by himself, even though he had a sexual partner.

The two elements that the patients had in common were their complaints of deficient desire and the nature of the immediate causes of their sexual symptoms. Although there were wide stylistic variations, every patient with HSD unwittingly down-regulated his/her sexual desire by selectively focusing on negative, while avoiding positive erotic input, and both patients with sexual aversion disorders displayed the typical link between fear and sex, as well as the well-reinforced sexual avoidance patterns.

TREATING SINGLE PATIENTS WITH SEXUAL DESIRE DISORDERS

According to some authors, sexual desire disorders are always caused by malignant interactions between the partners. Clinicians with this view recommend that treatment be conducted conjointly in all cases (Leiblum & Rosen, 1988; Masters et al., 1994).

While I agree that relationship problems are of primary importance in many instances, I take exception to the notion that conjoint treatment is mandatory or necessarily the treatment of choice in all cases. As a matter of fact, we have treated numbers of single patients with sexual desire disorders, as well as single patients with other psychosexual dysfunctions with good results. The first two case histories in this chapter describe the successful treatments of two middle-aged virgins with lifelong sexual avoidance, a woman and a man, who were each seen alone.

However, there is no question that the absence of a partner complicates the treatment and compromises the outlook for sexaphobic patients, simply because the treatment of choice for this disorder centers around a systematic program of *in-vivo* desensitization. This entails

*These outcomes are based on the patient's and therapist's evaluations at the termination of therapy. These are cited here only to illustrate the wide range of treatment results we have seen in clinical practice. Clearly, however, there is a need for systematic outcome and follow-up studies, which are in progress.

exposing the phobic patient very gradually to the sight, sound, touch, feel, smell and taste the of lover's body and genitalia, until his/her fear or revulsion diminishes. The availability of a cooperative, attractive, and above all trustworthy partner is clearly an invaluable asset for this procedure.

For example, "Ida and Ira Diamond," the young Orthodox Jewish couple (Case 5.5) described in Chapter 5, could not consummate their marriage on account of Ida's phobic avoidance of vaginal penetration.

This couple underwent the standard course of gradual, systematic *in-vivo* desensitization. At every step of treatment, Ira acted the devoted and cooperative partner. He allowed his wife to decide the pace of the extinction program, and he did not pressure her when she wanted to take extra time. Without resisting, he followed our suggestion to let her take complete control of the exercises, and he permitted her to guide his hands, his lips, and his penis during the therapeutic exercises. In addition, Ira unfailingly encouraged Ida's efforts and gains, and there is no question that his participation was an important ingredient in the successful outcome of this case.

The unavailability of a sexual partner presents an even greater handicap for women patients than it does for men. Hired sexual partners, such as sexual surrogates, masseuses, and prostitutes, can often substitute effectively for intimate partners for the purpose of conducting the therapeutic sexual exercises. But while this is quite acceptable and even customary for men, the majority of women in our society object to paying for sex, even in the context of therapy. Therefore, single sexually dysfunctional women who wish to have sex therapy must first solve the considerable problem of *attracting* a sexual partner to work with.

The risk of contracting AIDS from casual sexual partners is now diminishing this gender difference. For men are also becoming wary of sex with strangers and physicians have become reluctant to suggest surrogates. The limitations on surrogate therapy, together with the growing numbers of single men and women who are seeking help for their sexual difficulties, have sparked the development of new approaches for patients without partners.

Our method for treating sexually dysfunctional men and women without partners divides therapy into two phases. Phase I is devoted to improving the patient's sexual functioning primarily with the use of solo therapeutic exercises (Kaplan, 1989a, 1993a, 1995). The objective of the second phase of treatment, which is usually started while phase I is still in progress, is to support the patient's quest for an appropriate sexual partner.

CASE 8.1—"Greta Biedemeyer": Lifelong, Generalized Sexual Aversion and Avoidance in a 39-Year-Old Virgin with a Concomitant Panic Disorder*

This case, which was first mentioned in Chapter 5, illustrates several clinical issues. These include a successful treatment outcome, which occurred solely in response to behavioral and pharmacologic interventions, the adjunctive use of anti-panic medications, and the importance of working through the patient's traumatic memory of sexual abuse. Finally, this case affords a good look at some of the problems that are involved in treating a single sexaphobic patient.

"Greta Biedemeyer" was a 39-year-old, single, Austrian immigrant who requested treatment for her sexual aversion and avoidance of relationships with men on the advice of a friend who had been helped with her sexual problems at our clinic.

The patient had a severe, lifelong aversion to sex and was particularly repelled by the idea of kissing.

Greta was a virgin. She had not had intercourse, nor had she ever engaged in any sort of physical intimacy with a partner, not even holding hands. The very thought of meeting a man who might make sexual advances filled her with dread, and she had avoided any and all potentially romantic situations on that account. Thus, Greta had never dated or danced with a man, nor had she ever engaged in flirtatious banter. Declining social invitations that involved the presence of men, Greta generally spent evenings and weekends alone. Apart from her job as a bilingual secretary for the Roman Catholic Diocese and her volunteer work at a home for the aged, which she found gratifying, Greta led a lonely and pleasureless life.

The patient's aversion to and phobic avoidance of sex were limited to contact with a partner. Greta had no difficulty fantasizing and masturbating to orgasm when she was by herself, although she did this very infrequently.

This patient also had a history of a disabling panic disorder with agoraphobic features for which she had been treated the previous year at another facility. She had responded well to a course of imipramine in combination with cognitive therapy. When Greta became my patient, she was still on a maintenance dose of 75 mg of imipramine and she was functioning well in all spheres. She worked, she traveled without any difficulty, she was able to enjoy some holidays with her women friends,

*This case is further described in *Case Studies in Sex Therapy* edited by S. R. Leiblum and R. C. Rosen, Guilford Publications, 1995.

and she had experienced no further panic attacks since the end of her treatment. However, there had been absolutely no corresponding improvement in her sexual symptoms, which were as severe as ever.

Greta realized that her fear of sex was destroying her life, and she was now determined to seek help to overcome this problem.

Immediate Causes

The central core and immediate cause of Greta's sexual problem was her intense aversion to kissing, which could be traced directly to the sexual abuse she had endured as a child. As was mentioned in the section on sexual abuse (pages 124–125), Greta had been repeatedly molested by an elderly neighbor who lived down the hall when she was six to ten years old. The man would wait for her when she came home from school and drag her into his apartment, where he would hold her tightly while he pressed his "stinking" mouth on her lips. At the same time, he forced the child to rub his penis and would not let her go until he ejaculated. A shy, lonely little girl, raised by her widowed mother—a reclusive woman who was probably also agoraphobic—Greta told no one of her ordeals and suffered in silence. These repeated traumatic experiences had forged a link between feelings of disgust and aversion with kissing and sex.

A second tier of immediate causes of this patient's sexual problem, which would also have to be modified in therapy, was Greta's unattractive, anti-seductive appearance, which presumably served to protect her from unwelcome sexual approaches. This defense had originated in Greta's attempts as a little girl to become "sexually invisible" and unappealing in the vain hope that she could slip by her tormentor unnoticed.

Persons who are afraid of sex often adopt a countersexual persona and assume a cloak of sexual neutrality or unattractiveness in their efforts to avoid sexual relationships. Like Greta, these individuals often remain single and celibate.

Treatment

The challenge posed by trying to cure a lifelong, severe sexual aversion and avoidance, along with phobic social anxiety, in an obese, unattractive woman of 39 who had no sexual experience, had never dated, and had no partner nor any imminent prospects of finding one, was considerable.

As a first step, I became Greta's "good mother." A strong *positive transference* is an important ingredient in the success of this brief treatment method. An amiable transferential state boosts the therapeutic process by virtue of patients' wanting to please the therapist. In addition, this also allows patients to identify with the therapist and to adopt his or her more liberal and permissive sexual attitudes. A positive transference is especially important with sexually dysfunctional patients who, like Greta, experienced inadequate or destructive parenting and/or poor gender-appropriate role models during the critical phases of their psychosexual development.

Greta was "ready" for a good mother, and a firm therapeutic alliance was rapidly established on that basis. Thereafter, I gave Greta "grooming" and "appearance" homework. More specifically, after reassuring her that she was potentially an attractive woman (which she resisted, claiming that only "chubby chasers" would like her), I advised her to have a cosmetic "make over" consultation at an upscale department store and suggested that she clean and mend her clothes. I then asked her to wear her prettiest colored blouse to our next session. Greta was eager to win my approval, and I let her know that she had when she came in looking much better the following week.

Since Greta had no partner with whom she could conduct the therapeutic exposure assignments, I first tried to reduce her sexual anxiety and her phobic avoidance of kissing with *covert desensitization*. Towards that end, I asked her to watch kissing scenes on television and to practice visualizing couples kissing. But this had little effect.

I also attempted to "detour around" the patient's repugnance for kissing by pointing out that it was perfectly possible for her to make love to a man without necessarily allowing him to kiss her. Greta was skeptical of this cognitive maneuver, but a seed was planted in her mind that would sprout later.

At the same time, in every session we worked on uncovering and working through Greta's traumatic childhood experiences. As has been discussed in Chapter 6, it is not effective nor feasible to use behavioral exercises in the attempt to "bypass" a patient's fear or aversion to sex when this is due to sexual trauma. It makes more sense for the therapist to attempt to uncover and work through the patient's memories of the painful event(s), and so to enable her to respond positively to the therapeutic physical exposure exercises without being further traumatized.

During the initial therapy sessions, we reviewed in great detail the sexually abusive incidents Greta had endured and talked at length about how she had felt at the time. I made a special effort to clarify the destructive impact these events had on her psychosexual development and on her present problems. After a few sessions of this, Greta seemed to become a little bored by the topic, which suggested to me that she was beginning to come to terms with her painful memories.

Greta was making progress. In addition to her growing insight into the consequences of her traumatic childhood experiences, she also became visibly more attractive and cheerful. However, she continued to avoid social contact with men.

Treatment was at an impasse. It was apparent to me that no further meaningful progress could be made unless, somehow, actual partner-related therapeutic experiences could be arranged.

The Therapeutic Sigs

Greta had a lovely feminine speaking voice, which was seasoned with her charming Viennese accent, and I decided to use this asset as a starting point for helping her overcome her social anxiety and avoidance.

I asked the patient to place an advertisement in the personal columns of New York Magazine. I pointed out that she could expect to receive many letters from men who would want to meet her. In the attempt to forestall her anticipated objections, I reassured Greta that she would be entirely in control of the enterprise, as the letters would be addressed to an anonymous box number provided by the magazine. She could choose to call only those men whose letters appealed to her.

But Greta resisted this assignment. She claimed that only crazy men answer personal ads. She also maintained that she could not afford it.

At this point I confronted the patient with her resistance. I told her that I thought her objections to placing the ad were merely rationalizations and excuses for continuing her avoidance of men and sex. At the same time I balanced this relentless stripping away of her old defenses with my understanding and support. Thus, I was very warm and empathic with the difficulty of her situation, and I expressed my view sympathetically that her intense fears and avoidance of meeting men were entirely understandable under the circumstances, and that no one could fault her for this.

I also "joined the patient's resistance" by lowering my fee to compensate for the cost of placing the advertisement. Finally, with deep misgivings, Greta agreed to place the ad.

We then proceeded to compose the ad together. This turned out to be an excellent therapeutic opportunity to begin to modify the negative image Greta was projecting, which was one of the more effective defenses against sex in her considerable armamentarium.

In her initial draft of the ad, Greta described herself as fat and unattractive, while mentioning none of her positive qualities. The patient had no insight that this was an expression of her fear and avoidance of sex that practically guaranteed that no sane man would answer her ad.

With my steadfast support of the positives and my unrelenting vetoes of the negatives that Greta kept trying to slip into the text of the advertisement, she eventually composed an appealing, yet entirely honest description of herself, to which she received over 100 replies.

Greta was astonished and thrilled when she saw how many men wanted to meet her. However, she was also terrified of and very resistant to the idea of contacting them.

I then *reduced* the assignment. I suggested that Greta pick out the 25 most promising letters and call only three of these men each week. I tried to further decrease her anxiety by limiting the purpose of the phone calls so that these would be less threatening. I told Greta that the calls were only *exercises* meant for learning and practicing how to conduct a pleasant, appropriate social conversation with a man, but they were *not* to be the occasion for arranging dates.

We also rehearsed the phone calls. I advised Greta to start the conversations by telling each man that she liked his letter, but that she just wanted to chat and get to know him a little. For the time being, she was specifically asked *not* to agree to a meeting, if any of the men were to request this. In case a conversation became unpleasant, the patient was instructed to hang up the phone at once.

Despite the slow, careful pace of the desensitization program and despite my continuing support, amplified by our strong therapeutic alliance, all my attempts to bypass Greta's resistances with cognitive and behavioral tactics failed. Although she managed, with great apprehension, to make a few calls, she remained paralyzed by her intense anticipatory anxiety.

Psychodynamic Exploration of the Resistance

When it became clear that Greta's therapy was not moving forward despite my most artful "bypass" maneuvers, I shifted to a more "invasive," "insight-fostering" strategy. More specifically, I now attempted to fortify the behavioral program with psychodynamic explorations of the childhood roots and the deeper causes of Greta's sexual fears and of her resistances.

But Greta would have none of this. For example, during one week I gave Greta three assignments, but she had done only two. She had successfully carried out a masturbation/fantasy exercise with a vibrator, and she had attended her first session of Overeaters Anonymous. However, Greta had resisted her third and most important assignment, by failing to place any of the three prescribed calls to men who had answered her ad.

Dream work is often very useful in facilitating a patient's insight into the deeper meaning of his/her resistances, and in many of my cases the well-timed interpretation of a patient's dreams has catalyzed a genuine therapeutic breakthrough. Therefore, in an effort to illuminate the unconscious psychic infrastructure of Greta's tenacious resistance, I asked her if she had had any dreams that week.

Greta told me that she had dreamt that she had three umbrellas. She had given two away to a friend but kept one of the umbrellas for herself, "in case it rained."

I tried to interest the patient in considering the notion that this dream might be a metaphor for her inner conflicts about therapy and her resistance to giving up her defensive avoidance of men. I suggested that the umbrellas might symbolize her defenses, which she was being asked to give up in therapy. I proposed the idea that by doing two of the assignments she had given up two of her protective defenses or "umbrellas" against sex, namely she had allowed herself to experience erotic feelings by fantasizing and masturbating, and she was beginning to work on improving her appearance by trying to overcome her obesity. But, I said, the dream suggested that she was not yet ready to give up her "last umbrella," her ultimate defense against being hurt sexually again by a man, namely her avoidance of contact with potential sexual partners.

Greta was totally unimpressed by my clever interpretation and she dismissed my efforts as comparable to "Gypsy tea-leaf readings."

There were a number of *deeper underlying pathogenic issues* that presumably contributed to the origin and maintenance of this patient's sexual symptoms. I believe that the death of her father when she was very young could have made her particularly vulnerable to sexual assault by a "father" figure, while the emotional neglect by her inadequate, anxious, housebound mother might have predisposed the patient to becoming insufficiently assertive and self-protective with men.

These insights shaped my behavioral interventions. For example, my exceptionally protective "maternal" behavior towards Mary, and also my emphasis, while we role-played the phone calls, on modeling appropriate assertiveness with men. However, these deeper issues never came up per se in treatment.

I continued to see the patient for a total of 14 sessions in the clinic. Although it seemed that Greta had obtained no insight into her deeper conflicts, on an experiential level she had made slow but significant progress. Despite having lost no weight, her appearance had improved, she had become quite skilled and much more confident in her phone conversations with men, and the wounds caused by the trauma of her unfortunate childhood sexual experiences seemed to be healing. But Greta still had not had a single date with a man or even a face-to-face conversation.

The clinic closed for the summer and I saw her once again two months later in the fall. I was alarmed when Greta began the session by telling me that she had been "picked up by a policeman."

I feared that perhaps therapy had somehow unleashed an unsuspected latent psychopathic or self-destructive tendency in this patient, and that she had gotten herself into trouble. But Greta quickly reassured me that what she had meant was that a *cute* policeman had picked her up in the *park* and they were now having a pleasant sexual relationship, although she admitted that she still didn't care much for the kissing part.

Medication

Concomitant panic disorder complicates the treatment of sexual aversions and the phobic avoidance of sex, and medication can be helpful in these cases (see page 193).

Prior to becoming my patient, Greta had been successfully treated for her long-standing panic disorder with 150mg of Tofranil per day, in addition to cognitive/behavioral therapy.

She was still taking a reduced maintenance dose of 75mg of Trofanil daily while undergoing sex therapy. Although she had massive anticipatory anxiety, the patient experienced no actual panic attacks during the course of treatment. Therefore, there was no need to raise the dose of her medication, but neither was this discontinued. As a matter of fact, if this patient had not been taking anti-anxiety medication, I would not have hesitated to medicate her.

This case provides a good illustration of the dictum that anti-anxiety drugs alone do not cure sexaphobic patients. However, as has been discussed in the section on medications in sex therapy, in good responders, the adjunctive use of panic-blocking or anti-anxiety medications can reduce anxiety sufficiently during the *in-vivo* exposures to facilitate the permanent extinction of the sexaphobic responses in patients who might otherwise be too anxious to cooperate with or benefit from sex therapy.

It is of course impossible to determine what role, if any, the panic-blocking drugs Greta was taking had played in the successful outcome of her treatment. However, I suspect that, with the protection of medication, it would have been extremely difficult, if not impossible, for this patient to overcome her sexual aversion; at the very least, the process would have been much more stressful for her.

The next case was similar in several respects to the previous one.

Both patients suffered the malignant effects of incestuous early experiences, both were treated without partners, and in both cases there was a significant improvement despite the fact that neither patient gained much insight into his/her deeper conflicts.

CASE 8.2—"Bill Kangaroo": Lifelong, Generalized HSD and Sexual Avoidance in a 41-Year-Old Male Virgin

"Bill Kangaroo," a tall, handsome, blond, blue-eyed, single high school principal who has been mentioned in several previous chapters was an unhappy and reluctant 41-year-old virgin. This patient had never felt the slightest sensation of desire nor had he ever become erect in the presence of a partner. However, he masturbated regularly and without any difficulty while visualizing scenes that were reminiscent of his early incestuous experiences. As the reader will recall, Bill's first sexual experiences, which occurred about once a week between the ages of five, when his father died, to 14 when his mother remarried, was to stroke his mother's legs and thighs while she reclined on a couch dressed in only in a loose robe. Bill became highly aroused and often ejaculated during these sessions. He was fixated on this scenario, which became his permanent and exclusive sexual fantasy.

Bill consulted me because Georgia, the first woman with whom he had ever been in love, and the first with whom he had ever attempted sex, had urged him to do so.

In the past, Bill had systematically avoided sexual opportunities by relating to attractive women in an asexual way, like a "brother." But with her shapely, well-developed thighs, tall, athletic Georgia, a gym teacher at his high school, was the embodiment of his sexual fantasy. When she showed an interest in him, his defenses melted. However, despite his strong attraction to Georgia, he was totally unresponsive to her kisses, her caresses, and her attempts to stimulate him manually. As usual, he went into "neutral" in her presence, but after he got home from their dates he regularly masturbated to the fantasy of stroking her thighs and making love to her.

Awkward and shy during his adolescence, Bill found it as difficult as his early childhood. He experienced a great deal of separation anxiety and found it hard to leave his mother. In fact, the first time he left home, to go to college, Bill developed a severe disabling case of colitis.

He was forced to drop out of school, and his diarrhea and weight loss also made it impossible for the young man to function socially.

Then, after years of illness and misery, Bill made a remarkable recovery. He found an excellent therapist, whose approach was supportive and cognitive, and with his help Bill learned to control and stabilize his emotions, which is of prime importance for preventing recurrences of this stress-related inflammatory condition.

After his colitis improved, Bill finished college, went on to graduate school, and eventually became a successful and well-liked high school principal. His colitis has remained in remission, with the exception of some occasional minor flare-ups, which the patient had learned to manage extremely well.

This patient's diagnosis of hypoactive sexual desire disorder of the lifelong, global type is often associated with serious underlying psychopathology. A patient in his 40s who had never functioned sexually with a partner would generally be considered to carry a guarded prognosis with brief, psychosexual therapy.

Moreover, I had some misgivings about the emotional risks that sex therapy might pose for this rejection-sensitive, vulnerable man. I also had some apprehension about the potential for physical and psychological damage if therapy were to fail and if his lover were to leave him. However, I was so impressed by Bill's remarkable history of overcoming adversity that, despite my reservations, I accepted him for treatment.

The *immediate cause* of this patient's sexual avoidance is familiar. Bill approached all sexual opportunities, including his dates with Georgia, with apprehension. He became extremely tense and immersed himself in negative thoughts. "I am not in the mood, I don't feel strong enough for this, this is hopeless, why should I expose myself to rejection, I don't need this" was a fair sampling of his usual mental processes. It was much safer to go home and masturbate while thinking of the girls he had befriended than to try to date them and face the risk of starting a sexual relationship with its potential for rejection and pain.

Treatment

Bill's strengths promptly manifested themselves in his rapid response to treatment. With remarkably little resistance, he accepted the notion that he had been avoiding sex and that he had been turning himself off in sexual situations. He quickly learned to overcome his anticipatory sexual anxiety and to control his countersexual behaviors. In short order and with little ado, Bill stopped his negative obsessing, and managed to focus his attention on Georgia's lovely legs and her athletic body, which he loved.

At the same time, in order to forestall the resistances that are often mobilized by undigested memories of childhood sexual abuse or incest, I devoted a number of therapy sessions, as in the previous case, to reviewing Bill's early erotic experiences with his mother in great detail.

Within just a few weeks, Bill began to experience desire and erections while sitting in the car and while having dinner with Georgia.

Encouraged by Bill's rapid response, I decided that it was time for some therapeutic exercises with his partner. This was a little difficult because after the initial evaluation,which she attended, Georgia had resisted coming to the sessions, citing time pressures as her excuse. With my caveat to Bill to be sure to secure Georgia's acquiescence before commencing with any of my suggestions (which is always appropriate when giving assignments in the partner's absence), I suggested that Bill rub Georgia's legs while she sat reclining passively on a couch, scantily clad, just as his mother had done. Of course, this was an attempt to re-create the erotic incestuous scenes of his fantasy in order to divert the erotic power of that experience to Bill's current relationship.

However, this strategem was not effective. Bill did not feel aroused by stroking Georgia's legs, nor did he attain an erection. It was evident from this patient's reaction, that my assignment had backfired and evoked inhibition instead of desire.

However, Georgia was not easily discouraged. An extremely intelligent and intuitive woman, she ingeniously suggested that they reverse their roles. The next time the couple got together, she asked Bill to recline on her couch, while she stroked his nude thighs.

This time Bill felt extremely aroused and excited, and he had a strong erection. The following week, in response to Georgia's manual stimulation, Bill had his first adult ejaculation with a partner. An episode of successful intercourse, during which Georgia became extremely aroused and had multiple orgasms, followed shortly thereafter.

Partner Resistance

I was delighted with such good and rapid response, especially in such a potentially difficult case. But it was too early to celebrate, for as soon as it became clear that Bill was on the threshold of becoming entirely functional, Georgia abruptly announced that she had decided to stop seeing him, claiming that the demands of the relationship, added to the pressures of being a single mother (she was divorced and lived with her son) plus her strenuous job, were simply too much for her!

Since I was not seeing Georgia, I had no opportunity to analyze or work through her resistances. I felt helpless and concerned that my support might be insufficient to protect Bill from the emotional devastation of this rejection, and I feared that this might result in a recurrence of his colitis. I kicked myself (mentally) for having accepted a vulnerable patient who did not have a truly committed partner for treatment.

Bill did become mildly depressed for a brief time, which I thought was an appropriate response, and he continued to obsess about Georgia. But happily, except for some transient GI symptoms, he did not become seriously ill.

The therapy now shifted to helping Bill find a new partner. Sports-minded and aroused by women with athletic bodies, at my suggestion Bill joined a hiking club for single men and women. He enjoyed this so much that he also enrolled in a coeducational fitness center.

Through these activities he met a variety of attractive women. At first, he was hampered by his phobic sexual anxiety and avoidance, and by his old habits of sexual "invisibility" and his "brother" act. But fortunately, this patient was extremely responsive to cognitive interventions and behavioral strategies, and he eagerly carried out all my instructions and suggestions to help him overcome his social difficulties. Bill seldom showed any resistance to strategic suggestions, and he would often start a session by telling me with much animation, "Doctor, you will be proud of me. I was really nervous last week when you told me to (say hello, call someone up, focus on his date's legs, pay his dentist's attractive receptionist a compliment, etc.), but I screwed up my nerve and I did it! And Doctor, it worked!"

I was not about to interpret Bill's transferential distortions. Instead, I used his wish to please me to boost the power of my strategic suggestions to help him find a new sexual partner.

Bill's social skills improved and he became quite successful at attracting women. He also learned to make himself comfortable in sexual situations, and he became adept at focusing on the attractive features of his partners to arouse himself. He proudly reported that he was able to feel desire and have erections with a variety of women, even those who were not entirely his sexual ideal. But he continued to avoid actual sexual intercourse.

Resistance to Psychodynamics

One of the difficulties in this case was Bill's reluctance to work in a psychodynamic mode. He did not like to talk about his painful childhood and adolescence, and he could not remember his dreams.

I joined Bill's resistance to insight therapy, and I worked with him principally in a behavioral/cognitive/strategic mode for about two years of weekly sessions.

At the termination of therapy, Bill was regularly experiencing sexual desire in the "high-normal" range, and he was functioning normally. He had had a brief successful sexual relationship with an Oriental woman, and he was now dating an attractive, athletic social worker, a few years older than he, whom he had meet at a "singles" hiking event. This woman was closer to Bill's ideal, but Georgia remained his sexual fantasy.

The next patient, "Bud Player," can also be considered as a solo treatment case, for although Bud had a girlfriend, he kept his therapy a secret from her, and I never got to meet her.

This case provides yet another example of a patient whose libido improved to a high-normal level, although he obtained only limited insight into his deeper fears and vulnerabilities.

But the most novel aspect of this case was the use, in a physically normal man, of intra-cavernosal injections (ICI). The major purpose of pharmacologically provoked erections in this case was to "bypass" the patient's massive performance anxiety, as well as his intolerable feelings of sexual inadequacy, which were the immediate causes of the loss of his desire for sex.

CASE 8.3—"Bud Player": Intra-Cavernosal Injections in the Treatment of Acquired, Generalized Psychogenic HSD

Bud, age 45, was a handsome, dark-haired, bearded, charming, divorced, highly successful performer.

The patient was in a state of high anxiety when I first saw him because he had been unable to feel desire nor to function sexually with his new, extremely attractive, 23-year-old assistant, Tracy, with whom he was deeply infatuated. Bud was obsessed by the fear that Tracy was going to leave him if he did not make love to her soon.

Tracy accompanied Bud on his frequent concerts and performance tours. She was responsible for his travel arrangements, hotels, and bookings. When they were on the road, the couple usually shared a hotel room and slept in the same bed. Although mentally Bud found the young woman immensely attractive, he experienced absolutely no feelings of desire or arousal, nor did he have erections when they kissed, caressed, and slept in each other's arms. This was particularly shocking to this man because, before this, he had never experienced any sexual difficulties whatsoever.

One obvious currently operating *immediate cause* of this patient's lack of desire was the escalating cycle of his performance anxiety, impotence, and anticipation of failure, which made him feel totally inadequate and which drowned out any erotic feelings.

The patient made his own diagnosis of an additional, more subtle, *immediate cause* of his inability to function with the beautiful Tracy. He told me that for the past six years he had deliberately put a "lid" on his sexual feelings because his life since his divorce had been incredibly hectic and stressful. He told me that he had deliberately suppressed his sexual appetite because he felt that sexual relationships would have interfered with and taken him away from his career and his children, which were his two absolute priorities at this point in his life.

In other words, since his divorce, six years ago, Bud had protected himself from experiencing sexual feelings by deliberately erecting perceptual defenses to shield him from any and all erotic stimuli. If he did on occasion notice the beginnings of some erotic stirrings, he would quickly turn himself off by filling his mind with thoughts of the many responsibilities that preoccupied him.

This mental "brake" on his sexual desire had become habitual and automatic, and was no longer under his voluntary control. As a result, to his great frustration, when Bud was in bed with his beautiful partner, he did not know how to release the "brakes" and he felt "nothing."

Bud had no insight into some of the *deeper and more painful causes* of his sexual problem, namely that unconsciously he was protecting himself from experiencing yet another painful rejection. But this patient, even more so than "Greta" and "Bill," staunchly objected to my efforts to explore the unconscious meaning of his sexual symptoms and of his resistance to treatment.

I did manage to obtain a few scraps of historical information. From these, I surmised that the patient had been badly hurt by his self-absorbed, ignorant parents' constant rebuffs and what seemed an almost total lack of interest in the boy. Bud learned early on that the only way to get any attention or approval was through material success, which was all that seemed to matter to his impoverished clan.

Since his school days, Bud had put all his efforts into excelling and performing. Thanks to his drive and his God-given talent, he had succeeded brilliantly. His fame and his generosity had been effective in getting his family's attention, and in shoring up his self-esteem, until his wife's unexpected defection shattered him.

Bud had been married to his first wife Jane for 12 years and the couple had two children. Six years before, Jane had abruptly left him for another man, a neighbor. This had come as a complete shock to Bud. He had been in total denial and entirely unaware that his wife had been unhappy or discontented in any way. I suspected that she felt lonely because Bud did not know the meaning of intimacy. Since he did not recognize this, he had sincerely believed that their marriage had been good. "I did everything I was supposed to do, Dr. K," he said to me, obviously still hurt and perplexed, "I worked hard. I made lots of money for us; I bought her a beautiful house; we took great trips; I didn't screw around; I thought sex was fine, and I still can't figure out what went wrong."

Bud fought for and obtained joint custody of the couple's two little boys and he became the "perfect father." Compulsive, hyperconscientious, Bud imposed ultra-high standards of parenthood on himself. He carefully investigated the children's schools, lessons, and doctors; he cooked and shopped for the boys' clothes himself; he personally drove them to their schools and lessons and doctor appointments. No detail escaped him and nothing was too much effort during the 3½ days a week when they were in his care.

Bud took justified pride in the fact that both boys were thriving. And when he was not giving his all to taking care of his children, he gave "110%" to his demanding career. This talented, driven, achievement-oriented, compulsive, energetic man had not only succeeded brilliantly as a father but at the same time had achieved remarkable success in the highly competitive field of musical performance. During the summer months, when the boys were in camp, he committed himself to a heavy schedule of tours and concerts in the U.S. and around the world. In the off-season, he kept busy with recording sessions and promotional work, while also working on a book about American jazz.

Bud's compulsive parenting and his workaholicism had protected him against the emotional risks posed by love and sex for six years, but now he was obsessed with Tracy.

Since this patient's sexual deficit was total, and included the loss of his morning erections, I first had to rule out physical causes.

The tests revealed that his sex hormone profile and his nocturnal erections were normal. Therefore, concluding that Bud's sexual problem was psychogenic, I suggested a course of sex therapy.

Treatment

This man belonged to a culture that regards psychiatry with suspicion, and he was extraordinarily resistant to the process of psychotherapy. He felt threatened by the prospect of giving up his denial, strongly defended against admitting his vulnerabilities into conscious awareness, and was dead set against probing into the painful buried memories of past rejections. All Bud wanted from me was a "quick fix." He desperately wished to be able to function again, and he just wanted me to tell him what to do so as not to lose Tracy.

I was eager to help this unhappy man. I let him know that I "heard him," and I gave him all the practical advice I could think of. But he objected to everything I suggested.

He would not agree to try to communicate with his partner. ("She looks up to me. If she knew I had problems she would leave me for sure.")

He did not want to try SF with Tracy. ("That would make her split right away.")

He did not want to masturbate. ("That's kids stuff.")

He did not want to fantasize. ("But it's *Tracy* I want!")

He refused to consider bringing Tracy with him to the therapy session. ("Oh God! She must never know!")

He did not want to talk about his childhood. ("That was long ago. What difference does that make now?")

Bypassing Resistance with Penile Injection Treatments

After two totally frustrating sessions, I joined his resistance to intimacy, with me as well as with Tracy, and I offered to arrange a program of intracavernosal penile injection treatments (ICI) for him, although I reassured him that there was nothing physically wrong with him (Kaplan, 1993c; Wagner & Kaplan, 1994).

Bud was immediately receptive to the idea of a pharmacological solution to his problems. In fact, he pressured my busy colleague, Dr. Francois Eid, a urologist who specializeds in ICI, into giving him an early appointment.

Bud attained a satisfactory, pharmacologically provoked erection in Dr. Eid's office, and was given a solution of VIP and phentolamine and some sterile syringes to take home. He was thrilled.

Compulsive, achievement-oriented men like Bud are often so obsessed with their performance that they cannot feel desire and they lose sight of their partners' feelings. Under such conditions, it is impossible to translate the pharmacologically induced tumescent episodes into genuinely pleasurable, passionate lovemaking experiences with the partner. For this reason, this modality is much more successful with anxious men when this is combined with judicious sexual counseling (Kaplan, 1989b; Wagner & Kaplan, 1993).

I attempted to prepare Bud psychologically for using the injections effectively with his partner. I asked him to try to create a romantic mood before attempting to use the injections. More specifically, I suggested that Bud first engage in some intimate conversation and gentle foreplay with Tracy, and I admonished him not to use the injections unless he was feeling calm and to wait until he sensed that she was becoming aroused.

I further suggested that he initially conceal the fact that he was using ICI from Tracy; that after a reasonable period of foreplay, he could excuse himself, go to the bathroom, administer the injection, and return to the bedroom. I assured him that after about five minutes of further stimulation, in an intimate, relaxed ambiance he could expect to develop a "perfectly natural-looking and feeling" erection.

This is normally a very effective strategy for initiating ICI (Kaplan, 1993c). But Bud was too anxious and too impatient to follow my advice. When he got home he rushed right into the bathroom and injected himself, without even saying hello to Tracy. Not surprisingly, in this highly anxious, obsessive, adrenalin-laden, non-intimate state, the injections failed to produce the expected erection.*

Dr. Eid then gave him a stronger mixture of the medication, and with this, plus slowing down a little, Bud managed to give himself an erection that was firm enough to enable him to penetrate. He was jubilant! However, he did not get aroused enough to ejaculate and his frantic, prolonged thrusting did *not* make his astonished partner happy.

At this juncture, Bud was desperate enough about losing his relationship with Tracy to come in for a few counselling sessions.

Two of the major *immediate causes* of Bud's desire problem, his feelings of impotence and his performance fears, had been ameliorated by the injections. Therefore, it was time to shift the therapeutic objective towards trying to help him regain his feelings of sexual desire and also to get him to make more satisfying love to his partner. That meant that the other *immediate cause*, of Bill's sexual difficulties, his obsessive negative thought processes and his frantic behavior, which were interfering with his own and his partner's sexual pleasure, would have to be addressed.

To achieve these goals, Bud would have to learn to become more intimate, and more sensitive to his own as well as to his partner's feelings. He would also have to slow down and start letting erotic stimuli affect him again.

I used my evoked feelings to implement these objectives. More specifically, I faced Bud with the negative feelings that his obsessive behavior had evoked in me and suggested that if he was treating Tracy in the same inflexible, dismissive, insensitive manner that he had displayed towards me, she might become as frustrated and as ready to quit as I had been. This seemed to make an impression.

Since I had suggested the penile injections, Bud had begun to trust me a little and was now prepared to heed my advice, at least some of the time. He finally came to see that his driven, obsessive, non-intimate

*The adrenergic and sympathetic surge that accompanies intense anxiety can physiologically override the vasodilatory effects of the intra-cavernosal injections.

behavior, and not his erectile difficulties, posed the real danger to his relationship with his partner.

Bud gradually grew more confident. Soon he began to feel some stirrings of desire again, and he happily reported that his morning erections had returned. During our sixth and last session, he told me that he would now sometimes get an erection just by talking to Tracy on the phone. He was also ejaculating normally, but he had not yet risked trying intercourse without the injections. In addition, his desire had returned in full force. He happily told me, "Doc, I feel real horny—just like I did when I was a kid."

The improvement in this patient's desire and functioning was accompanied by only a sliver of insight into his deeper problems, which presumably centered around his vulnerability to rejection. Bud continued to deny the extent to which he had been hurt and shaken by his wife's leaving him for another man, and he had gained no insight at all into how this rejection had tapped into and rekindled his old childhood pain. He firmly brushed away my suggestion that his sexual difficulties had had anything to do with protecting himself from becoming vulnerable again.

After our sixth session, Bud felt secure about his ability to function with the injections, and he terminated therapy. One month later, he sent me one of his recordings.

This patient had lost his libido, at least in part, because he felt upset about and humiliated by his impotence. When his potency was restored with the help of ICI, he rapidly regained his sex drive.

This case is by no means unique in this respect. A number of our patients have experienced substantial increases in their libidos after the restoration of their potency. These cases are interesting in that they provide nice examples of the reciprocal feedback between erection and sexual desire (see page 109).

Misuse of ICI

I do not want to be misunderstood as suggesting that pharmacologic treatment for impotence is the answer for men who lack sexual desire for their partners. To the contrary, this would be a serious therapeutic error in most cases. While I consider bypassing performance anxiety a legitimate use of ICI, especially if this is done within a therapeutic context, I do not believe in using this modality to "bridge over" a patient's deeper emotional or sexual problems or to circumnavigate around a lack of desire for the partner if this is due to a fundamental incompatibility.

Patients who are deeply angry at their partners, those who are truly terrified about melding intimacy and passion, men who are genuinely not attracted to their partners, e.g., a homosexual man to his wife, or a man who has married a woman whom he finds repulsive, because of family pressure, like Dr. Raj (Case 5.2), should never be given ICI to enable them to have mechanical, undesired intercourse. That would be in some respects like teaching a woman to fake orgasm. This is ineffective at best; at worst, such misuses of this wonderful technology can result in serious emotional damage for both partners.

TREATING DYSFUNCTIONAL COUPLES WITH SEXUAL DESIRE DISORDERS

The last three patients, "Greta," "Bill," and "Bud," all had intrinsic sexual anxieties and conflicts that were essentially unrelated to their interactions with their partners. In these cases, the modification of the patient's self-generated sexual anxieties and antisexual behaviors was the chief objective of treatment. By contrast, the following three cases involve patients with partner-specific sexual desire disorders whose lack of sexual desire for their partners was due mainly to the couples' destructive relationships.

In these cases, the focus of treatment was on correcting the couples' faulty interactions, improving their communications, and in some cases helping them change their lifestyles so this would leave more time for romance.

The first case, "Nick and Toni Black," illustrates the successful resolution of a couple's low sexual desire problem by helping them to restore their deteriorated courtship behaviors.

CASE 8.4—"Nick and Toni Black": Inadequate Courtship Behavior and Low Sexual Frequency in a Fundamentally Sound Relationship

Thirty-nine-year-old Nicholas and 40-year-old Antonia had been married for 14 years and had two children, ages 4 and 6. The couple were seeking help because since the birth of the last baby, four years prior to the consultation, their sexual frequency had declined precipitously, so that their last encounter had been more than three months ago.

In the beginning of their relationship, Nick and Toni had enjoyed frequent, passionate and mutually satisfying sex. They missed this and both wanted to recapture the romantic, passionate aspect of their lives, which had somehow vanished.

An inquiry into the couple's current relationship and life together quickly revealed the *immediate causes* of their low sexual frequency: inadequate courtship behavior, in the context of a harried lifestyle that was not conducive to romance.

Nick and Toni operated a very successful restaurant which they had started together shortly after they married. They regularly worked closely together for 10 hours a day, six days a week. Besides their enthusiasm for good food and cooking, they also shared a deep love for their two children. They were so crazy about their kids that they would not hire sleep-in help. When they got home after their long day, they bathed and fed the children and read them stories. It was not unusual for them to feel so exhausted that all of them, kids and parents, would fall asleep on the bed together, fully dressed.

The restaurant and the kids took up so much of this couple's time and energy that there was virtually nothing left for sex or recreation.

I asked Nick and Toni to tell me in detail how they used to initiate sex in the beginning of their relationship, when they were still in school. With great enthusiasm, they both described their early romantic courtship and their passionate sex life. Nick would court Toni by bringing her flowers as well as by serenading her with song and guitar. Toni would flirt with him, often wearing nothing underneath her dress to entice him. They regularly had romantic dates. Nick used to delight in discovering great little restaurants to surprise Toni, and the couple would "talk sexy" and touch each other intimately throughout their leisurely dinner. By the time they got home, they were usually so aroused that they fell eagerly into each other's arms and made love.

When I asked them to compare this to the way they were now initiating sex, Toni gave me a disgusted look and told me that sometimes in the middle of the night or the early morning, when Nick found himself with an erection, he would "sort of grunt and roll over in the bed, grab me, and screw."

Nick conceded that his current courtship behavior lacked finesse, but he complained that he was reduced to "grunting and grabbing" his wife without preliminaries because she was no longer the pleasant, responsive woman that he had married, and he was feeling rejected and resentful.

Both Nick and Toni had colluded, unconsciously, in sabotaging their sex lives by creating a negative, antisexual ambience and a pressured lifestyle that left little room for courtship and romance.

On a *deeper level*, this couple's countersexual behavior was, at least in part, a reflection of their anger at each other, which had gradually and silently built up over the years.

Although both spouses took pride in the success of their restaurant,

Toni was chronically conflicted about not being able to spend more time with the children. Moreover, she secretly resented Nick's increasingly visible, dominant role in the business.

Nick was also angry. He saw Toni's ambivalence towards their beloved restaurant as a personal rejection and a betrayal, and he was hurt by and angry at his wife's increasingly critical and nonsupportive attitude towards him.

This struggle was played out in the bedroom. In a hundred ways, Toni let Nick know that she was too tired for sex and that making love with him was no longer a priority for her. He responded to this rejection with a silent rage that was expressed in his passive-aggressive withholding of tenderness and affection to the point where sex, albeit this now occurred infrequently, had become an angry, punishing act.

As has been discussed in Chapters 6 and 7, anger at the partner is a frequent and potentially serious cause of the loss of sexual desire. If the relationship is not basically sound and the anger between the pair is intense, these couples are not good candidates for a treatment that emphasizes the loving and intimate exchange of pleasure. In such cases, couples counseling before sex therapy is the indicated strategy.

But Nick and Toni's differences were relatively minor, and their marriage was basically solid. They truly loved each other and, most important, were still each other's sexual fantasy. Moreover, both spouses were free of significant psychopathology and had demonstrated the capacity to be loving committed partners.

This all suggested that the couple's underlying anger and their sexual difficulties might well be amenable to a brief course of sex therapy.

Treatment

The couple were somewhat taken aback when I told them that no one could have good sex under the circumstances they had created. This got their attention. I waited until this idea had sunk in, then I gave them a "date" assignment. The object of this exercise was to attempt to bring Nick and Toni back to their former romantic courtship mode, which had gotten lost in the debris of their pressured life.

The Therapeutic Sig

More specifically, to prepare for her date with her husband, I asked Toni to have her hair done, shower and use his favorite perfume, and wear her most becoming outfit. I also asked her not to put on her panties for her date with her husband. (This had been extremely arousing to him in the past.)

Nick was asked to shave and to shower and to wear his tightest jeans and sexiest shirt for their date (as I knew Toni loved to see him in that outfit).

I also suggested that they arrange coverage at the restaurant for the afternoon, so they could prepare themselves at leisure and be at their best for their date. In the therapy session, I asked Nick to pretend that his life depended on his putting Toni in a romantic mood and being able to seduce her.

I used the story of "The Seven Beauties," a film they both liked, to make the point that with the right motivation, seduction is possible even under the most unlikely circumstances. In Lena Wertmüeller's marvelous film, the Italian hero, played by Antonio Mastroianni, is about to perish in a Nazi camp, when he gets the idea that his only hope for survival is to seduce the director of the concentration camp, a grossly fat, tyrannical, sadistic, German woman who wears Jackboots and men's underwear. With the help of a whorehouse fantasy, our hero succeeds in making love to her despite being surrounded by murderous SS guards and snarling German shepherds, and he survives.

This was my indirect way of communicating to Nick that if he wanted to, he could surely succeed in seducing his wife, and that I was not interested in excuses.

The couple did not resist their assignment. Nick took Toni to a romantic restaurant, one that she had been wanting to go to, and he became his old seductive, courtly, flattering, and attractive self with his wife during dinner. Toni, for her part, looked lovely, and also reverted to her old warm, responsive and seductive behavior.

That night, for the first time in years, Nick and Toni made passionate love.

It goes without saying that one successful sexual experience does not equal a cure. Nonetheless, Nick and Toni's date was a breakthrough of sorts in that this showed them, far better that any words could, that they had not lost their capacity for a passionate sex life together, and that this was theirs for the taking.

Although not curative per se, an astute dating sig that taps into the couple's sexual fantasies as had been expressed by their former, successful courtship behavior can be a very powerful intervention. I have treated a number of cases, unfortunately not as many as I would like, where a few sensitively structured seduction assignments, boosted by therapeutic clarifications, succeed in awakening a couple's dormant sexual desire and getting them back to having sex on a regular basis again.

Termination

The obvious end-point of the treatment of patients who have sexual disorders is the improvement of their sexual functioning. However, treatment is generally not terminated until the couple have also gained a clear understanding of the immediate causes of their sexual symptoms, so that they can help themselves should the problems recur in the future.

Nick and Toni rapidly met these termination criteria. They began to behave like lovers again. Their sexual interest in each other rekindled, and the frequency and the pleasure of their sexual encounters increased.

Moreover, when I asked, "What did you learn from this," they revealed that they understood precisely how they had been sabotaging their sex lives, that is, by neglecting each other and by failing to keep up their romantic courtship behavior. Moreover, their responses to my question, "What would you do if you found you have had no sex for two weeks again," indicated that this couple had the information they needed to reverse an avoidance pattern should this resurface again.

Once again, while patients' understanding and control of the currently operating and immediate causes of their sexual problem is vital for the stability of the cure, insight into the deeper causes is not always necessary or, for that matter, always achievable as a condition for termination.

However, in this case, I thought that the couple needed some deeper understanding of their underlying struggle with each other, so that they would not start their sexual "cold war" all over again.

Therefore, before I discontinued treatment with Nick and Toni, we explored some of the hidden sources and earlier origins of their anger at each other.

I aimed my interpretations principally at the couple's maladaptive interactions. I confronted them with their self-destructive power struggles and I pointed out that they seemed to have formed "parental transferences" towards each other. However, I did not go into the deeper oedipal implications, nor did I face Nick with his negative projective identifications, which had contributed to Toni's rejecting attitude towards him. I felt that I could not resolve such complex issues in brief treatment and that this would not be necessary for a successful outcome. But my insights into these deeper dynamics influenced my interventions.

One important issue that emerged during the conjoint sessions was the hidden struggle, which had never been articulated by either spouse, about whose vision of their life together would prevail.

Although, like many couples, the Blacks had assumed that they shared the same goals, in actual fact these were very different. It turned out that Nick's vision of marriage was a partnership, albeit one where the male was the senior partner. Nick saw himself and Toni as King Theseus and Hippolyte, Queen of the Amazons, companions in arms, in their battle with life.*

Nick was angry because, while he was still putting all his efforts into their partnership, Toni was no longer an enthusiastic participant.

Toni had not been aware that she was really of two minds about her aspirations and that she was sending her husband mixed messages. On the one hand, Toni wanted to stop giving so much of herself to the business. She had been a "good girl" and worked very hard to build up the restaurant. Now, the childish part of her wanted a reward, to have "Daddy Nick" take care of her. And, on a more mature level, she genuinely longed to spend more time with the children.

But Toni also had another, a conflicting view. This modern young woman wanted to be an equal partner with her man. She was secretly envious and angry because Nick, who happened to be clearly the more talented chef, was becoming a highly visible star in the food world while she was playing an increasingly supportive, less glamorous, administrative role.

In her confusion and anger, Toni withheld the approval that her husband craved and she rejected the restaurant he identified with. This was particularly painful for Nick as it recalled the frustrations he had endured at the hands of his overcritical mother, whom he never had been able to please. He had no insight that on an unconscious level, he was subtly provoking and perpetuating Toni's anger.

I told the couple bluntly that I thought they had been treating each other badly. I confronted Toni with her cruelty to Nick, that she had been punishing him by withholding her support and approval.

Nick had to face the fact that he had become insensitive to Toni's feelings, that he was being provoking as well as selfish and bossy, and that his wife had been taking the rap for his mother.

At all times, I was careful to temper these potentially threatening, harsh, relentlessly confrontational interpretations with my continuous empathy and support for both partners, along with my expressed approval of the many genuine positives in their life together: their basic sexual attraction to each other, their success in work, their excellent parenting.

As Nick and Toni began to understand each other's deeper vulnerabilities, their power struggles and anger against each other abated. This

*It is significant that in the Euripidean version of the myth, Hippolyte was killed by a spear meant for her husband when she flung herself in front of him to protect him during battle.

made it possible for them to return to the empathic, supportive, loving, and sexy way they had treated each other in the beginning of their relationship.

This, plus their acceptance, albeit somewhat reluctantly, that if they wanted to maintain their sexual connection at the high level that they enjoyed they would both have to make a deliberate, conscious effort to maintain their courtship behaviors, satisfied me that treatment could be terminated without the risk of a rapid relapse.

I saw this couple for a total of 10 therapy sessions, plus one "booster" a year later. They told me that they had continued to get along much better. There had been a few brief flare-ups of their old anger. Further, they were having satisfying, passionate, and enjoyable sex, although not as often as they would have liked, and only when they could fit it into their busy schedule.

It should be noted that, for couples who are embroiled in bitter battles or are seriously incompatible, "Dating" and "Romantic Holiday" sigs cannot be expected to provide a "quick fix." These interventions are insufficient to repair more serious marital pathology, regardless of how sensitively constructed these are.

As an example I gave a similar "date" assignment to the "Blues," a middle-aged couple who had not had sex together for 16 years, but in this case the tactic did not succeed in restoring their former feelings.

CASE 8.5—"Belinda and Berny Blue": Long-Standing Sexual Avoidance in a Troubled Relationship

The husband and wife, "Belinda and Berny Blue," both went through the motions of complying with their "date assignment." On the afternoon before his "date" with his wife, Berny left his office early and had a massage in order to feel relaxed for the dinner he had arranged for them at a fine restaurant.

Belinda bought a new dress, had her hair done, and looked her elegant best. As they sat down at their candlelit table, she graciously complimented her husband on the chic place he had chosen.

He reported that he began to feel "pretty good." Unfortunately, Belinda could not hold on to these good feelings for more than a few minutes. Then, contrary to my explicit instructions to limit their conversation to pleasant, intimate matters and to avoid all unpleasant or controversial topics, she felt compelled to lament the fact that their wealthy friends were giving a super-expensive, highly elaborate 13th birthday or "bas mitzvah" party for their daughter, while their own more limited financial circumstances made a comparable extravaganza unfeasible for their own child, about to turn 13. Brenda expressed concern that this would be a psychological blow for their daughter.

His wife's clear implication that he was an inadequate provider compared to his friend and that he was letting his child down wounded and angered Berny. He began to feel the same unpleasant sense of tension that often bothered him when he was at home, and he became verbally abusive to Belinda. Clearly, the evening was a flop in terms of improving this couple's sex life.

However, the failure of this assignment provided me with the opportunity to confront the Blues with their destructive behavior and to suggest that they needed to explore the deeper causes of their sexual and marital problems.

The apparent cause of this couple's anger at each other and their consequent sexual avoidance turned out to be their long-standing, bitter, and seemingly ludicrous quarrel about where they should live! He yearned for the suburbs; she was desperate to have a beautiful city apartment.

This conflict, which began shortly after their wedding, had poisoned their lives. Neither felt they could compromise, and the resulting stalemate paralyzed them so that they never moved from their first tiny apartment, which had long ago grown far too crowded for a family of five. The result was that neither got what he/she wanted and they lived unhappily together for ever after. The couple had seen several therapists to try to resolve their dilemma, but they had resisted all attempts to release themselves from their self-imposed prison.

On a deeper level there were undoubtedly other, more complex issues that fueled this couple's ridiculous quarrel, their anger, and their sexual avoidance. I suspected that Belinda and Berny had unconsciously colluded to keep a safe distance between them because both were on some level afraid to commit themselves fully to the marriage. Unfortunately, I never got a chance to explore this issue, for shortly after commencing therapy, Berny received a diagnosis of prostate cancer and the couple discontinued treatment.

Anger was also the primary underlying cause of the sexual difficulties of the next couple, "Peter and Pearl Traveler," who were first mentioned in Chapter 6.

While not as malignant as the Blues', Pearl's anger was more intense and persistent than Nick and Toni's. This patient's sexual aversion to her husband did not abate in response to libido-enhancing behavioral assignments nor to insight into the deeper meaning of the marital power struggle. The resolution of this woman's anger and of the couple's sexual difficulty required the therapist to step in and take an active role in helping them make substantive changes in the politics of their relationship and in the circumstances of their life, so as to meet more of the wife's emotional needs.

CASE 8.6—"Peter and Pearl Traveler": Acquired, Situational Sexual Aversion in an Angry Wife

As the reader may recall, this couple's marriage was in a crisis because Pearl had recently learned that Peter had had sexual relations with another woman during one of his business trips. He had been compelled to disclose this because he had contracted a venereal disease for which they both needed treatment. Pearl felt utterly betrayed by Peter and she was livid with anger.

Even before this incident, Pearl's desire for sex was abnormally low. She did not become very aroused during foreplay, so that she always needed lubricants, and she had never had an orgasm. However, although Pearl was a passive sexual partner, she used to find the physical closeness involved in lovemaking quite pleasant and, in the past, she had never objected to having intercourse with her husband.

But after she learned about Peter's extramarital affair, Pearl developed a severe aversion to him. She now shuddered when he tried to touch her and she adamantly refused to have any sexual contact with him whatsoever. Although he felt guilty about his transgression, Peter was also sexually frustrated and increasingly angry with Pearl for not allowing him to make love to her, and he never ceased pressuring and pestering her for sex.

The *immediate causes* of this patient's sexual aversion to her husband were the negative thoughts, memories and feelings evoked by his touch or kiss ever since she had learned about his infidelities and sexually transmitted disease. However, Pearl also realized that she had never been a very good sexual partner, and she admitted that she bore some responsibility for her husband's having sought sex outside the marriage. Therefore, feeling that she should make an effort to become a better sexual partner, Pearl entered sex therapy. However, on a deeper level, her anger was so overwhelming that she did not want him to touch her.

Treatment

I saw this patient many years ago, when we were still routinely starting sex therapy with the sensate focus exercises. In retrospect, this couple's negative response to this assignment should have been predictable.

Peter eagerly looked forward to being permitted, after many months of having to abstain, to kiss his wife and to hold and caress her again.

But, although Pearl tried to comply with the SF assignment, she found his touch unbearable. When she stopped the exercise short, Peter had a predictable fit.

I then *reduced* the sensate focus exercises by limiting these to twice a week, while decreasing the time that Peter was to "pleasure" his wife to five minutes. At the same time, I tried to give Pearl more of a sense of control by suggesting that she let her hands "ride" over his while he caressed her.

In order to counteract Pearl's tendency to interrupt stimulation as soon as she began to feel aroused, I asked her to try to allow Peter to touch her as long as she could tolerate this, but I also told the couple that they were to stop the exercise at once if this got to be too unpleasant or intense for Pearl.

Pearl told me that "my negative tape starts playing in my head before we even make love—I wish you could give me a pill or something to get rid of it."

I tried to counteract her negative thought processes with fantasy, even though the aim of the sensate focus exercises is to heighten the person's awareness of touching and being touched, and erotic images are therefore not recommended. I suggested that she try to "tune out" her negative feelings towards her husband by "turning off" her "negative mental tape" and substituting one that contained pleasurable, erotic images while he was touching her.

Although Peter made every effort to cooperate, Pearl resisted every one of these cognitive and behavioral interventions, and she remained as repelled as ever by his touch.

It became increasingly clear that conjoint sexual exercises with the husband were not going to improve this couple's sex life. Therefore, I *joined her resistance* to having sex with Peter by interrupting the sexual homework assignments and I arranged to see her by herself for a few sessions, with the aim of exploring her resistances further. I also decided to begin to work on her anorgasmia, for and by herself.

I started Pearl on the standard treatment program we use for anorgasmia. (Kaplan, 1974, 1975, 1979; Barbach, 1976; LoPiccolo & Lobitz, 1978). This usually begins with attempts to "bypass" the patient's defenses against sexual feelings by getting her to absorb herself in erotic fantasy. In addition, for women like Pearl who had never had an orgasm by any means, we also introduce masturbation training.

As we explored Pearl's sexual history in greater detail, it became clear that the origin of her sexual anxieties and deficits could be traced to some extent to her strict Roman Catholic upbringing. But the destructive relationship she had had with her mother was also contributory. This narcissistic, self-involved woman took more care with her outfits than with her daughter, and never gave Pearl the maternal nurturing and encouragement which I believe to be vital for a healthy female psychosexual development. The mother was also extremely competitive with Pearl. When Pearl was a little girl, the mother interfered in her relationship to her father, and when Pearl started to socialize, mother would flirt with her dates.

With a strict parochial school education and such a narcissistic, competitive mother, it was not surprising that Pearl had severe body image problems, and she was sexually immature and insecure, although she was a truly beautiful woman.

In the attempt to provide a corrective emotional experience for this inadequately mothered woman, I played the part of the "encouraging mother" that she had never had. I took care to be unfailingly warm and encouraging to her, and I tried to counteract the sexually negative messages she had received as a child by giving her explicit "permission" to masturbate and to fantasize, and I congratulated her on every step of her sexual growth. Further, I took every opportunity to point out the fact that she was indeed beautiful and that her husband was very attracted to her.

The patient rapidly developed a strong positive transference towards me, and I used her eagerness to make me proud of her in the service of the therapeutic objective, by letting her know that what would please me most was for her to become a sexually fulfilled, happy woman.

Pearl responded rapidly to this treatment regimen, and after only six sessions she began to have orgasms by fantasizing and using her vibrator.

But Pearl's new-found sexuality did not transfer easily to her husband. To the contrary, she was still very angry at Peter, and she was finding the idea of resuming sex with him increasingly repellant.

Then, in what I took to be an acting out of her anger and her resistance to intimacy with her husband, Pearl began an affair with "Troubador," a handsome young artist. This was entirely out of character for this traditional woman, who had had a strict Roman Catholic upbringing and had been a virgin until her honeymoon.

Her lover's laid back, sensitive, artistic personality and his skillful, sensuous, intimate lovemaking were the antithesis of what she had experienced with her A-type, compulsive husband, and his performance-oriented, "macho" sexual style. Blind to the young man's shortcomings, Pearl became obsessed and fantasized running away with him. In a private session, Pearl reported that she was feeling intensely passionate, and that she was multiorgastic with her beautiful, bearded, blue-eyed young lover.

I was concerned that I might have been "too permissive." On the one hand, I was pleased that Pearl had finally claimed her own sexuality; on the other, I worried that in her transference to me she had invested me with unrealistic omnipotent protective powers and behaved as though I could shield her from the potentially destructive consequences of her acting out.

I confronted Pearl with the risks she was taking and with the fact that she was jeopardizing everything that was important to her with this affair, and I pointed out that if this were discovered I could not protect her. But I was very careful to balance my admonitions by letting her know that I was also truly glad that this lovely erotic experience had shown her that she was a sexually normal and desirable woman.

It was becoming clear that it was not going to be possible to bypass this woman's intense rage at her husband. Pearl had become so aversive to him that interactive homework assignments were still out of the question. Therefore, I shifted the therapeutic format once more, and I began to devote alternate sessions to seeing the couple together in the attempt to work through their interpersonal difficulties and seeing Pearl alone to clarify and resolve her resistances.

Some persons cannot forgive a partner for a betrayal. They never fully trust that person again, and they obsess about their partner's infidelity forever. But that is a minority. The majority eventually get over their spouse's extramarital affairs, and in many cases the couple's relationship actually becomes more intimate and honest as the crisis is worked through.

The process of healing the injury that is caused by a discovered extramarital affairs can be facilitated in therapy by helping the "guilty" party meet two conditions. For one, the "perpetrator" must genuinely understand and acknowledge the hurt that he or she has caused the other, and repent without qualification and without excuses. The second condition that seems essential for genuine forgiveness is that the person who was unfaithful must be prepared to reject the rival completely and to commit him/herself without qualification completely to the injured party.

Peter had done his best to fulfill both these conditions. He was obviously repentant, and he promised to take her along on all future business trips, if she wished. But this did not appease Pearl despite the insight she had gained into the resonance of the incident with old childhood injuries.

Her anger was no longer directed entirely at the affair. The crisis had made Pearl realize that she really hated the life they were living and that in many respects their marriage was geared to Peter's needs to the detriment of hers. This new awareness made her furious, and she also felt humiliated because she had allowed herself to get into such an exploited position.

Rage at the partner is especially toxic and persistent if the balance of power is extremely one-sided. We have a number of cases in our files wherein an "underprivileged" partner with a sexual desire disorder resisted treatment and failed to improve because of his or her deep, abiding, smoldering anger that defied therapeutic resolution.

Sometimes, such rage can be resolved only if genuine changes are made in the couple's power balance, and if the injured party feels that there has been just retribution.

But at times, even true repentance and equitable compensations are ineffective. For example, Alexandra Hollywood's (Case 6.3) sexual avoidance of her husband persisted until his death, although he had literally prostrated himself before her and had given her everything she asked for and more. Intellectually, Alexandra had long forgiven Alex for his attempt to take advantage of her, and she was no longer consciously angry. In fact, she felt warmly towards her husband, and she was unfailingly kind and caring to him after they reconciled, but she never had sex with him again.

The history of the Travelers' relationship revealed a similar considerable skew in the balance of marital power. During the early stages of their marriage, this traditional young wife had accepted her husband's absolute control over their finances and lifestyle. She had never questioned her lonely vigils during his long absences and the full responsibility of taking care of their three children while he was on his travels building a successful international electronics company. She had accepted this arrangement, even though this had prevented her from pursuing her own vocational interests and goals. She had dutifully agreed to Peter's building a "name architect" house in the Hamptons, which was his trophy but her burden on account of the constant business entertaining she had to do there. Further, she uncomplainingly complied with his compulsive, non-intimate, dictatorial, controlling, personality style, and she even converted to Judaism for him. As far as she was concerned, these were all part of their "deal." But his infidelity and his exposing her to disease constituted an intolerable betrayal. He had violated their implicit "contract," (Sager et al, 1971) while she had been faithful to her end of the bargain, and this caused the deep volcano of her long suppressed anger to erupt to the surface.

All these matters were aired and explored during the conjoint sessions. But it quickly became apparent that Pearl's anger at her husband and her sexual aversion were being kept alive by what she perceived to be the injustices and inequities in their marriage, and that she would never be satisfied unless substantive changes in the fundamental structure of their marital system and in their lifestyle could be made.

I shared this opinion with the couple, and since I believed that they would not be able to renegotiate their "contract" without "killing" each other along with their relationship, I offered to work with them on making such changes.

Fortunately, the Travelers were highly motivated to preserve their marriage. There was a basic bond between Peter and Pearl that had persisted despite all the turmoil. Moreover, since the high-desire, high-power partner, Peter, was sexually obsessed with his wife, he was willing to make considerable concessions in order not to lose her. For her part, Pearl was basically loyal to Peter, and despite her ambivalence, she too wanted to salvage the marriage.

This couple did make substantial changes in their life.

As she began to realize that she possessed considerable sexual power, Pearl became less childlike and timid vis-à-vis Peter, while he became more sensitive to her feelings.

He agreed to stop inviting business guests to the country every weekend and to sell their house in Connecticut, which abutted his precious golf club. The couple moved to the city where Pearl was freed from endlessly chauffeuring the children, entertaining Peter's clients, and supervising the house staff. Here she was closer to the cultural events she loved to attend while her husband was away on business. Soon after, at her request and with my encouragement, Peter helped Pearl apply to graduate school and he willingly paid the tuition for her studies. As she gained confidence in her ability to succeed in the academic world, Pearl felt more equal to Peter and her anger began to defuse.

The final consolidation of the Travelers' relationship occurred when one of their children was in a serious automobile accident while Peter was away on a business trip. As soon as he learned of this, Peter dropped everything and flew home from Europe at once to be with Pearl in their mutual crisis. This moved her deeply and melted away the last residues of her anger.

At the end of treatment, which went on intermittingly for about five years, this couple had made a total change in their lifestyle. Pearl's needs now received equal consideration with Peter's, and she was no longer angry at him. Her sexual aversion towards her husband finally dissipated and the couple wound up having "good enough sex" on a regular basis. Peter was more than satisfied, but Pearl never reached the heights of intimacy and passion that she had experienced during her brief, secret affair with Troubador.

TREATING SEXUAL DESIRE DISORDERS OF PATIENTS WITH MORE SEVERE INTRAPSYCHIC CONFLICTS.

The next case, that of "Joe Senator" and his fiancée Joan, has been cited in several sections of the book. This patient initially resisted the libido-raising behavioral assignments and cognitive interventions that can be so helpful for patients with low-desire states. But he began to respond after he gained insight into some of his deeper, unconscious sexual conflicts about melding sexual passion with emotional closeness and into his "mother" transference to his current partner.

This case provides an excellent example of how patients who fail to respond to behavioral and cognitive interventions can sometimes be salvaged by adding brief, insight-promoting modalities to the treatment regimen. Further, this case study illustrates how sexual fantasy can be deployed in sex therapy and also provides a good example of the benefits of a cooperative partner.

CASE 8.7—"Joe Senator": Lifelong, Partner-Specific HSD in a Fantasy-Dependent Man

The reader is reminded that "Joe Senator" was the 45-year-old lawyer whose engagement was in trouble because he had no sexual desire for his beautiful fiancée Joan, who did not want to proceed with the marriage until their sexual problem was resolved.

The immediate cause of Senator's deficient desire was his reluctance to use his "repulsive and crude" (his words) erotic fantasy, which consisted of berating his sexual partner with degrading, violent phrases, like, "You whore, you slut, you deserve a good fucking," while he was with Joan, whom he idealized and called his "angel."

Senator had always been able to masturbate and achieve normal erections and ejaculations, but only with the aid of his fantasy, which he sometimes amplified by muttering out loud. However, he had never been able to function with a partner, except once with a woman who inadvertently tapped into his fantasy when she whispered to him, "Call me a slut, Joe, tell me I deserve a good fuck." The following day this woman went off with one of his friends and he never saw her again. This seemed to reinforce his fear that his fantasy would drive women away.

In other words, this man was entirely dependent on this "slut" fantasy to incite his desire sufficiently to function, whether he was with a partner or by himself.

Joe accounted for his reluctance to summon up his obligatory fantasies when he was with his fiancée, on the grounds that these thoughts were "too hostile and crude and unworthy of this fine woman." But this was a rationalization. On a deeper level, this patient's avoidance of erotic fantasy with his partner was a reflection of his unconscious guilt and his unresolved conflicts about his sexuality.

The Partner

In cases such as this, where fantasy or erotica is a critical issue, it is of utmost importance to enlist the unqualified cooperation and approval of the partner.

When fantasy is an essential condition of a person's sexual functioning, a serious therapeutic dilemma is created if a partner strongly objects to her lover's imagining or acting out his particular fantasy, or to his bringing erotica into the bedroom.

Some women are offended or threatened by their partner's need for erotica or fantasy. They cannot and/or will not accept this and they insist that the partner must change and learn to become more "intimate." They object to extraneous sources of erotic stimulation because they want the partner to "love me for myself."

While I have sympathy for this position and empathy for the partner who feels shut out by her lover's focus on fantasy, unfortunately it is usually not possible or feasible to modify a person's inner "love map" or fantasy life. In most cases, it is much more practical and realistic to shift the aim of therapy to overcoming the partner's resistance to accepting her lover's needs for his fantasies.

These efforts may not succeed with partners who are too angry at their spouses, too rejection-sensitive, or too morally offended to be able to accept the other's enjoyment of images of different partners or of paraphilic sexual material or practices. A number of our treatment failures with desire disorder couples can be attributed to our inability to modify a partner's adamant refusal to permit her spouse to use or act out his erotic fantasy.

Fortunately, Joan had absolutely no objections to Senator's fantasy. In fact, despite her gentle demeanor and appearance, this ladylike woman was a marvelous sexual partner who welcomed anything that might help resolve her fiancée's problem.

Brought up with progressive sexual attitudes in a liberal, intellectual, secular home, and very eager to make the relationship work, Joan actively encouraged Joe to use and to express his fantasy. She even offered to dress up like a "whore" and to talk "smutty" for him. Senator winced when she said this, as that was not in concordance with his image of the "good woman" who was to be his lawfully wedded wife and the mother of his children. He had been programmed since early childhood, to protect and cherish "good" women, and to desist from "soiling" them with his sexual needs.

Treatment

Although Joe clearly had acquired his maladaptive sexual patterns in early life, as is usual, my initial strategy was to attempt to "bypass" these hypothetical deeper issues by simply trying to persuade the patient to stop withholding his crucial erotic fantasy when he was with his fiancée (see Chapter 7).

Having reassured myself that this would not be destructive to Joan or to the relationship, I devoted the next few sessions to working with Senator alone, to try to convince him to use his erotic fantasies and "dirty" language with his fiancée.

On the theory that this patient's unconscious guilt about his unacknowledged anger towards women was a contributory, *deeper cause* of his sexual difficulties, I tried to *reconceptualize* his irrational and maladaptive view that his sexual fantasy was potentially abusive to his partner. I pointed out that if he were to visualize his fantasy silently, while he and Joan were making love, she couldn't possibly feel hurt. Besides, she was obviously much more distressed by his not making love to her at all.

I balanced my "permission" to use his violent, misogynistic fantasies with my support of his protective and loving behavior towards his sweetheart, so as to underscore the notion that there is no dichotomy between using his violent fantasy and being a caring partner.

The Therapeutic Sigs

I first attempted to bypass this patient's resistance to doing his "homework" by asking him to *repeat* the initial therapeutic exercise, which was to use his fantasy with Joan. But he resisted once again.

"Doctor," Senator said to me in a plaintive tone of voice, "I have a devil on one shoulder saying 'Go ahead, have a good time, fuck her,' and on the other shoulder is an angel, telling me 'Don't do it, don't hurt her, she's a wonderful, loving woman,' and Doctor, I'm afraid the angel won."

I then *reduced* the assignment to provide a greater degree of separation between Senator's "bad" sexuality and Joan, whom he had cast in the role of the forbidden good "woman." This was to be a temporary or transitional stage of treatment. The ultimate aim of therapy was to slowly close the gap between his sexual passion and the tenderness he felt for his fiancée.

In the attempt to shape the patient's behavior gradually in the desired direction, I suggested for the assignment that Senator begin making love to Joan and to caress and pleasure her as intimately and tenderly as he knew how, and to stimulate her to orgasm, manually or orally. But the patient was admonished not to worry about becoming aroused himself, nor to attempt to ejaculate in her presence.

This part of the assignment did not evoke resistance, as Senator had no inhibition about giving his partner pleasure. In fact, he was a compulsive pleaser of women and took pride in being able to tell me, "Doc, I gave her so many orgasms that she could hardly walk."

Senator's greatest anxieties and his most intense resistances were mobilized by the prospect of letting himself go and immersing himself in the sexual experience with his partner. Joe simply could not allow himself to experience an unfettered surge of erotic passion when he was with his fiancée. For this, he needed his fantasy, and he could do that only when he was alone.

In the attempt to free up Senator's fantasies, I gave him another, a "reduced" assignment: I asked him to make love to Joan until she was satisfied. Then Senator was to go to the bathroom and masturbate by himself to his favorite "slut" fantasy. After he finished, he was to rejoin Joan and to hold her. The purpose of this maneuver was to begin to move Senator's sexual desire and his ejaculations gradually closer to Joan, physically as well temporally.

But he resisted carrying out this assignment. He claimed it would "not have been nice" if he had abruptly left his partner after they had such an intimate experience together, and this would surely hurt her feelings.

There comes a certain point in treatment, when it suddenly becomes crystal clear, that it will not be possible to bypass a patient's deeper conflicts, even with the most ingenious maneuvers. Joe's stubborn resistance to using his sexual fantasy with his partner was a case in point. The therapeutic behavioral assignments had made no impact on the patient's resistances, albeit these were greatly reduced, and neither did my cognitive restructuring of the meaning of erotic fantasy. Also the patient did not seem to be benefiting from my support and giving him "permission." I knew that it was time to shift into a psychodynamic mode.

The Shift to Psychodynamics

A closer scrutiny of Senator's history revealed additional details about the deeper, dynamic infrastructure of his "whore/madonna" split. The problem could be traced to the confluence of several factors. For one, the antisexual conditioning he had received from his church and the misogynistic messages from his father had acted in synergy with the patient's inner sexual conflicts. In turn, these were the residue of Joe's unresolved attraction to his seductive mother.

His mother's seductiveness had intensified the patient's early struggles with his sexual feelings for her. As an example, Senator remembered that on many occasions he had been allowed to watch his mother dress for the evening, and this had secretly aroused him. And, as the reader may recall, little Joe used to become excited when he watched his mother's breasts "accidentally" fall out of her robe, which happened regularly as she was preparing his breakfast. At the same time that he was being exposed to all this intense and forbidden stimulation, the boy was also being indoctrinated in his church with the idea that sexual feelings must be reserved for holy matrimony and being brainwashed by his father to believe that sex was only for "sluts" and was offensive to "good women." Because he was thoroughly intimidated by his father, Joe had no one to turn to help him sort out and deal with these emotionally powerful and confusing experiences and messages.

This man's sadistic, erotic fantasies and his desire to abuse "sluts" and "whores" grew out of his attempts as a child to cope with these traumatic events and difficult object relationships. He managed to eroticize the whole, sad scenario and to turn the tragedy (trauma) of his childhood into a sexual triumph (see Chapter 3).

However, he was now faced with the problem of translating his sadistic sexual fantasy, which had once been adaptive, into a normal sexual relationship with the lovely woman he loved.

In order to help this patient, I was not about to attempt the hopeless task of trying to change his fantasy, although that was what he would have wished. Rather, I would try to see if I could help him to overcome his resistance to using his fantasy in the service of his current love relationship.

As I shifted into a psychodynamic, insight-fostering mode, I kept probing more deeply into the patient's early history and interpreting the unconscious meaning of his associations and dreams with a view towards helping him gain insight into the underlying dynamics of his sexual desire inhibition. At the same time, I continued to give him sexual homework assignments, which the patient continued to resist.

During the eighth session, Senator brought in a dream in which he was the bartender in an "Old West-style" barroom. A gunman dressed in black came in brandishing a weapon and "made a ruckus." Senator "did not know whether to duck behind the bar or to leap heroically over the counter and challenge the bandit." He woke up in a cold sweat.

I sometimes ask patients to "change their dream," as if it were a movie that they were directing, in any way they like. I use this technique in the attempt to get patients in touch with their hidden strengths and resources, and to show them that it is often in their power to alter the destructive forces that they find overwhelming.

When I first asked Joe to change his barroom dream, he could not get himself to invent a scenario in which he played the role of "winner." Even in fantasy he could not see himself challenging the "bandit" with the "gun." But after a few tries and a little coaching, he finally came up with a scene where he "got a bigger gun" (than the bandit's) and disarmed him.

The patient's associations to the "weapon-wielding bandit" led straight to his father, who was described as an abusive, harsh, "son of a bitch" who regularly dealt out physical punishment to the patient and his brothers.

I asked Joe if he didn't want to "kill the son of a bitch." He laughed out loud and said no. He told me that he only wanted to take the gun *to keep the others from harm.*

Any psychoanalyst worth his/her salt could interpret this dream as a symbolic expression of the patient's unresolved oedipal conflict. However, I wanted to keep my interpretations on a level I thought would be ego-syntonic. Since the bandit could readily be seen as representing the threatening father, I told Joe that I thought that the dream might be a metaphor for his conflict with father figures.

Joe was thoughtful, and didn't say much.

The key intervention and the turning point in this case was my observation, later in the session, that in his dream Joe's primary motive had been *protective,* and *not* aggressive. In the dream, Joe's main concern had been to try to *shield* someone (perhaps his mother?) from a "ruckus" and from assault by the "bandit's weapon." I further suggested that this might symbolize Joe's view that sex is a "criminal act," "a ruckus" from which women should be protected. Perhaps, I ventured, by allowing himself to *feel sexual only towards women who were completely different from his mother,* "sluts" and "whores," he had really been trying to *shield* his mother from a "criminal" sexual assault.

As is usual in brief dynamic therapy, I kept my interpretations on a "middle" level of conscious awareness, as this is unlikely to mobilize resistance. Thus I did *not* equate the "bandit's weapon" with his father's penis, and I also refrained from commenting on the possible symbolic meaning of "unlawful entry" as representing his incestuous wishes. Nor did I mention the oral implications of his dispensing drinks in his dream.

I knew that Senator had always been guilty and ashamed about his sadistic sexual fantasies, believing that these showed him to be an evil person. My genuine empathy for his lonely childhood struggle with his sexual impulses, which I regarded as normal, helped him to become less judgmental and less punitive towards himself. This, plus my reframing of his sadistic, "dirty whore" fantasies and desires as the products of his valiant attempts to cope with his difficult childhood, seemed to make Joe receptive to the notion that he had only been trying to be "*good*," that he had not meant any harm. To the contrary, he had been attempting to *shield mother from his "outlawed" sexual impulses*.

The idea that by focusing his sexuality away from women who resemble his mother he had been trying to *protect* her seemed to intrigue him. Joe was extremely thoughtful as he took this in and muttered, almost to himself, "What do you know, all this time, I was really trying to protect her, hah! I never thought of it that way before."

The patient seemed to have experienced one of these rare genuine "aha!" reactions, one of those very few occasions when an interpretations really hits home, which is a very special high for the therapist.

In the following session, Senator admitted, with great shame and reluctance, that he sometimes imagined his mother as his "fantasy whore."

No wonder he had been reluctant to use the fantasy of "mother as whore" with his fiancée!

"I didn't know whether I could tell you this, I almost didn't, that's pretty sick, isn't it, Doc?"

I still do not quite understand what had transpired that allowed the patient to disclose his secret to me. In retrospect, I believe our interchange about the "bandit" dream in the previous session had made him feel that I truly understood and accepted him.

However it happened, I congratulated Senator on his openness and courage, and reassured him that incestuous fantasies were not uncommon. Moreover, his were certainly understandable in the light of his childhood. I said to him, in effect, that any boy with a good, healthy, sex drive like his, who was brought up under comparably difficult circumstances, would be likely to develop similar sadistic, "madonna/whore" erotic fantasies. To make this point more specific, I recapitulated the historic events that led to the sexual fantasies Joe was so ashamed of:

his sexy feelings towards his mother (which all boys have to some extent), a father who would have intimidated any child; plus all that guilt about sex that he was taught to feel in church, added on to his father's irrational messages that women are fragile creatures who need protection from male sexual violence.* All this could cause any boy to develop similar sexual desires and fantasies. It is merely a matter of cause and effect.

The process of "normalizing," "depathologizing," or "decriminalizing" a patient's aberrant or perverse sexual fantasies and desires can be powerfully reassuring. This can relieve the burden of guilt and shame that individuals who have perverse fantasies frequently carry. Moreover, the therapist's acceptance of what patients often regard as their "dark side,"also may have the effect of making them more amenable to insight and change.

This is exactly what happened with Joe. He did adopt a less judgmental and more rational view towards his sadistic sexual fantasies, and this provided me the opportunity to clarify the connection between Joe's unresolved sexual feelings for his mother and his vexing inhibition with his fiancée. More specifically, I was able to point out to Joe (and he was able to "hear" me) that he seemed to have developed a "mother transference" towards his fiancée Joan, and that this was blocking his sexual response to her.

This proved to be a critical insight. Shortly thereafter, the patient reported that he had finally used his fantasy with Joan, and that he had ejaculated intravaginally for the first time. He complained that he had not felt much sensation. I assured him that this, too, could improve, and thereafter treatment moved rapidly toward a successful conclusion.

CASE 8.8—"Doc Scotch": Lifelong, Severe, Partner-Specific HSD

The case of "Doc Scotch," the surgeon with a severe intimacy/passion split, has been cited several times. Like "Senator," the patient in the previous case, "Doc's" lack of desire was impervious to the libido-enhancing therapeutic homework assignments. This time, however, my attempts to salvage the case by incorporating psychodynamic insight-promoting measures into the behavioral/cognitive regimen did not succeed.

The *immediate causes* of this patient's partner-specific HSD were typ-

*This message was reinforced by Joan's brother, who had taken Senator aside at a family gathering and explained how fragile his sister was, and admonished Senator "to be sure not to hurt her."

ical. Doc focused his attention only on the negatives when he was with Marie, his loving, devoted girlfriend, and he strenuously avoided reacting to any of her positive qualities. In addition, he also kept his libido in check by making a "sister" out of her, thus tapping into the sex-suppressing power of the "incest taboo." But when he was with his bizarre, sadistic, fantasy girlfriend, Doc managed to tune out all the many obvious negatives, and he was wide open to erotic stimulation with her.

This patient's inability to feel passion in a close, long-term relationship was born of his horrendous, injurious, truly nightmarish childhood, which was dominated by repeated, cruel maternal rejections and abandonments.

The patient's father had left his mother before he was born. Doc had grown up hearing from his mother that his "father didn't want" him. His mother was a disturbed woman described as difficult, critical, demanding, fanatically religious, and constantly angry. The reader may recall that she placed Doc in a series of eight Roman Catholic foster homes from the time he was three months old. She would let the youngster stay with each set of foster parents for about a year, just time enough for him to form an attachment, and then she would abruptly remove him and place him in a new home. Her visits were erratic, and she typically left the child crying on the door step, uncertain if he would ever see his mother again.

When he was 12, Doc's mother relented and brought the boy home to live with her. But after he had been there for nine months, because he had broken a minor rule at the strict parochial school where he was enrolled, she had him committed to an institution for wayward boys.

Doc languished in this terrible place, surrounded by retarded and delinquent youths and the uncaring and occasionally brutal staff for five years, until miraculously this brilliant boy won a college scholarship to a Catholic college, and then another grant to support him through medical school.

These painful events had imbued Doc with a lifelong fear of intimate attachments. Although he was starved for affection, he had been damaged too severely to allow himself to feel passion for a woman towards whom he harbored tender feelings.

Doc was obsessed with Dotsie, the latest of a series of beautiful, but crazy, difficult, and sadistic women in his life. Dotsie, who was chronically in financial trouble, had a habit of asking Doc for inappropriate, outrageously expensive gifts. Her requests included large sums of cash, a gold Rolex watch, an alligator bag, expensive jewelry, designer clothes, and a weekend trip to Paris on the Concorde.

Doc would become furious each time she asked him for something. At first, he would angrily refuse her requests, but then he would become obsessed by the fear that she would never see him again if he didn't give her what she wanted, and he would then "surprise" her with the expensive trinket she wanted. Doc was chronically enraged at the demanding, exploitative Dotsie, whom he called a "gold digger," but he also felt very aroused by her and, while she actually allowed him to have sex with her only on very rare occasions, he frequently masturbated while fantasizing about her.

At the same time, Doc had a close relationship with Marie, a successful pediatrician who was crazy about him and who showered him with affection and attention and saw to it that he had a normal life. A remarkably intuitive, generous, and sensitive human being, Marie was the first woman with whom Doc had ever had a constructive, intimate, long-term relationship. Doc felt a deep affection for Marie, but he did not have the slightest sexual interest in her.

Doc had absolutely no insight into his underlying fears of intimacy, and he did not recognize the self-induced elements in his lack of sexual interest in Marie. He kept insisting that the fault lay simply in the fact that she was not attractive enough for him.

Treatment

Because there was a modicum of reality to this, in that Marie, while not exactly homely, was also not really "trophy" gorgeous, I joined his resistance to a romantic connection with her.

More specifically, I told the patient that I knew that he felt unattractive and insecure, and that he feared that because he was tall and skinny, balding, and from the wrong side of the tracks, no beautiful woman would want him. However, I further told him that this was a distortion, born of his unfortunate past. In reality, his quiet charm, sensitivity, and intelligence, and his outstanding success in his field, made him a most attractive and desirable man. I also said that I saw nothing wrong with his wanting a beautiful partner and that he most certainly could attract such a woman. Finally (and I meant it sincerely), I told Doc that I would be glad to help him overcome any psychological obstacles that stood in the way of his quest for a better looking partner.

It came as no surprise that Doc resisted this suggestion, on the grounds that he did not want to risk losing Marie, who meant a great deal to him. I think this was a real element. But I also believe that his reluctance to look for a truly beautiful companion, one who would not be flawed like his crazy girlfriend, also grew out of his insecurities, fears of rejection, and the conviction that he was unlovable.

Whatever his motives, Doc told me firmly that he would prefer my helping him feel more sexual towards Marie. Once he was committed to this course, we started right in by working on raising his awareness of his sexual sensations and of his emotional state. This took some doing, as Doc was remarkably defended and closed off, and he had almost no awareness of his physical sensations and his feelings. As an example, he typically failed to notice that his bladder was full, and he often had to rush to the bathroom, getting there just in time to avoid wetting himself.

My first assignment for this patient was not specifically sexual. I asked him to focus his attention on the sensations of his bladder periodically during the day and to attempt to urinate before he reached a state of urgency. I also had him lick a chocolate ice cream cone very slowly and to note the taste, texture, and temperature.

In response to my tireless confrontations and the therapeutic behavioral exercises, it finally began to dawn on him that he was putting himself into "neutral" or "reverse" when he was with Marie. But he still maintained that the problem would disappear if Marie were only better looking, and he even thought about offering to pay for plastic surgery for her.

The Therapeutic Sigs

The following sexual homework was assigned to increase Doc's libido with Marie. The exercises were designed to counteract his compulsion to obsess about the negatives and to "decentuate the positives"(see page 152). That weekend, when the couple were at Marie's secluded beach house together, after their usual foreplay Marie was to stimulate Doc orally, which they both enjoyed. This usually provoked an erection but not much arousal in Doc, as he seemed unable to immerse himself in the experience. I asked Marie to turn her back to Doc after he had become hard. He was then told to masturbate to orgasm, while looking at her backside and indulging in his favorite "dominatrix fantasy."

The rationale for this therapeutic exercise was to get Doc accustomed to feeling aroused in Marie's presence, and to try to bypass his fears of intimacy. I exploited the fact that I knew that Doc enjoyed anally oriented fantasies and that he had admitted that he found Marie's buttocks attractive.

Moreover, I gave the patient explicit "permission" and encouragement to "tune out" his partner and lose himself in his sexual fantasies.

Many patients with HSD feel liberated sexually if they are released from the pressure of having to relate intimately to the partner. This is what happened with Doc. He was able to stimulate himself to orgasm when she turned her back to him. In that position, he felt free to maximize the positive physical and psychic erotic input. At the same time, the "rear" view prevented Doc from obsessing about Marie's face, which he perceived as a negative.

Throughout all this, Marie was entirely agreeable and cooperative, and for the first time in their relationship, Doc became aroused enough to have a pleasurable ejaculation in her presence.

However, after this successful sexual exercise, Doc went through a period of increased avoidance of sex with Marie, while his obsession with the bizarre and exploitative Dotsie intensified.

Resistance

Typically, before Doc would meet Marie, he would put himself into "neutral" by relating to Marie as though she were the loving sister he had never had. Sometimes, he would reinforce his asexual position by silently obsessing and lamenting to himself, while he was getting ready for a date with Marie, that it was a shame that he was not meeting a more beautiful woman, a model or an actress, instead.

Doc's negative thought processes effectively neutralized all efforts on Marie's part to attract and seduce him and to satisfy him sexually.

Since he often masturbated before seeing Marie, as another way of diminishing his sexual feelings, I asked him not to ejaculate for 48 hours prior to seeing her. In a further move to counteract Doc's defenses against letting himself feel desire for his partner, he was asked to fantasize about making love to his current dominatrix before he entered Marie's bedroom, and he was to have sex with Marie only when he had succeeded in becoming aroused.

I further *reduced* the assignment by "prohibiting" intercourse, and suggested that he limit himself to stimulating himself to orgasm in her presence. This assignment was successful in that both partners became aroused and climaxed.

But after every "success" Doc became even more resistant. At those times, he often avoided sexual contact with Marie for weeks and even months. Yet, at the same time, during the therapy sessions he extolled Marie's virtues, talked at length about his fondness for her, and repeatedly appealed to me to help him increase his sexual feelings for her.

Doc kept a "safe" distance from Marie. He did not live with her, but they spoke on the telephone each day, and saw each other every Saturday. He made it a point to spend at least three weekday evenings without her.

I encouraged him to maintain this distance, as well as his occasional dominatrix and Dotsie excursions on the theory that these were "safety valves" for his fear of closeness.

According to the hypothesis advanced in Chapter 3, children tend to eroticize traumatic events and hurtful relationships and come to desire that which once hurt them. From that perspective it could be surmised that this man had eroticized his painful relationship with his mother. More specifically, I believe that Doc had sexualized his mother's awful behavior towards him, with the result that his sexual fantasies and desires were now fixated exclusively on sadistic, demanding, critical women like her. Unfortunately for this man, his masochistic desires were not confined to fantasy. Although he longed to share his life with a decent, loving woman, his malignant sexual desires dominated his object choices and limited these to women with whom it was impossible to develop normal relationships.

Psychodynamic Shift

In an attempt to resolve this patient's massive resistance to insight and to feeling more desire for Marie, I shifted the sessions to an insight-therapy mode, while continuing to prescribe structured, therapeutic, sexual homework assignments, as I had done in the last case.

Once, when Marie, in an uncharacteristic show of unkindness, berated him for some trivial oversight, Doc felt a flash of lust for her. But my attempts to confront him with the significance of this, fell on deaf ears.

Much of our therapeutic work involved exploring and attempting to resolve Doc's pathological relationship with his mother. I believed it critical that this patient gain insight into the connection between the abuse he had endured from his mother and his self-destructive attraction to women who treated him in the same cruel and sadistic manner that she had, and still did.

To this day, Doc was still being hurt and angered by his mother. She had become even more difficult as she aged, and just as relentless in her cruelty. Doc was still deeply engaged in the hopeless task of trying to please and appease her, and he had never learned to defend himself from her vicious attacks.

Doc was extremely resistant to any attempts to help him separate emotionally from his mother, and there was little progress in this respect.

I tried to work with Doc's dreams, but he resisted this as well.

Once, during what seemed to be a relatively less resistant phase of therapy, Doc had allowed Marie to persuade him to join her for a romantic weekend holiday. On the night before they left, he dreamt he was in bed with a beautiful woman, when two tigers leaped out of the wall and attacked and tried to devour them both.

I considered this a resistance dream, a "message" from his unconscious that sex with Marie was too dangerous for him, and also a warning of impending, aggressive self-destructive behavior.

But Doc did not give me the opportunity to interpret this "warning" dream in time.

Doc left for his weekend with Marie before we could discuss the dream. At dinner, this careful, meticulous, highly esteemed professional drank too much wine. On the way back to Marie's beach house, where they had planned to make love, Doc drove so unsteadily, that he was stopped by a policeman, arrested, and charged with drunk driving. The weekend was, of course, ruined, and the rapid intervention of Doc's attorney just barely saved him from a potential disaster, that could have cost him his professorship and his hospital privileges.

I saw this patient for three and a half years. I used every strategy I could think of, bringing all my creativity to bear on trying to help him, but I did not succeed.

I saw him conjointly with Marie for a while. This improved their communications but did not increase Doc's desire for her.

Among the avenues I explored was a referral to an excellent psychoanalyst, but Doc refused to see him.

To compensate for the lack of a normal family life, I suggested group therapy. He joined my group, but missed too many sessions.

I prescribed Desyrel. This improved his sleep and his erections, but did nothing for his lack of desire for Marie.

Doc benefited in significant respects from his therapy experience. He was no longer depressed and, apart from his sexual problem, he was living a normal life. However, in terms of the patient's desire disorder, this case was a definite treatment failure.

At the end of treatment, Doc and Marie were still together and closer than ever, but there was virtually no sex between them. Only on rare occasions did Doc managed to "tune out" with fantasy and to masturbate to orgasm in Marie's presence. But he never approached a normal level of sexual desire with Marie, and he continued his clandestine, obsessive affairs with his dominatrix fantasy women.

CHAPTER 9

Loss of Sexual Desire Due to Psychiatric Disorders in the Partner

HIDDEN PSYCHOPATHOLOGY IN THE PARTNER

Some psychiatric disorders are so obviously destructive to marital relationships—for example, alcoholism, substance abuse, psychopathy, and the major psychoses—that the spouse's lack of sexual interest poses no mystery. However, more subtle psychiatric conditions in the partner, particularly the milder *obsessive-compulsive states*, as well as *borderline* and *narcissistic personality disorders,* can also wreak havoc with a couple's sex life, and these conditions may go unrecognized.

Thus, in all too familiar scenario, the person who has lost his or her desire, not realizing that something is wrong with the partner, is baffled and assumes the entire blame for the sexual problem.

The dismay that the partner of such a person feels is amplified if the professionals they consult fail to recognize the partner's psychopathology and do not validate the logic of the sexually symptomatic partner's feeling of distress.

The following case is typical.

CASE 9.1—"Arlette and Arthur Beaver": Obsessive-Compulsive Disorder in the Husband; Sexual Aversion in the Wife

Arlette, a beautiful, 36-year-old physician came to the initial session by herself. She was in considerable distress when she told me her problem: "Arthur is handsome. He is a passionate lover, he's brilliant, he's a responsible father, and very generous to me. But I have a sexual problem. I can't stand for him to touch me anymore. He is very upset about this and of course he's right. We haven't had sex for six months. I really don't want to keep on living under this pressure. I feel like running away, but we have two wonderful little kids and he is a really good father. I am so conflicted. You must help me get over my neurosis. Do you think it could be Oedipal? My father - - - etc."

This patient went on to describe her sexual aversion, which was specific to her husband.

In the first year of their relationship, Arthur and Arlette were seeing each other on alternate weekends only, because they lived in different cities. During this period, these attractive, sexually open young people had enjoyed a passionate, and mutually satisfying sexual relationship. One year later, after they began to live together in a small apartment, Arlette's desire began to wane. Nevertheless, six years ago they married and now they have two small children whom they both adore.

After the birth of their second child, three years prior to our initial consultation, Dr. Beaver found her interest in sex with her husband declining even further. Then, about two years ago, her "quiet" lack of interest began to turn into an active aversion. By the time I saw this couple, Arlette was avoiding all physical contact with her husband. The last time she had agreed to have sex with him was six months ago. She had found this experience "unbearable."

Arlette's work as a pediatrician gave her ample excuses to avoid physical contact with her husband. On the grounds that she had early rounds at the hospital, she always went to bed before Arthur and was invariably fast asleep by the time he came to bed. Moreover, she carefully kept to the edge of her side of the bed, all night, in order to avoid his touch even during sleep.

Arthur loved his beautiful wife very much. He was devastated by her refusal to make love with him, while she felt increasingly pressured and guilty about avoiding sex. When she first began to dislike sex, Arthur became angry and constantly pressured her to make love. When this got him nowhere, he became despondent and begged her to go into therapy to solve what they both considered to be "her sexual problem."

Arlette saw a well known female analyst who apparently attributed her problem to an unresolved Oedipal conflict. The analyst, although she had never seen the husband, felt that Arlette had formed a parental transference towards Arthur, and was acting out her unresolved ambivalence towards her father with her husband.

When Arlette's sexual aversion did not improve after a year of psychoanalytic treatment, Arthur pleaded with her to join him in marital therapy.

The Beavers then saw a reputable marriage therapist. He misinterpreted Arthur's compulsive behavior (described below) as a pathological "need to control" his wife and he felt that the core of Arlette's sexual problem was a power struggle between the couple that played itself out in the bedroom. In addition, this doctor felt that the couple's difficulties were complicated by their "inadequate communications."

As a result of couples therapy, the Beavers' anger at each other diminished. But there was no corresponding improvement in Arlette's sexual aversion to her husband; if anything, it seemed to be getting worse. In a final attempt to save their marriage, this couple sought sex therapy.

Like many persons who are married to difficult spouses, Arlette had not admitted the extent of her husband's pathology to herself. Moreover, this had escaped their therapists' notice, as well. This was because Arthur appeared to be functioning well. In fact, his compulsive devotion to his job, his obsessiveness about the details of every project, and his fanatical perfectionism contributed greatly to Arthur's success in his computer business. But these same personality traits were a disaster in his personal life.

My evaluation of Arlette indicated that she did not have an intrinsic sexual problem and that her sexual aversion was clearly specific to her husband. I came to this conclusion because this young woman's psychosexual development was perfectly normal, she had never suffered any sexual trauma, she had a negative psychiatric history, she was brought up in a sexually liberal home where she developed healthy sexual attitudes, and she had been fortunate in her good relationships with both her parents. Moreover, prior to her marriage she had enjoyed a number of successful sexual affairs. In fact, she had been very responsive and passionate with Arthur in the beginning of their relationship.

Arthur was also free of sexual difficulties, and he was by Arlette's own admission a caring and creative lover.

When evaluating couples with sexual difficulties, I find it useful to obtain a detailed picture of their current life together (see Chapter 5), which I did when I saw the Beavers in a subsequent conjoint session. This clearly illuminated the destructive impact that the husband's obsessive-compulsive behavior was having on the couple's relationship and on Arlette's sexuality.

HSK: What happens when your husband comes home? How do you feel when you hear his key in the door? I'd like to hear all the details.

Arlette: Well, when he gets home, he first goes through all his mail carefully; then he hands me notes about what I have to do.

HSK: What was on the list last night?

Arlette: Let's see. Buy theater tickets, arrange for repairs of the freezer and a lamp, plus a long list of household purchases. He also reminded me to make dental appointments for the children, and to call the liquor store about a charge.

HSK: What happens then?

Arlette: He then looks around to see if the house is tidy. If there are any toys lying about, and Dr. Kaplan, my kids are two and four, so something is always out of place, he gets hysterical. We have to stop everything else and pick them all up and put them away neatly. After everything is in order, he takes a shower and that can take an hour and then he changes into his leisure clothes. But before we can have dinner, he insists on putting his towels, underwear, and shirt into the washing machine and laundering them.

Only after all this is done, does he kiss me and the children and we settle down to eat. After dinner, he goes to his study and works with his computer.

Later in the interview:

HSK: Do you have a good time when you go out together?

Arthur: We have a great time, she always looks beautiful. She's an excellent dancer. I am so proud of her.

Arlette: He is also an excellent dancer and we go out to great restaurants. He knows all about wines and can discuss vintages with the somalier for hours.

HSK: That sounds great.

Arlette: Yes, but I'm usually in a lousy mood when we go out.

Arthur: Yes, Doctor, she often spoils our evenings out together with her miserable moods.

HSK: Why is that?

Arlette: Well, before we go out, he usually makes me change my outfits six or seven times. When he finally finds the dress he likes, then I have to change the jewelry, my shoes, and my bags until he is satisfied with my appearance. I want to please him and look nice for him, but by the time I'm finished with all these changes, I feel grumpy and then I become a real bitch.

HSK: What would happen if you were to refuse; what if you told your husband that you don't feel like changing one more time?

Arlette: Our other therapist (the marriage counselor) explained to us that we are in a power struggle, and that Arthur is trying to control me. He told me that I have the right to assert myself and to say "No." I tried. But Arthur gets so frantic and enraged that it's simply not worth it; it's easier to give in."

It turned out that Arthur had a number of obsessive-compulsive rituals that included, among others:

1. He checks the towel for dampness after Arlette goes to the bathroom, to make sure that she has washed her hands.
2. He gets to work 15 minutes early every day to vacuum his office rug.
3. He spends at least one hour a day in the shower. He has a clock attached to the shower wall and ritualistically washes each part of his body for a specified length of time.
4. He has a habit of buying extras of everything. For example, he recently bought four identical expensive briefcases of a kind that he likes; he regularly insists on buying large quantities of paper towels and toilet paper, which, Arlette complained, clutter up their country and city homes. When they were first married he bought 10,000 condoms.

Clearly, Arthur met the criteria for obsessive-compulsive disorder (OCD) (APA, 1994).

Obsessive-compulsive disorders and traits still tend to be underdiagnosed. Yet, such problems in the partner are frequently the critical factor in a person's loss of sexual interest.

The husbands and wives of individuals with *narcissistic and borderline personality disorders* are also predisposed to develop sexual desire disorders, and in moderate cases, these may similarly escape the professional's attention as a factor in the symptomatic partner's sexual problem. But the recurrent emotional storms, irrational angers, obsessive jealousies, self-absorption and unreasonable feelings of entitlement, the lack of empathy for the partner, and the ambivalence that invariably taints their love relationships, together with the inability of persons with these personality disorders to lead a happy, orderly, tranquil existence, can make life a virtual hell for the patient's family. It is not surprising that this often creates ambivalence and the withdrawal of sexual interest in the spouse. The following case illustrates the erosive effects on the sexual aspect of the marriage of the wife's borderline personality disorder.

CASE 9.2—"Solomon and Sarah Weiser": Borderline Personality Disorder in the Wife; Loss of Sexual Desire in the Husband

Dr. Solomon Weiser, age 54, was a handsome, charming, slim, impeccably dressed, successful radiologist. He had been married for 28 years to Sarah, a highly intelligent, obese, but attractive woman, aged 52. The couple had four grown children.

The Weisers had been referred to me by their internist after Sarah had complained that her husband's impotence was "ruining her life."

I saw Mrs. W. once, by herself, for evaluation. During the session, she explained that her husband was impotent because of his poor relationship with his mother, and that he was hostile to women on that account. She was eager for him to "get help," but she refused to join him in conjoint therapy.

She was greatly offended and furious with me when I asked her (to test her capacity for insight and her flexibility) if she thought there was anything *she* could do to improve the relationship.

I "blew it" with this question. Mrs. W., who met the criteria for borderline personality disorder and who displayed the exquisite oversensitivity and paranoia that one sees with some of these individuals, took this as an accusation that I thought she was too fat, and that her weight was responsible for her husband's impotence. She was greatly offended and refused to see me again. Paradoxically, however, she was more eager than ever for me to treat Sol, but only on the condition that I would see him alone.

Since Mrs. W. had a therapist of her own (who did not seem to realize that his patient's hostile behavior was jeopardizing her marriage), I agreed to see Dr. Weiser by himself, with the goal of improving his sexual functioning with his wife.

The couple's marriage had always been marred by the ebb and flow of Sarah's emotions. Her calm periods alternated periodically with violent emotional storms. When she was in one of her good moods, Mrs. W. could be warm, charming, witty, and attractive. But, subject to recurrent episodes of depression and agitation, she was often in a diffuse rage, and would then express violent anger at her husband and also strike out at others, to the point where her relationships with her children were strained.

At times, there was no discernible reason for her outbursts, but being extremely rejection-sensitive, some of her mood swings were clearly triggered by what she perceived to be slights on the part of her husband. Sarah's moods predictably deteriorated when Sol was away at a conference or when he came home late from a meeting, but she was at her worst when he did not have sex with her for a while.

The last episode of depression and violent rage was triggered by Sol's enjoying an animated conversation with an attractive, single woman who was seated next to him at a dinner they both attended. In one of her typical explosive episodes, Sarah carried on, wept, moved out of their bedroom, berated Sol for ruining her life and threatened to divorce him.

Mrs. W's obsessions centered around having intercourse with her husband. She seemed to take this as a benchmark of Sol's feelings for her, and she tormented him if more than a week went by without having relations with him. At these times she seemed to feel great emotional pain and she would lapse into one of her angry, depressed, and agitated moods. The only thing that could make her feel better was having sex with Sol.

Sarah was a compulsive binge eater, and in recent years she had become seriously overweight. Her thighs were now so heavy that oral sex had become mechanically difficult and this was a "turn off" for Sol. But she refused to diet on the grounds that, "if I lost weight, you still wouldn't make love to me, you are destroying me, you are impotent—you should get help."

Sapped by the recurrent emotional storms, it was not surprising that Sol's urge to have sex with his wife had indeed decreased. He was now making love to her out of a sense of duty, without much desire. He approached sex with enormous apprehension because he knew that should he lose his erection (which was happening with increasing frequency), she would berate him, accuse him of impotence and of ruining her life. Thus, performance anxiety had become a definite etiological factor in this case.

His wife's constant accusations of sexual inadequacy had so undermined Sol's sexual confidence that, about six months prior to our consultation, for the first time in his married life, he had started an affair with his office nurse. I believe that part of Sol's motivation was to reassure himself and to reaffirm his manhood. He had no trouble feeling erotic desire or having erections with this easygoing, accepting, sexually open woman who made him "feel like a hero" and he felt none of the performance anxiety which had become habitual with his wife.

But despite all their difficulties, Sol really cared deeply about his wife; in fact, when she was in one of her good moods, he was very happy with her. He admired her intelligence and the wit she displayed when she was "her normal self," and he appreciated her loyalty and the support she had given him during the early struggling years when he was in school.

Despite his medical training and his keen intelligence, Dr. W. did not recognize that there was anything wrong with his wife. On one level, he bought his wife's theory that he was at fault for her emotional illness and that she would recover from her mood swings and her depressions if he were to have intercourse with her more frequently and if he became a "better" husband. He was eager to try to improve the relationship.

In fact, the project to "rescue" his wife from her despair was right up Dr. W's alley, because he was a "problem solver," and he took enormous pride in working out seemingly impossible clinical and financial conundrums.

This pattern began when, as a boy of 12, after his father had died leaving the family penniless, he rescued his mother and his younger siblings from their financial plight. This took heroic efforts that included holding down two jobs while putting himself through school. His successful efforts on behalf of his mother and younger brothers made him feel proud and worthy of love. Now he simply could not accept that there wasn't anything he could do to solve the problems in his marriage, and to relieve his wife's chronic unhappiness. This ran counter to his omnipotent "rescuer" fantasies, which formed the foundations of his self-esteem.

Treatment

The evaluation had revealed that the patient's erectile problem was psychogenic, probably due to a combination of performance anxiety and insufficient desire, and that he was a good candidate for treatment.

At first, I joined Sol's resistance to admitting that his wife had serious psychiatric problems that were not of his making and to giving up his irrational belief that a better sex life would cure these. We proceeded to work on his agenda, namely, on improving his potency and thereby his marriage.

I began by trying to raise Sol's level of awareness of his wife's emotional vulnerability, and I gave him some "be nice to your partner outside the bedroom" sigs (see Chapter 7). In other words, I encouraged Sol to try to become more sensitive and solicitous to Sarah, apart from sex. More specifically, I suggested that he compliment her more often and bring her gifts on occasion. I specifically asked Sol to be especially attentive to Sarah on the days that he had his sessions (she knew his schedule exactly) so that she would not feel threatened by his therapy.

This made things a little better between them. Encouraged, Sol was eager to begin to work on his performance anxiety. He learned to use erotic fantasies to heighten his desire. This gave him confidence and diminished his apprehension about making love to his wife; in short order, his potency, as well as his sexual desire, improved.

Sol began to look forward to making love to Sarah again, and instead of the oral and manual techniques he had been forced to rely on in recent years (which his wife scorned as "substitutes" and "excuses" for his "impotence"), the couple had several episodes of successful intercourse. In addition, with my encouragement, Sol also continued to make a conscious effort to become a "better" and more attentive husband. He stopped sleeping with his nurse.

Sure enough, Sarah seemed happier for a while, and Sol was in seventh heaven. But predictably, it did not take long for Sarah's depressions, rages, binge eating, accusations, and lamentations about how he had ruined her life to start all over again.

When this happened, Sol's anger erupted. He began to resent and to resist using his sexual fantasies to enable him to "service" his wife.

OBJECT CHOICE: WHY DO PEOPLE CHOOSE DIFFICULT PARTNERS?

The evaluation of persons who are involved with emotionally difficult partners must include a consideration of their object choices.

Some authorities feel that the choice of a neurotic partner is a sign of neurosis in the chooser and that such individuals are destined to repeat this pattern.

Our experience does not support this position entirely. Some of our patients clearly do have a pattern of repeatedly choosing destructive partners. This was illustrated in the case of "Lucinda Skier" (Case 6.2), the beautiful young woman with the horrendous family background, who had a string of awful relationships and a phobic avoidance of attractive and suitable partners.

But some people just have the bad luck to end up with a difficult partner simply because of their youthful naïveté and lack of experience. In such cases, after they extract themselves from their abusive partner, they often go on to an excellent marriage with healthier, gentler, and kinder individuals.

We have also seen a number of couples wherein an apparently well-integrated and well-functioning individual married and stayed with a difficult, narcissistic, borderline, abusive, psychopathic, schizophrenic, or alcoholic person. These puzzling combinations can be explained, at least in part, by the special knack that certain emotionally troubled men and women have for attracting normal, supportive partners, satisfying them sexually, getting them to form attachments, and taking care of them for life.*

In yet another variation, a person who superficially appears "normal" remains with a frankly disturbed lover because that person represents his or her sexual ideal or fantasy. In such cases, the desire for the crazy loved one remains intense and obsessive, no matter how much suffering this may cause. A sadomasochistic pattern of this sort is evident in the following case.

CASE 9.3—"Harvey and Honey Gross": Narcissistic Personality Disorder in the Wife; Masochistic Desire in the Husband

Harvey Gross was a 58-year-old stockbroker who had contracted Parkinson's disease a year prior to the initial consultation. He was agitated because Honey, his attractive wife, with whom he was obsessed, had been avoiding sex. Honey had always given her husband a bit of a hard time about making love, but ever since he had developed the illness she had become more avoidant than ever, and she had recently asked him to move out of their bedroom.

The patient's neurological disorder was well controlled by medication, but his wife "could not bear" the side effect. This was actually rather mild and consisted of occasional involuntary motor jerks. Harvey had consulted a string of distinguished neurologists in the attempt to seek a solution, all to no avail. The doctors had convinced him that it was his wife who needed help and, in great frustration, Harvey consulted me to see if I would treat Mrs. G's "desire disorder."

But Honey Gross did not have a genuine desire disorder. She was deliberately withholding sex to manipulate her husband and to "punish him" for becoming sick and thus "raining on her parade."

This patient was a highly narcissistic woman who was so completely self-involved and had such an absurd sense of entitlement that she saw her husband's illness strictly as her personal calamity and seemed incapable of even the slightest empathy for his suffering.

"What about me? How could this have happened to me," she lamented in outrage during one of our individual sessions.

*Dr. Richard Kogan pointed this interesting adaptive pattern out at one of the Wednesday conferences.

Despite his illness, Harvey continued to work a fourteen-hour day, plus a long commute to the suburbs, so that his wife and children would not have to reduce their luxurious lifestyle. But Honey was not moved by the efforts her husband was making on her behalf. In fact, when Harvey came home utterly exhausted after his long and grueling work day, she often made outrageous demands on him, despite the fact that they had a full-time maid and she usually spent the day resting and indulging in expensive services such as massages and a personal trainer. These demands involved mostly personal errands and odious household chores.

I felt great sympathy for this man's suffering, until it dawned on me that Honey's selfish behavior did not diminish his lust. In fact, Harvey seemed to become aroused by her cruelty, and undoubtedly, on an unconscious level, he somehow encouraged this.

After she had been exceptionally demanding, he would plead with her to make love to him. Sometimes, she would promise to do so if he met various requests, such as scrubbing the toilets thoroughly or neatly recopying all the addresses in her rolodex. At those times he would literally knock himself out to meet all her demands, no matter how unreasonable these might seem. But then, when he was ready and eager to make love to her, she would often renege, telling him she was just not in the mood.

In another of Honey's sadistic scenarios, she would begin to make love with him and then stop abruptly if he had the slightest involuntary motor movement, claiming that this had turned her off.

On the rare occasions when she allowed him to make love to her, she was orgastic and he was ecstatic.

This woman's narcissistic behavior meshed with this man's masochistic erotic fantasies. These had their origins in his unresolved, ambivalent attachment to his mother, who had been similarly narcissistic and cruel to him. This was another example of the erotization of cruel, wounding childhood experiences and object relationships, which were transmuted into erotic excitement. Thus, his wife's narcissism and her sadistic demands, which could, would, and should put off a normal man, only heightened his sexual desire.

Etiology of the Loss of Sexual Interest in Partners of Difficult Persons

The fundamental, underlying causes of the appropriate loss of sexual interest in a disturbed and destructive partner and those of the pathological inhibition of desire for a healthy, attractive, and suitable partner are, of course, very different. However, the same *immediate psychopath-*

ogenic mechanisms that down-regulate the individual's sexual desires are operative in both situations.

Immediate Causes: Selective Focus on Negatives

More specifically, in both instances the person unknowingly suppresses his or her sex drive by selectively focusing on negatives about the partner and/or actively avoiding positive erotic stimulation (see Chapter 6). In one case, however, the suppression of sexual desire is *functional,* in that the person is turned off by the partner's truly disturbed behavior. This serves to protect him against a disadvantageous liaison. On the other hand, the negatives that dysfunctional, neurotic persons dwell on with regard to their nice, heathy lovers, are trivial, imagined, and/or exaggerated, and in some cases actively elicited by the individual, and this is definitely to their disadvantage.

The observation that the psychological "turn-off" mechanisms that serve to decrease sexual desire in appropriate as well as in inappropriate circumstances are identical lends support to the hypothesis that was advanced earlier (Chapter 2) that psychogenic HSD represents the patient's unwitting subversion of the normal sexual controls in a dysfunctional manner, for neurotic purposes.

An example may make this clearer. At one time during therapy, Arthur Beaver went to a great deal of trouble and expense to give Arlette a surprise birthday party luncheon. He gathered together her best friends from various times in her life: high school, college, and medical school. They came from all over the country and Arlette was pleased and touched. But she could not tolerate these good feelings towards Arthur for very long, and she quickly changed the focus of her attention to her annoyance at Arthur's repetitive checking his watch, and urging her to hurry so they would not be late for the lunch. Arlette's choosing this one, trivial negative over the many positive, loving, and pleasurable aspects of his thoughtful gift, which she could have cathected, "tricked" her sexual-motivation regulatory mechanism into remaining "turned off," and this allowed her to maintain her defenses against responding to Arthur's seductive attempts to win her back.

The following is another example of the sexually suppressing power of the selective focus on negatives (which in this case were real and substantial). One of my patients was a man who suffered from migraines. He had avoided sex with his chubby, extremely compulsive wife for the past 16 years. As we explored the unhappy details of their life together, the immediate causes of his lack of desire for her became clear. This man's wife, whose OCD was only partially responsive to medication and who was left with a good deal of residual compulsive symptomatology, insisted on weighing herself three times each morning, stark naked, on three different scales ("I have to check so there's no mistake," she told me in one of our conjoint sessions), while he had to kneel down and record her weight (she was nearsighted and could not make out the numbers on the scale by herself). This man told me, "Every time I feel horny, in my mind's eye I see her standing on the damn scale with her big fat ass in my face. That's the first thing I see every morning, and the first thing I hear is her telling me to hurry up and record the stupid numbers. As soon as that little scenario enters my mind, my sexual interest is gone with the wind."

Deeper Causes: Valid Partner Rejection

The rejection of a desirable partner, with the concomitant loss of sexual interest of patients with sexual desire disorders, is based on his/her neurotic problems, or the couple's conflicts about sex, love, and intimacy, and has no basis in reality. However, the rejection of a disturbed partner is valid and can not be considered a psychiatric disorder.

There are many normal persons who simply cannot or will not accept their partners' aberrant behavior. These men and women lose their sexual desire, and/or develop aversions as an unconscious protest and an expression of their anger and despair about their terrible life with the disturbed individual. It is almost as if on some level they feel that if they were to allow themselves to enjoy lovemaking with the partner, this would constitute their condoning his/her destructive behavior, and/or would be tantamount to giving up all hope for a better life.

However, such negative reactions are not inevitable. Some equally normal persons who are married to someone with significant emotional and mental problems take little notice of, or simply accept, the partner's craziness without taking this personally or letting this spoil the other aspects of their lives.

These flexible folks focus predominantly on the attractive erotic aspects of the relationship, with the result that they are not "turned off" sexually, as was the case with "Tim and Mary" (see page 188).

As another example, one of my patients was married to a handsome, wealthy man who had considerable obsessive-compulsive personality traits. This woman was attracted to her compulsive husband and they enjoyed a good sex life together. She told me during an individual session, "Sure he can be a royal pain—but then I think of how much better I'm off with George, who is basically so kind, than I was in my first marriage to that abusive son of a bitch. Then I just tune out George's little craziness and we go on with our life. And besides, Doctor, he is a marvelous lover. He is compulsive about giving me an orgasm every time."

Another patient who was deeply attracted to his beautiful, borderline girlfriend paid as little attention as possible to her mood swings and irrational angers, and focused instead on her lovely face and voluptuous body. He was perfectly happy with their love-making and with their life.

Sexual obsessions represent the other side of the "selective focus" mechanism. Persons who are in the grip of a sexual obsession are unable to perceive the most glaring negatives of their love object or of the disadvantages of their situation. They can only see their loved one's positive and attractive qualities, which they tend to exaggerate greatly.

TREATMENT ISSUES

The Therapist

The therapist, by virtue of the power vested in him by the therapeutic transference, is often in a highly influential position with regard to the destinies of the relationships of the couples he is treating. In order to avoid unwittingly misusing this power when treating couples where one partner has lost his/her sexual desire on account of the other's psychopathology, the therapist must become as aware as possible of his own unconscious biases and countertransferences regarding the relationship. This is an important issue in all couples therapy, as was discussed in Chapter 7, but the therapist's insight in this regard is especially critical in these cases.

For example, if a therapist should overidentify with the "normal" partner, he might be tempted to "rescue" the healthy one from a "sick" marriage (possibly because he remembers his father's suffering due to his mother's emotional problems, or perhaps because his own first marriage was to a disturbed person), and serious damage may be done to a relationship that is potentially good for both partners.

Novice therapists often make the mistake of attempting to "normalize" an "abnormal" relationship without first ascertaining how good or how bad the basic "fit" between the partners is, and without understanding what must be changed in order for them to be happy together. A common, well meaning error on the part of therapists who are not accustomed to thinking in a systems mode is to encourage the "normal" partner to "assert" him/herself and "set limits" for the more difficult spouse. But this well meaning intervention could have disastrous results in unconventional relationships whose stability may depend on the healthy partner's unqualified support of and acquiescence to the needs and wishes of the "sicker" or more vulnerable spouse.

Similarly, the happiness of some of these skewed pairs may not rest on a "politically correct" balance of power. For example, a couple with a compulsive partner may be better off with a marriage based on the reality that the compulsive person needs a certain amount of control and predictability in order to function, and the therapist's attempts to foster his or her own value system of perfect equality can only end badly.

Another example is the inappropriate imposition of traditional American mental health ideals of "better communications" or "increased intimacy" on an emotionally claustrophobic couple whose happiness may be based on the enjoyment of silent companionship and respect for each other's privacy.

It goes without saying that many couples benefit immensely from overcoming their resistances to intimacy and from learning to listen to and to communicate their feelings to each other. However, like every other intervention, these too must be individualized in their application, and they must meet the patients' needs, not those of the therapist.

The Therapeutic Alliance with Couples

The doctor-patient relationship can become complicated when one of the partners has a significant degree of psychopathology.

A firm therapeutic alliance with both partners is an essential ingredient in every sex therapy case. This is especially important and also especially difficult to establish when one of the partners has a personality disorder and/or is especially rejection-sensitive or emotionally fragile.

In couples therapy, the formation of a therapeutic alliance requires that both partners feel deeply understood by the therapist, and that both firmly believe that the doctor is a trustworthy ally and does not favor one over the other.

The therapist has to be pretty nimble to succeed in this delicate balancing act. On the one hand, it is important to validate the symptomatic patient's feelings of distress about the real problems he/she has had to cope with in the relationship. Towards this objective, the therapist must let the individual who has lost his/her desire know that the partner really *is* difficult and that anyone might have problems with coping with that person. At some point the therapist should communicate empathy for the individual's understandable frustrations and suffering in the relationship and admiration of his or her patience and fortitude.

At the same time, it is also vital that the therapist avoid projecting too negative a view of the disturbed partner and remain steadfast in support of the relationship, so as not to threaten the other and "sicker" partner.

To maintain the balance of both partners' therapeutic alliance, it is wise to couch discussions of the partner's psychiatric problems in terms of excessive "sensitivity" or "vulnerability," rather than using words with negative connotations, like "mental illness," "sickness," or "pain in the ass." It is wise, too, to acknowledge the genuinely positive aspects of the relationship on an ongoing basis.

The difficulty of staying in contact with both partners was briefly touched on in the description of "Tim and Mary's" treatment in Chapter 7 (Case 7.1). In that case, I spent the lion's share of the sessions supporting the fragile partner with the personality disorder, Mary, to the point that when we reviewed the videotapes at the Wednesday seminar, the whole group, including myself, suffered from severe tedium. And yet, my "over-support" of Mary was essential not only for engaging Mary in treatment, but also for providing a model for Tim as to how he would have to behave if he wanted to live in peace with his wife.

Once again, finding the right balance requires a good deal of therapeutic agility. At the same time that one lends support to the sexually symptomatic partner, it is also necessary to confront the emotionally disturbed one, in this case it was Mary, with the destructive effects that her aberrant behavior was having on the relationship.

Typically, the sexually symptomatic partner is relieved to hear that the sexual problem is not entirely his or her doing. Further, the therapist has an advantage in that the partner with the psychiatric disorder is often terrified of losing the other, and his/her belief that the therapist can show how to save this valued relationship strengthens the therapist's influence, which is invaluable in this form of treatment.

This is what happened with Tim and Mary (Case 7.1) and also with the Beavers (Case 9.1).

Mary admitted that she was depressed and took my advice to try medication. She proved to be an excellent responder to low doses of Prozac, so that her mood, flexibility, and ability to engage in therapy improved dramatically after she was medicated.

Arthur, the OCD husband, agreed to commit himself to a pharmacological-cognitive therapy program once I had confronted him that he was risking losing his wife on account of his compulsive behavior. Arlette, touched by Arthur's efforts, softened towards him, grew more accepting, and for a while supported his effort to change.

In the end, however, the Beavers were a treatment failure. Arthur's compulsive symptoms improved only moderately in response to treatment, and Arlette, who had become irreversibly disillusioned with her husband, resisted all my efforts to help her to "tune out" Arthur's obsessions and compulsions, and to focus on the positives of their life together. A beautiful and financially independent woman, she had ample opportunity to find a less difficult relationship and she was simply not willing to go through the effort of accommodating to Arthur's difficult personality.

Patients with Personality and Obsessive Compulsive Disorders Have a Guarded Prognosis

Patients who have personality disorders are notoriously difficult to engage in therapy, and they tend to resist change in all spheres of their lives, including their sexual behavior. These difficult characteristics probably account for the fact that the prognosis for the improvement of sexual desire disorders is significantly less favorable when either partner has a personality disorder than for couples in which neither carries this diagnosis.

CHAPTER 10

Organic Sexual Desire Disorders: Low Sexual Desire Due to Medical Conditions, Drugs, and Age

Many lines of evidence have established beyond question that the experience of sexual desire and the normal regulation of sexual motivation require that the neurological substrate that transmutes the perception or fantasy of an attractive sexual partner into subjective feelings of sexual lust must be anatomically intact and supplied with a normal complement of hormones and neurotransmitters.

As was discussed in Chapter 2, biological foundations of sexual desire have been scientifically established by a variety of experiments that involved surgical, chemical, and electrical manipulations of certain pathways and regions of the limbic system and most particularly the anterior medial nuclei of the hypothalamus, the so called "sex centers" of the brain. These studies have repeatedly demonstrated that the surgical or chemical impairment of these structures effectively destroys an animal's sexual motivation and its ability to respond to sexual stimulation. Similarly, the long and extensive history of the castration of males of many species, including roosters (capons), Bulls (oxen), stallions (geldings), and man (eunuchs or castrati), has left no doubt about the importance of adequate levels of testosterone for normal male sexual functioning and desire. More recent studies have demonstrated a similar correlation between androgens and female sexuality.

In a modern life, there are a number of endocrine abnormalities, general medical conditions, and pharmacologic substances that replicate the surgical and chemical experiments and the castrations that deplete libido, as was cited above. These result in clinically significant losses of sexual desire and constitute the organic sexual desire disorders.

In addition, although DSM-IV has specifically separated sexual impairments due to age from organic sexual disorders due to drugs and medical conditions, I take exception to this position.

I have taken the position that it is important from a clinical perspective to distinguish sexual impairments due to medications and hormone abnormalities from the normal, age-related decline of sexual desire and functioning, (Kaplan 1989b). However, because age-related decline in sexual functioning is clearly physiological and not psychological in nature and also because the management of the decrease of sexual desire due to drugs, disease states, and old age is similar, a case can be made for subsuming all of these conditions under the category of organic sexual desire disorders.

DESIRE DISORDERS DUE TO HORMONES

The three most commonly observed *endocrine abnormalities* that are associated with decreased sexual desire in clinical practice are: 1) the *post-menopausal female urogenital estrogen-deficiency syndrome*; 2) *androgen deficiencies in men and women*; and 3) *hyperprolactinemia*. Hyper- and hypothyroidism may also result in a decline of libido, but this is seen less frequently.

1. *The Female Urogenital Estrogen-Deficiency Syndrome*

After reviewing the voluminous publications on estrogen replacement, Sherwin summed up the role of E in female sexuality as follows: "This literature has repeatedly demonstrated that although E replacement alleviates atrophic vaginitis and associated dyspareunia in post-menopausal women, it is without effect on the libidinous aspect of sexuality, such as desire and arousal" (Sherwin, Gelfand, & Brender, 1985, p. 350).

In other words, as was pointed out in Chapter 3, contrary to popular misconceptions, estrogen is not essential for the experience of sexual passion in women, and a deficiency of this hormone will not per se result in loss of libido.

However, estrogen deficiency is a major *indirect* cause of the loss of sexual interest in post-menopausal women because this results in the *female urogenital estrogen-deficiency syndrome* (Wagner, 1986; Semmens & Wagner, 1982).

This condition is characterized by atrophic changes of the female genitalia. More specifically, in the absence of E, the vaginal mucosa atrophies and becomes thinner, and there is a loss of or a marked decrease in vaginal lubrication. In addition, postmenopausal women who do not take estrogen replacement and those who don't have intercourse on a regular basis may experience some atrophy and shrinking of the vaginal tissues. These changes result in discomfort and pain on intercourse. The friction produced by the penis as it rubs against the tight, dry and more friable vaginal mucosa often produces painful irritations, erosions, and even frank open lesions of the vaginal tissues. Traumatic genital lesions are common in women who engage in vigorous coitus, especially if no lubricants are used. These vaginal lesions can be severe enough to preclude intercourse and lead to a loss of desire for sex.

Impact on the Partner

Vaginal dryness due to E deficiency can also make penetration more difficult for the partner. Moreover, the postmenopausal decrease in ovarian E production also results in a gradual regression of some of the female characteristics that are attractive to men, such as smooth skin and the feminine genital aroma. This, added to the aforementioned lack of vaginal lubrication, can precipitate functional difficulties and decreased sexual desire in the partners of postmenopausal women.

Etiology of the Female Urogenital Estrogen-Deficiency Syndrome

Since estrogen is synthesized and secreted largely by the ovaries, the loss or impairment of these glands results in the signs and symptoms of estrogen deficiency (Sherwin, 1985). Therefore, unless they receive E replacement, *all postmenopausal women develop some degree of the urogenital E-deficiency syndrome after menopause* (Wagner, 1986). This condition occurs irrespective of whether the menopause is due to the natural, age-related atrophy of the ovaries, bilateral surgical oophorectomy, or damage to the patient's ovaries by chemotherapy with cytotoxic agents or radiation.

Treatment

Estrogen replacement, orally or by transdermal patch, is highly effective in relieving dyspareunia and restoring the vaginal physiology to its freely lubricating, more resilient, premenopausal state. Unless this is medically contraindicated, E is the treatment of choice for female postmenopausal urogenital estrogen-deficiency syndrome (Notolewitz, 1989).

The local application of vaginal premarin creme is also excellent for reversing vaginal atrophy, but, since there is massive absorption of estradiol through the vaginal walls (Fruhjelm et al., 1980) and a substantial amount of the hormone spills into the general circulation, this is not advised for women who have histories of breast, uterine, or ovarian cancer, or for those who should not take estrogens for other medical reasons.*

Fortunately, there are several reasonably good alternatives for the relief of vaginal dryness for postmenopausal women who should not or don't want to take estrogens. These include nonhormonal vaginal lubricants, such as "Astroglide," a commercial water-based preparation and pure vitamin E oil, which some clinicians recommend.

There are also two possibly safe, or at least safer, estrogen preparations on the horizon that might one day solve the problem of estrogen deficiency dyspareunia and the associated loss of sexual interest in postmenopausal women who cannot take systemic estrogens.

Nova pharmaceuticals in Denmark has developed a low dose estrogen vagipository called *Vagifem*, which consists of a pellet that contains 25 mgm of estradiol in a slow-release resin. In this vehicle, low doses of estrogens are released very slowly into the vagina in amounts that are sufficient to restore the premenopausal physiology of the vaginal mucosa and lubrication in the great majority of patients. The evidence is convincing that when E is administered in this form, the hormone does not penetrate significantly into the rest of the body, where it could harm women who should not take estrogens. This conclusion is based on studies that showed that virtually no measurable estradiole can be detected in the patient's bloodstream after the administration of Vagifem. Further evidence of the fact that the E that is delivered to the vaginal tissues by Vagifem does not, for all practical purposes, escape beyond the vagina is that this very rarely causes endometrial proliferation (Mattson et al., 1989; Mettler & Olsen, 1991; Eriksen & Rasmussen, 1992). Hopefully, this promising preparation will soon be available in the United States.

---

*Estrogen is considered too risky for women with histories or strong family histories of neoplasms of estrogen-sensitive organs such as the breasts, uterus, or ovaries, or precancerous conditions of these organs. Thromboembolic disease states and hepatitis are among numbers of other contraindications for E administration. However, recent findings regarding the relative safety of administering estrogen to women with histories of breast cancer (Lobo, 1993) have made some oncologists more flexible about prescribing low doses of E in some cases.

Another estrogen preparation for which claims of reduced risk from the perspective of carcinogenesis have been made is *estriol*, the so-called "safe" metabolic form of estrogen. I mention this here only for the sake of completeness, because unlike Vagifem, which has a solidly researched basis on human subjects, scientific evidence regarding the safety of this form of estrogen is not conclusive, although animal studies are promising. Apparently, estriol is used by European physicians, but is not available for clinical use in this country (Follingstad, 1978).

Postmenopausal women who seldom have vaginal intercourse are at a higher risk of developing severe, disabling vaginal dryness, tight and spastic muscles, as well as a narrowing of the vagina. These changes make it difficult or impossible to have vaginal intercourse. The systematic use of vaginal dilators is highly effective for stretching and rehabilitating the vaginal musculature of these patients. This is also useful for the prevention of postmenopausal shrinking of the vaginal barrel. Finally, the periodic rhythmic contraction of vaginal muscles, the so-called "Kegel exercises," have been recommended for improving and maintaining vaginal muscle tone (Klein-Graber & Graber, 1978).

2. *Androgen Deficiency in Men and Women*

The sex-regulating centers of the male and the female human brain are unable to function without normal levels of bioavailable T. In the absence of this hormone, men as well as women completely lose the urge to have sexual intercourse, so that even an attractive, willing partner leaves them cold.

The Hypogonadal Syndrome in Males

The clinical effects of a lack of androgen in males depend on the age at which this occurs. Individuals in whom the loss of T takes place prior to puberty never masculinize properly, develop an eunuchoid habitus, and will also lack sexual motivation when they mature (Segraves, 1988b; Schiavi & White, 1976; Davidson & Rosen, 1992). Moreover, Money concluded on the basis of his work with hermaphrodites that individuals who are deprived of T prior to a critical period may not develop the capacity to fall in love (Money, 1961).

Clinical observations of adult male patients who are T-deficient due to injuries to their testes or to anti-androgen medications—for example, sex offenders and cancer patients—indicate that when adult, sexually experienced men are deprived of T, the full hypogonadal syndrome may not develop immediately. However, eventually the absence of T robs all men of their sexual appetite. (Segraves, 1988b; Segraves & Segraves, 1992; Davidson & Rosen, 1992).

The first sign of surgical or chemical castration is usually a complete or severe loss of libido and of the urge to copulate, along with the disappearance of spontaneous fluctuations of desire. This is generally followed, in time, by a progressively diminishing responsiveness to sexual stimulation (Schiavi & White, 1976; Segraves, 1988b).

Several lines of evidence indicate that the effect of T is mainly on the desire phase of the sexual response cycle, while the erection reflex is probably not directly affected by T deficiency. Thus, the ability to have erections may be maintained for some time in sexually experienced men after surgical or chemical castration, although most hypogonadal men eventually become impotent. Segraves has summed this up very well in his excellent review of male hypogonadal states: "The explanation that I favor is that androgen activation of CNS receptors and social learning are both necessary for male sexual behavior. With castration, the urge to copulate is dramatically reduced. However, sexual activity may be maintained in certain men by other psychological factors, such as the desire for physical closeness, the fear of displeasing the partner, or the need to reaffirm one's manhood" (Segraves, 1988b, p. 279).

Etiology of Male Hypogonadism

The etiology of T deficiency in males may involve any or all occurrences or agents that interfere with testicular synthesis and secretion of androgens, or with the bioavailability of circulating T. Common causes include physical injury to the testes by accident, surgical castration, or radiation; disease states that destroy testicular tissue, such as mumps, bilaterally undescended testicles, hydrocoele, the degenerative effects of the aging process, and cytotoxic chemotherapy; and a number of drugs with anti-androgen effects (see Tables 7 and 8).

The Female Androgen-Deficiency Syndrome (FADS)

T is the libido hormone for women as well as for men, albeit the physiological levels that are required for normal motivation in women are much lower (see Chapter 3).

Until very recently, this condition has not been investigated or documented as extensively in women as in men. For this reason, we conducted a study of the psychosexual effects of female androgen deficiency; this confirmed that T deficiency produces comparable sexual deficits in adult men and women (Kaplan & Owett, 1993). More specifically, we compared 11 women who had either undergone a total abdominal hysterectomy with bilateral salpingo-oophorectomy or had cytotoxic chemotherapy-induced menopause, and who all had very low circulating T levels (>10ng/dl), with 11 women who all had the same clinical profiles but whose T levels were in the normal range (30–55ng/dl). All the subjects in both groups reported that they had had normal sexual feelings and responses prior to their treatments.

We found that, like men with T deficiencies, the low-T women in our study all reported that they had lost their libido completely, along with spontaneous fluctuations of sexual desire, and they all experienced a loss of or a marked decrease in their previously normal responses to sexual stimulation and in their ability to have orgasms (see Table 6).

In addition, decreased frequency of sexual activity was reported by the low-T group. Typically, these women ceased being interested in masturbation or in fantasizing, and they seldom engaged in these activities except occasionally as a "test" to find out if their sexual feelings had returned. They also reported having sex less frequently with their partners.

The women with T deficiencies all described the decrease in their sexual feelings in strikingly similar terms. When complaining about the loss of their spontaneous feelings of sexual desire, these women will typically tell you, "I used to feel horny, at least two or three times a week. I could just be lying down or taking a bath, and I would just feel sexy. Then I might fantasize or masturbate or, if he was around, approach my partner. That just hasn't happened since my chemo (or hysterectomy)." Another patient in the study put it this way: "I used to be a '10' (sexually), and now I am barely a '1.'"

Like men, women with T deficiency-related losses of libido often report that they no longer engage in erotic fantasy. Some of our subjects made deliberate efforts to conjure up their previously arousing erotic fantasies, but they were all disappointed to find that the old scenarios had lost their erotic power. For example, one of our "low T" subjects reported that in the past she would become highly aroused if she fantasized about a handsome man in jeans masturbating. After her illness and chemotherapy, she could still visualize the masturbation scene, but this now left her completely "cold."

Female patients with androgen deficiency-related desire disorders are also similar to hypogonadal men who tend to complain about their diminishing ejaculations, in that women experience a loss or a significant decrease in their orgastic pleasure and sensations. In other words, like men, androgen-deficient women lose their normal, premorbid capacity to experience pleasurable sexual climaxes.

Some female low-T patients lose their ability to climax altogether. Those who retain some capacity to achieve orgasms usually report that they now experience these as far less pleasurable, and their sensations are less intense. They tend to complain that their orgasms, such as they were, had become briefer and consisted of fewer and weaker vaginal spasms. In addition, the sensations tended to be much more localized to the genitalia in the T-deprived women, and the "rush" of a total experience was lost to these patients. Typically, these women expressed a sense of frustration about the loss of their orgastic capacity: "Since my hysterectomy (or my chemo), my orgasms are non-events—it's just a little blip—it's hardly worth the effort." Or, "Now it's just like a little sneeze" is another typical refrain.

Our low-T subjects often voiced their distress about losing their erotic clitoral sensations and the erotic sensations that were once evoked by stimulation of their nipples. As one patient put it, "When he uses his tongue on my clitoris, it feels like he is licking my elbow." This is similar to the complaints of some T-deficient older men that their penis, especially around the glans, has lost its former sensitivity.

All of our patients wished that they could have their old pleasurable orgasms back. Some patients used vibrators in the attempt to compensate for the loss of their clitoral sensitivity and for their raised orgastic thresholds. Those who succeeded in achieving a climax in this manner told us that they had to press the vibrator very hard against their clitoris, and that they had to double and triple their premorbid stimulation time in order to feel any erotic sensations whatsoever, and in order to achieve even the diminished orgasms of which they were still capable. Another patient put it this way: "I really have to grind it (the orgasm) out. But it's a real project."

In other words, all the low-T subjects noticed and complained about the fact that the T-deficiency states had raised their orgasm thresholds. Table 6 compares the sexual effects of T deficiency in men and women.

Causes of T Deficiency in Women

Under normal circumstances, 50% of female androgens are produced by the ovaries and 50% by the adrenal gland. Circulating female androgens increase at puberty and, except for minor fluctuations during the menstrual cycle, remain at a constant level until about a decade before the menopause, when a slight and gradual decline in ovarian T production begins. However, in most healthy women this is not clinically significant and the ovaries continue to secrete sufficient amounts of T to maintain female libido at a normal level for some time after cycling stops. In addition, in many women the adrenal gland picks up the slack after menopause, so that circulating T levels and female libidos continue at a level that is sufficient for normal sexual functioning well into the postmenopausal years, when T production declines to significant and noticeable levels in old age (McCoy & Davidson, 1985; Sherwin, 1988, 1991; Longcope, 1991a, 1991b; Vermuelen, 1976).

But the destructive effects on female libido seem to be more profound if the loss of the sources of T is sudden. Thus, a number of excellent studies have documented that clinically significant T deficiency states are not uncommon in women after surgical removal of both ovaries during hysterectomy and after chemical damage to the ovaries by cytotoxic chemotherapy for cancer (Sherwin et al., 1985; Sherwin, 1985; Chakravarti et al., 1977; Rose & Davis, 1980; Kaplan, 1992b; Kaplan & Owett, 1993).

TABLE 6

The Effects of Androgen Deficiency on Males and Females

A—Hypogonadal males display the following clinical characteristics:*

1. Sexual desire and fantasy are absent or markedly decreased; spontaneous fluctuations of libido are absent.
2. Erection may be retained, but is usually lost eventually.
3. Ejaculation is absent or markedly decreased.
4. Erotic penile sensitivity is decreased.
5. The sexual symptoms are global.
6. The onset of the patient's sexual complaints occurs after a physical event or events that can be associated with impaired androgen production or bioavailability (e.g., castration, anti-androgen medications ([See Table 7]).
7. The circulating T levels are below the normal range for males (300 ng/dl–1,200 ng/dl).

B—Androgen deficient females display the following clinical characteristics:

1. Sexual desire and fantasy are absent or markedly decreased; spontaneous fluctuations of libido are absent.
2. Orgasm is absent or markedly decreased.
3. There is a loss of erotic nipple and clitoral sensitivity.
4. The sexual symptoms are global.
5. The onset of the patient's sexual complaints occurred after a physical event or events that can be associated with impaired androgen production (e.g., natural, surgical or chemical menopause ([See Table 7]).
6. The circulating T levels are below the normal range for women (25 ng/dl–100 ng/dl).

*This table includes only the sexual manifestations of T deficiency and omits all mention of cognitive, metabolic, and other physiologic changes.

As in men, clinically significant androgen deficiencies can occur in women as a result of certain drugs, for example contraceptives, that bind circulating free-T molecules so tightly that they become biologically unavailable to the T receptors of target organs (Bancroft et al., 1991).

Profound Psychological Reactions of Women to the Loss of Their Libido

Like hypogonadal male patients who are on anti-androgen medications for the adjuvant treatment of prostate cancers, the T-deprived women in our study were all dismayed about the loss of their ability to respond to their partners. One patient said, "I never missed sex so much when he was away, but I always got very turned on when he kissed me or touched me. Before I got sick, I could always get hot if we watched an erotic videotape together. But now I just can't feel a thing, no matter what we do." Or, "Now he has to work on me for hours for me to feel anything, and even then it isn't much—it's a real bummer."

The medical establishment has long been sensitive to the devastating effects that the loss of libido and impotence can have on men. But doctors have been less aware that it is also a terrible thing for a woman to lose her sex drive and her ability to climax. Thus, many of our female cancer patients who had acquired T deficiency from chemotherapy with cytotoxic agents or from oophorectomies found the loss of their erotic feelings more devastating than the diagnosis of cancer, the loss of their breasts, or the loss of their childbearing capacity. Mourning for their lost erotic feelings was a reoccurring theme for our FADS patients just as it was for our hypogonadic male patients.

Effects on Sexual Relationship

The majority of our low-T patients continued to enjoy the cuddling or nongenital aspects of sexual contacts with their husbands and lovers. Many appreciated their partners' continuing sexual interest in them and were relieved that they had not lost their sexual powers and that they had retained their ability to provide their men with sexual gratification. Others experienced sexual contact as neutral. However, some of the women who lost their capacity to experience erotic pleasure eventually developed true sexual aversions and could no longer tolerate any physical contact with their partners. These women typically became angry when they had intercourse since they felt nothing, while they observed their partners' obvious sexual pleasure.

Partner Response

It is of interest to note that the husbands of women who lost their libido tended to become more disturbed by their wives' lack of responsiveness than by the loss of their wives' breasts or postmenopausal vaginal dryness.

Once again, we see a gender parallel in that wives of hypogonadal men who lose their libido as a result of orchiectomy or treatment with antiandrogen cancer medications, such as Lupron (leuprolide acetate) and Flutamide, tend to feel rejected and sexually turned off even though the men may do their best to provide them with erotic stimulation, and they understand intellectually that the husband's lack of sexual interest has a physical basis.

TREATMENT OF ANDROGEN-DEFICIENCY STATES

Males

It is beyond the scope of this text to cover the topic of androgen replacement therapy in detail, and the reader is referred to the many excellent publications that are available on this topic (Wilson & Foster, 1992; Goodman & Gilman, 1993; Davidson & Rosen, 1992). The present discussion is limited to some general principles of T replacement for men and women that are pertinent for sex therapists.

The symptoms of T deficiency in adult males are entirely and rapidly (in two to three weeks) reversed simply by the administration of physiological amounts of T. Unless this is medically contraindicated,* T replacement is the treatment of choice when there is an absolute deficiency of endogenous androgens, while hypogonadal states that are drug-induced can be reversed simply by discontinuing the medication.

The aim of replacement therapy is to restore the patient's circulating bioavailable T to physiologically correct male levels. In most laboratories the norms for adult men range between 300 ng/dl and 1,200 ng/dl for long-term T replacement maintenance therapy (Davidson & Rosen, 1992). In order to avoid atrophy of the testes, some andrologists prefer to switch to or add low doses (5mg) of Clomid (clomiphene), an infertility drug that stimulates testicular synthesis and secretion of testosterone.

The administration of T to men whose levels are in the normal range

*The administration of exogenous T is not considered safe for men with histories of prostate or breast cancers, and cardiovascular congestive states, among other contraindications.

is subject to controversy. While T usually does not raise the libido of eugonadal men and the practice is frowned upon by more conservative endocrinologists (because this exposes the patient to some medical hazards), some middle aged and older men, whose androgen levels are in the low-normal range, do report an increase of their sex drive and their feelings of well being in response to supplemental testosterone treatment (Davidson & Rosen, 1992). This has been our experience as well.

It may be speculated that since the normal range of circulating T in men is very wide (300 ng/dl to 12,000 ng/dl), the low-normal levels of some of these men actually represent hypogonadal states, relative to their prior higher levels.

Therefore, it is my practice to suggest brief trials of T injections for nondepressed men over 50 who complain of a global loss of sexual interest, and who have low-normal circulating bioavailable T levels and no medical contraindications, on the theory that they may be suffering from an occult male menopausal hormone deficiency.

Different textbooks and clinicians vary somewhat in their recommendations regarding doses, schedules, and preparations of T for replacement therapy for males (Wilson & Foster, 1992; Goodman & Gilman, 1993; Sherwin, 1988; Davidson & Rosen, 1988).

The usual replacement regimen currently used by the endocrinologists and andrologists we work with in the New York City area is 150cc to 300cc of one of the long-acting T esters, ethanate or propionate, in aqueous solution, administered by intramuscular injection every two or three weeks. The dose and time schedule are adjusted until the patient reports a return of his normal libido. In addition, because of the wide range of both the normal values and the individual responses to T, I always check the patient's T and free-T levels periodically to determine at what level that particular patient feels sexually "normal." Since it may take two to three weeks for the patient's libido to increase, once the proper dose is administered, in my experience a three-month trial provides ample time to determine if T therapy will be effective and to adjust the dose and the administration schedule to the patient's specific needs.

Recently, *Testaderm*, a transdermal testosterone preparation in the form of a patch,* has become available, which obviates the need for injections. *Testaderm* delivers 4 mg or 6 mg of dihydrotestosterone daily through the scrotal skin. The manufacturers supply convincing evidence that this transdermal delivery system is as effective (or more so) in providing physiologically normal male levels of androgens as I.M. injections, that the T patch mimics the normal physio-

*Testaderm is supplied in patches that deliver 4 and 6 mg of T per day.

logic secretion more closely, and that the patch is safer than oral or injected T. (Cunningham et al., 1989; McClure et al., 1991; Davidson & Rosen, 1992).*

Females

The treatment of female androgen deficiency is also the replacement of testosterone, but this must be with low, physiologically correct doses of androgens. The therapeutic window between normal libido and virilizing side effects for women can be attained with about 10% of the amount that men need. However, when circulating T falls below this 10% minimum level, women lose their libido and responsiveness just as hypogonadic men do.

The issue of whether to prescribe T for women whose circulating T levels fall into the normal range** is even more complex than it is for men. Biologically normal, regularly cycling women who complain of low libido do not seem to benefit from supplemenatary androgens (Bancroft et al., 1991, I & II; Segraves, 1988b). However, some women who receive high doses of androgens for metastatic breast cancer report a surge of libido, suggesting that in some cases supraphysiologic doses of androgens could raise female libido.

Physiologic doses of T pose little risk, and I consider a brief trial is justified in postmenopausal women with a global loss of libido whose T levels are abnormally low, > 25ng/dl or in the low-normal ranges (25–35 ng/dl). However, T has no place in the treatment of premenopausal women with normal T levels, nor in postmenopausal women with high or high-normal T levels. Because of the danger of virilization, supraphysiologic doses of androgens should never be prescribed for women as a sexual stimulant under any condition.

With low, physiologic doses of T, which produce serum levels that are within the normal physiologic range for women, 25–110 ng/dl or about 10% of the normal male levels, the unwelcome symptoms of virilization that tend to occur with the higher male levels are a rarity.

It has been speculated that the fact that the low amounts of T that would be inadequate to maintain libido in men are effective for women may be due to the greater neuronal sensitivity of females to T (Sherwin, 1988). Whatever the reason, it is unlikely to be a biological accident that

*A comparable T patch for women is still in the developmental stage (personal communication, Alzea Corporation).

**Laboratories vary widely in what they label the lower limit of normal T for women. We consider this to be 20–25 ng/dl, on the basis of a survey of current medical texts, as well as our own clinical experience (unpublished study).

the brains of female mammals, including humans, have a normal sexual response to low T levels that do not virilize the peripheral tissues.

"Estratest" is a clinically available oral preparation that contains low, nonvirilizing doses of methyl testosterone and esterified estrogen.* This product has been well researched (Notolewitz, 1990; Longcope, 1991a,b; Gambrel, 1990). The manufacturers of "Estratest" have met the FDA criteria for efficacy and safety, and the preparation is currently recommended and prescribed as replacement therapy for postmenopausal women. However, because it contains estrogens, Estratest is contraindicated for patients for whom parenteral E poses a risk. Women with T deficiency-related low libido who cannot take estrogen have the option of treatment with low doses of T by itself.

In our experience, women with androgen deficiency states tend to do well in terms of regaining their libido with about 10% of the male dose, in the form of 10 to 30 ml of one of the long-acting T esters in aqueous solution by intramuscular injections every two or three weeks, or by oral methyl testosterone 5 mg two to four times a week.

A number of our patients with FADS have reported that the daily application of 2% testosterone propionate in petrolatum to the clitoris and labia is beneficial in increasing clitoral sensitivity, and some report that their desire also increased. In the absence of controlled studies, it is difficult to rule out placebo effects, but since the downside is minimal, this is worth trying. The ointment can be prescribed to supplement oral or parenteral T replacement, or by itself.

Physicians Are Reluctant to Prescribe T for Women.

Androgen replacement for men is a common practice that is well described in numerous publications and texts. But for women, this has been a neglected area of medicine.** Moreover, many physicians feel reluctant to and are often curiously resistant to prescribing T for their women patients. In part, this reflects a valid concern about the potential

---

*"Estratest HS" contains 0.65 mg estrogens and 1.25 mg methyl testosterone, and "Estratest" is made up of 1.25 mg estrogens and 2.5 mg testosterone.

**All of the standard textbooks we reviewed described male hypogonadism and its treatment in detail, while none made any mention of androgen deficiency and its treatment in women. However, the signs and symptoms of the virilizing effects of (excessive) T administration to female patients were cited in all. The texts we reviewed included: *Cecil Loeb Textbook of Medicine* (Wynoarden et al. (Eds), 1991); *Williams Textbook of Endocrinology* (Wilson & Foster (Eds), 1992); *Clinical Pathology* (Howanitz, Howanitz & Henry, 1991); *Goodman and Gilman's Pharmacology* (Goodman, Gilman, Rall, Nies & Taylor (Eds) 1990); *Harris Textbook of Medicine* (Branareld, Isselbacker, Perdersderf, Wilson, Martin & Fanci (Eds), 1987; PDR, 1994.

virilizing effects of this "male" sex hormone, which includes the growth of facial hair, the development of acne, and the irreversible deepening of the voice, etc. But once again, these unwelcome symptoms of virilization of the peripheral tissues occur only if women are overdosed with high amounts of testosterone that exceed the normal physiologic range for females.

The effectiveness of T replacement for women who lack this hormone, in contrast to the ineffectiveness of other treatments, is illustrated by the very first case of female androgen deficiency that I recognized.*

CASE 10.1—"Beatrice Kurt": Hypoactive Sexual Desire Disorder Due to Androgen Deficiency

The patient was a 46-year-old married woman who complained bitterly about her lack of sexual desire and difficulty in having orgasms. This problem had begun 10 years previously after she had undergone a successful course of chemotherapy for Hodgkin's disease. Prior to her illness, this woman had been highly sexual and responsive, and she and her husband had enjoyed an unusually active and passionate sex life.

The patient had experienced the usual unpleasant side effects of chemotherapy with cytotoxic agents: nausea and vomiting, depletion of energy, hair loss, cessation of her menses, and also the loss of her desire for sex. She soon recovered, however, and her hair, menstrual periods, energy, and even her vaginal lubrication came back, but her libido did not.**

The loss of Mrs. Kurt's sexual feelings were very painful for this couple and they had sought individual and couples therapy with several reputable therapists during the 10 intervening years. These psychological treatments had not been effective in restoring Mrs. Kurt's libido, and the couple came to the sex therapy as a "last resort."

I could not detect any emotional problems to account for this patient's sexual symptoms on a psychological basis. More specifically, depression and marital disharmony were ruled out. In fact, this woman loved her husband deeply, and he was very good to her. Moreover, she lubricated normally, and intercourse, while not erotic, was physically comfortable. Furthermore, the patient's psychiatric examination and history indicated that her psychosexual development had been entirely normal and that she was free of significant sexual conflicts.

---

*This case was described in a previous publication (Kaplan, 1992b).

**The resumption of normal cycling, as well as the lubrication-swelling response, indicated that the patient's ovaries had recovered their capacity to synthesize and secrete estrogen.

However, the clinic picture was reminiscent of the T-deficient post-hysterectomy women I had been seeing, and therefore I ordered hormone tests. These revealed that this patient's T and FT levels were 0 (this was confirmed by two repeated testings).

This patient's libido and her orgastic ability were completely restored in less than a month with bimonthly injections of 15 ml of testosterone ethanate in aqueous solution, without any additional psychological intervention.

The patient expressed the joy she felt, which is typical of those who recover their lost libido, in a letter to me, signed by both spouses, in which she referred to T replacement as a "medical miracle."

HYPERPROLACTINEMIA

Hyperprolactinemia, or prolactinemia, refers to an elevation of serum prolactin (Prl) above normal levels. This is associated with a loss of libido in men and women even though their T levels may be normal. This abnormality can be produced by a number of disease states that range from trivial to serious, and by dopamine blocking medications, as well as by stress (Bancroft et al., 1984; Davidson & Rosen, 1992; Segraves, 1988a,b).

The most serious condition that is associated with a high serum prolactin level is prolactin-secreting adenoma of the pituitary gland. In the early stages of prolactin-secreting pituitary adenomas, before other physical or neurological signs and symptoms begin to appear, the elevation of serum Prl may be the only sign of the disease, and the gradual loss of libido, possibly accompanied by impotence, may be the sole clinical symptom. Since prolactin levels are not routinely checked by physicians, patients with prolactinemia-associated losses of libido are often erroneously cleared medically and referred to therapists for psychological treatments.

Malignant prolactin-secreting pituitary macro adenomas are potentially lethal and must be medically, surgically, or radiologically treated promptly, for this tumor can spread and become inoperable. Since these patients often cannot be clinically distinguished from those with global psychogenic HSD or from those with androgen-deficiency states, it is imperative to include Prl levels in addition to T levels in the diagnostic workup of every patient who complains of a generalized loss of sexual desire.

The following case provides a dramatic illustration of the importance of measuring Prl levels in these patients.

CASE 10.2—"Professor Lucky": Hypoactive Sexual Desire Disorder Due to Prolactinemia in a Man with Psychological and Marital Problems

The patient was a 54-year-old professor of psychology who was born in England. He held an appointment on a distinguished Canadian faculty. Over the past 18 months, he had progressively lost his sexual interest in his wife of 22 years, and he was also beginning to develop erectile difficulties.

Professor L. complained that he no longer felt spontaneous surges of sexual desire, and that he had lost his urge to fantasize. Moreover, making love to his wife, which had been very arousing in the past, no longer excited him. And, although he usually could, with sufficient stimulation, obtain an erection, lately these had lasted only a short time and were not as firm as they used to be. Further, he described a marked decrease in his ejaculatory sensations. Prior to about two years ago, when the patient first began to note his progressive loss of sexual interest, he had always functioned without difficulty.

About six months prior to the consultation, during his annual medical examination, the patient had mentioned the problem to his internist, and he was reassured that physically "everything was fine." The doctor suggested that his was a common complaint that was to be expected at his age.

Professor Lucky was a highly intelligent and well-educated researcher who, in addition to his other credentials, had acquired psychoanalytic training. The professor had thought deeply about his problem and had formulated a plausible hypothesis about the possible dynamics of his diminishing libido.

Two years ago, around the time he began to notice a decrease in his sexual interest, he had discovered that his wife had been having an affair with the chairman of his department. He was devastated. However, he had done his best to try to forgive the contrite and guilty Mrs. Lucky, whom he loved dearly. Nonetheless, he attributed his sexual symptoms to his remaining unconscious anger at her and his fear of putting himself at emotional risk once more. Further, he told me that this episode had rekindled old buried oedipal issues that involved competition with his father. This had been a major theme during his training analysis.

Patients can certainly develop desire disorders and lose their libido on account of such traumatic rejections, especially if, like Professor Lucky they have residual underlying oedipal problems. Thus this patient's self analysis sounded believable.

But I was a little concerned about the possibility of organicity because the patient had also told me that his loss of desire was across the board. He no longer had A.M. erections nor had he felt like masturbating or fantasizing in recent months.

This type of global loss of libido does not necessarily indicate an organic etiology, for the same clinical picture could also have been produced by the patient's depressive reaction to his wife's unfaithfulness. However, I wanted to be certain that Professor L's problem was entirely psychogenic, so I asked him to have our standard battery of hormone tests* done in Toronto. While assuring him that this was probably an unnecessary caution, we made plans for the professor and his wife to come to New York for treatment.

The next communication from Professor Lucky was a note written in a shaky hand, which arrived a month later, informing me that the tests had revealed an abnormally high prolactin level and that he had just been operated on for a sizable pituitary tumor.

On a follow up visit one year later, Professor L. had made a complete recovery. His prolactin levels had returned to normal and his sexual interest in his wife, who had been wonderfully supportive and loving during his surgery and recovery, had also returned.

SEXUAL DESIRE DISORDERS DUE TO MEDICAL CONDITIONS AND DRUGS

The list of disease states that can affect libido adversely is huge and encompasses every disease that causes chronic pain, debility, malaise, and psychological embarrassment in addition to those that result in erectile difficulties or dyspareunia. Far too many to enumerate in this chapter, these include such common ailments as arthritis, advanced cardiovascular and renal diseases, chronic obstructive pulmonary diseases, neurological diseases such as multiple sclerosis and Parkinson's disease, chronic inflammatory diseases, cancer, thyroid conditions, many kinds of chronic infections, and various gynecological and urologic conditions.

The majority of these disease states produce a decrease of sexual desire indirectly by sapping the patient's strength, destroying his/her feeling of well-being, interfering with intercourse, and/or making him or her feel unattractive or self-conscious. However, there are a few disease states that decrease libido *directly*, by virtue of producing androgen-deficiency states or by raising the patient's prolactin levels.

Similarly, there is an extensive list of prescription drugs and recreational substances that may impair the sex drive.

---

*The test battery consisted of serum Testosterone, free Testosterone, Prolactin, FSH, LH, Estrogens, and a Thyroid Profile.

A variety of mechanisms have been implicated in the libido-decreasing effects of medications. These include antagonism or tight binding of testosterone, increase of prolactin, the favoring of serotonin over dopamine in the brain, and a variety of pharmacodynamic actions that have not yet been elucidated. In addition, drugs that impair erection or orgasm may have secondary, deleterious effects on the sex drive.

It is beyond the scope of this book to present a comprehensive review of all the illnesses and medications that can potentially reduce libido. Further, to do so would constitute an unnecessary replication of the excellent works on these topics that have been published elsewhere.

To orient clinicians who work with sexually dysfunctional patients, I have listed in Tables 7 and 8 the most common medical conditions, prescription medications, and recreational drugs that have been implicated in lowering the sex drive.

The tables were prepared in consultation with Dr. R. Taylor Segraves. For further information, the reader is referred to excellent comprehensive reviews in two scholarly chapters by Dr. Segraves: "Drugs and Desire" and "Hormones and Libido," in *Sexual Desire Disorders: Update for the 90's* (Leiblum & Rosen, 1988). "Aging and Drug Effects on Male Sexuality," a chapter by R.T. Segraves and K.B. Segraves in *Erectile Disorders: Assessment and Treatment* (Rosen & Leiblum (Eds), 1992), and "Hormonal Determinants of Erectile Dysfunctions" by J.M. Davidson and R.C. Rosen in that same volume are also excellent resources. For additional medical and pharmacologic references, the 9th edition of Goodman and Gilman's *Textbook of Pharmacology* (Goodman & Gilman, 1993) and *Williams Textbook of Encrinology*, 8th edition (Wilson & Foster, 1992) provide authoritative and up-to-date information.

Organic and Psychogenic HSD: Differential Diagnosis

Psychogenic sexual desire disorders are far more common than desire disorders due to hormones or drugs, especially in patients below the age of 50. However, it goes without saying that organic factors must be ruled out in every case involving a global loss of sexual desire prior to considering sex therapy. Not only is it incumbent on the clinician to make sure that physical conditions that might require medical intervention are detected, but it is also clearly unethical to recommend expensive, time-consuming psychological treatments that will do the patient with physical problems no good.

The loss of libido in patients whose sexual complaints are due to diseases or are drugs-induced *is always global or generalized, simply because these stressors undermine the physical substrate upon which the experience and regulation of sexual desire depend.* Therefore, if the lack of desire does not occur in all situations—for example, if the patient has not lost his or her desire to fantasize and to masturbate, organic causes are ruled out and psychogenocity is established even though he/she is no longer responsive to the partner.

However, mild organic deficits can provide exceptions. In the beginning stages of a hormone problem, when the deficit may still be only partial, as in perimenopausal states or in the early stages of a slow-growing prolactinoma, patients may attempt to compensate for their dropping T levels by increasing the sexual stimulation. Such cases may present with a "pseudo-specific" clinical picture.

In other words, patients with *partial organic* deficits may still manage to reach a climax, albeit this is possible only with the prolonged use of a vibrator and intense fantasy, while they no longer becomes aroused with the less intense stimulation provided by sexual intercourse with the partner. This may be mistaken for a genuinely situational and, therefore, psychogenic desire disorder.

Situational Deficit: A Subtle Diagnostic Issue

The situational pattern of decreased desire is not always obvious on the initial evaluation because patients may not be entirely forthcoming about their sexual feelings, and even skillful probing does not always elicit this information.

For example, one of the patients in the FADS study was a 47-year-old married woman who had undergone a mastectomy with adjuvant chemotherapy (CMF) for breast cancer three years prior to the interview. During the initial evaluation, Mrs. S. complained sadly that she had lost her sexual desire totally. She reported that since her illness she did not respond to her husband nor could she have orgasms masturbating by herself.

Mrs. S. had consulted me because her unresponsiveness was becoming a problem in this couple's marriage. His wife's mastectomy had not diminished the attraction she held for Mr. S. and he was eager to continue to have sex with her on a regular basis, but her lack of sexual interest and her avoidance of sex was a growing source of anger and tension between them.

It was only some time later that the patient admitted that on one occasion, after she had recovered from the effects of her surgery and chemotherapy, her husband had taken her on a luxurious trip to Europe. There she learned that her son had received a prestigious international award and she remembered feeling elated. That night, she did have one

TABLE 7*
Common Medical Conditions That May Decrease Sexual Desire

A— **DISEASES THAT CAUSE TESTOSTERONE DEFICIENCY STATES IN MALES:**
castration, injuries to the testes, age-related atrophic testicular degeneration, bilateral cryptorchism, Klinefelter's syndrome, hydrocele, varicocele, cytotoxic, chemotherapy, pelvic radiation, mumps orchitis, hypothalamic-pituitary lesions, Addison's disease, etc.
Conditions requiring anti-androgens drugs, e.g., prostate cancer, antisocial sexual behavior, etc.

IN FEMALES:
bilateral salpingo-oophorectomy, adrenalectomy, hypophysectomy, cytotoxic chemotherapy, hypothalamic-pituitary lesions, Addison's disease, androgen insensitivity syndrome, etc.
Conditions requiring anti-androgen drugs, e.g., endometriosis, etc.

B— **CONDITIONS THAT CAUSE HYPERPROLACTINEMIA:**
pituitary prolactin-secreting adenoma, other tumors of the pituitary, hypothalamic disease, hypothyroidism, hepatic, cirrhosis, stress, breast manipulation, etc., and conditions requiring Prl raising medication, e.g., depression, psychosis, infertility, etc.

C— **CONDITIONS THAT DECREASE DESIRE VIA UNKNOWN MECHANISMS:**
hyperthyroidism, temporal lobe epilepsy, renal dialysis, etc.

D— **CONDITIONS THAT CAUSE ORGANIC IMPOTENCE (Indirect cause of low sexual desire in men):**
diabetes mellitus, arteriosclerosis of penile blood vessels, venus leak, penile muscular atrophy, Peyrones disease, Lariche's syndrome, steal syndrome, sickle cell disease, priapism, injury to penis, etc.

E— **CONDITIONS THAT CAUSE DYSPAREUNIA (Indirect cause of low sexual desire):**

IN FEMALES:
urogenital estrogen-deficiency syndrome—normal age-related menopause, surgical menopause, chemical menopause, irradiation of ovaries; endometriosis, pelvic inflammatory disease, vaginitis, herpes, vaginismus, cystitis, etc.

IN MALES:
herpes, phymosis, post-ejaculatory syndrome, etc.

F— **ALL MEDICAL CONDITIONS THAT CAUSE CHRONIC PAIN, FATIGUE, OR MALAISE (Indirect cause of low desire):**
arthritis, cancer, obstructive pulmonary disease, chronic cardiac and renal insufficiency, shingles, peripheral neuropathy, trigeminal neuralgia, chronic infections, traumatic injuries, etc.

*Tables 7 and 8 were prepared in consultation with Dr. Taylor Segraves.

TABLE 8
Commonly Used Pharmacologic Agents That May Decrease Sexual Desire*

A— **ANTI-ANDROGEN DRUGS*:** cyproterone* and depo-provera* (for sex offenders), Flutamide* (for prostate cancer in men, virilizing syndromes in women, precocious puberty in boys, etc.), Luprin,* a Gonadotropin releasing hormone analog (for prostate cancer, used together with Flutamide, also for endometriosis in women); Cytotoxic chemotherapeutic agents* (Adriomycin, Methotraxate, Cytotoxin, Fluorouracil, Cisplatin, etc.).

B— **PSYCHOACTIVE DRUGS:**

1. *Sedative-Hypnotics:* loss of desire dose-related: in low doses, dysinhibition may cause increase in desire; high doses and chronic use reduce desire. Alcohol; Benzodiazepines (Valium, Ativan, Xanax, Librium, Halcion, etc); Barbiturates (phenobarbital, amital, etc.); Chloral Hydrate, Methaqualude, etc.

2. *Narcotics** (Heroin, Morphine, Methadone, Meperadine, etc.).

3. *Anti-Depressants:* (Dopamine blocking and serotonergic) SSRIs* (Prozac, Zoloft, Pacil); Tricyclics (Tofranil, Norpramin, Amitriptyline, Aventil, Clomipramine*); MAOIs* (Nardil, Marplan), Lithium Carbonate, Tegretal.

4. *Neuroleptics (increase Prl):* Phenothiazine (Thorazine,* Thioridazine) Prolixin,* Stellazine, Mellaril, etc.); Haldol,* Sulpride.*

5. *Stimulants:* loss of desire is dose-related: low, acute doses may stimulate libido; high doses and chronic use reduce sex drive. (Dexadrine, Methamphetamine, Cocaine).

C— **CARDIAC DRUGS:**

1. *Antihypertensives:* (Hydrochlorothiazide,* Chlorthalidone,* Methyldopal,* Spironolactone,* Reserpine,* Clonidine, Guathedine,* etc.).

2. *Cardiac Drugs:* Beta adrenergic blockers* (Endoral, Atenelol, Timolol, etc.); Calcium blockers** (Nifedipine, Verapranil, etc.).

D— **DRUGS THAT BIND WITH TESTOSTERONE:**

1. Tamoxifen, Contraceptive Agents, etc.

E— **MISCELLANEOUS DRUGS:** Cimetidine* (for peptic ulcer); Pondomin* (serotonergic appetite suppressor); Diclorphenamine, Methazolomine (for glaucoma); Clofribrate, Lovastatin (anti-cholestrol); Steroids (chronic use for inflammatory conditions), (Prednisone, Decadron, etc.).

*All the drugs listed have been reported to result in the loss of sexual desire and/or in erectile problems. However, the frequency with which sexual side effects occur varies considerably, and the drugs that have a very high incidence of decreased libido have been marked with *.
**Long-acting calcium channel blockers are more likely to decrease desire and impair erection than the short-acting preparations.

"glorious" sexual experience with her husband during which she became entirely absorbed in her sexual feelings and had multiple orgasms. But since then, for the past year, she had again felt "nothing."

This patient had regained her normal premorbid sexual response only once in the three years since her mastectomy and chemotherapy, but that was enough to indicate that her physical capacity for arousal was still intact and that her problem was psychogenic. As I expected, her testosterone level turned out to be within the normal range (39 mg/dl) and it did not surprise me when she responded rapidly to therapy.

A brief course of psychosexual therapy helped Mrs. S. come to grips with her underlying depression, which had been a major factor in the loss of her libido. In addition, the couple benefitted from working conjointly with one of our sex therapists on improving their sexual communications.*

Establishing Endocrine Causes of Low Sexual Desire

Once again, organic and psychogenic HSD are both manifestations of the pathological down-regulation of sexual motivation, albeit in one case the central "sex centers" are rendered physiologically inoperative, while in the other they are inhibited on a psychological basis (See Figure 2 in Chapter 2). It follows that the clinical features of organic sexual desire disorders are often identical to those of psychogenic HSD. Unless the symptom is clearly situational, it is impossible, even for an expert, to make the differential diagnosis solely on the basis of a psychiatric or sexual history.**

Moreover, the diagnostic process is further complicated because patients with low sexual desire due to T deficiencies and elevated prolactin levels or who take drugs with sexual side effects often appear to be perfectly healthy physically, without any medical signs or symptoms.

For these reasons, the diagnosis of hypoactive sexual desire disorders due to hormone abnormalities *can be confirmed with certainty only by positive laboratory findings*, such as low-T or free-T levels, abnormally elevated levels of prolactin, hypo- or hyperthyroidism.

To reiterate the point that was made in Chapter 5, the pretreatment workup of patients with complaints of generalized low desire should always include specific tests to detect those patients with relatively few

---

*The therapist was Trudy Owett, MSW from our group.

**In the study of FADS, which was described above, more than half of the women with normal T levels whose sexual deficits were presumably psychogenic complained of a global loss of libido and a generalized lack of responsiveness that were no different from the symptoms reported by patients with low T levels.

occult hormonal and metabolic problems that can cause a loss of sexual desire in apparently healthy, otherwise asymptomatic men and women.

The endocrine workups that have been recommended for screening patients with complaints of low sexual desire by various authorities differ somewhat, but all include T and Prl (Davidson & Rosen, 1992). As part of our diagnostic procedure, we use the following battery of tests: Testosterone, bioavailable testosterone, prolactin, total estrogens, LH, FSH, and a thyroid profile for men. For female patients, the tests are the same except that estradiol is substituted for estrogens (Kaplan & Owett, 1993). We have found that this battery picks up the great majority of occult endocrine causes of low sexual desire. However, some have argued that this is too expensive and that only the T and Prl levels should be done initially, to be followed by other tests, if indicated (Segraves, 1992).

Diagnosing Drug-Induced Sexual Disorders

If drug-induced sexual abnormalities are suspected, the diagnosis is made on the basis of a history that indicates that the patient's loss of libido coincided with commencement of the medication. The diagnosis of drug-induced loss of desire is confirmed by discontinuing the agent in question and/or substituting a drug with a more favorable side-effect profile and observing the patient to determine if his or her libido returns to normal.

Diagnosing Low Desire and Sexual Aversion Due to Painful Sex

Once again, every patient should be specifically asked if he/she experiences discomfort or pain during or after intercourse or orgasm. If the answer is affirmative, he or she must receive a careful physical examination of the genitalia to determine if there is a medical basis for the complaint prior to the therapist's instituting any sort of "sexual homework" (see also Chapter 5).

THE TREATMENT OF ORGANIC DESIRE DISORDERS

Treatment of Underlying Medical Conditions

It is impossible to provide a meaningful discussion herein of the treatments for the various disease states that may directly or indirectly impact on sexual motivation, as this would encompass a number of medical and surgical specialties. However, therapists who work with sexually dysfunctional patients should have some familiarity with the diagnostic procedures and treatments their patients will be undergoing.

This information will help in making appropriate referrals. For this reason, I have listed in Table 9 some of the current treatments for the most common medical conditions implicated in low sexual desire states.

Managing Drug Induced Low-Desire States: Discontinuation, Substitution, and Antidotes

Decreased sexual desire due to the side effects of medication may complicate the treatment of psychiatric disorders as well as such medical conditions as cancer, coronary artery disease, hypertension, peptic ulcer, and autoimmune diseases, among others. Further, drug-induced *erectile dysfunction* and anorgasmia often decrease sexual desire on a secondary basis.

Discontinuation and Substitution

The first-line strategy in managing the loss of libido due to drugs is to discontinue the agent in question if this is medically prudent and feasible, and/or to substitute a drug with equivalent therapeutic actions but with a more favorable side-effect profile.

As a common example, the SSRIs, MAOIs, and heterocyclic antidepressants have frequently been implicated in producing a variety of sexual dysfunctions, including a decrease of sexual motivation (See Table 8) (Segraves, 1988b,c, 1992; Segraves & Golden, 1992; Segraves & Segraves, 1992; Segraves, 1995).

If the patient's history suggests that his sexual problems may be due to the Prozac or the Nardil he is taking for his depression, a substitution with Wellbutrin and/or Desyrel is indicated and will frequently solve the problem.

As another example, Beta adrenergic blockers such as Endoral or Atenuate are known to produce a decrease of sexual desire in a substantial proportion of patients. This problem, which may lead to noncompliance, can often be reversed by switching the patient to a short-acting calcium channel blocker, such as Verapamil, which the patient is advised to take after he has finished having sex.

Antidotes

In cases where discontinuation or substitution is not feasible, certain antidotes have been recommended by a number of medical sex therapists.

TABLE 9
Treatment Options for Common Physical Causes of Low Sexual Desire

1. *For the Complications of the Female Postmenopausal Urogenital Estrogen-deficiency Related Dyspareunia and Vaginal Dryness:* E replacement is the Rx of choice; Alternative remedies include non-steroidal vaginal lubricants. Dilators are indicated for spastic, shrunken vaginal muscles. Surgical repair of cystocele and rectocele.

2. *For the Loss of Libido Due to Androgen Deficiency in Men and in Women:* replacement with gender-appropriate doses of T is the Rx of choice. A less effective option is the administration of medications with aphrodisiac effects (e.g., Wellbutrin, Eldepril, Desyrel).

3. *For the Loss of Libido Due to Hyper-prolactinemia:* treatment of the underlying condition. If this is a prolactin-secreting adenoma: bromocriptine, surgery and/or radiation, etc.; change of medication if drug-related.

4. *For Decreased Libido Associated with Thyroid Abnormalities:* replacement therapy or other thyroid treatments.

5. *When the Loss of Libido Is Secondary to Depression:* psychotherapy and antidepressant medications (preferably with antidepressant drugs that are minimally sexatoxic).

6. *If the Loss of Libido Is Drug Induced:* a drug-free trial and/or switch to a different medication or antidotes such as Yokon, Periactin, Bethanecol, etc., in consultation with a medical specialist.

7. *For Organic Male and Female Dyspareunia:* urologic or gynecologic treatment of underlying conditions in consultation with urologists and gynecologists.

8. *For Low Libido Due to Organic Impotence:* penile injection treatments (ICI), penile implants, change of sexatoxic medication, and/or antidotes; sexually stimulating drugs (e.g., Yokon, Wellbutrin, Desyrel).

9. *For Low Libido Due to Female Genital Dysfunctions:* sex therapy plus dilators, vibrators, lubricants, change of sexatoxic medications and/or antidotes; sexually stimulating drugs (e.g., Wellbutrin, Desyrel).

For the *loss of libido* due to MAOIs and TCAs in males, Yohimbine 10 mg one hour prior to having sex (Segraves & Golden, 1992; Segraves & Segraves, 1992) or Yohimbine 4.5 mg tid plus pentoxiphilline (Trental) 400 mg tid (Korenman & Viosca, 1993) has been recommended. Further, Yohimbine has also been used in the attempt to override the *erectile and libido problems* caused by a variety of antihypertensive and other cardiac drugs.

For *anorgasmia* caused by Anafranil and the SSRIs in both genders, Periactin (cyproheptadine) 4–8 mg one to two hours before sex (Segraves & Golden, 1992), and also Mytonochrol (bethanecol) 10–20 mg taken one to two hours before sex is reportedly effective in some patients (Segraves, 1992, 1995).

The Treatment of Hypoactive Sexual Desire Due to Combined Factors

Minor physical deficits and the patient's and/or the partner's inadequate emotional responses to these often act in synergy to escalate a partial physical deficit or impairment into a major sexual disability and/or a total loss of interest in sex. In fact, we see more cases where the patient's low libido is due to combined organic-psychogenic factors than ones exclusively caused by drugs or disease states, especially in older patients.

Treating the Physical Problems First

The first step in the management of low-desire patients who have physical problems is to see to it that these are treated with appropriate medical measures (see Table 9). After the medical treatment has been completed and the physical problem has been remediated as far as this is possible, the patient's sexual status should then be reevaluated to determine if he/she needs further psychological treatment.

Integrated Medical and Psychological Treatment

Hormone replacements and other medical treatments such as ICI are most likely to be effective in terms of restoring the quality of the patient's lovemaking with his/her partner if these are administered within the context of psychosexual therapy and/or by a doctor who sees beyond the patient's hormonal status and deals with the totality of the couple's relationship, including its sexual aspects. Above all, clinicians who work with these patients should be knowledgeable about human sexuality and sensitive to the emotional meaning that the loss of sexual feelings has for the patient and for the partner.

Conditions that require both medical and psychiatric treatments are best treated in consultation with the patient's own physician or psychiatrist. For example, a urologist who specializes or is expert in ICI should start the patient on the pharmacologic injection treatment program. The urologist conducts a urologic examination to clear the patient medically for the injection procedure, adjusts the medication to the patient's specific physiologic requirements, instructs the patient in the self-injection technique, and supplies him with sterile solution and syringes for use at home.

But compliance is ultimately better if the sex therapist then works with the patient and/or couple to help them translate the mechanical tumescent episodes into sensitive, passionate, lovemaking experiences (Kaplan, 1993c; Althof et al., 1987; Turner et al., 1989).

As another example, if a patient's antihypertensive medication is suspected as the culprit of his low sexual desire, his cardiologist should be consulted to decide on a therapeutic strategy that is minimally sexatoxic. For example, it might be medically safe for the patient to discontinue his clonidine and/or perhaps to substitute on ACE inhibitor antihypertensive agent like catapril, which tends to have fewer and less serious sexual side effects.

Nonpsychiatric sex therapists might want to consult with a pharmacologist colleague to determine if their low-libido patient should be taking antidepressant medication and, if so, to ascertain if one of the dopaminergic, non-sexatoxic antidepressants like Wellbutrin or Elderpril (see Chapter 7) might be effective, or if a trial of an antidote for the side effects of his current medication, such as cyproheptadine or yohimbine, is warranted.

Similar considerations, that is, working closely with the patient's urologist, oncologist, or gynecologist, are advisable when estrogen and/or androgen replacement is indicated after hysterectomy, prostatechtomy, chemotherapy, etc.

The following case, that of "Sofia and Selwyn Chain," illustrates the logic of a combined medical-psychological approach in a hypogonadal man with a long-standing sexual dysfunction.

CASE 10.3—"Mr. and Mrs. Chain": Long-Standing Marital Dissatisfaction and Hypoactive Libido in a Man with Mild Hypogonadism

Mrs. Sophia Chain, a 42-year-old housewife, was in tears when she consulted me. She had recently been rejected by her lover, Heinz, a married neighbor with whom she had been carrying on a passionate, clandestine extramarital affair for five years. Attractive and stylish, Sofia told me that she had entered into the relationship with Heinz because her husband, Selwyn, age 61, made love to her only on rare occasions. Even in the beginning of their marriage 10 years ago, the couple had never had sex more than once a month, and recently much less often than that.

Sophia had felt rejected and hurt and also frustrated by her husband's lack of sexual attention until Heinz, described as an articulate and charming man, the opposite of her silent, awkward husband, seduced her, and they began to make "beautiful love" secretly, once a week.

Six months before the consultation, Sofia had undergone a mastectomy for breast cancer.*

She made an excellent recovery, but she was in great emotional pain because after the operation, Heinz had rejected her. He kept making lame excuses for not seeing her, and when she finally confronted him, he told her bluntly that he wanted to end their affair.

Heinz' loss of interest had devastated Sofia. She told me that she was hoping to get him back and, as a first step, was planning to have reconstructive surgery. She had consulted me mainly because she wanted to know if I, as an expert on sexuality, thought there was anything else she could do to get Heinz to desire her again.

Almost as an afterthought, near the end of our session, Sofia told me that Selwyn had been extraordinarily loving and attentive to her during her illness, and she wanted to know if I thought there was anything that could be done about improving her sexual relationship with her husband.

I told the patient that I would have to see her husband before I could comment on this matter, and I scheduled an appointment with the Chains for an evaluation four weeks later.

However, because of Mr. Chain's age and the history of long-standing low sexual frequency, I wrote out a prescription for hormone tests. I asked that this be done in the couple's own community, so that the results would be available prior to our scheduled visit.

It turned out that Mr. Chain had a low T level (180 ng/dl). I conferred with his local physician by telephone. After repeating the test and obtaining a slightly lower level, he accepted my suggestion to get Mr. Chain started on a trial of T-replacement therapy.

The doctor almost sabotaged treatment by telling the patient that many men function perfectly well with that kind of T level and that the injections probably wouldn't work.

But they did. By the time I saw the couple, the husband had received

*The patient's lymph nodes were negative and she received no adjuvant chemotherapy, and hormone problems were not an issue.

two injections of 250cc of testosterone propionate. He reported happily that he felt a definite increase in his sexual feelings and, in fact, the Chains had had sex twice in the past two weeks, which was an all-time record for them.

The evaluation of this couple's sexual interactions revealed several important contributory *psychological causes* of this husband's low sexual desire and frequency.

For one, Selwyn was a premature ejaculator. When he was young, he had compensated for his poor control by having intercourse twice in a row. But this strategy began to fail as he approached the age of 50, which, incidentally, was also around the time of the couple's marriage.

In addition, Selwyn was a shy man. He was quite in awe of and intimidated by his beautiful, glamorous wife, and he was desperately afraid to fail in her eyes. He did not know how to tell her that he feared he might ejaculate too fast, and rather than risk the humiliation of a sexual failure, he found it easier simply not to approach her. Mr. Chain also told me that he figured that his wife didn't find him attractive because she never let him know she did.

Sofia's part of the problem grew out of her narcissism and her excessive rejection sensitivity. She had misinterpreted her husband's reticence as a personal rejection, and she had no understanding or empathy for his feelings. In fact, she felt so wounded and insulted, and she was so totally absorbed in her own sense of rejection, that she had never tried to reassure or encourage him.

Both spouses felt bad in their own way about the lack of sex in the marriage, and they responded in their characteristic fashions. He withdrew, and suppressed his sexual feelings, while she stepped outside the marriage to seek sexual solace, and also to express her anger.

It was not clear when Mr. Chain's hypogonadism had begun, nor how much, if at all, this had contributed to his low sex drive earlier. But although androgen replacement seemed to be helping him at this point, it was also clear that while this was an essential first step, hormones would not by themselves solve this couple's complex sexual and interpersonal problems.

In addition to hormone replacement, if the Chains' sexual relationship was going to improve on a permanent basis, he would need to overcome his performance anxiety, learn better ejaculatory control, and improve his sexual and communication skills. On her part, Sofia would have to become more forthcoming and more encouraging to her husband in the bedroom. These objectives would require that the couple commit themselves to a course of sex therapy.

They were eager to do this and they did very well. After 10 sessions, Mr. Chain's sexual desire, as well as his ejaculatory control, improved. I couldn't tell how much this was due to testosterone and how much to the fact that he now realized that his wife desired him. Their relationship became somewhat more intimate, although Mr. Chain's lack of introspection was a limiting factor in this regard.

At the end of treatment, the couple were having sex on a regular basis although, according to Sofia, their lovemaking never became as sensuous and erotic as it had been with her lover, Heinz. Nevertheless, she felt much better, "like a woman again" when she saw that her husband adored her with or without her breast. I am also happy to report that Sofia's obsession with Heinz disappeared completely.

AGE AND THE LOSS OF SEXUAL DESIRE

Many elderly patients and couples are troubled by the decrease of their libido and their sexual frequency. Most often, these complaints are the result of a combination of organic and psychological factors, for many aging patients overreact to the normal physiological decline of their sexual functioning and desire because they believe in the myth that getting older entails the loss of sexuality.

However, a number of studies involving thousands of men and women between the ages of 50 and 100 (Brecher, 1984; George & Weiler, 1981; Palmore, 1970, 1974; Starr & Weiner, 1981; Todarello & Boscia, 1985; Weitzman & Hart, 1987; Schiavi, 1990; Schiavi & Schreiner-Engel, 1990; Schiavi et al., 1990; Schiavi et al., 1994) are unanimous in their findings that asexuality is not an inevitable consequence of aging. More specifically according to all these studies, healthy 70-year-olds with available partners have sex on the average of once a week.

In actual fact, sex is one of the last biological functions to fall prey to the aging process, and there are countless older people who are retired, who are grandparents, who are wearing hearing aids or reading glasses, and even some who are confined to wheelchairs who are still enjoying making love (Kaplan, 1987).

Age-Related Changes in Sexual Functioning

I do not mean to suggest that we retain our full youthful sexuality all our lives. Older patients should be apprised that there are certain inevitable, age-related changes in sexual physiology and in sexual desire, but that these do not have to mean the end of their sex lives. If aging couples are able to adapt to and compensate for certain age-specific changes in their sexual responses, most can potentially remain sexually functional until advanced old age.

Clinicians who work with older patients should understand that the sexual aging process affects men and women differently. Moreover, age does not result in a general sexual decline, but has a specific and different impact on each of the three phases of the human sexual response cycle (Kaplan, 1990a).

Following is a brief summary of those age-related biological changes that are of special clinical significance because of their roles in the pathogenesis of the sexual disorders of the elderly.

Male and Female Orgasm

The refractory period for ejaculation in men increases considerably with age. In other words, the time that must elapse before men can climax again lengthens from a few minutes at the age of 17 to a few days when they reach 70. In females, orgasm is not appreciably affected by age, so that women remain potentially multi-orgastic throughout life.

Male and Female Arousal (Excitement)

Unlike young men who can have spontaneous erections in response to physical *or* psychic stimulation, older men, as the ability to experience spontaneous erections declines and penile sensitivity decreases with age, require increased and concomitant physical stimulation of their genitalia as well as psychic erotic input in order to obtain and maintain their erections.

In addition, erections tend to become less firm with advancing age, due to the gradual deterioration of penile muscles and blood vessels (Andersson & Wagner, 1995; Davidson & Rosen, 1992; Kaplan, 1989b; Wagner, 1990, 1993). However, under ordinary circumstances penile erections remain rigid enough for penetration throughout life. The length of time that an erection can be maintained decreases with age and, most important from the perspective of sex therapy, erections as well as desire become progressively more vulnerable to the physiological concomitants of emotional stress and anxiety (Kaplan, 1990a).

Certain disease states, such as diabetes and arteriosclerosis, and a number of drugs can produce erectile deficits that mimic the normal, age-related decline, as described above. I have suggested the term *presbyrectia* to distinguish these normal signs of penile aging from such pathological conditions (Kaplan, 1989b).

The female arousal response of pelvic vasocongestion and vaginal lubrication-swelling also declines with age as the older woman develops the female urogenital estrogen-deficiency syndrome described on page 268 (Wagner, 1986).

In addition, the vaginas of parous women often become stretched and lax and develop rectoceles and/or cystoceles, which further compromise the integrity and functional capacity of the female sexual organs.

Male and Female Sexual Desire

The effects of the aging process on *sexual desire* are gender-specific and highly variable. Some persons lose their interest in sex entirely after the middle years, while others maintain a high level of sexual motivation until advanced old age (Schiavi, 1990a,b; Segraves & Segraves, 1992).

For most *males*, sexual desire peaks at age 17 to 18. At that age, young men personify the "high-normal-2" level of desire. Thereafter, the male sex drive gradually declines. The midlife decrease of male libido, which is known as the "male menopause," typically becomes noticeable around the age of 50 to 60, when most normal men have become "low-normal-3s" (see Chapter 4).

Many *females* in our society don't reach their sexual apogee until their late 30's or early 40's, and female sexual desire may not decline significantly until years after menopause (McCoy & Davidson, 1985; Leiblum et al., 1983; Sherwin, 1992; Bachman et al., 1985).

These gender differences in the rise and fall of the sex drive are reflected in the common scenario of the newlyweds' distress because the young husband's desire exceeds that of his bride's, while complaints regarding sexual discrepancies in older couples are typically in the other direction.

Pathogenesis: The Interaction of Physical and Psychological Factors

The physiologic processes and causes of the age-related decline of sexual desire are not well understood. It is generally assumed that these must be related, at least in part, to the general physical aging and deterioration of the central nervous system, which has to affect the sex centers to some degree. Further, it is believed that the decline of sexual desire with aging parallels to some extent the normal drop in testosterone production (Segraves & Segraves, 1992).

It goes without saying that psychological factors are also important in the pathogenesis of the age-related decline of male and female libido.

For one thing, even in a putative monogamous species like humans, long-term familiarity with the partner can induce sexual satiety. This, together with some inevitable decline in the older person's youthful attractiveness, are significant elements in many cases.

Another important etiologic factor that needs to be considered when one treats older patients with deficient sexual desire is the *powerful negative feedback effect* that the age-related slowing of the genital responses may have on sexual desire. In other words, the aging man's growing awareness of his progressive difficulty with obtaining and maintaining his erections, the loss of penile firmness, his diminished penile sensitivity, and his less forceful ejaculations, along with his greater vulnerability to his partner's responses, may all add up to impact negatively on his desire for sex.

Similarly, the menopausal woman's vaginal dryness and other signs of advancing age can also exert strong psychological dampening effects on the female libido.

From a psychological perspective, the net effect of these real and perceived physiological changes is to increase the man's sexual vulnerability and his dependency on his partner. As he ages, he will increasingly have to count on her to supply him with the extra stimulation and support that he now needs in order to function.

Older women, on the other hand, have to cope with the insecurity that comes with knowing that they have lost the bloom of their youthful sexiness and that they are now handicapped in the competition for men. Sexual aging is particularly difficult for women who are single, but married women are by no means immune.

Healthy Adaptations: Maintaining Sexual Functioning

In the light of all this, one might wonder how it is that so many older people manage to remain sexually active. And a great many do, despite considerable physical impairment. Our extensive clinical observations* of older patients have made it clear that loving couples who have harmonious marriages, who enjoy an intimate and caring relationship that includes a commitment to each other's pleasure, and who are also sexually open and free of significant sexual conflicts intuitively adapt to these physical changes of aging without missing a beat.

Elderly couples who have worked out a good "fit," who are emotion-

*We have seen 1,974 men and women who were over the age of 50 with sexual complaints between 1972 and 1992 at the Payne Whitney sexual dysfunction clinic and in our private practice group.

ally close, empathic, and attuned to each other's feelings, and who communicate well, sense each other's diminishing capabilities and increasing vulnerabilities. They instinctively help each other to function by "accentuating the positives and decentuating the negatives" more than they ever did before.

The sensitive wife knows, without a word being spoken, that her husband is now more dependent on her for stimulation and support, and much more vulnerable to becoming impotent if she makes any performance demands. As a result, she is now extra careful not to criticize his sexual performance and not to ask him for things he can no longer do, such as, for example, to wear a condom.

She is instinctively protective of his feelings and, realizing that her elderly husband now functions better in the mornings, she does not make a power struggle out of preferring evening sex. She is not offended by, nor does she comment on, the fact that he no longer has spontaneous erections when he approaches her. She simply supplies him with more intense and active penile stimulation, perhaps trying oral sex, which can be very helpful for older men, and she does this without necessarily being asked. She does not expect her husband to maintain his erection as long as he has done in the past. With tact and sensitivity, she encourages him to climax at his own rhythm, and accepts his gift of manual or oral stimulation without making him feel that he has failed her. And most important, she goes along with his new or increasing need for fantasy and erotica to boost his weakened libido. Should he experience an occasional erectile failure, she minimizes this and reassures him that she will be available when he is ready to try again, and that he will have better luck next time. Moreover, postmenopausal women who value their sexuality are aware that their vaginal dryness is a "turn off" for their partners, so they make sure to use plenty of lubricants before making love.

The same sensitivity, flexibility, and generosity are required of the partner of the aging women. If he wishes her sexual interest to remain high, he must be sensitive to the greater physical vulnerability of his wife's aging genitalia, and he will be gentler now and more patient in his lovemaking. He is more attentive to his foreplay skills, in order to compensate for his diminishing penile "staying power." He does not take the use of a lubricant by his wife as a personal rejection, nor as a loss of her femininity and attractiveness, but encourages her to protect herself. Similarly, he encourages clitoral play and he is positive about the use of a vibrator to help her have orgasms. He encourages her to fantasize and he looks for erotica that she may find exciting.

If she likes to have sex more often then his lengthened refractory period allows, he does not become defensive or nasty. He derives pleasure from making love to his wife in ways that end in a climax for her, but not necessarily for him. Also, he becomes more attentive, and makes an effort to make his mature partner feel desirable and attractive. And most important, he is very careful never to threaten his postmenopausal wife with complimentary comments about or behaving seductively towards younger women.

Maladaptation: Premature Loss of Sexual Desire

Sexual difficulties follow in the absence of such ideal conditions between the sexual partners. If these normal age-related changes occur in a setting of latent marital hostility, physical impairments can escalate into severe sexual disabilities as the angry partners "decentuate the positives and accentuate the negatives," which older people can ill afford.

More specifically, the older man's increasing emotional and physical dependence on his partner can set the stage for old, hidden marital struggles to erupt into the open. In a common scenario, a long-suffering wife who had felt helplessly intimidated, controlled, and dominated by her husband for many years now takes the opportunity offered by his sexual vulnerability to finally express her pent-up anger. She "castrates" him by passive-aggressively remaining passive and withholding her sexual availability and encouragement, without which he can no longer function.

On the other side of the coin, this period of vulnerability may also be the occasion for an angry husband, who feels threatened and despondent because he is having trouble functioning, to punish his wife inside the bedroom and also outside by blaming her for his sexual difficulties, withdrawing from her, physically and emotionally, or by threatening her with other women.

Sexual dysfunctions and premature losses of sexual desire can also develop if either partner has been imbued with Puritanical feelings of sexual shame or guilt. Deeply ingrained antisexual attitudes can make it difficult for a couple to avail themselves of the aphrodisiacal power of fantasy and erotica to boost their aging libidos.

Treating the Older Patient with Low Sexual Desire

If the patient's libido has not improved to a satisfactory level after his or her physical rehabilitation has been brought to an optimum level, be this by means of T replacement, the healing of vaginal lesions, or a change of medication, a program of psychosexual therapy or sexual rehabilitation may then be instituted.

The first step in the treatment of age-related desire disorders is to educate the couple about the normal age-related physical changes in their sexual responses and to help them to accept more realistic sexual goals. It goes without saying that the emphasis should be on the couple's remaining assets, along the theme of "true, something has been lost, but much endures and you can make the most of this."

The overriding therapeutic strategy for boosting the sluggish sex centers of the infirm, the medicated, and the aged is to increase the input of erotic stimuli, the sexual incenters, while at the same time eliminating, as far as it is possible, the negative stressors and sexual suppressors to which these patients are becoming progressively more vulnerable.

The following is a sampling of some of the therapeutic tactics we use with older couples to implement this basic theme:

1. *De-emphasis of Coitus.* Intercourse, which can generate performance anxiety because this becomes increasingly difficult for men as they age, is de-emphasized as the be-all and end-all of sex. Instead, couples are encouraged to spend more time kissing, caressing, and stimulating each other's erotogenic body parts and genitalia.

2. *Morning sex.* An attempt is made to shift the couple away from evening to morning sex in order to take advantage of the male circadian rhythm, which causes the T levels of males to peak in the early morning hours.

3. *Fantasy and Friction.* The synergy between physical stimulation of the genitalia and the erotogenic zones of the body and erotic psychic input is exploited. Patients are encouraged to use and explore sexual fantasy and erotica and are also offered sexual skills training. The *simultaneous use of physical stimulation and fantasy* is especially helpful for bypassing the lack of novelty as well as the actual and perceived loss of the long-term partner's sexual attractiveness when these issues are material in a particular case.

4. *Enhanced Genital Stimulation.* The use of lubricants is encouraged not only to protect the older woman's more fragile genitalia, but also to facilitate intromission of the older man's less rigid penis. Lubricants and vibrators are also good for enhancing male and female genital sensations; this can have a positive feedback effect on sexual desire.

5. *Improved communication,* In addition to helping the couple update their ineffective sexual techniques, the therapist should make a concomitant effort to *improve their communications and their tolerance of intimacy.* These qualities are even more important for maintaining and

improving a couple's sexual pleasure than the most advanced lovemaking skills.

The sort of combined medical-sex therapy approach that has been outlined above is often successful with healthy, harmonious, older couples who are well motivated to remain sexually active. However, some older patients are intransigently moralist and rigid in their sexual attitudes, and resist trying the new sexual techniques they need to accommodate to the aging process. Further, the passage into older age can reawaken preexisting sexual and emotional conflicts. These, too, can rob the person of the flexibility and closeness with the partner that he/she needs to make the changes that are necessary to continue to function despite the inevitable progression of physical deficits.

The following case illustrates a treatment failure in an older man with a loss of libido who had a concomitant personality disorder, which got in the way of treatment.

Like many aging men, this patient was unprepared for the normal, minor, presbyrective changes and a mild age-related decline in his libido; he misinterpreted these as signs that sex was over for good. Therapy was complicated in this case by the patient's narcissistic distortions, which made the idea of modifying his sexual behavior painful and intolerably insulting for him.

Such narcissistic defenses are some of the most common sources of resistance* against the immensely helpful strategy of the patient's committing himself to making a conscious effort to put himself into a receptive mood instead of simply sitting around and waiting in vain for his old spontaneous surges of erotic lust to make their appearance.

CASE 10.4—"Warren Fountain": Age-Related Decline of Sexual Desire in a Man with a Narcissistic Personality Disorder

The patient, "Warren Fountain," the privileged, third-generation scion of a wealthy family, met the diagnostic criteria for narcissistic personality disorder, although he was functioning quite well. In part this was the result of extensive psychoanalytic help as well as the choice of an excellent partner.

WF was 68 years old when he consulted me in a state of depression and despair because he had (in his words), "totally lost my libido" since he contracted Lyme disease on his country estate one year prior to the visit.

The sexual status examination revealed that the frequency of WF's

*We are indebted to Dr. Richard Kogan for this insight (Wednesday conference).

morning erections had decreased, and he had clearly lost the spontaneous surges of desire and fantasy to which he had been accustomed. Further, he was not as responsive to his wife as he had been prior to his illness.

The patient was distraught by his inability to make love to his wife and he also mourned the loss of the high sex drive he had enjoyed since his adolescence. For example, he no longer got a charge out of watching scantily dressed women, and he sadly told me, "I just don't feel like a man anymore."

In other words, WF had been accustomed to a "high-normal 2" sex drive and he was now overreacting to the fact that his level of sexual desire had fallen to a "low-normal 3." Although this is normal for a man in his late sixties, this patient was having trouble coping.

WF reported that he had not had sexual relations with his wife for the past six months because he had lost his sexual confidence after having problems keeping his erection on a few occasions.

This man's sexual difficulty was really not surprising, because the Fountains had been making love in the same way for the past 25 years, since the beginning of their marriage. Their sexual routine was as follows: The husband would initiate lovemaking when he felt "horny" (which used to happen frequently). His wife, a beautiful Frenchwoman, was his sexual fantasy, and he was accustomed to becoming aroused and instantly erect whenever he approached her. It was his habit to stimulate her manually or orally to orgasm, while she remained totally passive, which he liked. Exciting his wife was WF's sexual fantasy, and he would remain aroused and erect during the process without any physical stimulation of his genitalia. After she had an orgasm, he would penetrate and they would have intercourse. Sometimes she would climax again.

This routine had been very effective for 25 years. However, it was no longer working because the patient was now trying to initiate sex without feeling "horny." He was approaching his wife mainly as a "test," and he was filled with negative anticipations whenever he did. He now typically lost his erection while he was stimulating his wife and he would then become discouraged and withdraw. It never occurred to him to ask his wife to touch or stimulate his penis. On her part, Chantelle Fountain was a supportive partner in that she never complained, but neither had she ever offered to help him.

As has been discussed previously, when a sexual impairment is global, it is always important to rule out physical causes. Therefore, I did a workup in this case, which showed that the patient's hormone profile was perfectly normal. The only positive finding was marginal. NPT testing for three consecutive nights with a portable home monitor revealed that the frequency and the durations of the patient's nocturnal tumescent episodes were on the low side. The record also showed that his nocturnal tumescent periods were confined to the morning hours.

These findings ruled out a hormonal basis for the decrease in WF's libido. However, his age, the history of Lyme disease, and the results of the NPT indicated that there was probably a modest physical decline in WF's erectile capacity, which is a normal finding in a man in his late sixties. More important, the tests also documented that there was plenty of remaining erectile reserve, so that he should be able to function perfectly well providing he approached lovemaking with flexibility and a positive frame of mind.

Warren was sorely disappointed when I told him that I believed his problem was nothing more than a normal, age-related decline in male sexual functioning. I speculated that the process had probably been accelerated by his Lyme disease* and suggested that there might be some improvement in his erections over time.

I further gave him what I considered to be good news—that although there was evidence of some minor physical changes in the level of his sexual capacity, just as he had suspected, this was undoubtedly greatly amplified by his negative emotional reactions. I reassured him that he had sufficient remaining capacities to enable him to function much better than he was now doing. All that he would have to do to improve his functioning would be to come in with his wife for a few therapy sessions so he could learn how to put himself into an erotic mood and to modify his sexual techniques to compensate for his deficit.

I naively thought that this was good news. But the patient did not want to hear this. In fact, he took my suggestion that he might have to make a conscious effort to raise his own desire and that he would have to learn to become a "better lover" as a painful and humiliating personal insult.

WF flatly refused to ask his wife to join him for conjoint therapy. Instead, he requested "hormone shots"** because nothing less than the complete return of his premorbid libido, without any effort on his part, was acceptable to him.

The case was a treatment failure. This narcissistic man would not or could not comply with a therapeutic program that would entail changing the long-standing habits to which he was accustomed. Irrationally,

*Neurological and sexual sequelae are not uncommon with Lyme disease.

**I saw this patient, in 1978, before ICI became clinically available. Today, I might very well suggest this alternative to a resistant patient like Fountain.

he felt he was entitled to his youthful virility and he strongly resisted any suggestions to the effect that he would have to change his sexual behavior and his stance vis-à-vis his wife. Unfortunately, this immature man equated the admission of any vulnerability or "imperfection" as tantamount to playing the role of a sexual cripple begging for favors.

I joined WF's resistance to sex therapy and to the idea of changing his sexual behavior. Although the tests had ruled out hormone deficiencies, at his request I referred the patient to an andrologist who specialized in testosterone replacement therapy, on the chance that the injections might have a placebo effect. I also hoped that the door had been left open should he ever want to reconsider therapy in the future.

Should We Be Treating Low Sexual Desire in Older Couples?

Because patients with sexual desire do not respond as well to treatment as those with genital phase disorders, and because those who are helped tend to relapse with greater frequency, some clinicians have become pessimistic about treating low sexual desire and low sexual frequency in long-term relationships. During a recent sex therapy conference in Copenhagen (June, 1994), R. Gunther Schmidt of Germany raised the question of whether the loss of sexual interest in the partner after some years might not be a normal phenomenon, and suggested that it is inappropriate to treat these couples (personal communication).

I am among the many who disagree. Even though there is no doubt that prolonged familiarity with one's partner is, in fact, often associated with a decrease of sexual desire, and that new love objects in novel settings are erotically stimulating for men as well as for women, and even though it is unlikely that our treatment of sexual anorexics will ever match the excellent results that are par for the course for psychogenic erectile dysfunctions and for orgasm disorders, my positive clinical experiences with almost 2,000 happy, sexy, elderly men and women who have been with their partners for 20, 30, and even 40 years make me much more optimistic than Dr. Schmidt.

The data indicating that novelty is, in fact, a powerful aphrodisiac have, of course, not been ignored in my thinking. This has been incorporated into our treatment format by the introduction of fantasy, erotica, and variety in sexual stimulation, as was described in the previous section.

I do not believe that enduring romantic love is an illusion. Further, I am convinced by our clinical experience that a long-term, enjoyable sexual connection is a realistic goal for many healthy older couples. In fact, with the sex therapy approach outlined above, combined with appropriate medical management of age-related physical problems, the poor outcome in the last case is actually quite atypical. As a group, older men and women who are less fragile and more flexible and secure emotionally and sexually than Mr. Fountain, and who have an intimate, caring relationship with their partners, have surprisingly positive responses to therapy, especially if they have had good sex in the past. The therapeutic process helps them accept their transition from the "high-normal" level of desire of their youth to the "low-normal" eroticism of maturity, and to accommodate to the inevitable physical deficits of the aging process by "accentuating the (remaining) positives and decentuating the negatives."

References

Althof, SE; Badner, DR; Turner, LA; Levine, SB; Riesen, CB; Kursh, ED & Resnick, MI : Intracarvenosal injection in the treatment of impotence: A prospective study of sexual, psychological and marital functioning. *J. of Sex and Marital Therapy, 13*, Fall, 1987.

Althof, SE : Psychogenic impotence: treatment of men and couples. Chapter in *Principles and Practice of Sex Therapy*, Leiblum, SR & Rosen, RC (Eds). Guilford, New York, 1988.

American Psychiatric Association: *Practice Guideline For Major Depressive Disorders*; Supplement, *Am. J. Psychiatry, 150*, No. 4, April, 1993.

Andersson, EK & Wagner, G : Physiology of penile erection. *Physiological Reviews, 75* No. 1, January 1995 (191–236).

Angst, J; Scheidegger, P & Stable, M: Efficacy of meclobamide in different patient groups. *Clinical Neuropharmacology, 16* (Supp 2) 1993 (555–562).

Apfelbaum, B : Retarded ejaculation: a misunderstood syndrome. Chapter in *Principles and Practice of Sex Therapy*, Leiblum, SR & Rosen RC (Eds). Guilford, New York, 1988.

Araoz, DL & Bleck, RT : *Hypnosex*, Arbor House, New York, 1982.

Arletti, R; Benelli, A & Bertolini, A : Oxytosin involvement in male and female sexual behavior. Chapter in *Oxytosin in Maternal, Sexual and Social Behaviors*, Pederson, CA; Caldwell, JD; Jirikowski, GF & Insel, TR (Eds). *Annual Review N.Y. Academy of Science, 652*, New York, 1992.

Assalin, P : Clomipramine in the treatment of premature ejaculation. *J. Sexual Research, 24*, 1988 (213–215).

Assalin, P & Ravart, M : Compulsive sexual behaviors: etiology, clinical manifestations and pharmacological treatment. *Canadian J. of Human Sexuality, 2*, No. 4, Winter, 1993 (221–226).

Bachman, GA; Leiblum, SR; Sandler, B; Ainsley, W; Narcissian, R; Shelden, R & Haymans, HN : Correlates of sexual desire in post-menopausal women, *Maturitas, 7*, 1985 (211–216).

Bancroft, J; O'Carral, R; Lukas, K & Shaw, RW : The effects of bromocryptine on the sexual behavior of hyperprolactinemic men. A case study. *Clinical Endocrinology, 21*, 1984 (131–137).

Bancroft, J; Sherwin, BB; Alexander, GN; Davidson, DW & Walker, A : Oral contraceptives, androgens, and the sexuality of young women I: A comparison of sexual experience, sexual attitude and gender role in oral contraceptive users and non-users. *Archives of Sexual Behavior, 20*, No. 2, 1991 (p. 106).

Bancroft, J; Sherwin, BB; Alexander, GN; Davidson, DW & Walker, A : Oral contraceptives, androgens, and the sexuality of women II : The role of androgens. *Archives of Sexual Behavior, 20*, No. 2, 1991 (121–134).

Barbach, LG : *For Your Self: The Fulfillment of Female Sexuality.* Archer/ Doubleday, Garden City, 1976.

Basic Endocrinology. Greenspan, FS (Ed). Appleton and Langer, San Mateo, California, 1991.

Batten, M : *Sexual Strategies: How Females Chose Their Mates.* Tarcher/ Putman, New York, 1992.

Bell, AP & Weinberg, MS : *Homosexualities, A Study of Diversity Among Men and Women.* Simon & Schuster, New York, 1978.

Berliner, D : New research suggests that romance begins by falling nose over heels in love. *Wall Street Journal*, April 7, 1993.

Birch, HG & Bitterman, ME : Reinforcement learning: the process of integration. *Psychological Review, 56*, 1949 (367–383).

Brecher, EN and the editors of Consumer Reports Books: *Love, Sex and Aging.* Little Brown, Boston, 1984.

Buspar: Seven year update. *J. Clinical Psychiatry, Monograph Series; Supplement,*12, May, 1994.

Caldwell, JD : Central oxytosin and female sexual behavior. Chapter in *Oxytosin in Maternal, Sexual and Social Behaviors*, Pederson, CA; Caldwell, JD; Jirikowski, GF & Insel, TR (Eds). *Annual Review N.Y. Academy of Science, 652*, New York, 1992.

Carney, A; Bancroft, J & Mathews, A : Combination of hormonal and psychological treatments in female sexual unresponsiveness. *Br. J of Psychiatry, 133*, 1978 (339–347).

Cecil Textbook of Medicine, 19th Edition, Wyngarden, JB; Smith, LH Jr. & Bennet, JC (Eds). Saunders, Philadelphia, 1991.

Chakravarti, S; Collins, WP; Newton, JR & Opram, DH : Endocrine changes and symptomatology after oophorectomy in premenopausal women. *British J. of Ob-Gyn, 84*, 1977 (769–775).

Cooper, AM : The unconscious core of perversion. Chapter in *Perversions and Near Perversions in Clinical Practice.* Fogel, GI & Meyers, WA (Eds). Yale University Press, New Haven, 1991.

Crenshaw, T : The sexual aversion syndrome. *J. Sex and Marital Therapy. 11*, 4, 1985.

Crenshaw, TL; Goldberg, JP; & Stern, PC : Pharmacologic modification of psychosexual dysfunction. *J of Sex and Marital Therapy, 13*, No. 4, Winter, 1987 (239–251).

Cunningham, GR; Cordero, E; Thomby, JI : Testosterone replacement with transdermal replacement systems: Physiologic testosterone and elevated dihydrotestorone levels. *JAMA, 26*, No. 17, 1989 (2525–2530).

Davidson, JM & Rosen, RC : Hormonal determinants of erectile functioning. Chapter in *Erectile Disorders: Assessment and Treatment.* Rosen, RC & Leiblum, SR (Eds). Guilford, New York, 1992.

Dollard, J & Miller, NF : *Personality and Psychotherapy.* McGraw-Hill, New York, 1950.

Dreverts, WC; Burton, H; Videen, TO; Snyder, AZ; Simpson, Jr., JR & Raichle, ME: Blood flow changes in human somatosensory cortex during anticipated stimulation. *Nature 3T3* January 1995 (249–251).

DSM-III: The Diagnostic and Statistical Manual of the American Psychiatric Association, 3rd Edition. American Psychiatric Press, Washington DC, 1980.

DSM-IIIR: The Diagnostic and Statistical Manual of the American Psychiatric Association, 3rd Edition Revised, American Psychiatric Press, Washington DC, 1986.

DSM-IV: The Diagnostic and Statistical Manual of the American Psychiatric Association, 4th Edition. American Psychiatric Press, Washington DC, 1994.

Elia, I : *The Female Animal.* Henry Holt, New York, 1986.

Eriksen, PS & Rasmussen, H : Low-dose 17B-estradiol vaginal tablets in the treatment of vaginitis: A double-blind placebo controlled study. *European J. of Obstetrics & Gynecology and Reproductive Biology, 44*, 1992 (137–144).

Fakelman, KA : Hormone of monogamy: The prairie vole and the biology of mating. *Science News, 144*, No. 22, November 1993 (360–365).

Faludi, G : A new possibility in the treatment of anxiety. *Orvosi Hetilap, 135*, August, 1994 (1807–1813).

Follingstad, AH : Estriol, the forgotten estrogen? *JAMA, 1*, No. 239, January 2, 1978 (593–594).

Freud, S : A child is beaten: a contribution to the study of perversion. *In Collected Works of Freud: Standard Edition*, Hogarth, Toronto, 1964.

Friedan, B : *The Fountain of Age.* Simon & Schuster, New York, 1993.

Fruhjelm, M; Karlgen, E & Carlstrom, K : Intravaginal administration of congegated estrogens and postmenopausal women. *Int. J Gynecol & Obstet., 17*, 1980 (335–339).

Gambrel, RD : Androgen therapy for the management of menopause. In monograph, *Hormone Replacement Therapy and the Role of Androgens in the Menopausal Patient.* Pragmaton Press, Chicago, 1990 (10–11).

George, LK & Weiler, SJ : Sexuality in middle and late life. *Arch. General Psychiatry, 38*, 1981 (919–923).

Goodman & Gilman's, The Pharmacological Basis of Therapeutics, 9th Edition: Gilman, AG, Rall, TW, Nies, AS & Taylor, P (Eds). Pergamon Press, New York, 1993.

Gross, MD : Reversal by bethanecol of sexual dysfunction caused by anticholinergic antidepressants. *American J. of Psychiatry, 139*, 1982 (1193–1194).

Harlow, HF : The nature of love, *Am Psychologist, 13*, No. 673, 1958.

Harlow, HF & Harlow, MK : *The Affectional Systems of Non-Human Primates. Vol 2* of *Behavior in Non-Human Primates*. Schrier, AM; Harlow, HF & Stollnitz, R (Eds). Academic Press, New York, 1965.

Harlow, HF & Janersberg, HE : Sex differences in passion and play. *Perspective in Biology and Medicine, 17*, 1974 (348–360).

Harrison's Principles of Internal Medicine, 11th Edition, Braunwald, E; Isselbacher, KJ; Petersdorf, RG; Wilson, JD; Martin, JB & Fauci, As (Eds) McGraw-Hill, New York, 1987.

Herman, JB; Brotman, AW; Pollack, MH; Falk, WE; Biederman, J & Rosenbaum, JF : Flouxetine induced sexual dysfunction, *J. Clinical Psychiatry, 51* No. 1, 1990 (25–27).

Howanitz, JH; Howanitz, PJ & Henry, JB : Evaluation of endocrine functioning. Chapter in *Clinical Diagnosis and Management by Laboratory Methods, 18th Edition*. Henry, JB (Ed). BW Sanders, Philadelphia, 1990.

Insel, TR : Oxytocin: A neuropeptide for affiliation: Evidence from behavioral, receptor, autoradiographic and comparative studies. *Psychoneuroendocrinology, 17*, 1992 (3–35).

Insel, TR & Shapiro, L : Oxytosin may be linked to bonding. *ADAMHA News*, February 1992.

Insel, TR; Carter, CS & Shapiro, J : The role of central vasopressin in pair-bonding in monogamous prairie voles. *Nature, 365*, October 7th, 1993 (545–548).

Kaplan, HS *The New Sex Therapy*. Brunner/Mazel, New York, 1974.

Kaplan, HS : *The Illustrated Manual of Sex Therapy*, New York Times Books, New York, 1975.

Kaplan, HS : Hypoactive sexual desire. *J. of Sex and Marital Therapy, 3*, No. 1, Spring, 1977.

Kaplan, HS : *Disorders Of Sexual Desire*. Brunner/Mazel, New York, 1979.

Kaplan, HS; Kohl, R; Pomeroy, WB; Offit, AK & Hogan, B. Group treatment of premature ejaculation, chapter in *Handbook of Sex Therapy*. LoPiccolo, J & LoPiccolo, L (Eds) Plenum, New York, 1979.

Kaplan, HS : Sex, Intimacy and the Aging Process. *J. American Academy of Psychoanalysis, 18*, No. 1, Spring, 1980 A.

Kaplan, HS : An integrated approach to brief sex therapy. Chapter in *The Interface Between the Psychodynamic and Behavioral Therapies*. Marmor, J & Woods, SM (Eds). Plenum, New York, 1980 B.

Kaplan, HS : New developments in human sexuality. Chapter in *American Handbook of Psychiatry, 7*, Arietti, S (Ed). Basic Books, New York, 1981.

Kaplan, HS; Fyer, AJ & Novick, A : The treatment of sexual phobias: The combined use of anti-panic medication and sex therapy. *J. Sex and Marital Therapy 8*, Spring 1982.

Kaplan, HS : *The Evaluation of Sexual Disorders: Psychological and Medical Aspects*, Brunner/Mazel, 1983.

Kaplan, HS : *Monograph: The Comprehensive Evaluation of Disorders of Sexual Desire*. American Psychiatric Press, Washington DC, 1984.

Kaplan, HS & Moodie, LJ : Therapies for psychosexual dysfunctions. Chapter in *Volume on Psychosexual Therapies for the APA Commission on Psychiatric Therapies*. American Psychiatric Press, Washington DC, 1984.

Kaplan, HS : *Sexual Aversion, Sexual Phobias and Panic Disorder.* Brunner/Mazel, New York, 1987.

Kaplan, HS : *PE: How To Overcome Premature Ejaculation.* Brunner/Mazel, New York, 1989 A.

Kaplan, HS : The concept of presbyrectia. *International J. of Impotence Research, 1*, 1989 B.

Kaplan, HS : Sex, Intimacy and the Aging Process. *J. American Academy of Psychoanalysis, 18*, No. 1. Spring, 1990 A.

Kaplan, HS : The combined use of sex therapy and intrapenile injections in the treatment of impotence. *J. of Sex and Marital Therapy, 16*, No. 4, Winter 1990 B.

Kaplan, HS : Psychiatric evaluation and therapy. Chapter in *World Book on Impotence Research*, Lue, T (Ed), Smith-Gordon, London, 1992 A.

Kaplan, HS : The sexual side effects of the treatments for breast cancer. *J. of Sex and Marital Therapy, 18*, 4, Winter, 1992 B.

Kaplan, HS : Psychogenic impotence: Update, chapter in *Current Therapy in Endocrinology and Metabolism. 5th Edition.* Bardin, WC (Ed). Decker, Philadelphia, 1993 A.

Kaplan, HS : The myth of the new impotence: update for the 1990's. Chapter in *New Concepts of Feminine Psychology: Women Beyond Freud.* Berger, M (Ed), Brunner/Mazel, New York, 1993 B.

Kaplan, HS : The psychiatric aspects of injection treatment. Chapter in *The New Injection Treatment for Impotence.* Wagner, G & Kaplan, HS (Eds). Brunner/Mazel, New York, 1993 C.

Kaplan, HS : The post-ejaculatory pain syndrome. *J of Sex and Marital Therapy, 19*, No. 2, Summer, 1993 D.

Kaplan, HS & Owett, T : The female androgen-deficiency syndrome. *J. of Sex and Marital Therapy, 19*, No. 1, Spring, 1993.

Kaplan, HS : Update: Psychosexual disorders. Chapter in *Psychiatry*, Michels, R & Covenar, Jr., JO (Eds). Lippincot, Philadelphia, 1995.

Kaplan, P: The use of serotenergic reuptake inhibitors in the treatment of PE. *J. of Sex and Marital Therapy 120* Winter, 1994, (321–324).

Kernberg, OF : Barriers to falling and remaining in love. *J. American Psychoanalytic Association, 22*, 1974A (486–1115).

Kernberg, OF : Mature love: Pre-requisites and characteristics. *J. of American Psychoanalytic Association. 22*, 1974 B (743–768).

Kernberg, OF : Boundaries and structures in love relationships. *J. American Psychoanalytic Association, 25*, 1977 (81–114).

Kinsey, AC; Pomeroy, WB & Martin, CE : *Sexual Behavior in the Human Male*, Sanders, Philadelphia, 1948.

Klein, DF : Anxiety reconceptualized. In *Anxiety: New Research and Changing Concepts.* Klein, DF & Rabkin, JG (Eds), Raven Press, New York, 1980.

Klein, DF; Gittelman-Klein, R; Quitkin, F & Rifkin, A : *Diagnosis and Drug Treatment of Psychiatric Disorders.* William & Wilkins, Baltimore. 1980.

Klein, DF & Rabkin, JG (Eds) : *Anxiety: New Research and Changing Concepts.* Raven Press, New York, 1980.

Klein, DF : Sexual disorders and medications. In Kaplan, HS, *Sexual Aversion, Sexual Phobias and Panic Disorder.* Brunner/Mazel, New York, 1987.

Klein, DF : The definition and pharmacology of spontaneous panic and phobias: A critical review. Chapter in *Psychopharmacology and Anxiety*, Tyrer, PJ (Ed), Oxford University Press, New York, 1989 (135–162).

Klein, DF : False suffocation alarm response, spontaneous panics and related conditions: An integrative hypothesis. *Archives of General Psychiatry, 50*, April 1993 (306–317).

Klein, M : *Envy and Gratitude & Other Works, 1944–1963*. Delacorte Press, New York, 1975.

Klein-Graber, G & Graber, B : Diagnosis and treatment of pubococcygeal deficiencies in women. *Handbook of Sex Therapy*. LoPiccolo, J & LoPiccolo, L (Eds). Plenum, New York, 1978.

Kline, MD : Fluoxetine and anorgasmia, *American J. of Psychiatry, 146*, 1989 (804–805).

Korenman, S & Viosca, S : Treatment of Vasculogenic sexual dysfunction with Pentoxifylline. *J. of the American Geriatric Society, 41*, April, 1993 (363–366).

Kupferman, I : Hypothalamus and limbic system motivation. Chapter in *Principle of Neural Science*, 3rd Edition, Kandel, ER; Schwartz, JH & Jessell, TM (Eds) Elsevier, New York, 1991 (751, 755).

Lal, S; Rios, O & Tharundayil, JX : The treatment of impotence with trazadone: A case report. *J. Urol, 144*, 1990 (819–820).

Lamont, AJ & Anderson, L : Gender differences in psychological responses to infertility treatments. *Canadian J. of Human Sexuality, 2*, No. 3, 1993 (129–140).

Lazarus, AA : A multimodal perspective on problems of sexual desire. Chapter in *Sexual Desire Disorders*. Guilford, New York, 1988.

Leiblum, S; Bachman, G; Kernman, E; Colburn, D & Schwartzman, L : Vaginal atrophy in the post-menopausal woman: The importance of sexual activity and hormones. *JAMA, 16*, No. 249, 1983.

Leiblum, SR, Previn, LA & Campbell, H : The treatment of vaginismus. Chapter in *Principles and Practice of Sex Therapy*, Leiblum, SR & Rosen, RC (Eds). Guilford, New York, 1988.

Leiblum, SR & Rosen, RC : *Sexual Desire Disorders*, Guilford, New York, 1988 (p. 2).

Lesko, LM; Stotland, NL; & Segraves, RT : Three cases of anorgasmia associated with MAOIs. *Am. J Psychiatry, 159*, No. 101, October, 1982 (1353–1355).

Liebowitz, M : *The Chemistry of Love*, Harper Brown, New York, 1983.

Liebowitz, M : Antidepressants in panic disorder. *Br. J Psychiatry, Supplement, 155*, 1989 (46–52).

Lief, H : What's new in sex research? Inhibited sexual desire. *Medical Aspects of Human Sexuality. Vol II*, October, 1977 (94–95).

Lief, HI : The evaluation of inhibited sexual desire: Relationship aspects. Chapter in *The Comprehensive Evaluation of Disorders of Sexual Desire*, Kaplan, HS (Ed). American Psychiatric Press, Washington DC, 1985.

Lobitz, C & LoPiccolo, J : Low sexual desire. Chapter in *Principles and Practice of Sex Therapy*, Leiblum, SR & Previn, LA (Eds). Guilford Press, New York, 1980 (29–64).

Lobo, RA : Hormone replacement therapy: Oestrogen replacement after treatment for breast cancer? *Lancet, 341*, May, 1993.

Longcope, C : Androgen production in women. Monograph, *Managing Menopausal Symptoms: Meeting the Challenge of the 90's*. Pragmaton Publications, Chicago, 1991 A (4–7).

Longcope, C : Androgens and the menopause. In monograph, *Controversies in the Management of Menopause*, Pragmaton Press, Chicago, 1991 B (5–7).

LoPiccolo, J & Lobitz, WC : The role of masturbation in the treatment of orgasmic dysfunction. Chapter in *Handbook of Sex Therapy.* LoPiccolo, J & LoPiccolo, L (Eds). Plenum, New York, 1978.

LoPiccolo, J & LoPiccolo, L, Eds : *Handbook of Sex Therapy.* Plenum, New York, 1978.

LoPiccolo, J : *Low Libido States*. Lecture, presented at the meeting of the American Association of Sex Therapists, Philadelphia, 1979.

LoPiccolo, J : Management of psychogenic erectile failure. Chapter in *Contemporary Management of Psychogenic Erectile Failure*, Tanagho, E; Lue, T & McClure, R (Eds), Williams & Wilkins, Baltimore, 1988.

LoPiccolo, J & Friedman, JM : Broad-spectrum treatment of low desire: Integration of cognitive, behavioral and systemic therapy. Chapter in *Desire Disorders*, Leiblum, SR & Rosen, RC (Eds). Plenum, New York, 1988.

LoPiccolo, L : Low sexual desire. Chapter in *Principles and Practice of Sex Therapy*, Leiblum, SR & Previn, LA (Eds), Guilford, New York, 1989.

LoPiccolo, J : Postmodern sex therapy for erectile failure. Chapter in *Erectile Disorders*, Rosen, RC & Leiblum, SR (Eds), Guilford, New York, 1992.

Lorand, S & Schneer, H : Sexual deviations II: Fetishism, transvestitism, masochism, sadism, voyeurism, incest pedophilia, and bestiality. Chapter in *Comprehensive Textbook of Psychiatry, 1st Edition*. Kaplan, HI & Freedman, AM (Eds). Williams & Wilkins, Baltimore, 1976 (p. 981).

Masters, WH & Johnson, VE : *The Human Sexual Response.* Little Brown, Boston, 1964.

Masters, WH & Johnson, VE : *Human Sexual Inadequacy.* Little Brown, Boston, 1970.

Masters, WH, Kolodny, RC & Johnson, VE : *Textbook of Sexual Medicine.* Little Brown, Boston, 1979.

Masters, WH; Johnson, VE & Kolodny, RC : *Heterosexuality.* HarperCollins, New York, 1994.

Mattson, LA; Cullberg, G; Erikson, O & Kutson, F : Vaginal administration of low-dose oestradiol—effects on the endometrium and vaginal cytology. *Maturitas, 11*, 1989 (217–222).

McClure, RD; Oses, R & Ernest, ML : Hypogonadal impotence treated with transdermal testosterone. *Urology, 37*, No. 3, 1991 (224–228).

McCoy, N & Davidson, JM : A longitudinal study of the effects of menopause on sexuality. *Maturitas, 7*, 1985.

McEwen, BS; Davis, PG; Parsons, B & Pfaff, DW : The brain as a target for steroid hormones action. *Am. Rev. Neurosciences, 2*, 1979 (65–112).

McEwen, BS : Gonadal receptors in the developing and adult brain. Chapter in *Fetal Neuroendocrinology.* Ellerdorf, F; Gluckman, P & Parvizi, N (Eds). Perinatology Press, Ithica, New York, 1984.

Mettler, L & Olsen, PG : Long-term treatment of atrophic vaginitis with low-dose oestradiol vaginal tablets. *Maturitas, 14*, 1991 (23–31).

Michel, G : *Behavioral Differences in Nonhuman Primates*, Van Norstad/Reinholt, New York, 1979.

Money, J : Components of eroticism in man: Hormones in relation to sexual morphology and sexual desire. *J. of Nervous and Mental Diseases, 132*, 1961.

Money, J : *Gender Identity.* Lecture, Cornell Medical College, New York, 1976.

Money, J : *Love and Love Sickness.* Hopkins University Press, Baltimore, 1980.

Money, J : *Love Maps*, Irvington, New York, 1986 (p. 36).

Money, J & Lamacz, M : *Vandalized Love Maps: Paraphilic Outcome of Seven Cases in Pediatric Sexology.* Prometheus Books, Buffalo, New York, 1988.

Moore, FL : Evolutionary precedents for behavioral actions of oxytosin and vasopressin. Chapter in *Oxytosin in Maternal, Sexual and Social Behaviors.* Pederson, CA; Caldwell, JD; Jirikowski, GF; Insel, TR (Eds). *Annual Review NY Academy of Science, 652*, New York, 1992.

Mowrer, OH : On the dual nature of learning : A reinterpretation of "conditioning" and "problem solving." *Harvard Educational Review, 17*, 1974.

Nessel, M : Yohimbe and Pentoxifylline in the treatment of erectile dysfunction. *American J. of Psychiatry, 151* No. 3, March 1994 (453).

Notolewitz, M : Estrogen replacement therapy: Indications, contraindications and agent selection. *American J. of Obstetrics and Gynecology, 161*, 1989 (1832–1841).

Notolewitz, M : *Managing Menopausal Symptoms: Meeting the Challenge of the 90's.* Monograph, Pragmaton Press, Chicago, 1990 (2–4).

Noyes, R; Reich, J; Christianson, J; Saelza, M; Phael, B; & Coryell, WA : Outcome of panic disorder. *Arch. Gen. Psychiatry. 44*, 1990 (809–818).

Palmore, E (Ed) : *Normal Aging*, Durham, NC, Duke University Press, 1970.

Palmore, E (Ed) : *Normal Aging II*, Durham, NC, Duke University Press, 1974.

Papez, JW : A proposed mechanism of emotion. *Arch. Neurology and Psychiatry, 38*, 1937 (725–743).

Pedersen, CA; Caldwell, JD; Jirikowski, GF & Insel, TR (Eds). *Oxytocin in Maternal, Sexual and Social Behaviors. Annual Review, New York Acad. Sci., Vol 652*, New York, 1992.

Person, ES : *Dreams of Love and Fateful Encounters.* Norton, New York, 1988.

Physician's Desk Reference, 48. Medical Economics, New Jersey, 1994.

Rappaport, JL; Ryland, DH & Kriete, M : Drug treatment of acral lick: An animal model of obsessive-compulsive disorder. *Archives of General Psychiatry, 49*, July, 1992 (512–521).

Roiphe, H & Galenson, E : *Infantile Origins of Sexual Identity.* International Press, New York, 1981.

Rose, DP & Davis, TE : Effects of adjunct chemo-hormonal therapy on ovarian and adrenal function of breast cancer patient. *Cancer Research, 40.* November, 1980.

Sager, CT; Kaplan, HS; Grundlach,RH; Kremer, M; Leuz, R; & Royce, JR : The marriage contract. Chapter in *Progress in Group and Family Therapy.* Sager, CT & Kaplan, HS (Eds), Brunner/Mazel, New York, 1971.

Scharff, DE : *The Sexual Relationship: An Objects Relation View of Sex and the Family.* Reatledge & Kegan, London, 1982.

Schiavi, RC & White, D : Androgens in male sexual functioning. *J. of Sex and Marital Therapy, 2*, No. 3, Fall 1976 (228).

Schiavi, RC : Sexuality and aging men. In *First Annual Review of Sex Research.* Bancroft, J (Ed). *Society for the Scientific Study of Sex I.* Philadelphia, 1990.

Schiavi, RC & Schreiner-Engel, P : Nocturnal penile tumescence in aging men. *J. Nervous and Mental Disorders, 147,* 1990 (766–771).

Schiavi, RC; Schreiner-Engel, P; Mandeli, J; Schanzer, H & Cohen, E : Healthy aging and male sexual functioning. *J. Gerontology, 43,* 1990 (146–150).

Schiavi, RC : Interview, psychometric and psychophysiologic strategies to assess sexual disorders. *J. Clinical Psychiatry Monograph, 10,* No. 19, 1992.

Schiavi, RC; Mandeli, J; Schreiner-Engel, P : Sexual satisfaction in healthy aging men. *J. of Sex and Marital Therapy, 20,* No. 119, 1994.

Schreiner-Engel, P & Schiavi, RC : Life-time psychopathology in individuals with low sexual desire. *J. Nervous and Mental Diseases, 174,* 1986 (646–651).

Schwartz, MF & Masters, WH : Inhibited desire: The Masters & Johnson Institute treatment method. Chapter in *Sexual Desire Disorders.* Leiblum, SR & Rosen, RC (Eds). Plenum, New York, 1988.

Segraves, RT : Drugs and desire. Chapter in *Sexual Desire Disorders,* Leiblum, SR & Rosen, RC (Eds). Guilford, New York, 1988 A.

Segraves, RT : Hormones and libido. Chapter in *Sexual Desire Disorders,* Leiblum, SR & Rosen, RC (Eds). Guilford, New York, 1988 B.

Segraves, RT : Sexual side effects of psychiatric drugs. *International J. of Psychiatry and Medicine, 18,* 1988 C (275–289).

Segraves, RT : Sexual dysfunction complicating the treatment of depression. *J. Clinical Psychiatry Monographs, 10.* May, 1992 (75–78).

Segraves, RT & Golden, J : *Medication Often Causes Sexual Dysfunction in Depressed Patients.* Presented at the US Psychiatric Congress, New York, 1992.

Segraves, RT & Segraves, KB : Aging and drug effects on male sexuality. *Erectile Disorders: Assessment and Treatment.* Rosen, RC & Leiblum, SR (Eds), Guilford, New York, 1992.

Segraves, RT, Saran, A, Segraves, K & Maguire, E : Clomipramine versus placebo in the treatment of premature ejaculation. A pilot study. *J of Sex and Marital Therapy, 19,* No. 3, Fall, 1993, (198–201).

Segraves, RT : Antidepressant-induced orgasm disorder. *J. of Sex and Marital Therapy, 21,* No. 3, Fall, 1995 (87–92).

Semmens, JP & Wagner, G : Estrogen deprivation in vaginal functioning in post-menopausal women. *JAMA, 248,* 1982 (245–448).

Sherrington, CS : *The Integrative Action of the Nervous System.* Yale University Press, New Haven, 1906.

Sherwin, BB : Changes in sexual behavior as a function of plasma sex steroid levels in post-menopausal women. *Maturitas,* 7, 1985 (225–233).

Sherwin, BB; Gelfand, MM & Brender, W : Androgen enhances the sexual motivation of women. *Psychosomatic Medicine, 47,* No. 4, July–August, 1985 (p. 350).

Sherwin, BB & Gelfand, NM : The role of androgen in the maintenance of sexual functioning in oophorectomized women. *Psychosomatic Med., 49,* 1987 (397–409).

Sherwin, BB : A comparative analysis of the role of androgen in human male and female behavior: Behavioral specificity, critical thresholds, and sensitivity. *Psychobiology, 16* (4), 1988, (416–425).

Sherwin, BB : The psychoendocrinology of aging and female sexuality. Chapter in, *Annual Review of Sex Research, 2*. Bancroft, J (Ed) Society for the scientific study of sex; Lakeside, Ohio, 1991 (181–198).

Sherwin, BB : *"Aging and Sexuality: A Biopsychosocial Perspective."* Invited Lecture, Annual Meeting of the Society for Sex Therapy and Research. Montreal, March, 1992.

Spiegel, D; Blume, JR; Kraemer, H & Gotheil, E: The effects of psychosocial treatment on survival of patients with metastatic breast cancer. *Lancet, 45*, October, 1989.

Starr, BD & Weiner, MB : *The Starr-Weiner Report on Sexual Sexuality in the Mature Years*. McGraw-Hill, New York, 1981.

Stoller, RJ : *Perversion: The Erotic Form of Hatred*. Pantheon Book, New York, 1975.

Stoller, RJ : The term perversion. Chapter in *Perversions and Near Perversions in Clinical Practice*. Fogel, GI & Meyers, WA (Eds). Yale University Press, New Haven, 1991.

Stotland, NL : *Psychiatric Aspects of Reproductive Technology*. American Psychiatric Press, Washington DC, 1990.

Sullivan, G : Increased libido in three men treated with trazodone. *J. of Clinical Psychiatry VI, 46*, 1988 (202–203).

Symons, D : *The Evolution of Human Sexuality*. Oxford University Press, Oxford, 1979.

Tiefer, L & Melman, A : Interview of wives: A necessary adjunct in the evaluation of impotence, *Sexuality and Disability, 6*, 1983 (167–175).

Tiefer, L & Melman, A : Comprehensive evaluation of erectile dysfunction. Chapter in *Principles and Practice of Sex Therapy, Update for the 1990s*. Leiblum, SR & Rosen, RC (Eds). Guilford, New York, 1989.

Tiefer, L : Discussant, *Psychological evaluation of the impotent male*; Consensus Development Conference on Impotence, Department of Health and Human Services, Bethesda, Md, December 7th, 1992.

Todarello, O & Boscia, SM : Sexuality in aging: A study of a group of 300 elderly men and women. *J. Endocrin. Invest., 8*, 1985.

Turner, AL; Althof, ED; Lenice, SB; Riesen, CB; Bocheer, DR; Kursh, ED & Resnick, MI : Self-injection of papaverine and phentalomine in the treatment of psychogenic impotence. *J. of Sex and Marital Therapy, 15*, Fall, 1989.

Verlust, J & Heyman, JR : An interactional approach to sexual dysfunctions. *American J. of Family Therapy*, 7, No. 4, 1979 (19–35).

Vermuelen, A : The normal activity of the post-menopausal ovary. *J. Clin. Endocrinology and Metabolism, 42*, 1976 (1917–1929).

Wagner, G : The influence of oestrogen on vaginal physiology—symptomatology of oestrogen deprived women. Chapter in, *The Urogenital Oestrogen Deficiency Syndrome*. Samisoe, G & Eriksen, PB (Eds.) Copenhagen, *Proceedings of the International Workshop*, November, 1986.

Wagner, G; Gerstenberg, T & Levin, RJ : Electrical activity of corpus carvenosum (EACC) during erection and flaccidity of the penis. *Am J. Urology*, 1990.

Wagner, G : Erection and Impotence. Chapters in *The New Injection Treatment for Impotence*, Wagner, G & Kaplan, HS (Eds). Brunner/Mazel, New York, 1993.

Wagner, GM & Kaplan, HS : *The New Injection Treatment for Impotence.* Brunner/Mazel, New York, 1993.

Waxenberg, SE; Drellick, NG & Sutherland, AN : The role of hormones in human behavior I: Changes in female sexuality after adrenalectomy. *J. Clinical Endocrinology 19*, 193, 1959.

Waxenberg, SE; Finkbiener, JA; Drellick, MD & Sutherland, AN : The role of hormones in human behavior II: Changes in sexual behavior in relation to vaginal smears of breast-cancer patients after oophorectomy and adrenalectomy. *Psychosomatic Medicine Volume XXII, No. 6*, 1960 (435–439).

Weitzman, R & Hart, J : Sexual behavior in healthy married elderly men. *Arch. Sexual Behavior, 16*, 1987 (39–44).

Wilson, JD & Foster, DW (Eds) : Williams Textbook of Endocrinology, 8th Edition. Saunder's, Philadelphia, 1992.

Wolpe, J : *Psychotherapy with Reciprocal Inhibition.* Stanford University Press, Palo Alto, 1958.

Zajecka, J; Fawcett, J; Schaff, M; Jeffries, H & Guy, C : The role of Serotonin in sexual functioning: Flouxetine associated orgasm dysfunction. *J. Clinical Psychiatry, 52*, No. 1, 1991 (66–68).

Zilbergeld, B & Ellison, CR : Desire discrepancies and arousal problems in sex therapy. Chapter in *Principles and Practice of Sex Therapy*, Leiblum, SR & Previn, LA (Eds), Guilford Press, New York. 1980.

Zilbergeld, B : The man behind the broken penis: Social and psychological determinants of erectile failure. Chapter in *Erectile Disorders: Assessment and Treatment:* Rosen, RC & Leiblum, SR (Eds), Guilford, New York, 1992 A.

Zilbergeld, B : *The New Male Sexuality.* Bantam, New York, 1992 B.

Zohar, J; Kaplan, Z & Benjamin, J : Compulsive exhibitionism successfully treated with Fluoxamine: A controlled case study. *J of Clinical Psychiatry, 55*, No. 3, March, 1994 (86–88).

Name Index

Subject Index